New Dimensions in Ethnohistory

Papers of the Second Laurier Conference
on Ethnohistory and Ethnology

Huron College
University of Western Ontario
May 11–13, 1983

Edited by

Barry Gough
Department of History
Wilfrid Laurier University

and

Laird Christie
Department of Sociology and Anthropology
Wilfrid Laurier University

Canadian Ethnology Service.
Mercury Series Paper 120

Canadian Museum of Civilization

© Canadian Museum of Civilization 1991

Canadian Cataloguing in Publication Data

Laurier Conference on Ethnohistory and Ethnology
(2nd: 1983, Huron College)

New dimensions in ethnohistory: papers of the
second Laurier Conference on Ethnohistory and
Ethnology

(Mercury series, ISSN 0316-1854)
Paper/Canadian Ethnology Service,
ISSN 0316-1862 ; no. 120)
Includes an abstract in French.
"Huron College, University of Western Ontario,
May 11-13, 1983"
ISBN 0-660-12911-6

1. Ethnohistory — North America — Congresses.
2. Ethnology — North America — Congresses.
3. Indians of North America — Congresses.
I. Gough, Barry M., 1938- . II. Christie, Laird.
III. Canadian Museum of Civilization. IV. Canadian
Ethnology Service. V. Title. VI. Title: Papers of the
second Laurier Conference on Ethnohistory and
Ethnology. VII. Series. VIII. Series: Paper
(Canadian Ethnology Service); no. 120.

GN345.2.N58 1991   970.004'97   C91-098560-X

Printed and bound in Canada

Published by
Canadian Museum of Civilization
100 Laurier Street
P.O. Box 3100, Station B
Hull, Quebec
J8X 4H2

Cover illustration: The Covenant Chain, reprinted
with the permission of the New York State
Historical Association.

Production Coordinator: Debborah Brownrigg

Cover Design: Francine Boucher

Canadä

Abstract

The papers in this volume represent ethnohistorical research by a number of scholars on North American native peoples. They were presented at the Second Laurier Conference on Ethnohistory and Ethnology held at Huron College, University of Western Ontario, May 11–13, 1983.

Résumé

Les articles publiés dans ce livre représentent la recherche ethnohistorique de plusieurs universitaires sur les peuples autochtones d'Amérique du Nord. Ils ont été présentés à la deuxième Conférence sur l'ethnohistoire et l'ethnologie qui a eu lieu au collège Huron de l'University of Western Ontario, du 11 au 13 mai 1983.

PREFACE

The papers in this volume represent work presented at the Second
Laurier Conference on Ethnohistory and Ethnology held at Huron College,
May 11-13, 1983. The two Laurier Conferences had their roots in discussions
among Anthropologists and Historians at Wilfrid Laurier University, the
University of Waterloo and the University of Western Ontario during
1979-80. The focus of our talk was the need for a relatively small
gathering of anthropologists and historians who might, while presenting the
results of their own research, engage in conversations about substantive,
theoretical and methodological issues relevant to the disciplinary
partnership which has for more than thirty years sustained Ethnohistory as
an academic field.

Our hopes were happily realized in the first conference, held at
Wilfrid Laurier University in late October of 1980. We were most grateful
to those scholars who responded to our call for papers, in particular to
Bruce Trigger who agreed to present the keynote address of the conference.

The format proved to be serendipitous. The arrangement of plenary
sessions at which all participants had opportunity to act as discussants,
and the involvement of the audience seemed to provide exactly the kind of
setting required for informal input and interaction. "The conversation of
all was a course of lectures to each," as Newman envisioned for his ideal
university.

For those of us who were primarily listeners, the opportunity to hear
William Fenton, Bruce Trigger, James Axtell, Francis Jennings and Wilcomb
Washburn (to neglect the other names on what is virtually a roster of
currently active and productive ethnohistorical scholars) present and
exchange views on anthropological and historical scholarship was one which
could not have been replicated in the conventional large scale setting of a
major conference.

We were encouraged to repeat the conference in 1983, and tentatively
considered a rotating series, using the facilities of Wilfrid Laurier and
Huron College (University of Western Ontario) for future meetings, possibly
on a triennial basis.

We are grateful to Douglas Leighton of Huron College who, along with
his most complaisant and cooperative fellow faculty and staff members at
Huron, gave us three delightfully pleasant and intellectually refreshing
days in an ideal academic environment. The whole committee, Barry Gough,
Douglas Leighton, Elizabeth Graham, Laird Christie and David McNab, was
responsible for the architecture of the conference, the choice of
presenters, chairs and discussants; everyone present felt the benefits of
its work.

This collection of papers represents the conference in only the sketchiest and most skeletal fashion. What is lost in all such proceedings is the discussion which illuminated, augmented and enriched the original papers. Most of all, the "conference in the round" provided, as reports of papers cannot, important contributions to the dialogue which inspired its organization in the first place—talk between historians and anthropologists about how they pursue their crafts.

In a wry conclusion to his contribution to Shepard Krech's collection of papers on the Keepers of the Game debate, Indians, Animals and the Fur Trade (1981), Dean Snow remarked:

> "Anthropologists will continue to drive historians crazy with their sloppy source criticism and other technical failings. Historians will continue to drive anthropologists crazy with notions of cause and effect that seem to lie outside the bounds of known human behaviour. But out of this collective madness comes scholarship that is much better stuff than it could ever be if we stayed behind our disciplinary fences."

Hopefully Laurier I and II and such colloquia as may follow will contribute their bit to this "collective madness."

We acknowledge our thanks to P. Coulas, Programmes Administrator, Canadian Ethnology Service, Canadian Museum of Civilization/Musée canadien des civilisations, Hull, for assistance in bringing this work into print. We are grateful to our several contributors for their help and their patience in completing this publication.

Barry Gough
Laird Christie
Wilfrid Laurier University

v

CONTENTS

Preface.. iv

Amerindians in Renaissance Europe,
by Olive Patricia Dickason... 1

Prehistoric and Historic Linkages: Problems and Prospects,
by Adolph M. Greenberg and Ronald H. Spielbauer........................ 25

Southern Boundary of the Lenape: Cultural Interaction and
Change in the Early Contact Period 1550-1610,
by Marshall J. Becker... 43

Preachers, Priests and Pagans: Catholic and Protestant
Missions in Colonial North America, by James Axtell.................... 65

Miscegenation in Eighteenth Century New France,
by Cornelius J. Jaenen.. 79

Native Christianity in Eighteenth Century Massachusetts:
Ritual as Cultural Reaffirmation, by Kathleen J. Bragdon.............. 117

Russian Orthodox Missionaries and the Tlingit of Alaska,
1880-1900, by Sergei Kan... 127

From Sorel to Lake Winnipeg: George Nelson as an Ethnohistorical
Source, by Jennifer S. H. Brown...................................... 161

"The Great Mart of all this Country": Lewis and Clark and
Western Trade Networks, by James P. Ronda........................... 175

Indian and Non-Indian Fisheries for Klamath River Salmon:
Environment and Culture Change on the Northwestern
California Frontier, by Arthur F. McEvoy............................ 191

Pawnee Usage of Bundle Beliefs and Practices,
by Morris W. Foster... 213

Native North American Trickster-and-Vulture Tales,
by Pierre Ventur.. 225

The Indian Rights Association and the Ghost Dance Uprising,
by William T. Hagan.. 269

The Gitskan Incident of 1888, by I. V. B. Johnson..................... 281

AMERINDIANS IN RENAISSANCE EUROPE

by

Olive Patricia Dickason

1

ABSTRACT

Beginning with Columbus' capture of ten West Indian islanders in 1492, the practice of transporting New World native peoples to Europe was carried on by the Spanish, French and English for some three centuries. While early attempts by the Spanish to engage in wholesale removal of Indians as slaves failed because of the rapid decline in Caribbean Indian populations (as well as the notable lack of success the Europeans experienced in preserving captive Indians alive), the transport of individuals and small groups to meet monarchs, learn the languages and customs of Europeans and undergo religious instruction, continued as a regular feature of voyages of exploration and colonization.

This paper explores the motives for the transport of native North Americans, European impressions of their Indian "guests" (and, reciprocally, Indian ideas about European society and culture) and the consequences of such visits for European images of and interest in the New World.

2

AMERINDIANS IN RENAISSANCE EUROPE[1]

Olive Patricia Dickason

The days of first contact between Europeans and Amerindians were also the days of an active two-way traffic across the Atlantic. If Europeans came to the New World to conquer and settle, Amerindians went to Europe to meet with kings and princes, and to take part in those ceremonial occasions that were so dear to the Renaissance heart. Europeans had come to take over the New World; Amerindians were taken to Europe to be seen and wondered at, to be used as pawns in the struggle between monarchs for the privilege of exploiting American riches. Europeans came voluntarily to America, often to make their fortunes there; Amerindians usually went involuntarily to Europe, particularly during the sixteenth century, where they were fortunate if they survived.

These Amerindian visits were more frequent than documented instances indicate. Early explorers kidnapped New World men for display in European courts as proof of where they had been, which led to Amerindians being taken to train as interpreters and guides for subsequent voyages. Very quickly, the French added their own dimension to the practice, and sought to circumvent Spanish and Portuguese New World claims by bringing over Amerindians to request the protection of His Most Christian Majesty. Similarly, France asserted her right to evangelize and, by extension, to colonize, by staging some spectacular ceremonies for the baptism of New World visitors. On a small scale, missionaries brought Amerindians to Europe for public appearances to enlist support for their evangelical projects. As colonization developed, so did the practice of sending over Americans (as they were sometimes called), especially children and young people, for indoctrination in European ways. France became particularly active in this regard. She also encouraged chiefs and headmen to come to court in order to strengthen French-Amerindian alliances, and attempted to transform enemies into friends by sending over prisoners of war, in contrast to the Spaniards, who used them as slaves. When the French court sought to solve a manpower problem by using a group of such prisoners as galley slaves, the outcry from the colony was such that the project was dropped. The expense of visits proved to be high in proportion to the results obtained, and eventually they were discouraged. By the latter part of the seventeenth century France saw fewer such occasions, and by the time of her defeat in North America in eighteenth century, they had all but ceased. Britain's continuing colonial presence in the northern parts of the New World meant that Amerindians continued to arrive on her shores; but this had never been a frequent occurrence, as the British had not encouraged them as had the French. Because France, more than any other European colonizing nation, developed the political potentialities of these visits, and sought to use them as a means of building her empire, her experiences invite particular consideration.

Columbus began the movement of Amerindians to Europe when he brought back six West Indian islanders whom he presented to the Spanish court. Actually, he had taken ten, but one had died at sea and three others had been too ill upon landing at Seville to proceed further; eventually, the six survivors were baptized at Barcelona. One stayed in Spain with Don Juan of Castile and learned Castillian, only to die in two years.[2] Of the others, three survived long enough to return with Columbus on his second voyage. Upon his arrival in the West Indies, the Admiral released one in the hope he would act as an ambassador. The other two escaped.[3] On his second voyage, Columbus brought thirty Amerindians as prisoners of war from Hispaniola; they were sold in Seville as slaves.[4] The extent of the resistance that the Spanish were meeting from Amerindians is indicated by the report that 600 others were sent over as war captives that same year, 1494, also to be sold as slaves in Seville.[5] In 1495, the number brought over was given as 500.[6] In 1496, Don Barthelemy Columbus, brother of the Admiral, sent 300 islanders to Spain for having taken arms against the Spanish.[7] That same year, Columbus estimated that he could export as many slaves as could be sold, about 4000.[8] Vespucci reported that on his first voyage to the West Indies, 250 Amerindians were taken as prisoners of war, of whom 222 survived the trans-Atlantic crossing to be sold at Cadiz.[9]

Such traffic quickly reduced to a trickle, however, owing to the rapidity with which Amerindians died in the Old World. In addition, the source of supply was dwindling: of an estimated 300,000 Amerindians on Hispaniola, two-thirds had disappeared within a few years after the Spanish conquest.[10] In view of all this, official sentiment in Spain veered against importation of Amerindians. This was illustrated by the cool reception accorded Esteban Gomez, when he returned from his voyage in 1525 along the coast of New England and Cape Breton with his ship's hold filled with Amerindians, "people of both sexes, all innocent and half-naked, who had lived contentedly in their huts." Gomez's action contravened express instructions he had received before setting out on his search for the Northwest Passage.[11] His return to Spain was marked by an incident that was to become a favourite with sixteenth and seventeenth century chroniclers. In the confusion of his arrival, the report ran through the streets to the court that he brought back "clavos" (cloves) rather than "esclavos" (slaves). When Charles V learned the truth he was not at all pleased, and ordered the captives to be set at liberty. Their subsequent fate is unknown. It was not until 1550 that an ordinance outlawed the bringing of Amerindians to Spain.[12]

In the meantime, a spectacular group of Aztec musicians, singers, dancers and jugglers arrived under official auspices in 1528 to be presented at the court of Charles V. They had come in the entourage of Hernan Cortés, and proved to be so successful that the enterprising conquistador, seeking to legitimate his natural children, sent the jugglers to entertain the Pope.[13] The sensation was such that a Polish magnate, famous for his vanity and predilection for the exotic, asked diplomat Jan Dantiscus to intervene with Cortés to make him a gift from the New World--even if it were just an Amerindian.[14] On another occasion, Pietro Martire (Peter Martyr), the Italian at the Spanish court who chronicled early voyages of discovery, invited Amerindian Francisco Chicorana to dinner, and found him not unintelligent. Francisco for his part entertained his host with ingenious recipes for making giants, a custom which he said was practiced in the New World for making kings who could be looked up to. Martire was dubious, but in any event reported Franciso's tale.[15]

The earliest account we have of Amerindians from the northern regions being brought over to the Old World concerns the Portuguese Gaspar Corte-Real in 1501, the same year the explorer was destined to disappear on a voyage to Greenland and the North American mainland coast.[16] Corte-Real's Amerindians were different enough from the by-now familiar islanders and Brazilians to arouse considerable interest in Lisbon:

> The hair of the men is long, just as we wear ours,
> and they wear it in curls, and have their faces
> marked with great signs, and these signs are like
> those of the [East] Indians.... Their manners and
> gestures are most gentle; they laugh considerably
> and manifest the greatest pleasure.... In fine,
> except for the terribly harsh look of the men, they
> appear to me to be in all else of the same form and
> image as ourselves.[17]

The reaction of another observer was that the King of Portugal would be pleased with this new source of slaves who appeared to be fit for every kind of labor; according to reports, this new land was well populated.[18] Two years later, 13 July 1503, four Portuguese ships returned to Lisbon loaded with dyewood and Amerindians, who, however, were probably Brazilians rather than northerners.[19]

Earlier, three men had been brought from Newfoundland to England, according to John Stow's Chronicle. An entry which begins "18.Henry VII Ad 1502" reads:

> This yeere were brought unto the king three men
> taken in the new found island, by Sebastian Caboto
> before named, in anno 1498, these men were clothed
> in beasts skins, and eat raw flesh, but spake such
> a language as no man could understand them, of
> which three men, two of them were seene in the
> kings court at Westminster two yeeres after clothed
> like Englishmen, and could not be discerned from
> Englishmen.[20]

If the evidence of this account is to be credited, these New World men must indeed have been very adaptable. In another instance, the adaptation worked differently: when Sir Martin Frobisher brought Inuit along with a kayak to England in 1577, Queen Elizabeth allowed them to hunt on the Thames and did not exempt the royal swans from their attentions, much to the amazement of the English public.[21]

The first New World visitor to France of whom there is a record appears to have flourished. His name was Essomericq, and he came over from Brazil in 1503 with Captain Binot Paulmier de Gonneville of Honfleur. De Gonneville had gone to the New World to trade, taking a selection of merchandise which indicated that he possessed a clear idea of the type of item which would interest the natives.[22] He had remained with the Carijó (Guaraní) in Brazil for six months; upon his departure, his host, Arosca, had agreed to allow his son to accompany the French on the understanding that he would be returned in approximately twenty months. De Gonneville was not able to fulfill this promise because on his voyage back he lost everything as a result of two attacks by English pirates on the Channel. When he finally reached France, the young Brazilian apparently took to his new life. On the voyage over he had already indicated his willingness to try out French ways by accepting baptism after nearly dying of scurvy. Essomericq is reported to have married a relative of de Gonneville's, to have established a family, and to have lived in France until 1538.[23] His great-grandson, Abbé Jean Paulmier de Courtonne, canon of Lisieux, wrote a memoir to Pope Alexander VII in which he argued for the establishment of a French mission in the "third world", as he referred to the Americas.[24] He asked that he be sent as a missionary, for which he felt he was particularly suited, because of his birth and his calling.[25] In recounting his ancestor's story, the Abbé said that de Gonneville had arranged Essomericq's marriage "which made him an ally" in order to recompense him for the good treatment the French captain had received in Brazil.[26] In his arguments in favour of the missionary enterprise, the Abbé showed himself well informed about the New World, as well as about procedures for founding missions.

There is no record of the fate of the next Amerindians known to have arrived in France, seven "homines sylvestres" who were reported in Pamphili Eusebius's chronicle to have come to Rouen in 1509 equipped with a bark canoe so light that a man could easily carry it on his shoulder.[27] The French noted that these men ate dried meat, drank water, and did not know about wine, bread or silver. It is usually assumed that they were brought to France by Captain Thomas Aubert, one of Jean Ango's pilots, known to have sailed from Dieppe in 1508.[28] The Jesuit missionary Pierre Biard wrote that in 1508 Captain Aubert brought some natives "whom he exhibited to the wonder and applause of France."[29] However, there is no proof that these were the same as the seven men of Eusebius's chronicle. A curious contemporary account tells of a French ship encountering a bark canoe off the English coast in which were seven men with broad, bronze faces, crossed with "stigmate" (probably tattoos) outlining their jaws like "livid veins", who ate raw meat and drank blood.[30] On arriving in Normandy six of these men quickly succumbed, but the seventh was sent to the court of Louis XII as an object of curiosity.[31]

A few years later the story was told of a young Amerindian woman successfully resisting capture. The incident occurred during the voyage of Giovanni da Verrazzano along the coast of North America in 1524. The young woman raised such a fuss that the sailors let her go; however, they kept a boy whom they brought back to France.[32] Among the French, such incidents seem to have continued on a desultory and individual level. There were exceptions to this, of which Jacques Cartier provided the most notable examples. On his 1534 voyage he brought back the Stadaconans Taignoagny and Domagaya. As they continued to be known by their native names, it can be inferred that they were not baptized; France was not yet using such visits as a means of legitimizing her claim to colonize in the Americas by having her Amerindian guests publicly proclaim their friendship and ask for French protection. It can be speculated, however, that Cartier did have short-range motives: he took the Stadaconan brothers not only to act as guides and go-betweens for his second voyage that he was even then hoping to make, but also as an aid in obtaining the necessary commission. In all of this he was successful; the two learned to speak French and upon their voyage back guided Cartier to Stadacona and later acted as interpreters. This was not the explorer's first such action; in 1527, he had brought a girl from Brazil, who had been baptized 30 July 1528 at Saint-Malo with Cartier's wife, Katherine Des Granches, acting as godmother.[33] There is no indications as to what had prompted him in that particular case.

On his second Canadian voyage (1535-36), Cartier's kidnappings increased in scale, as he not only retook Taignoagny and Domagaya, but also their father Donnacona and other head men, a total of about six.[34] On this occasion Cartier appears to have wanted spokesmen of stature to appear before the French king to tell him about Canada, as their land was called; apparently, a colonization project was already in train. Donnacona was at least partly responsible for being taken, as he had been telling Cartier tales of white men on the Saguenay who wore woolen clothes and who possessed immense quantities of gold.[35] Donnacona may have been trying to tell Cartier what he thought the explorer wanted to hear; but he also may have been recounting reports of Spaniards to the south which had filtered through native trade routes. The chieftain was only too successful; Cartier took him to tell his stories to François I. The Spanish historian Andrés González de Barcia wrote that Cartier arrived back in Saint-Malo, 9 July 1536 with his guests "who were travelling contentedly in the hope of returning quickly to Canada with a good share of wealth."[36] None of the group survived, however, to accompany the French in 1541 on their first colonizing attempt in North America. A little girl, apparently one of the children who had been presented to Cartier, seems to have reached adulthood. However, it is not known whether she returned to her native land.

That François I approved of Cartier's action is indicated by his payment of fifty écus for the maintenance of the Amerindians during two years in Saint-Malo.[37] We also get a hint of this approval in the wording of François I's commission dated 17 October 1540 for the colonization of Canada. He mentions transporting and maintaining Amerindians to train as guides and interpreters for French enterprises in the New World.[38]

By this time Rouen and Saint-Malo had become centres for bringing in Amerindians, Rouen for Brazilians in connection with the dyewood trade, and Saint-Malo for Canadians in connection with the fur trade. Their stay was usually for a few months. Jacques Noël, one of Cartier's nephews, was among those who carried on this practice. In applying in 1587 with sea captain Etienne Chaton de la Jannaye for a monopoly of the Canadian fur trade, Noël claimed to have brought several Amerindians to France to be trained as interpreters.[39] This custom, also used to prepare for colonization, was well established long before the birth of New France.[40] It was a formula that proved useful to the English as well, at least during the first days of settlement.

By mid-sixteenth century it was fashionable in France for both royalty and wealthy nobles to have Amerindians in their entourages. This custom was to continue until well into the next century: for instance, some boys taken captive by the Tupinambá in Brazil and sold to their French allies were sent to Henry II of France, who in his turn made gifts of them to various nobles.[41] When Chevalier Nicholas Durand de Villegaignon returned to France in 1558, in effect abandoning the colony he had begun three years earlier in Brazil, be brought back Brazilians of both sexes whom he distributed among friends, keeping half a dozen for himself and his brother. Similarly, François Gravé Du Pont, a naval captain-turned-fur trader who was associated with Champlain, in 1602 presented Henry IV with Amerindians from Canada. One of these was the young son of Begourat, a Montagnais chief, who had been sent by his father on the strength of favourable reports of two fellow tribesmen who had previously made the trip with Gravé Du Pont.[42] The lad was installed as a companion to the Dauphin in the Château Saint-Germain, where he died the following year.[43]

Something of the role of Amerindians at court is indicated by a report from Paris dated 23 March 1668 to the effect that Louis XIV had gone to Versailles "where he intends to divert himself upon the Lake with several guilt [sic] boats which are there provided for him; where there are also Hiroquois with their Gondolas brought from the Indies, made of one entire piece of bark, in which they row with extraordinary swiftness."[44] While Amerindians were kept as curiosities, there existed a certain interest in their particular skills: as the above quotation indicates, their deftness as canoemen was much admired. So was their technique for making fire with two dry sticks; a demonstration of this was put on for Henry IV at Fontainebleau in 1605.[45]

By this time--the beginning of the seventeenth century--Amerindians were appearing in pageants, so characteristic of Renaissance Europe's social and political life. These pageants incorporated aspects of a Roman triumph, as when Charles IX entered Bordeaux 9 April 1565, and was honored with a procession of captives from a dozen nations, including "sauvages américains et brésiliens." Each group made a submission to the King in its own language, which was then interpreted for the King. Charles's entry into Troyes in March of the previous year had also included Amerindians, one of whom had been mounted on a horse masquerading as a unicorn.[46] At that time unicorns had been reported in Norumbega, today's New England.

New World men were on occasion expressly transported to Europe to participate in such events, as in the celebrated entry of Henry II and Catherine de Medici into Rouen in 1550. This was a pageant so lavish that books were published about it, beginning with one the following year.[47] One of the most important tableaux illustrated life in Brazil; fifty natives were supplemented with 150 sailors who had frequented the New World sufficiently to be able to speak a native language, as well as portray tribal customs and manners. But Rouen's interest lay in more than native lifeways; an aspect of the presentation was its enactment of the gathering and preparation of brazilwood, important at that time as a source of red dye. Rouen was a principal centre for this trade. There was also a political purpose; a Tupinambá addressed a poem to the King, asking him to expel the Portuguese, enemies of his people and, incidentally, of the

French. Henry was sufficiently impressed to send an expedition the
following year to map the Brazilian coast and to report on its inhabitants.
Four years after that, in 1555, Villegaignon established a French colony at
Rio de Janeiro, with Henry's moral and material support. However, the
colony did not flourish, and was eventually destroyed by the Portugese in
1560.

Not unexpectedly, Renaissance Europe soon combined this fondness for
display for social, commercial, and political purposes with its concern for
souls. By mid-sixteenth century, New World men brought to France were being
baptized as soon as possible.[48] By early in the seventeenth century, the
French had transformed these baptisms into affairs of state. The most
spectacular of such occasions, if one is to judge by the popular interest
aroused, occurred in 1613 when François de Razilly[49] brought a group of six
Brazilians to France under the care of the Capuchin Père Claude. The
Tupinambá had agreed to come as a delegation to present their homage to the
French King, and to ask for help in the form of missionaries and soldiers,
artisans and merchandise.[50] The occasion was prompted by a French attempt
to establish a colony in Tupinambá territory on the island of Maragnan in
the mouth of the Amazon, a region that was claimed by the Portuguese. Upon
arrival, the delegation was welcomed at a reception at Havre de Grace, or
Le Havre, including a church service during which the Tupinambá recited
aloud the Pater Noster and Ave Maria in their own language. Their entry
into Paris almost a month later took on the aspects of a triumph;
fashionable Paris turned out in such numbers that the press of the crowd
forced the Capuchins to retreat with their exotic charges into their
convent. But still the visitors came, so that the King was constrained to
send protecting guards. Cloistered nuns were allowed to see them. "Who
would have thought," mused Claude, "that Paris, used to the strange and
exotic, would have gone so wild over these Indians?"[51] However, at least
one contemporary Frenchman was not so impressed. François de Malherbe, poet
and critic, did not believe that the Brazilians, their dancing, or their
possessions, would encourage colonization: "I do not think," he observed
sourly, "that this booty will arouse much desire in those who have not been
[to Brazil] to go there."[52]

In making their formal submission to the King, the Tupinambá referred
to their people, before the arrival of the French, as living a miserable
life, without law and without faith.[53] One could wonder if they believed
the words put into their mouths by the enterprising Capuchins. In any
event, they provided the King with the occasion to consent publicly to the
sending of twelve Capuchins, as well as soldiers, to Maragnan, as duly
reported in Le Mercure François.[54] Three of the Brazilians quickly
succumbed under the pressures of an unaccustomed life style; the other three
were prepared for baptism at the Church of the Capuchins, which was richly
decorated for the occasion.[55] The Tupinambá were dressed in white taffeta,
each being led by two white-robed priests to the baptismal font obscured by
yards of white taffeta. The Bishop of Paris officiated, and the King and
Queen Regent were godparents; Claude interpreted. In the concluding
procession, the Tupinambá carried lillies and wore tall hats decorated with
fronds of feathers. Claude's book on the Maragnan expedition was published
in 1614; the part dealing with the entry into Paris and the baptism
frequently appeared in the anthologies so popular at this period. The

Brazilians also became a favourite with illustrators, particularly in their baptismal finery or wearing French dress. Despite all this interest and effort, the colony at Maragnan was also destroyed by the Portuguese, in 1615.

Another spectacle occurred in 1637 when two Montagnais girls were baptized in the great convent of the Carmelites in Paris. As with the Tupinambá, the occasion was marked with a host of fashionable and important participants and guests, including the Princess de Condé as godparent.[56] Besides being an affirmation of the re-establishment of New France in Canada following the English occupation of 1629-32, this was a glittering social event in its own right.

The successful plantation of New France on the St. Lawrence provided a new dimension for the practice of sending over Amerindian children to be educated in the French manner. When the Jesuits embarked on this policy in 1634, they were following in the footsteps of their colleagues in Brazil, as well as in those of the Recollets who had preceded them in New France, and who had begun sending over boys in 1620.[57] Being a continental power dependent on her armies, France was reluctant to part with her nationals in the numbers needed for successful colonization, so she turned to educating Amerindians to be Frenchmen. Such a policy had been encouraged by early reports of the docility of Amerindians, and the widely-held belief that they were culturally a "tabula rasa" awaiting the imprint of European civilization. The Jesuits in particular believed that the best way of recasting of Amerindian children into the French mould was by isolating them from their native cultures. This could be most effectively achieved, the reasoning went, by sending them to France, where, under ideal conditions for such an experiment, it should be possible to so condition the children that once returned to their native lands they would live and act like Frenchmen. To quote Jesuit Paul Le Jeune, superior at Québec from 1632 to 1639:

> I see no other way than that which your Reverence
> suggests, of sending a child every year to France.
> Having been there two years, he will return with a
> knowledge of the language, and having already
> become accustomed to our way, he will not leave us
> and will retain his little countrymen.[58]

In 1635 he noted optimistically that "the Savages are beginning to open their eyes and to recognize that children who are with us are well taught." The next year, in 1636, he again wrote in the same vein, concerning a lad he was sending over as a "gift" to M. De Noyers, secretary of state: "I have great hopes that so good a hand will return him to us some day, so well educated that he will serve as an example to the people of his nation."[59]

However, Le Jeune's high hopes were not realized. One of the difficulties lay in keeping the children alive in France. If they survived, another serious problem was soon encountered: the tendency of these children, despite their indoctrination in French ways, to revert to their native cultures at the first opportunity, or else to become misfits in both cultures, the French as well as their own. The Huron Louis Amantacha had been sent to France in 1626, where he was baptized as Louis de Sainte-Foy,

and returned a little over two years later.[60] Louis was in New France when
it fell to the English in 1629; when the French repossessed their colony in
1632, they found that Louis had reverted to his traditional ways. The
failure was somewhat mitigated by Louis's continuing interest in cementing
the French-Huron alliance, until he was taken by the Iroquois and heard of
no more. There was no such mitigation in the case of the Montagnais,
Pierre-Antoine Pastedechouan, who had grown up in France, and who had also
been in New France during the English occupation.[61] Pierre became a misfit
in both societies; in the end, only the missionaries were prepared to endure
him, and that solely for the sake of learning his native language.
Eventually, in 1636, he was reported to have died of starvation in the
woods. Thus ended the high hopes the French had entertained at his baptism,
when the Prince de Guémenée had stood as his godfather. The French
naturally blamed the influence of the English for these failures, although
some wondered if the Amerindians had been instructed sufficiently to be able
to maintain their newly acquired cultural orientations upon being returned
home "without shepherds."[62] The temptation existed to attribute the
program's lack of success to the perversity of Amerindians, or perhaps to
their alleged devotion to the devil.

Failures in education and assimilation aside, the diplomatic aspects of
these European visits remained. In 1638, the son of Iwanchon, a Montagnais
captain, laid his "crown" of porcelain beads (wampum) at the feet of
Louis XIII "as a sign that he recognized the great Prince, in the name of
all nations, as their true and lawful monarch." The King and Queen
responded by showing him their Dauphin, and making the Montagnais a present
of six suits of clothing "entirely of cloth of gold, velvet, satin, silk,
plush, scarlet and everything else in keeping." Back in Québec the young
man displayed these gifts to Governor Charles Huault de Montmagny, "who
deemed it advisable to distribute them among several of the nations
present. Therefore three splendid suits were given to this young
Savage—one for himself, one for his son, and the third for his father. The
three other suits were presented to Christian captains of different
nations." Decked out in their European finery, these Captains led the
Amerindian section in a procession for the feast of the Assumption of the
Virgin. Sending an Amerindian costume to the Dauphin, the chiefs explained:
"It is not a present that we make him, for his riches are far greater than
ours; but it is a metawagan—a small toy to amuse his little son, who may
perhaps take pleasure in seeing how our children are dressed."[63]

The French custom of sending war prisoners to France was described by
an Englishman as "the great and most effectual means they have taken for
confirming of their Indians, and for the subverting or corrupting or ours."
According to John Nelson, a Scottish merchant who toward the end of the
seventeenth century was a prisoner at Québec and who reported on his
observations,

> they have from time to time transported into France
> some of the most eminent and enterprizing Indians
> (not only of their own, but of ours whom they have
> happened to take their prisoners) for no other
> intent than to amaze and dazzle them with the
> greatness and splendour of the French Court and

Armie where the King hath so thought it worth his
countenancing as to send them into Flanders, where
the Armies have been expressly mustered before
them, to show their greatness.

As a matter of fact, added Nelson, "there are actually at this instant now
in Versailles six Sagamos or chiefs sent from Canada, Hudsons Bay and Nova
Scotia to sollicite such help and assistance against us."[64]

By the time Nelson penned his observations in 1696, the French had been
sending Amerindian war prisoners to France for more than half a century.
One of the most noted of these was the Mohawk Honatteniate, who arrived at
Havre de Grace on 7 December 1649. Known to the French as Le Berger, he had
been ransomed several years before by Montmagny from Pieskaret, the
Algonquin captain who had waged his own private war against the Iroquois
with such success that he had become a legend in his own time.[65] Le Berger
had returned to his own people, but did not forget that he owed his life to
the French. He opposed the killing of Father Isaac Jogues in 1646. Two
years later he decided to give himself up to the French, which he did while
on a hunting expedition near Trois-Rivières. The French, however, were
convinced he had come to spy, and did not believe him when he showed a scar
on his arm where he claimed to have taken a blow intended for Jogues. They
shackled his feet. To prove his sincerity, Le Berger arranged for some
fellow Iroquois to be captured, but they all managed to escape, except
Le Berger, who determinedly remained. The French, fearful that one day he
might return to his own country with information he had gathered while at
Trois-Rivières, decided to send him to France. On board the ship, the
sailors bound him for fear he would escape; in the morning, he would be
found free from his fetters. This happened several times, so that the
sailors began to wonder if he were a sorcerer.[66] The sight of Havre de
Grace so astonished him that he did not speak for two hours. Although it
was December, he preferred to go barefooted rather than to confine his feet
in French shoes and stockings. He also went bareheaded. Injuring his foot,
he was lodged in the hospital at Dieppe where the nuns reported that "he
took his repast, not as a Barbarian, but as a temperate man; for although he
was tall and powerful, he ate rather sparingly." Eventually, he was taken
to Paris, where he was lodged in a house for recent converts; there he
died. The concluding remark in the Jesuit Relations concerning Le Berger
was to the effect that it was estimated that he had eaten fifty men in his
day.

The most celebrated incident in the history of New France concerning
sending Amerindians to Europe occurred when Governor Jacques-René Brisay de
Denonville transported thirty to sixty Iroquois war prisoners for service as
galley slaves.[67] A terse note in Le Mercure Galant reported the arrival of
the Iroquois destined for galley service, to see if they would be useful for
it.[68] The experiment--if that is what it can be called--aroused bitter
criticism at the time. Jesuit Jean de Lamberville, for one, felt that it
threatened his work among the Iroquois, particularly as the prisoners
included "some who had been to France often."[69] Lahontan also had some
sharp words on the subject.[70] As early as 1663 it had been proposed to
destroy the Iroquois either by killing or by sending their best men to serve
in the galleys.[71] Talon wrote in a similar vein three years later;[72] in

1684, Governor Joseph-Antoine Le Febvre de La Barre was urged to take as many Iroquois prisoners as possible for service in the galleys.[73] The fate of most of the Iroquois who were sent over for this purpose can only be surmised; that at least some of them were sent to Marseilles is suggested by an account that concerns the expenses of four Iroquois travelling to that city.[74] Perhaps the cries of outrage from the colony had their effect, or perhaps the Iroquois died too quickly to be of much use as galley slaves. Or perhaps it was political pressure exerted of Amerindian allies back in New France; in any event, the survivors were released more than a year later, in 1689.[75] According to de Lamberville, only 13 returned to Canada; he claimed the rest had died of destitution.[76] This episode is unique in the history of New France. When Louis de Buade de Frontenac returned in 1689 for his second term as governor, he brought three of the surviving Iroquois with him.[77] One of these, Orecone, became Frontenac's inseparable companion.[78] Orecone became renowned for his exploits in the French cause, which he explained "with a modesty rare among Indians, that he still had not done enough to repay his father Onontio."[79]

In the meantime, the English, remained convinced that the French policy of sending influential Amerindians to France was producing better results than it actually was. Nelson makes this clear:

> In regard to our Indians, no better methods can be
> taken, than by imitating the French, both as to
> their encouragements at home, as also to have some
> chiefs of the diverse nations of the Indians to be
> sent into England whereby to give a counterpoise
> unto the French reputation and greatness.[80]

But the French had slowly become convinced that the policy had only produced useless expense, at least as far as Amerindian chiefs were concerned.[81] First of all, Amerindian delegates displayed a tendency to consider themselves as equal even to the French King, in spite of all the pomp and circumstance with which he was surrounded; second, even when they were suitably impressed with French might, they were seldom able to convince their fellows in the New World of this. So that in terms of gaining new alliances or cementing existing ones, such visits proved ineffective, which finally led the French to discourage them.[82] Unofficial or casual visits also came to be disapproved, an attitude that intensified during the eighteenth century. In 1740, the unauthorized passage to France of a Micmac and his interpreter drew severe official displeasure on the head of the captain involved.[83] The Micmac, Denis d'Esdain, was given red cloth, gold braid, gold fringe, beads and ribbon in assorted colours. Missionary Jean-Louis Le Loutre was instructed to inform d'Esdain of the value of these gifts, while at the same time impressing upon him that he would have been even better treated if his visit has been authorized.[84]

As for Amerindians, they seldom regarded going to Europe with any particular enthusiasm, to say the least. Early European travellers reported, with apparent surprise, that while Amerindians travelled much in their own countries they were not eager to go to Europe. Jean Ribault discovered this during his attempt to colonize "La Floride" (today's Carolina coast) in 1562-65. He was under instructions from the Queen to bring back two Amerindians, presumably for her entourage. Ribault obtained the consent of an Amerindian "King," who named two men whose first reaction was that they were being especially favoured. The two quickly changed their minds when they realized they would be leaving their homeland. The best efforts of the French to cajole them into accepting their lot proved fruitless, and they escaped, carefully leaving behind the clothing and other items their hosts had given them.[85] Similarly, Jean Mocquet, geographer to the King, in 1617 told of a young Caribbean Indian who had indicated a willingness to go to France under the impression that "France" was the ship in which the French were sailing. Upon learning the truth he sought to escape; the French tied him, but he freed himself from his bonds. By that time, they were too far out to sea for the young man to swim back to shore. Frustrated, he vented his fury on a shipmate, an Amerindian belonging to an enemy tribe. The captain ordered the belligerent one to be whipped, to which his only reaction was to tense his shoulders and not utter a sound, which greatly impressed the French in view of the welts caused by the lashes. Eventually, Mocquet presented him to the King.

The loneliness that Amerindians experienced in Europe was suggested by Mocquet's story of Yapoco, whom he saw in Paris with Claude's group. Mocquet had known Yapoco in Brazil; the latter, upon seeing a familiar face from his homeland, clung to Mocquet and embraced him, recounting his experiences in France.[86]

What were the reactions of Amerindians to Europe? Outside of Montaigne's celebrated interview with three Brazilians in Rouen, in which they expressed surprise at the social inequalities they saw in French society, there are very few reports of Amerindian impressions of Europe from the sixteenth or even the seventeenth centuries. We have already noted that the accounts of Amerindians who had sailed to France with Gravé Du Pont had influenced Begourat to allow his son to go. Obviously, impressions must have been expressed in terms of cultural experiences; thus the son of Iwanchon told of "rolling cabins drawn by moose."[87] In another case the visitor, seeing the street of metal workers' shops in Paris, wondered if the coppersmiths were not relatives of the King and the copper trade a privilege of the seigneurs.[88] In the New World, reports of such masses of people and houses seemed incredible. "They have bribed you" was an understandable reaction.[89] It is also entirely possible that Amerindians, once they recovered from their first astonishment, were not so overwhelmed by European cities as Europeans would have liked to assume. From the beginning, Amerindians were loyal to their own cultural values and displayed a preference for their own way of life. Typical was Louis of Dominique, who after some time in France wanted only to return to his own people. Asked if he had regrets about leaving France after having lived in Paris and consorted with princes and the royal courts, and having seen the city's beautiful buildings, he replied that he liked his own country better.[90] The instant he was back on his native soil, he shed his European garments and reverted to his traditional way.[91]

Europeans were misled by their preconceptions of Amerindians as "poor savages" who could not help but be impressed by Europe's sophisticated civilization. Europeans, no less than Amerindians, were the prisoners of their lexicons, capable of perception "only in their own manner." The truth was that Amerindians had a sophistication of their own. Le Clercq recounted a story of some ladies at the French court who ridiculed a group of chiefs for their manner of painting themselves. The chiefs' retort was that the ladies should look to their own makeup, which with its black "beauty spots" made the women look as though they were in mourning.[92] The French began to perceive something of this cultural self-confidence when they observed that New World men were quite as devoted to their own self-interest as were the French, and were equally as willing to avail themselves of every means at their disposal to gain their own ends. Thus chiefs who were impressed with French power in Europe reacted by trying to win it to the service of their own particular interests. The French found themselves not overawing simple savages but negotiating with accomplished diplomats. Little wonder that their initial enthusiasm for bringing chiefs to France waned.

The European society to which Amerindians were exposed was not one in which living conditions were necessarily more comfortable than those of the New World. The gap in living standards was less during the days of first contact than it was to become later. Neither did Amerindians find a society with less violence than their own; rather, they found one in which for all practical purposes it was the prerogative of privileged groups,[93] which the state would have liked to restrict even further. To Amerindians, this was unacceptable, as in their own non-state societies they were accustomed to considering each man his own master, whether in trade, warfare or religion. They were astonished to see poverty in the midst of opulence; it did not accord with their practice of sharing, which, if not always even, was always inclusive.[94] What the Amerindians saw in Europe only confirmed them in the belief that they were at least equal, if not superior, to the French, both as individuals and in respect to their civilizations. The people in France, for their part, continued to regard Amerindians as curiosities; except for Montaigne, few Frenchmen seem to have considered that they had anything to learn from these exotic visitors.

In 1725, more than a century after the visits began, a group of Illinois chiefs were received in Paris in terms strongly reminiscent of those which had been accorded to Claude's Tupinambá in 1613; overwhelming enthusiasm and very little comprehension. France had been having difficulties with her alliances in the Great Lakes region, and so the Illinois chiefs were welcomed in high places and by distinguished personages in the hope that their visit presaged a firmer commitment to the French cause in the colonial wars against Great Britain. The occasion was reported in Le Mercure de France in the same vein as that of the earlier event.[95] The romantic notion of the "noble savage" was also a factor; within a few decades, Jean-Jacques Rousseau would boost its long-since established popularity by lending it an aura of intellectual respectability. In the meantime the British, having learned to appreciate the services of their Mohawk allies in the colonial wars, lionized visiting chieftains: Queen Anne's four American kings, for instance, in 1710; and Joseph Brant in 1785-86. An earlier visit that had been made much of, that of Pocahontas in 1616, coincided with the launching of English colonization in Virginia in territory controlled by the lady's father, Powhatan. Interestingly enough, the pictorial record of Amerindian visitors to England is much better than for those who went to France: the English commissioned leading artists to paint portraits of their exotic guests, if they were important enough, something the French never did. The fact that Claude's Tupinambá were illustrated at all is indicative of the extraordinary level of interest aroused in Paris by that particular visit.

While it can hardly be argued that these visits at any time had a major influence in the sweep of events that overtook the Americas, there can be little doubt that they were an effective means of arousing European public interest in the New World. Especially during the sixteenth century, many more Europeans saw Amerindians in the Old World than in the New. However, early attempts to use these visits as a source of information about the New World soon proved unsatisfactory, as Amerindians quickly detected what Europeans wanted to hear, and told whatever tales they felt would ensure their early passage back to their native lands. Undeterred by this, and perceiving other possibilities, the French excelled in developing techniques for using these visits as instruments of empire. Despite that fact, or perhaps because of it, Amerindian visits contributed very little toward understanding or sympathy between the two worlds. Even for the French, such an aim had been encouraged only to the extent that it served more important goals, such as challenging Spain, Portugal and the Vatican on their division of the world. France was more interested in winning Amerindians to her service than she was in Amerindians for their own sake, or for that of their civilizations. It is ironic that the best ethnographic records of Amerindians during the days of first contacts with Europeans were compiled by the Spanish, whose reputation concerning their relationship with New World peoples is hardly an enviable one, particularly in contrast to that of the French: the "black legend" versus "French and Indians."

FOOTNOTES

1. This paper is largely drawn from the sixth chapter a chapter in my book
   The Myth of the Savage and the Beginnings of French Colonialism in the
   Americas, (Edmonton: University of Alberta Press, 1984). Some
   additional information has been included.

2. Gonzalo Fernández de Oviedo y Valdés, L'Histoire naturelle et generalle
   des Indes, isles et terre ferme de la grand [sic] mer oceane...
   [tr. J. Poleur] (Paris: M. De Vascosan, 1555), bk II:17v.

3. Pietro Martire d'Anghiera, De Orbe novo de Pierre Martyr Anghiera, tr.
   avec commentaires par Paul Gaffarel (Paris: E. Leroux, 1907), IV:2.

4. Paul Gaffarel, Histoire de la découverte de l'Amérique depuis les
   origines jusqu'à la mort de Christophe Colomb, 2 vols. (Paris: Arthur
   Rousseau, 1892), II:417; Martin Fernández de Navarrete, Relations de
   quatre voyages..., 3 vols. (Paris: Treuttel et Würtz), I:469.

5. Margaret T. Hodgen, Early Anthropology in the Sixteenth and Seventeenth
   Centuries (Philadelphia: University of Pennsylvania Press, 1964), III.
   There is some doubt about this report as there is no word that the
   captives arrived in Seville (Carl O. Sauer, The Early Spanish Main
   (Berkeley and Los Angeles: University of California Press, 1969),
   87n25).

6. Navarrete, Quatre voyages, I:492.

7. Bartolomé de Las Casas, Oeuvres, ed., J.A. Llorente, 2 vols. (Paris:
   Alexis Eymery, 1822), I:256; Antonio de Herrera y Tordesillas, Histoire
   générale des voyages et conquestes des Castillans dans les isles et
   terre ferme des Indes Occidentales, tr. N. de La Coste, 3 vols. (Paris:
   N. et J. de La Coste, 1659-71), I:188.

8. Bartolomé de Las Casas, Histoire des Indes occidentales..., (Lyon: Jean
   Caffin et F. Plaignard, 1642), II:323; Gaffarel, Histoire de la
   découverte, II:418.

9. Amerigo Vespucci, The First Four Voyages of Amerigo Vespucci, (London:
   Bernard Quaritch, 1893), 22-23. The authenticity of this voyage,
   supposed to have occurred in 1497-98, has been disputed. Some have
   assigned this episode to Vespucci's accepted 1499 voyage with Alonso de
   Ojeda.

10. Arthur Percival Newton, The European Nations in the West Indies
    1493-1688, (London: A. and C. Black, 1933), 13.

11. Pietro Martire d'Anghiera, De Orbe Novo, tr. and ed. Francis Augustus MacNutt, 2 vols. (New York: Putnam's, 1912), II:418-420.

12. Antonio de Herrera y Tordesillas, The General History of the Vast Continent and Islands of America, Commonly Called the West-Indies..., tr. Captain John Stevens, 6 vols. (London: J. Batley, 1725-26), VI:339.

13. Bernal Diaz del Castillo, Historia verdadera de la conquista de la Nueva-Espãna, (Madrid, 1632), ch. cxcv, ff. 226v-227.

14. Janusz Tazbir, "La Conquête de l'Amérique à la lumiè de l'opinion polonaise, "Acta Poloniae Historica, XVII (1968), 7.

15. Martire, De Orbe Novo (MacNutt, ed.), II:258, 267-268.

16. The account was first published in Fracanzano da Montalboddo's Paesi novamenti retrovati e Novo Mondo da Alberico Vesputio Florentino intitulato (Vicenza, 1507).

17. Dispatch of Alberto Cantino from Lisbon to Hercules d'Este, Duke of Ferrara, 17 October 1501, reproduced in Henry Percival Biggar, ed., The Precursors of Jacques Cartier 1497-1534, (Ottawa: Government Printing Bureau, 1911), 64.

18. Letter of Pietro Pasqualigo to the seignory of Venice, 18 October 1501. Reproduced by Biggar, Precursors, 66.

19. Henry Harrisse, The Discovery of North America, (Amsterdam: N. Israel, 1961), 128, 694.

20. John Stow, Annales, or a General Chronicle of England, Begun by John Stow: and augmented with matters Foraigne and Domestique, Ancient and Moderne, unto the end of this present yeere, 1631, by Edmund Howes (London, Richard Meighen, 1631), 483-484. The visit of the three Amerindians is also reported by Richard Hakluyt, The Principal Navigations, Voyages, Traffiques and Discoveries of the English Nation, 12 vols. (Glasgow: James MacLehose, 1903-1905), XII:19.

21. John Rigby Hale, "A World Elsewhere," in The Age of the Renaissance, ed. Denys Hay (London: Thames and Hudson, 1967), 335. Likely Inuit had long since been seen in Denmark and perhaps in Norway. See Tryggvi Oleson, Early Voyages and Northern Approaches 1000-1632, (Toronto: McClelland and Stewart, 1963).

22. Paul Gaffarel, Les Découvreurs français du XIVe au XVIe siècles..., (Paris: Challamel, 1888), 86-87; Armand d'Avezac, Campagne authentique du voyage du Capitain de Gonneville... (Paris: Challamel Ainê, 1869).

23. Charles de Brosse, Histoire des Navigations aux terres australes...,
    2 vols. (Paris: Durand, 1756), I:102-20; Charles-André Julien, Les
    voyages de découverte et les premiers établissements (XVe-XVIe siècles)
    (Paris: Presses Universitaires de France, 1948), 19-20. For a
    different version, see John Hemming, Red Gold (London: Macmillan,
    1978), 11-12.

24. Jean Paulmier de Courtonne, chanoine de Lisieux, Mémoire touchant
    l'établissement d'une mission chrestienne dans le troisième monde,
    autrement appellé la Terre australe, meridionale, antarctique et
    inconnue..., (Paris: C. Cramoisy, 1663), 178.

25. Ibid, introductory letter.

26. One could speculate if Voltaire had this story in mind when he wrote
    L'Ingenue, a play about a "Huron"--really a Frenchman raised by
    Hurons--who came to Europe.

27. Gaffarel, Découvreurs français, 128. This is a translation of a Latin
    account which appeared in the chronicle of Eusebius as updated by
    Prosper and Mathieu Paulmier. Hemming says the seven men were from
    Brazil (Red Gold, 12).

28. Giovanni Battista Ramusio, A la découverte de l'Amérique du Nord, tr.
    Général Langlois and M. J. Simon (Paris: Centre de Documentation
    'André Thevet', 1933), 113; Harrisse, Discovery of North America, 181;
    William Francis Ganong, Crucial Maps in the Early Cartography and
    Place-Nomenclature of the Atlantic Coast of Canada (Toronto:
    University of Toronto Press, 1964), 197.

29. Reuben Gold Thwaites, Jesuit Relations and Allied Documents, 73 vols.
    (Cleveland: Burrows Bros., 1896-1901), III:39.

30. Raccolta di documenti e studi pubblicati dalla R. commissione
    colombiana pel quarto centenario dalla scoperta dell'America (Rome,
    1892), part III, vol. II:377. This citation is taken from Pietro
    Bembo's Historia Veneziana (1530).

31. Ch. de La Roncière, Histoire de la marine française, 6 vols. (Paris:
    Plon-Nourrit, 1901-1923), III:139.

32. Ramusio, Navigations et voyages, 100.

33. René Maran, Les pionniers de l'Empire... (Paris: Albin Michel, 1943),
    104, 97.

34. The figure ten usually given refers to Cartier's statement that he
    returned with ten Amerindians. (Henry Percival Biggar, ed., The
    Voyages of Jacques Cartier [Ottawa: Acland, 1924], 249). That number
    would have included the four children who had been presented to him at
    Stadacona and Hochelay.

35. Ibid., 201, 221.

36. Anthony Kerrigan, ed., Barcia's Chronological History of the Continent of Florida Containing the Discoveries and Principal Events which came to Pass in this Vast Kingdom, (Gainesville: University of Florida Press, 1951), 20.

37. Henry Percival Biggar, ed., A Collection of Documents Relating to Jacques Cartier and the Sieur de Roberval, (Ottawa: Public Archives, 1930), doc. LXXVI, March 1538/39.

38. Ibid., 69-70.

39. H.H. Michelant et Alfred Ramé, eds., Voyage de Jacques Cartier au Canada en 1534... (Paris: Librairie Tross, 1865), part II:37.

40. Recollet Gabriel Sagard prepared for his journey to Huronia in 1623 by learning something of the language beforehand, apparently in France. (The Long Journey to the Country of the Hurons, ed. George Wrong [Toronto: Champlain Society, 1939], xvi).

41. Jean de Léry, Histoire d'un voyage fait en la terre du Brésil (Lausanne: Bibliothèque Romande, 1972), 78-79.

42. Pierre-Victor-Palma Cayet, Chronologie septenaire de l'Histoire de la Paix entre les Roys de France et d'Espagne, 2 vols. (Paris: J. Richer, 1605), II:415-16.

43. A.-L. Leymarie, "Le Canada pendant la jeunesse de Louis XIII", Nova Francia, I, 4 (1926), 168-69; Guillaume de Vaumas, L'Eveil missionnaire de la France d'Henri IV à la fondation du seminaire des missions étrangères (Lyon: Impr. Express, 1942), 43.

44. The London Gazette (No. 348) 1668, new item "Paris March 23"; in Burney Collection of Newspapers, British Museum. For an admiring view of New World watercraft, in this case a kayak, see César de Rochefort, Histoire naturelle et morale des isles Antilles de l'Amérique... (Rotterdam: A. Leers, 1658), 189.

45. Jean Mocquet, Voyages en Afrique, Asie, Indes orientales et occidentales... (Paris: J. de Heuqueville, 1617), 80-1.

46. Gaffarel, Histoire du Brésil, 136; Gilbert Chinard, L'Exotisme américain dans la littérature française au XVIe siècle (Paris: Hachette, 1949), 105.

47. C'est la deduction du somptueux ordre plaisantz spectacles et magnifiques theatres dresses et exhibes par les citoyens de Rouen... (Rouen: Robert le Hoy et Jehan dictz du Gord, 1551). A manuscript describing the event, illuminated in color, and bound in velour, is in the Bibliothèque Municipale de Rouen. Thomas Galiot described the two-day event as being superb and magnificent in his Inventaire de l'histoire journalière (Paris: Jacques Rezé, 1599). See also

Ferdinand-Jean Denis, Une Fête brésilienne célébrée à Rouen en 1550...
(Paris: J. Techener, 1850); Paul Gaffarel, Histoire du Brésil français
au seizième siècle (Paris: Maisonneuve, 1878), 130-136. At the time
of the entry, Rouen had been a major centre for trade in brazilwood for
half a century. To this day Rouen remembers its Brazilian connection.
In 1969 La Foire de Rouen featured ballets "brasiliana" as a major
attraction. The event was reported in Paris-Normandie, 19 mai 1969.

48. An example of such a ceremony is contained in Jean La Vacquerie, De
multiplici haereticorum tentatione, per 10. vacquerium Roiensem,
(Paris, 1560), 56ff.

49. François's brother, Isaac, was Lieutenant-General of New France,
1632-35.

50. A contemporary account of this event can be found in Troisième tome du
Mercure François, seconde continuation (Paris, 1617), 164ff.

51. Claude [d'Abbeville], Histoire de la Mission des Pères Capucins en
l'Isle de Maragnan et terres circonvoisins (Paris: François Huby,
1614), 339v-340.

52. Lettres de Malherbe [à Peiresc], dediées à la ville de Caen (Paris:
J. J. Blaise, 1822), 258.

53. Claude, Maragnan, 341v-42.

54. Troisième tome du Mercure François, seconde continuation, 174.

55. Gilbert Chinard, L'Amérique et le rêve exotique (Paris: Robert
Laffont, 1969), 22-4. Chinard gives the impression that all six were
baptized and died afterward. This is not borne out by either Claude's
account nor by that in Le Mercure François. Neither does Claude
mention a plan to marry the Tupinambá to suitable devots, as Chinard
claims.

56. Thwaites, Jesuit Relations, XI:99-101. A contemporary report of this
type of event is found in Joseph Le Ber's Départ pour le Canada en
1639. Lettre inédite d'une Ursuline (Soeur Cécile de Sainte-Croix)
(Dieppe: La Vigie de Dieppe, 1939).

57. Coppie de la lettre Escripte par le R.P. Denys Jamet, Commissionaire
des PP. Recollestz de Canada a Monsieur de Rancé, grand vicaire de
Pontoyse, 15 aoust 1620 (Paris, 1620), 7. Recollect Chrestien Le
Clercq told of one such lad who "had been shown what was most important
and beautiful at Paris and elsewhere, and the most holy spots."
Unfortunately, the boy died at sea on his way back to Canada. (Le
Clercq, First Establishment of the Faith in New France, tr. and ed.
John Gilmary Shea, 2 vols. (New York: J.G. Shea, 1887), I:181-83.

58. Thwaites, Jesuit Relations, IV:85.

59. Ibid., IX:105.

60. The story of Louis is in the <u>Dictionary of Canadian Biography</u> I, s.v.
    "Amantacha." Louis's baptism in the Cathedral of Rouen had been
    another of those religious spectaculars that characterized this age of
    Roman Catholic missionary zeal. Sixte Le Tac describes the event in
    <u>Histoire chronologique de la Nouvelle France ou Canada, depuis sa</u>
    <u>découverte (1504) jusques en l'an 1632</u> (Paris: G. Fischbacher, 1888),
    136-38.

61. <u>Dictionary of Canadian Biography</u>, I, s.v. "Pastedechouan"; Thwaites,
    <u>Jesuit Relations</u>, IV:107-09; VI:87; VII:67-71; and IX:69-71.

62. Ibid., II:87.

63. Ibid., XV:223-227; 237.

64. Edmund Bailey O'Callaghan and John Romeyn Brodhead, eds., <u>Documents</u>
    <u>Relative to the Colonial History of the State of New York</u>, 15 vols.
    (Albany: Weed Parson, 1853-87), IV:206-11. "Mr. Nelson's Memorial
    about the State of the Northern Colonies in America", 24 September
    1696. This compilation will be hereafter referred to as <u>New York</u>
    <u>Colonial Documents</u>.

65. For something of Pieskaret's story, see Cadwallader Colden, <u>History of</u>
    <u>the Five Nations</u>... (New York: W. Bradford, 1727), 8-15. For
    Honatteniate (Le Berger) see Thwaites, <u>Jesuit Relations</u>, XXXVI:21-45,
    and <u>Dictionary of Canadian Biography</u> I, s.v. "Honatteniate."

66. For another example of an Amerindian freeing himself from bonds, see
    <u>infra</u>, 27.

67. Thirty-six were sent according to Jean Leclerc, <u>Le Marquis de</u>
    <u>Denonville, gouverneur de la Nouvelle-France 1685-1689</u> (Montreal:
    Fides, 1976), 194-95. This is the figure given by Jesuit Thierry
    Beschefer (Thwaites, <u>Jesuit Relations</u>, LXIII:278). However, a report
    in <u>Le Mercure Galant</u> datelined November 1687, places the figure at
    between fifty and sixty.

68. <u>Le Mercure Galant</u> (nov. 1687), 102.

69. Thwaites, <u>Jesuit Relations</u>, LXIV:249.

70. Louis-Armand de Lom d'Arce, Baron de Lahontan, <u>Voyages</u>...dans
    <u>l'Amérique septentrionale</u>..., 2 vols. (Amsterdam: François l'Honoré,
    1705), I:109ff. The argument has carried over to this day. W.J.
    Eccles has taken the position that Denonville's action had not been
    planned beforehand ("Denonville et les galériens iroquois," <u>Revue</u>
    <u>d'Histoire de l'Amérique française</u> XIV, 3 [1960], 408-29).

71. PAC (Public Archives of Canada), AC (Archives des Colonies), C11A
    2:36v-37. Memoire pour la Nouvelle France, de La Rochelle, 22 janv.
    1663.

72. PAC, AC, C11A 2:214v, de Talon à Québec, le 11 nov. 1666.

73. PAC, AC, C11A 6:289v, de Versailles à De La Barre, 31 juillet 1684.

74. PAC, AC, F1A 4:36, "Estat de la depense que le Roy veut," 1 mars 1688. The item concerns the payment for fifty livres for the subsistence of the Iroquois.

75. Leclerc, Denonville, 199-200.

76. Jean Leclerc, "Denonville et ses captifs Iroquois: Jean de Lamberville et les quarante delegués Iroquois," Revue d'Histoire de l'Amérique française, XV, 1 (1961), 53-54. He is citing a letter written by de Lamberville dated 23 June 1695 (Thwaites, Jesuit Relations, LXIV:243). Later, Leclerc took issue with de Lamberville, citing official directives that the galley slaves be well treated. (Denonville, 195-96).

77. PAC, AC, C11A 10:220v, Frontenac au ministre, le 15 novembre 1689.

78. PAC, AC, F3 7: 154v, "Explication de trois colliers que deux Iroquois portent aux...Indiens catholiques de Canada," 9 février 1694.

79. PAC, AC F3 6:401-401v, "Relation de ce qui c'est passé...le 27 novembre 1690 jusqu'au 15 octobre 1691."

80. O'Callaghan and Brodhead, New York Colonial Documents, IV:208.

81. PAC, AC, B 57:639, Maurepas à Beauharnois, 8 avril 1732.

82. Americans were later to have a similar experience when they attempted to impress hostile Amerindians by bringing their chiefs to Washington, where they were wined and dined, met the president and had carefully arranged opportunities to see American military might. The reports of these delegates to their fellow tribesmen were not only often doubted, they were sometimes openly scoffed at, and the delegates themselves ran the risk of being regarded as traitors because they had associated with the Long Knives on their own ground. See K.C. Turner, Red Men Calling on the Great White Father (Norman, University of Oklahoma Press, 1951).

83. PAC, AC, B 76:83v, Maurepas à Guillot, 1 mai 1740.

84. PAC, AC, C11B 23:74-74v, Du Quesnel à Maurepas, 19 octobre 1741.

85. René Goulaine de Laudonnière, L'Histoire notable de la Floride située es Indes Occidentales... (Paris, Jannet, 1853), 27-31.

86. Mocquet, Voyages en Afrique, 94-95, 98.

87. Thwaites, Jesuit Relations, XV:235.

88. Nicolas Denys, The Description and Natural History of the Coasts of North America (Acadia), ed. William F. Ganong (Toronto, Champlain Society, 1908), 441. Sagard had observed: "Since they reckoned that the greatest captains in France were endowed with the greatest mind, and possessing so great a mind they alone could make the most complicated things, such as axes, knives, kettles, etc., they concluded therefore that the King, being the greatest captain and chief of them all, made the largest kettles, and regarding us in the capacity of captains they used sometimes to offer us kettles to mend." (Long Journey, 183).

89. Thwaites, Jesuit Relations, LXVIII:215. This reaction was reported for a visit in 1725.

90. Maurile de Saint-Michel, Voyages des isles Camercanes, en Amérique qui font partie des Indes occidentales... (Mans: Hierosme Olivier, 1652), 143.

91. Ibid. Similarly, Sieur de La Borde reported that the love of Amerindians for their own land was so great that individuals brought to France never wanted to stay there. ("Relation de l'origine des moeurs," 16, in Henri Justel, comp., Recueil de Diverses Voyages Faits en Afrique et en l'Amerique... [Paris: Louis Billaine, 1674].)

92. Le Clercq, New Relation, 97-8.

93. War was traditionally the principal activity of the nobles. (Robert Mandrou, Introduction à la France moderne (1500-1640) [Paris: Albin Michel, 1961], 148).

94. Thwaites, Jesuit Relations, VI:287-89.

95. "An Indian Delegation in France, 1725," eds. Richard N. Ellis and Charlie R. Steen, Journal of the Illinois State Historical Society, LXVII, 1 (1974), 385-405.

PREHISTORIC AND HISTORIC LINKAGES: Problems and Prospects

by

Adolph M. Greenberg and Ronald H. Spielbauer

ABSTRACT

Examining the Selkirk and Blackwater artifact assemblages from Ontario, Manitoba, Saskatchewan and northern Minnesota and the ethnohistorical linkages which have been posited between these archaeological cultures and the historic Ojibwa, this paper highlights some of the problems which arise from attempts to tie rigid material assemblage typologies to historical cultural descriptions. It is argued that only a processual definition of cultural patterns (e.g. Cree and Ojibwa) in which such variables as resource scheduling, settlement/site distributions and demographic arrangements are incorporated into a dynamic adaptational model will yield clarity on the problematic linkages between archaeologically defined cultures and historic ethnic groups.

PREHISTORIC AND HISTORIC LINKAGES: PROBLEMS AND PROSPECTS

Adolph M. Greenberg
and
Ronald H. Spielbauer

Despite years of research by eastern subarctic archaeologists and
ethnologists, incontrovertible linkages have not been established between
archaeologically identified cultures and historically known populations.
Although central to much of anthropological thought on cultural evolution
and culture change, the treatment of this issue in the literature for the
most part, has been tangential to other, more specifically defined research
problems.

For archaeologists, the problem is in ascertaining not only what is
diagnostic of the archaeological assemblage, but also what ties this
assemblage to the historic occupation that overlays it. On the other hand,
there exists a similar problem for the ethnologist/ethnohistorian:
isolating those aspects of the cultures of historically known populations
that are identifiable in and provide links to the archaeological record.
Thus, linking historic Algonquian groups with prehistoric archaeological
assemblages using either ceramic or lithic types remains a vexing issue
(Bishop and Smith 1975; Pollock 1975; Wright 1971). Additionally, the
present-day distribution of Algonquian ethnic units does not correspond well
with prehistoric populations (Pollock 1975, Wright 1965). Moreover, an
approach which groups sites or components on the formal requirements of
containing similar artifact assemblages will not necessarily produce
archaeological culture units which are equivalent to either the ethnologists' conception of a "culture" (Trigger 1968:18) or the ethnohistorians'
documented tribal designation.

This paper examines, using both the Blackduck/Selkirk question and the
historic group identities question, some of the many dimensions of the
problem of prehistoric and historic linkages. We will offer criticism of
extant work and suggest lines for future research. It is our contention
that the problem is not insurmountable. It will not only require some
painful rethinking on a number of ideas and concepts presently embedded in
anthropological thought, but also require the establishment of a rapprochement between archaeology and ethnology.

TRADITIONAL APPROACHES: ARCHAEOLOGY

The traditional strategy utilized by archaeologists in establishing
linkages between historic and prehistoric populations has been the direct
historical approach. This approach was implicitly used in interpreting the
New World archaeological record in the 1880's by Cyrus Thomas (1894) in his
study of the mounds and earthworks of the Ohio and Mississippi Valleys. In

the 12th Annual Report of the Bureau of Ethnology, Thomas concluded that
these structures were clearly the work of the American Indian and that
different mounds had been built by different tribal groups (Knudson
1978:473; Sharer and Ashmore 1979:54; Willey and Sabloff 1974:50). In the
southwestern United States, F.H. Cushing (1886, 1890) and Kroeber (1916)
utilized the same approach to trace a connection between contemporary Pueblo
peoples and their ancestors (Knudson 1978:473; Sharer and Ashmore 1979:54;
Willey and Sabloff 1974:114).

The direct-historical approach, as later refined by Strong (1935) and
Wedel (1938), is based upon the principle of working from the known to the
unknown in the archaeological record (Steward 1942). The known are living
or historically recorded peoples and the unknown are their prehistoric
ancestors for whom no written records exist (Fagan 1981:362; Sharer and
Ashmore 1979:53). Generally, in using this approach, focus is on a small
local area for which a succession of cultural periods are worked out. A
culture can be derived from such a local sequence by following the
assumption that "...all the people of a given period belonged to a single
cultural group, or if it is obvious that they did not, by separating them
into two or more groups through the process of cultural classification"
(Rouse 1972:76-77).

The process of cultural classification is crucial to the application of
this approach, and in using it one moves backward in time from artifacts and
sites identified with historic groups to similar and earlier archaeological
assemblages and sites. The method works, however, only so long as a given
cluster of artifacts remains coherent and recognizably distinct from those
of other prehistoric societies (Sharer and Ashmore 1979:54). The
application of the direct historical approach has been successful in many
cases since many American Indian cultures or their historically known
representatives were found or are found residing in the same area originally
occupied by their ancestors (Knudson 1978:473). But it is not applicable in
all areas and it has been recognized as having serious limitations
(Hickerson 1970:20). Generally, confidence in the interpretations made
decrease as one moves from historic to prehistoric to telehistoric sites
(Fagan 1981:363). But when an archaeological site is found to contain both
indigenous and historic European materials in association, the identification of the original ethnic group can often be established on the basis of
historic records. Following this identification, the direct historical
approach can be used to trace the culture of the ethnic group back into time
(Wright 1981:91). In fact, this is what has been done with the Selkirk and
Blackduck archaeological assemblages and their purported links to Cree and
Ojibwa respectively.

Selkirk was first named by MacNeish (1958) in southeastern Manitoba,
but Selkirk sites have since been identified in a core area distributed
north of Southern Indian Lake in Manitoba, west to Lac Ile à la Crosse in
Saskatchewan, south to the Saskatchewan River, and east into northwestern
Ontario (Wright 1981:92). Selkirk assemblages have been characterized on
the basis of a lithic and bone tool inventory and primarily a distinctive
fabric impressed ceramic ware (Wright 1981:92).

Selkirk ceramics are grit tempered fabric impressed wares manufactured with a modeling technique. In vessel form they occur as globular to elongated globular vessels which have vertical to outflaring rims and flattened lips. Decoration varies according to named types such as Alexander Fabric Impressed, Sturgeon Falls Fabric, Impressed Sturgeon Punctate, and Clearwater Lake Punctate—which have been grouped together under the general category of Winnipeg Fabric Impressed Ware (Anfinson 1979:231). These ceramic types would be placed in the Late or Terminal Woodland prehistoric period and have been recorded in the area of northwestern Ontario, east and central Manitoba, east-central Saskatchewan, and northern Minnesota (Anfinson 1979:231).

Selkirk sites evidence a lithic assemblage which includes small triangular or side-notched triangular projectile points, a wide variety of scraper forms, bifacially-flaked knives, bifacially-flaked celts with ground bit edges, hammerstones, manos, anvils, abraders, and more rarely wedges (Anfinson 1979:231; Pollock 1975:20; Wright 1981:92). Bone when preserved on Selkirk sites is found used in a variety of forms including awls, flaking tools, fleshers, arrow shaft straighteners, and tubular beads (Wright 1981:92).

Selkirk has been dated via C 14 to a time frame of 810 AD to 1620 AD, and historic Selkirk sites have been reported from Saskatchewan, Manitoba, and Ontario where documentation would seem to indicate that Selkirk is attributable to the historically-known Cree (Anfinson 1979:231; Bishop and Smith 1975:54; Wright 1981:92). The Cree, thus, apparently had a long period of cultural development in the region, and Wright (1981:94) has suggested that Selkirk ceramics may have developed out of the preceding Middle Woodland Laurel period.

However, Selkirk apparently had a very close relationship with contemporaneous cultural developments to the south, for example, with Sandy Lake and Blackduck (Anfinson 1979:232; Wright 1981:94). The nature of these relationships is not well understood at the present time.

Blackduck as a name of a local Late or Terminal Woodland assemblage was first used by Wilford (1955) in Minnesota. It is found distributed in a core area from the north end of Lake Winnipeg south into northern Minnesota, west to the Red River in Manitoba and east to the Michipicoten River (Anfinson 1979:23; Fitting 1978:55; Wright 1981:94). It is found, thus, distributed for the most part within the distributional area of Middle Woodland Laurel wares, and has been interpreted as being clearly related to this proceeding cultural period (Anfinson 1979:24; Wright 1981:94). Its ceramics have as well been described as showing great affinity to the Selkirk ceramics of Ontario and Manitoba (Anfinson 1979:24). Blackduck sites have been dated by C 14 to a period ranging from AD 620 to 1560, and historic Blackduck sites in Ontario have shown European trade goods (Wright 1981:94).

Pottery is the most distinctive characteristic of Blackduck. The ceramics are grit tempered wares manufactured with a paddle and anvil technique if cordmarked or modeled if formed in fabric containers (Anfinson 1979:26). In form, vessels are characteristically round or globular, with constricted necks and sub-conoidal bases, flaring rims and flattened and usually thickened lips. Decoration or surface treatment includes cordmarking, punctation, brushing, and comb stamping done in such a manner as to imitate cord wrapped stick impression (Anfinson 1979:26-27; Fitting 1978:55; Pollock 1975:16). Other artifact associations found with Blackduck assemblages include small triangular and side-notched triangular projectile points, a variety of scraper and knife forms, tubular drills, steatite and clay pipes, bone awls and needles, unilaterally barbed bone harpoons, bone flakers and spatulas, cut beaver incisors, bear canine ornaments, and copper fishhooks, gouges and beads (Anfinson 1979:24).

There has been much disagreement concerning the ethnic classification of Blackduck. Wilford (1955), MacNeish (1958), Hlady (1964) and Bishop and Smith (1975) have argued for linkages with the Siouan-speaking Assiniboin who split off from the Yanktonai Sioux. By contrast, Wright (1965, 1967, 1968, 1972) and others (Anfinson 1979; Dawson 1974:92, 1976; Lugenbeal 1978; Mason 1981:392-393) have argued for linkages with the Ojibwa. The latter argument having been made on the basis of evidence derived from archaeological site distributions, ethnohistorical data, and supporting evidence from linguistics, ethnology, and physical anthropology (Anfinson 1979:24; Dawson 1976:167; Wright 1981:94).

There is abundant evidence indicating a long and close interrelation- ship between Selkirk and Blackduck (Anfinson 1979; Dawson 1976 and Wright 1972, 1981). Consequently, the boundary lines between the two appear to be rather amorphous. Similarly, Wright has noted that much of MacNeish's Selkirk material from southeastern Manitoba may be regarded as Blackduck and that the lithic assemblages reported for each are very related, with the exception of a reported relative scarcity of wedges and bone tools from Selkirk sites. Analogously, ceramics deriving from both pottery traditions have been found on the same sites; and although generally one ceramic tradition may be found dominating, there are instances of the two pottery styles occurring in roughly equal frequencies on the same site (Wright 1981:94). Wright (1981:94) has explained the occurrence of these different ceramics by suggesting that both Selkirk and Blackduck may be seen as products of two related Algonquian-speaking populations, and by virtue of female marital mobility. Additionally, ceramics from historic Ojibwa components appear to be the products of borrowing from more than one ceramic tradition. Wright (1965:200) has indicated that the Ojibwa reside in an extensive area which placed them in contact with a wide variety of pottery producing peoples. This coupled with their nomadic life style and accentuated by both the effects of the fur trade and Indian conflicts may be interpreted as contributing to the mixtures seen. This borrowing of foreign ceramic traditions may relegate the value of ceramics to a different role from that seen with groups which are active in the development of a single ceramic tradition (Wright 1965:200). The lithic assemblages linked to Ojibwa groups on the other hand do not show the same mixture as that seen with ceramics. Wright (1965:216) has interpreted this as possibly indicating an indigenous Ojibwa material culture, and he further suggests that it may be the lithics which will provide a basis upon which spatial and temporal relationships may be established.

TRADITIONAL APPROACHES: ETHNOHISTORY

The question of group identities for various boreal forest Indian
populations is the area of ethnohistorical research most germane at present
to establishing links with prehistoric populations. In short, if it is
possible to unequivocably identify the groups or "Nations" mentioned in
seventeenth-century records, then the question of what cultural groups
overlay either Selkirk or Blackduck in the early historic period will be
resolved and an effective connection potentially made. The issues
surrounding the "origin" of the "northern Ojibwa" provide an example of the
difficulties in doing so.

For quite some time the assumption was that the Ojibwa had always
inhabited the boreal forest zone north and west of Lake Superior
(E. S. Rogers: personal communication). Hickerson (1966:8) challenged this
view, though indirectly, largely on the basis of historical evidence and
arguing that the Shield region north of Lake Superior was a wasteland
without permanent residents prior to the intrusion of Europeans in the later
seventeenth century. This area, according to Hickerson (1966:8), was first
populated by Cree who under the stimulation of the fur trade moved down from
Hudson Bay. Subsequently, this region was occupied by roving bands of
proto-Ojibwa, offshoots of the unilineal descent groups which had until then
resided in clan-named villages associated with extensive fisheries along the
north shore of Lake Huron (Hickerson 1966:10-11). In the areas west of Lake
Superior, these proto-Ojibwa lineage segments had seemingly displaced the
aboriginal Cree and Monsoni-Cree inhabitants by the mid-eighteenth century
(Hickerson 1967:47).

Along similar lines, Bishop (1970, 1974, 1976; Bishop and Smith 1975)
believes that the historical data prove conclusively that the precontact
Ojibwa were marginal to the boreal forest, residing instead in a richer
ecozone on the northern shore and immediate hinterland of Lake Huron and
northeastern Lake Superior. Unlike Hickerson, Bishop believes that the
Shield country north and west of Lake Superior was already occupied at
contact--but by Cree and Assiniboine, who over the next century, gradually
shifted to the west. Into this territorial vacuum moved roving bands of
Ojibwa, as well as other Algonquian-speakers from the southeast. The
historic Ojibwa, according to Bishop (1976:40), migrated and dispersed over
an area at least ten times as large as that their ancestors had occupied at
contact with a commensurate increase in population.

In a review of the documents for the seventeenth century, Greenberg and
Morrison (n.d.:8) have reached a different conclusion regarding the identity
of boreal forest groups at contact as well as the "Origin" of the Northern
Ojibwa. They argue that scholars like Hickerson, Bishop, and Ray
(1974:3-23) have made two unwarranted assumptions. The first is equating
Kilistinon with those contemporary Algonquians speaking the language now
known as "Cree." The second is equating "Ojibwa" and Ojibwa-speaker. Thus,
when Bishop and Smith ask (1975:54): "What was the identity of the Indians
north and west of Lake Superior at contact? Ojibwa, Cree or Assiniboin?"
they are applying misleading and invariant linguistic and cultural
categories to the historical documents (Greenberg and Morrison n.d.:8). The
groups known today as Northern Ojibwa may have inhabited the boreal forest

at least since contact. What had been seen as migration, or as general population movement was, very likely, the diffusion of the term "Ojibwa" to ethnic units known at contact under a host of different names--among them Kilistinon or Cree, Monsoni, Muskego, and Gens des Terres (Greenberg and Morrison n.d.:4). It has also been suggested that both recent scholars and some early European observers, may have confused mobility for purposes of trade and warfare--an undisputed fact--with mobility for subsistence purposes (Greenberg and Morrison n.d.:31). Data on group identity, on the other hand, has led to the suggestion that the changes in Northern Ojibwa subsistence documented by Bishop (1970:10) took place within a relatively fixed "hunting range" system, perhaps similar to the one he postulates for a later period (Greenberg and Morrison n.d.:31).

THE TRADITIONAL APPROACHES EVALUATED

Assessing the work of both archaeologists and ethnohistorians, it would appear that the arguments for a linkage are based primarily on spatial dimensions and the correctness of ethnohistorical interpretation. Thus, the parameters of both Selkirk and Blackduck horizons are worked out for a specific time frame while the group identities of boreal forest cultures are deciphered. This suggests strongly that one follows the other in a specific area. This is conventional anthropological wisdom. It is also, we suggest, conventional anthropological ignorance, and for the following reasons.

Haag (1961:19) has expressed the view that the development of the Midwestern or McKern Taxonomic Method was stimulated in part from a dissatisfaction with the application of the direct historical approach. As he notes this approach appeared to promise greater order in archaeological work and lead to its interpretation as a genetic system more than as a taxonomic system. "...it seemed axiomatic that all manifestations having similar traits or a measure of similarity, were of common origin (Haag 1961:19)." Although this approach met with criticism and underwent changes in formulation and application, it has been seen as a significant constructive development (Griffin 1943:327-41; Guthe 1948:9).

Following Taylor (1967:139), however, we would suggest that culture classifications such as those traditionally employed by archaeologists, e.g., with the McKern system or its modifications, are not classifications of cultural entities or of archaeological materials in a cultural sense, and except by chance, there can be no necessary connection between groupings based on these systems and aboriginal ethnic units, tribal, or cultural groups. Inherently, taxonomic system themselves do not justify such an interpretation because they have been constructed on the basis of empirical types and classes and not on the basis of cultural ones.

> ...Attributes of quantity and quality, of provenience and association, and of their respective affinities have not been utilized in creating the categories.... How can it [then] be expected that types, created with so little regard for cultural data, will, when classified, yield a picture of the cultural relationships that once existed? (Taylor 1967:139).

Trigger (1968:19-20) points out still other difficulties with the traditional taxonomic approach. No single social or political unit can be linked isometrically with a single material culture pattern. As he notes, there are many examples of peoples sharing material culture yet having different cultural affiliations, socially, politically, linguistically. Contrary situations can also be found.

> ...a uniform material culture does not constitute proof that the people associated with it necessarily had a strong sense of common identity anymore than differences in material culture prove the lack of such a sense of identity (Trigger 1968:20).

Equally serious problems obtain in the ethnohistorical approach, even though considerable data can be and has been marshalled to promote specific points of view. In addition, given the focus of the research and the serious examination of the documents, remarkable strides have been made in the group identity question. However, there remain serious problems not only with the documents but also with the approach.

Several years ago, Fisher (1969) had shown the dangers inherent in the formal typological method of classifying cultures, and it would seem that the problems persist. Clearly, the application of blanket tribal designations like Cree or Ojibwa has created false impressions of cultural homogeneity or discreteness, disguising local ecological and social variability in ethnic categories. It has already been shown that the ambiguity found in the historical and anthropological usage of "tribal" designations frequently lead to mistaken theories of population movement. Along similar lines, to call the residents of the interior north and west of Lake Superior "Northern Ojibwa" creates more problems than it solves. For example, this tribal appellation, only extant in anthropological parlance, masks the type of local ecological and social variability suggested recently by archaeologists (Pollock 1975; Dawson 1976) and ethnologists (Rogers and Rogers 1980). As Trigger (1968:17) has noted, if an archaeological concept of culture is to correspond with the ethnological conception of representing the total life ways of a people who share a common tradition, then the definition of such a culture must be able to include within it the variations found within such a pattern. This end, however desirable, can not be attained through the use of any rigidly defined set of formal characteristics or similarities as seen amongst components. In addition, rigid types disguise the fundamental links that exist between groups such as the "Northern Ojibwa" and the "Algonquian" of western Quebec and northeastern Ontario (Greenberg and Morrison n.d.). In an assessment of the group identity question, Edward S. Rogers (1969:36) and Wright (1965:190-191) have noted that we are dealing with a confusing variety of terms: broad designations of either European or Indian origin; territorial names; indigenous clan-totem names, perhaps; and differing names for the same groups of people. Add to this the archaeological and linguistic designations and we get a most unwieldly and unproductive scenario for the disentanglement of critical issues in anthropological thought found in the existing data on the prehistoric and historic populations of the eastern subarctic.

NEW DIRECTIONS AND PROSPECTS

Trigger (1968:16, 23) has raised two questions which are directly relevant to the problem of interpreting and reconstructing cultural units and establishing ethnic identities: 1) whether similarities in material remains can be used to infer identity of such diverse cultural aspects as language, social structure, and ideology; and 2) whether the various artifact types found in components may be treated as equivalent (or equal) in their representation of the culture, or whether instead that each artifact type must be treated independently in terms of its own specific historical significance. In answering these questions, Trigger (1968:8-9) has pointed out that both Edward Sapir (1921) and Franz Boas (1940) noted the need to study race, language, and culture separately, essentially as independent variables. Sapir and Boas' work showed that the diffusion of culture traits may result in similar cultures being shared by physically and linguistically distinct peoples. Trigger (1968:25) has also pointed to the inherent limitations of defining cultures and interpreting historical events through comparisons of formal similarities or differences found among artifact sets deriving from different archaeological components, an argument akin to Fisher's (1969) criticism of ethnological types and culture area classification. The historical significance of different artifact types or categories may vary from culture to culture for ecological or cultural reasons. Only through an analysis of the functional roles can one infer the historical significance of an artifact or trait in the society (Steward and Setzler 1938).

These problem areas were examined briefly by Trigger (1968) in a discussion of the results of Wright's (1965) study of five historic 'Ojibwa' sites in Ontario. Wright found no consistent assemblage of ceramic traits which could be used to demonstrate close geographical or temporal relationships. Pottery, instead, seems to be a more sensitive indicator of contacts than of Ojibwa ethnic identity. Trigger (1968:23-24) interpreted this as being probably a reflection of the relative unimportance of ceramics among hunting peoples of the region. The greater degree of similarity seen amongst lithic tools was suggested by Wright (1965) to be a better basis for determining spatial and temporal relationships and as well as possibly being an indigenous material culture. However, Trigger (1968:24) has suggested that the lithic assemblage may represent an important part of the technology used in exploiting the environment. If this were the case, then widespread similarities in lithic assemblages are not any better as indicators of a common ethnic identity. Thus Trigger (1968:24) concluded that neither ceramics nor lithics are good indicators of ethnic relationships.

As we have already noted, Taylor (1967:139) has criticized the position that types of taxonomic categories created without regard for cultural data will, when classified, evidence cultural relationships. That some types come from a given site or geographic area is not proof that they should be grouped together culturally. Instead, in order to have some degree of assurance of cultural relationship more than just formal similarities and spatial propinquity are needed (Taylor 1967:140). These attributes are, however, leads which may be fruitfully followed in ascertaining what was culturally related as opposed to what appears to be similar in appearance or located within a limited geographic/spatial domain.

The problem is in constructing classifications of archaeological data which reflect cultural relationships. In doing this, a pragmatic approach must be adopted, that is, the criteria which are chosen should reflect these relationships, and their use is justified by their applicability to the problem (Taylor 1967:146). To quote Taylor (1967:145):

> To put it most simply, the archaeologist first separates his material empirically on the basis of space, defining a local human group; then he separates it inferentially on the basis of cultural cohesiveness, defining a cultural group; then he constructs a cultural context for this cultural group, and finally he compares this context with others similarly derived, typing and classifying them in order to bring out what he considers to have been their cultural relationships.

This approach conforms rather closely to the definition of an archaeological culture suggested by Trigger (1968:22). An archaeological culture may be defined as a group of communities which share a similar material culture but no greater range of variation than might be expected within a single cultural tradition. A culture is thereby defined in terms of similarities found among communities, and while there is no specification of the degree of similarity, there is the stipulation that the definition of a culture should reflect a total lifeway.

With this approach (Taylor 1967:144-145; Trigger 1968:23), the community or component may be seen as the basic unit. These units may then be linked by any criteria such as artifact types, language, social-political organization, economic relations, etc. The overall patterns which emerge when different criteria are applied may differ. This flexibility, however, allows the archaeologist to examine archaeological data on its own terms rather than within the rigid taxonomic categories of an arbitrarily defined culture. Similarly, ethnohistorians would be well advised to exercise caution in the categorization of boreal forest ethnic units until a clearer understanding of the historical usage of tribal appellations is forthcoming (see Greenberg and Morrison n.d.). Otherwise, we may persist in the establishment of linkages between ethnological and archaeological types and not between populations of ethnic units, thereby contributing, perhaps, to a disregard for some probable and significant variations in Cree and Ojibwa culture types, prehistorically and historically.

We would argue that these problems will not be resolved unless there develops a rapprochement between archaeology and ethnology. For this to occur, the extant theoretical dualism noted by Fisher (1969) as characterizing not only archaeology and ethnology, but also the assessment of precontact versus postcontact change must be critically reexamined. We would suggest at this point that the work of Thomas (1972, 1973) and Jochim (1976, 1981) might serve as two examples of the kinds of research that both archaeologists and ethnologists could employ in establishing linkages. Their approach does not place reliance upon clear-cut artifact evidence, but rather attempts to provide an explanatory and predictive framework for the archaeological analysis of hunters and gatherers, especially where there is a lack of explicit evidence about subsistence-settlement patterns (Jochim 1976:83). This model, couched in ecological anthropology and drawing heavily on the problem-solving attributes of human beings, is based on explicit assumptions concerning the subsistence/settlement strategies of band societies, derived from ethnographically known populations. By focusing our attention on the structuring of the relationship of a group to its natural environment, it is possible to examine exploitive activities specifically and their implications for settlement patterns and demographic arrangements. These seem to be the areas of clearest articulation between human populations and their environment (Jochim 1976:9). This model should generate predictive statements which can be tested with data obtained from both archaeological and ethnohistorical research where it has been pointed out that the nature of resource and subsistence activities is considered to be the primary factor conditioning both site placement and demographic arrangements (Jochim 1976:12). It should be possible, therefore, for ethnohistorians to develop a data base on these activities for any given group, construct a subsistence strategy model for it, and yield a number of predictive statements that can be tested in the archaeological record. Conversely, the same avenue of inquiry should be open to the archaeologist. Though we have some reservations regarding the treatment of cultures in isolation from an historic context, this model and similarly-constructed ones have the unique advantage of providing a common ground between two, often disparate, research interests. There already exists a tradition in subarctic ethnology of ecological studies (see Rogers and Smith 1981). Further refinements in the analysis of the subsistence and settlement behaviour of groups over time should provide both archaeologists and ethnologists with the kinds of data necessary for establishing linkages. Moreover, this approach would have the added advantage of providing us with a processual definition of Cree or Ojibwa cultures based on inter-relationships among such variables as resource scheduling, settlement/site distribution, and demographic arrangements rather than trait inventories. Therefore, we argue, as Jochim (1976:83) does, that "the neat geographical patterning" of space into culture areas "is deceptive and poses the danger of encouraging a view of environments and cultures as fixed and simple whole units." A new approach, implied in Thomas and Jochim's research, contemplates a culture concept that transcends traditional, linguistic, archaeological, and ethnological research. This would not merely be a mixing of normative, behavioural, and trait inventory approaches, but is instead the application of a comprehensive model of behaviour in a variable and problematic environmental setting. This approach would not only have the benefit of helping to establish linkages, but also would add meaningful dimensions to the perplexing problem of rendering intelligible the assumed distinctions between pre- and post-contact culture change.

REFERENCES

Anfinson, Scott F., (ed.)
    1979   A Handbook of Minnesota Prehistoric Ceramics. Occasional
             Publications in Minnesota Anthropology No. 5. Minnesota
             Archaeological Society, Fort Snelling.

Bishop, Charles A.
    1970   "The Emergence of Hunting Territories Among the Northern
             Ojibwa." Ethnology 9:1-15.

    1974   The Northern Ojibwa and the Fur Trade: An Historical and
             Ecological Study. Toronto: Holt, Rinehart and Winston.

    1976   "The Emergence of the Northern Ojibwa: Social and Economic
             Consequences." American Ethnologist 3:29-54.

Bishop, Charles A., and M. Estellie Smith
    1975   "Early Historic Populations in Northwestern Ontario:
             Archaeological and Ethnohistorical Interpretations." American
             Antiquity 40(1):54-63.

Boas, Franz
    1940   Race, Language and Culture. The Macmillan Company, N.Y.

Cushing, Frank H.
    1886   A Study of Pueblo Pottery as Illustrative of Zuni Culture
             Growth. Bureau of American Ethnology, 4th Annual Report,
             pp. 467-521. Washington, D.C.

    1890   "Preliminary notes on the Origin, Working Hypotheses, and
             Primary Researches of the Hemenway Expedition." Seventh Inter-
             national Congress of Americanists, Berlin, pp. 151-194.

Dawson, K.C.A.
    1974   The McCluskey Site. National Museum of Man, Mercury Series,
             Archaeological Survey of Canada, Paper No. 25. Ottawa.

    1976   "Historic Populations of Northwestern Ontario." In, William
             Cowan, ed., Papers of the Seventh Algonquian Conference,
             pp. 157-174.

Fagan, Brian M.
    1981   In the Beginning, An Introduction to Archaeology, Fourth
            Edition. Little Brown and Company, Boston.

Fisher, Anthony D.
    1969   "The Cree of Canada." Western Canadian Journal of Anthropology
            1(1).

Fitting, James E.
    1978   "Regional Cultural Development, 300 B.C. to AD 1000." In,
            Bruce G. Trigger, ed., Northeast Handbook of North American
            Indians, Vol. 15. Smithsonian Institution, Washington, D.C.

Greenberg, Adolph M., and James Morrison
    n.d.   Group Identities in the Boreal Forest: The Origin of the
            Northern Ojibwa Ethnicity. In press.

Griffin, James B.
    1943   The Fort Ancient Aspect. University of Chicago Press, Chicago.

Guthe, C.E.
    1948   "Twenty-Five Years of Archeology in the Eastern United States."
            In, J.B. Griffin, ed., Archaeology of the Eastern United
            States, pp. 1-12. University of Chicago Press, Chicago.

Haag, William G.
    1961   "Twenty-Five Years of Eastern Archaeology." American Antiquity
            27(1):16-23.

Hickerson, Harold
    1966   "The Genesis of Bilaterality Among Two Divisions of Chippewa."
            American Anthropologist 68:1-26.

    1967   "Land Tenure of the Rainy Lake Chippewa at the Beginning of the
            Nineteenth Century." Smithsonian Contributions to Anthropology
            2:37-63.

    1970   The Chippewa and Their Neighbors: A Study in Ethnohistory.
            Holt, Rinehart and Winston, N.Y.

Hlady, Walter M.
    1964   "Indian Migrations in Manitoba and the West." In, Walter M.
            Hlady, ed., 10,000 Years of History in Manitoba, pp. 25-53.
            Papers of the Manitoba Historical and Scientific Society,
            3rd Ser., Vol. 17, Winnipeg.

39

Jochim, Michael A.
    1976   Hunter-Gatherer Subsistence and Settlement: A Predictive
            Model. Academic Press, N.Y.

    1981   Strategies for Survival: Cultural Behavior in an Ecological
            Context. Academic Press, N.Y.

Knudson, S.J.
    1978   Culture in Retrospect: An Introduction to Archaeology. Rand
            McNally, Chicago.

Kroeber, Alfred L.
    1916   "Zuni Potsherds." Anthropological Papers of the American
            Museum of Natural History, Vol. 18, Pt. 1:7-37. New York.

Lugenbeal, Edward
    1978   "The Blackduck Ceramics of the Smith Site (21 KC3) and Their
            Implications for the History of Blackduck Ceramics and Culture
            in Northern Minnesota." Midcontinental Journal of Archaeology,
            Vol. 3(1):45-68.

MacNeish, Richard S.
    1958   An Introduction to the Archaeology of Southeast Manitoba.
            National Museum of Canada, Bulletin No. 157. Ottawa.

Mason, Ronald J.
    1981   Great Lakes Archaeology. Academic Press, N.Y.

Pollock, John W.
    1975   "Algonquian Culture Development and Archaeological Sequences in
            Northeastern Ontario." Bulletin of the Canadian Archaeological
            Association 7:3-53. Ottawa.

Ray, Arthur
    1974   Indians in the Fur Trade: Their Role as Trappers, Hunters, and
            Middlemen in the Lands Southwest of Hudson Bay 1660-1870.
            University of Toronto Press, Toronto.

Rogers, Edward S.
    1969   "Band Organization Among the Indians of Eastern Subarctic
            Canada." In, Contributions to Anthropology: Band Societies,
            David Damas, ed., National Museums of Canada, Bulletin No. 228,
            Anthropological Series No. 84, pp. 21-55. Ottawa.

Rogers, E.S., and Mary Black Rogers
    1980   "Who Were the Cranes? Groups and Group Identity Names in
            Northern Ontario." Paper presented to the Conference on
            Algonian Archaeology, Calgary, Alberta.

Rogers, Edward S., and James G.E. Smith
    1981   "Environment and Culture in the Shield and Mackenzie
            Borderlands." In, Handbook of North American Indians, Vol. 6,
            Subarctic, pp. 130-144. The Smithsonian Institution,
            Washington, D.C.

Rouse, Irving
    1972   Introduction to Prehistory, A Systematic Approach.
            McGraw-Hill, N.Y.

Sapir, Edward
    1921   Language, An Introduction to the Study of Speech. Harcourt,
            Brace and World, Inc., N.Y.

Sharer, Robert J., and Wendy Ashmore
    1979   Fundamentals of Archaeology. Benjamin/Cummings Publ. Co.,
            Menlo Park, California.

Steward, Julian H.
    1942   "The Direct Historical Approach to Archaeology." American
            Antiquity 7(4):337-343.

Steward, Julian H., and F.M. Setzler
    1938   "Function and Configuration in Archaeology." American
            Antiquity, 4:4-10.

Strong, William D.
    1935   "An Introduction to Nebraska Archaeology." Smithsonian
            Miscellaneous Collections Vol. 93, No. 10. Washington, D.C.

Taylor, Walter W.
    1967   A Study of Archeology (Reprint of 1948 edition). Southern
            Illinois University Press, Carbondale.

Thomas, Cyrus
    1894   Report of the Mound Explorations of the Burial of Ethnology.
            12th Annual Report of the Bureau of Ethnology. Washington,
            D.C.

Thomas, David H.
    1972   "A Computer Simulation Model of Great Basin Shoshonean
            Subsistence and Settlement Patterns." In Models in
            Archaeology, D.L. Clarke (ed.). Methuen, London.

    1973   "An Empirical Test of Steward's Model of Great Basin Settlement
            Patterns." American Antiquity 38(2):155-176.

Trigger, Bruce G.
    1968   Beyond History: The Methods of Prehistory. Holt, Rinehart and
            Winston, N.Y.

Wedel, Waldo R.
    1938   "The Direct-Historical Approach in Pawnee Archaeology."
            Smithsonian Miscellaneous Collections, Vol. 97, No. 7.
            Washington, D.C.

Wilford, Lloyd A.
    1955   "A Revised Classification of the Prehistoric Cultures of
            Minnesota." American Antiquity 21(2):130-142.

Willey, Gordon R., and Jeremy A. Sabloff
    1974   A History of American Archaeology.   W. H. Freeman and Company,
            San Francisco.

Wright, James V.
    1965   "A Regional Examination of Ojibwa Culture History."
            Anthropologica N.S., 7(2):189-227. Ottawa.

    1967   "The Pic River Site: A Stratified Late Woodland Site on the
            North Shore of Lake Superior." National Museum of Canada
            Bulletin 206:54-99.

    1971   "Cree Culture History in the Southern Indian Lake Region."
            Anthropological Series 87, National Museum of Canada Bulletin
            232:1-31. Ottawa.

    1972   "Ontario Prehistory, an Eleven-Thousand-Year Archaeological
            Outline." Archaeological Survey of Canada, National Museum of
            Man, National Museums of Canada. Ottawa.

    1981   "Prehistory of the Canadian Shield." In, June Helm (ed.)
            Subarctic, Vol. 6, Handbook of North American Indians,
            pp. 86-96. Smithsonian Institution. Washington, D.C.

SOUTHERN BOUNDARY OF LENAPE:
Cultural Interaction and Change in the Early Contact Period,
1550-1610

by

Marshall J. Becker

ABSTRACT

Delineation of boundaries or buffer zones which separated native
American peoples enables us to identify these specific groups more clearly.
The territorial borders or boundary areas for any people often prove
essential for recognizing their cultural integrity. Although this chore may
seem simple the actual process is not easy in the historic period and quite
difficult for the prehistoric period.

Recent studies have begun to clarify the aboriginal situation regarding
the northern boundary of the Lenape. Various documents relating to the populations in present Delaware and Maryland, coupled with some archaeological
evidence.

SOUTHERN BOUNDARY OF THE LENAPE: CULTURAL INTERACTION AND CHANGE IN THE
EARLY CONTACT PERIOD 1550-1610

Marshall J. Becker

The Lenape, the native inhabitants of the lower Delaware River valley,
are well known and often mentioned in various aspects of American colonial
history. They are often identified by the term "Delaware," particularly
after 1740. In many respects they are best known for their interactions with
William Penn, who systematically purchased all of their land rights on the
west side of the Delaware and then protected their de facto land holdings in
the colony. Their activities and cultural behaviour often is discussed, but
usually from data derived from after 1740, by which time all of the main
Lenape bands had left their homeland and taken up residence along the
waterways of the Susquehanna drainage and even further to the west.

Recently, attention has been focused on Lenape lifestyles at the time of
European contact, around 1600 A.D., in order to understand the impact of
colonization on these people. As part of a comprehensive program aimed at
reconstructing their lives before contact, in order to document the ways in
which the Lenape responded to European trade and colonization, an attempt had
been made to delineate their borders in 1600. This is important for two
reasons. First, clarifying their territorial limits helps to identify the
Lenape as such; second, border changes show us how the Lenape responded to
political and economic change and how they developed alliances which enabled
them to operate successfully in their homeland for nearly one hundred and
fifty years after European contact.

The rapidly growing literature on frontiers and boundaries (see Juricek
1966) demonstrates that the delineation of cultural and/or political borders
is an area of considerable interest at this time. The applications of this
body of data to questions involving the Lenape have been discussed elsewhere
(Becker in press) and need not be reviewed here. This paper will focus on
the evidence which suggests the extent of the Lenape realm before and up to
1600 and how and why changes occurred in the early 17th century.

The significant question which must be answered at this point relates to
the means by which we can define the boundaries of a foraging
(hunting-gathering) society, which was loosely organized into bands, at a
point in time prior to the beginning of historic records for the area. Two
principal approaches have been used in this reconstruction. First, the
archaeological evidence from the Late Woodland period (ca. 900 A.D. to about
1600 A.D.) has been reviewed (see Stewart et al. 1983), with particular
emphasis on the terminal aspects (ca. 1450-1600 A.D.). The distribution of
archaeological sites is determined to see (1) if there is a general pattern
of presence or absence, and (2) if sites cluster in any given region leaving
zones in which sites with relatively significant occupation are absent.

Relative clustering of sites in a physiographic region, with an absence of related sites around them, suggests the existence of a buffer zone or boundary area between territories. Second, records of land sales can be examined in minute detail for evidence of territories claimed by the native peoples. Lenape, and presumably other native Americans, were scrupulously honest in their land sales. Only rarely does any evidence of unusual native claim appear, and generally these reflect ambiguous circumstances involving buffer zones such as will be noted below. By "upstreaming," or inferring that land "ownership" generally was inherited through kinship, we can determine the gross outlines of the territories owned by the Lenape by what they sold over the course of some sixty years.

Much of our information regarding Lenape land holdings derives from the deeds and related documents or indentures recording the sales of parcels of all sizes. Long before William Penn and his agents arrived in the New World and began the systematic purchase of all the lands held by the various Lenape bands, tracts large and small had been sold to various Dutch, Swedish, and even possibly English (New Haven) traders and settlers. The examination of some of these will be necessary to reconstructing the southern Lenape border.

Examination of the deeds recording the sales of lands between known Lenape bands to William Penn and his agents in the years just after 1680 provides a great deal of agreement. The most southerly of Penn's purchases, made on 2 October 1685, secured a tract of land which reached southward to Duck Creek (land between Duck and Chester Creeks and backward from the Delaware as far as a man on a horse can ride in 2 days: Penna. Archives, Series I, Vol. 1:95-6). From this evidence one may infer that Duck Creek was about at the southern border of Lenape territory. The general release treaty of 17 September 1718, which confirmed all of Penn's previous purchases, covered all the land from Duck Creek to the Lehigh River, as can be tabulated by reviewing all previous purchases (Colonial Records of Penna. III:320-321). Duck Creek today forms the southern branch of the Smyrna River, which enters Delaware Bay about 45 km. south of Wilmington. However, the present Leipsic River appears to have been Lindeström's (1925 map) "Ancke Kijlen," or the Great or Old Duck Creek. Old Duck Creek (Leipsic River) is the most northerly of the streams which exits at the south end of Bombay Hook island.

Since the 3 "lower counties" in colonial Pennsylvania, now part of Delaware, were near to the Maryland colony and in an area contested by the Governor of Maryland, Penn may have been uninterested in making purchases deep into that troubled region. On the other hand, Duck Creek may have been the southern boundary of the Lenape realm in 1680, with the area to the south either owned by other people or a vacant buffer zone separating the Lenape from their neighbours to the south.

A deed of 7 June 1659, granting all the lands between Bombay Hook and Cape Henlopen to the Dutch, is signed by the elders of six different bands all of whom appear to be related. Since this document suggests that the lands contiguous with those sold by the Lenape were claimed by another group we should determine if this group, the Ciconicins (also Siconese and variously spelled) were related to the Lenape or separated in some way from them. Two pieces of information suggested a possible relationship, requiring that a thorough investigation be conducted. First, a band generally believed to have the same name, Siconysy (also Siconese), is described from the Jersey side amidst several bands generally assumed to be related to the Lenape. Second, an expansion of Susquehannock power down the Susquehanna River about 1600 and across to the Delaware, probably by 1610 or 1620, was very disruptive to Lenape settlement. This led to the assumption that the Ciconicins may have been the southernmost Lenape band in 1600, living in northern Delaware. The Susquehannock thrust could be seen as splitting these people: driving some south and some across the river. A careful review of the evidence, however, suggests that the Ciconicins are unrelated to the Lenape and allows us to reconstruct the southern Lenape border in 1600 with some certainty. What follows is the evidence which leads us to this conclusion.

THE ARCHAEOLOGICAL EVIDENCE

On the lower reaches of the Susquehanna River, just north of the mouth of Octorara Creek, excavations at the Conowingo Site (18-CE-14) in 1981 revealed ceramics which indicate the presence of Lenape in the 16th century. When first found these ceramics were grouped into four categories. One part of the full collection of ceramics originally was classified as Potomac Creek (McNamara 1982:17) and believed to be within the range of cultural traditions related to the Susquehannock people. Subsequent re-evaluation of this part of the ceramic collection, and discussion with Jay Custer, led to the identification of some of this 1981 material as being in the Minguannan tradition. Minguannan ceramics, named for the Minguannan Site (36-CH-3) on White Clay Creek, are generally thought to be proto-Lenape or contact Lenape in origin.

Excavations in 1982 at the Conowingo Site added ceramic material which appears to reinforce the identification of Minguannan Ware, which appears to represent the Late Woodland occupation of the area. Minguannan Ware overlies Mockley Ware (Middle Woodland?), which in turn is over early Middle Woodland Wolfe Neck Ware (McNamara n.d.:5). McNamara (n.d.:7) views this riverine orientation as providing the most stable resource zone and agrees with Custer (1982:35) assuming that this environment lends itself to the development of sedentary lifestyles. Both then conclude, in the absence of any direct evidence, that by Late Woodland times these people adapted were growing some maize as well as using anadromous fish. While recognizing that the Lenape grew crops of supplementary grains (maize, peas) this intermittant use of these riverine resource areas does not imply "agriculture," but probably reflects traditional Lenape use of maize as a supplemental winter food resource.

In short, this ceramic evidence suggests that the Lenape realm extended out to the Susquehanna River at least around 1550-1600. Some verbal reports of Minguannan ceramics being recovered on the west side of the river in the same area, in excavations conducted many years ago, reinforce the idea that the Lenape were using that area in the late 16th century.

Correlated with this evidence from northeastern Maryland is the extensive data gathered by D. Griffith regarding Late Woodland cultural movements in the area of modern Delaware. On the basis of site distributions (indicating increasing concentration in the area of Cape Henlopen, Griffith (1980:37) suggests that there were pressures from cultural movement (expansion) into northern Delaware from about 1360 A.D. until the Contact Period. The area of expansion extends down to approximately Bombay Hook. According to Griffith's interpretation (1980:40) the entire region from north of Duck Creek to well south of Bombay Hook became a buffer zone in the Late Woodland/Contact Period. The distribution of archaeological sites in the region surrounding Cape Henlopen suggests that the inhabitants of this region were distinct in space from the Lenape on the other side of the buffer zone. Burial patterns (ossuaries) clearly relate the population in the Cape Henlopen area with peoples on Maryland's eastern shore and with their neighbours in Virginia.[1] These people in the Cape Henlopen area belong to the Slaughter Creek Complex, defined by their use of Townsend ceramics. In general, Griffith (1983) describes their culture as extremely similar in overall pattern to that of the Lenape.

The interpretation of these data seems to reflect the expansion of the Lenape, followed by or perhaps propelled by the growing power of the Susquehannock in southern New York. Although Shenks Ferry ceramics (proto-Susquehannock) are found about 1100 A.D. all the way down to Maryland and over to the upper Schuylkil Drainage and even touching the Delaware River, the Proto-Lenape appear to expand again, perhaps after 1350.

The movement of the principal Susquehannock village from southern New York down to the Washington Borough site (near Harrisburg) about 1550 A.D. signals a new shift in their power. Fueled by trade goods, including steel hatchets and guns, they rapidly dominated the Susquehanna Valley, and moved into the Delaware Valley after 1600. All of this activity was in response to the growing trade with Europe, which appears to have been concentrated in the region north of Manhattan Island.

In the area of the Chesapeake Bay and Delaware River exploratory ships and at least one group of missionaries came in the 1570's (Lewis and Loomie 1953). This Spanish mission on the Chesapeake, which lasted but a few years, may have been exterminated, but quite possibly the few individuals were absorbed by the native people in the area. Quite possibly these Spanish blended into a population such as the Lenape, who were always noted for their considerable cultural flexibility.

Growing trade with Europeans, particularly by the successful Susquehannock, brought considerable change to the entire Susquehanna Valley. By the time of the John Smith expedition up the Susquehanna River in 1608 the native peoples all along the top of Chesapeake Bay had felt the power of the Susquehannock (Smith 1965:427). The Lenape using the lower Susquehanna River appear to have been ejected by the early 1600's. Although specific identification of the year or years when major hostilities began cannot be fixed, the Susquehannock expansion here probably was felt during the period from 1590 to 1600. This correlates with the Dutch claim that they had built a fort on the South (Delaware) River by 1598 (Fernow 1877:iii) and subsequent note of a commercial venture to that area under Captain Hendrickson in 1614.

These activities would have attracted the Susquehannock, who had opened a clear path to the Chesapeake by 1600. This ability to get their furs to traders by a southern route may have been a reason for relocating the Susquehannock village so far down on the Susquehanna River. These people positioned themselves for trade with western parts of the area as well as for markets to the south and northeast. With relatively free access to the Virginia area, and any boats that came by, the Susquehannock had two outlets for furs: the Chesapeake and overland to the mouth of the Hudson River.

Since trade and other activities along the Chesapeake must have been disrupted extensively by the 1622 Powhatan uprising against the English, the Susquehannock may have begun to expand over into the Delaware Valley at that time. By the 1630's (Myers 1912: passim) the Lenape along the upper reaches of Delaware Bay had been cleared away before Minquas power. This intrusion is known to have forced some Lenape across the river; others may have moved south to occupy the region of their kin around Bombay Hook. Possibly this problem led to the sharing of resources in the buffer zone which separated them from the Ciconicins.

THE DOCUMENTARY EVIDENCE

An earlier publication (Weslager 1949) reviewed what was known of the people called the Ciconicins in the light of existing documents. This paper intends to carry this study forward using additional information. Consideration of the entire socio-political situation generated by European trade and changing political alliances in the 17th century also should illluminate what we know about these people. This should aid us in under-standing the configuration of the southern Lenape border and how it changed through time.

The detailed accounts left by Captain John Smith concerning the lands of the Potomac River and Chesapeake Bay frequently note the Chickahamania River and its people, the Chickahokin (Smith 1965:424, 467, 521-2). The Smith map (1965: facing p. 540) places the "Chickahokin" east of the Tockwaghs, which suggests that they may be related to the "Ciconicins" recorded by later voyagers. However, this association is tenuous at best.

While most may have gone unrecorded one can be certain that there were numerous direct contacts between Europeans and the Ciconicins as well as various bands of Lenape prior to the earliest Dutch purchase of lands in this area in 1629. During the 53 active years (1629-1682) prior to the arrival of William Penn, who brought with him a Royal patent which provided exclusive rights to purchase lands directly from the native inhabitants of his land "grant," the activities of the Swedes, Dutch, and English of the Duke of York period were great. Among the primary activities of these pre-Penn populations was the purchase of land from the native inhabitants to establish legitimate claims to the area or parts of it at low cost. This land could have been gained by "conquest" from the Lenape and others. But the early traders did not have the military ability to do so; nor did they wish to generate hostilities with these natives were more than eager to sell their furs as well as their territorial "rights." From the native point of view such sales were strategically important in establishing allies in their wars with hostile neighbours.

These early land deeds are important to us as documents from which we can infer the boundaries of these various native groups as well as gain insights into social structure, population distribution, and other features of native life.

On 1 June 1629 the Dutch purchased "ye Land now called Swanendale" from a band of natives identified as the "Ciconicins" (Penn Mss. HSP: Paper relating to the three Lower Counties, Vol. 15:15; see also Dunlap 1954). Twelve natives are mentioned in the text, but the signature section of the document is missing. The names of these grantors, beginning with Aixtanun, may provide evidence which enables us to determine what became of the Ciconicins.

The Ciconicin sale of land in 1629 can be seen as a strategic maneuver with dual rewards. The lesser value of this sale derived from the scant material goods gained. Far more important would be the gain of an ally against the Lenape and Minquas to the north. The Dutch who were to occupy this area would act as allies to the Ciconicin in an unstable political situation. The danger to the Ciconisins from their enemies now shifted to the Dutch traders.

After the purchase of 1629, two Dutch ships were sent to colonize the area. One was captured, but the Walvis arrived in the spring of 1631 and planted a colony on the Horn (Hoere) Kill, naming it Swanendael. More land was purchased and the colony grew, but in the fall of 1632, 32 of the 33 colonists were killed and the colony destroyed (Johnson 1911:170-1). This led the Dutch to focus their trade at their station on the east side of the river (Ft. Nassau, built ca. 1623). The clear identification of the Hoerenkill with Ciconicin activity derives from several references such as on the deed of 7 June 1659 in which the "Hoerekil" is noted as called the river "Siconece" by the owners, and also in J. Alrichs' letter of 16 August 1659 in which he notes that the "new fortification and settlement were made at the Whore or Sickoneysincks kill, which have been daily visited." (O'Callaghan 1858 II:71).

Archaeological evidence suggests that the people making Townsend ceramics were concentrating in the region of Lewes, Delaware, in the period after 1400. Possibly these people were developing a focal base camp (settlement/village) in that area and only hunting in the remainder of their territory. Thus the people known as Ciconicins at contact may have had a relatively large "village" site on the Hoerenkil but hunted all the way up to Bombay Hook, where their lands were contiguous with the neighbouring Lenape.

The Ciconisins were not designated by name when Beauchamp Plantagenet, in December of that year 1659, provided a description of New Albion. In this tract he notes that "Sir Walter Rawley seated and left 30 men and four pieces of Ordnance, at the Creek neer Cape Iames, by the Dutch called Hoarkill, by us Roymont, and by the Indians Cui Achomoca;..." (Force 1836:17). Although this account is slanted in such a way as to attract colonists, it provides one piece of information which is important. The native name of the Hoerenkil River and the name of the people is always given as Ciconicin, except that this time the land area is designated by another native name: Cui Achomoca. Subsequently, Plantagenet notes that Roymont is a good place for a fort. He repeats that "Rawley" had left a troop there 60 years before, and that the Dutch later had left 15 men and a fort to cultivate the rich soil of the five-mile broad neck across to the Roymont River, which Plantagenet believed flowed to the Chesapeake (see Smith 1965:429 on an earlier search for Raleigh's town). In noting that this was a good place to plant tobacco Plantagenet inserted scant reference to the native people (Force 1836:26): "and trade: And there is a poor Indian of fourteen men only, and weak to hinder any...."

Certainly Plantagenet wished to play down any thought that the natives might provide a military threat to potential settlers, particularly since the very area of the Swanendael massacre about sixteen years before. These facts may have caused Plantagenet to discount the size of the group he mentions, who must have been the Ciconicin.

Only a few years later, in 1654, Peter Lindeström's voyage took him around Cape Henlopen to the Haert Kill, which is noted as Blommer's Kill on his map and can be identified as the Hoerenkill/Sickoneysinck Creek. Lindeström notes that the "savage tribe, living there, Sironesack by name, is a powerful nation and rich in maize plantations" (1925:153-4). The Hoerenkil, a stream lying immediately west of Cape Henlopen, is where Lewes, Delaware now stands.

Lindeström (1925:173) noted that the entire shore was unoccupied from "Sandhock to Cape Henlopen, on the west bank"...; with Sandhock being the location of Fort Casimir/New Castle. If the Ciconicins gathered in a single large village during the summer, but hunted along this coast during the winter, Lindeström's passage may have taken place when no one was using this area. In fact, during the period from about 1650 to 1665 the Lenape also were aggregating into a series of relatively dense "settlements," and probably using the rest of their realm as a hunting area during the winter.

In June of 1654 Lindeström (1925:130) records the meeting between several Lenape elders from the settlements around the mouth of the Schuylkyl and the new Director, Johan Rijsingh. The Swedish deeds of purchase to lands in this area were reviewed, with the names of Lenape grantors being read. After this reading one of the Lenape elders asked for the loan of a boat so two Lenape could go to the Hoerenkil to visit the great sachem Tentackan. They wished to beg Tentackan to remove the dangerous spirit which he had sent with the Swedish boats. Tentackan appears to have been the "chief" (in the true sense of the word) of the Ciconicins.

Of considerable importance in identifying the southern Lenape boundary are two documents written only a month after the Lenape chiefs met with Director Rijsingh. On July 8, 1654 two instruments were drawn up involving the sales of land stretching from the area of "Sandhock" (New Castle) to the north (see Johnson 1911:766-7 and facing 564). The Swedes received a confirmation deed from the Lenape covering previous purchases of land "around" the Sandhock and on up the Delaware to the mouth of the Christina River. The second deed was to "Tamakongh or the Sandhock with the surrounding lands" specifically, and also included lands from Fortress Christina on up the river, particularly noting Naamans Point to Marikens Point. These sales are distinct from those which the Ciconicins made to the

Dutch in 1659, and the two sets may describe not only the native boundaries but the spheres of influence of the European traders.

On 7 June 1659 a deed was drawn up covering the sale of the entire stretch of land "lyinge between Boempies Hook and Cape Hinlopen..." to the Dutch (Weslager 1949). A Dutch original of this document is noted by Fernow (1877:243) who describes it as "Too defective, to be readable." Fortunately, a translation in English survives at the Historical Society of Pennsylvania (Philadelphia) and it is this copy that Weslager (1949) has published. This deed notes the sale, by the native owners, of the land area along the coast as indicated above and "2 or 3 days Walking up Into the Country or about therty Myls...." The first person mentioned in the text of the deed (Weslager 1949:10) is "Neckosmus or Teotacken" and he is the first signatory (as Neckakosmus) of the 16 who put their marks to this document.[4] The seventeen individuals mentioned in this text are associated with at least six distinct tracts of land, all of which were sold in this single agreement. The land sold stretches for 70 km. along the Delaware Bay and 30 miles (Dutch?) into the interior. We cannot tell if the 30 miles noted in this contemporary English translation of the Dutch deed altered the distance into an English linear measurement or if Dutch (or German) miles were intended. Usually one Dutch mile equals 3 or 4 English. Each of the six tracts is represented by from 1 to 6 individuals, suggesting that several small extended family groups claimed ownership of the various areas referred to in the text. Note should be made that the area in question has five large stream drainage systems and one small one (Little River), and the six tracts may correlate with these geophysical realms.

In June of 1659 the Dutch settlement already established at the Hoerenkil gained formal ownership of the region. Their precarious position, protected by a small fort, did not prevent natives from raiding. By August of 1659 J. Alrichs reported that "the maize crop, etc., is now injured by the Indians, and in this manner the hospital is robbed and bread taken out of the mouth, which we, from weakness, cannot prevent. (O'Callaghan 1858 II:71). Presumably these raids were not the work of the Ciconicins but of other groups who had been previously harassing the Ciconicins. Quite probably the willingness of the Ciconicins to sell their land reflected difficulties engendered by hostilities with other natives and the land sale was a means by which the Dutch could be secured as allies.

What became of the Ciconicins after 1659 only can be demonstrated by tracing each of the individuals to determine where they may have gone and with whom they associated. At present only a single reference in 1676 to an "imperor of those indyans" on the Hoerenkil, who is not named, reflects continuity in residence of these people and possibly the presence of Teotacken/Tentackan at that date.

In 1669 the Maryland colony began a formal war against the Wiccomiss, who lived along the eastern shore of the Chesapeake (see Marye 1938, 1939): The Wiccomiss[5] were allied with their former enemies, the Minquas, and also allied to a group known as "Mathwas" whom Marye (1938:150) believes to be the Lenape but who may have been the Ciconicins. During this period the Maryland colony was vigorously pressing its claims for territory along its northern border. Jennings (1982) suggests that the Marylanders wanted an excuse to invade Lenape territory so that they could claim the area by right of conquest. Marye (1938:150) believes that the Wiccomise (or Whorekill) path connected the head of the Sassafras River with the Whorekills (Cape Henlopen). If so this route would pass through an area just beyond that which I believe to be Lenape controlled.

The problems of native rights and colonial purchases at the Hoerenkil re-emerged in 1676. On 11 May of that year Captain Cantwell wrote to Governor Andros (Fernow 1877:545-7) noting problems with settlers on the Horekill who feared for title to their land. Cantwell notes:

> y[e] Indyans Declares how far y[e] Dutch has had y[e] said
> Bay southward of y[e] horekill sum people are Doutfull it
> may Ly vnd[r] Baltemore and will not take it vp;...Y[e]
> ould indyan[s] sayes that y[e] Dutch when they had bought
> y[e] Land they did sett vp something w[ch] I supose may be
> y[e] armes and sum indyans thus promise to show ye very
> place. There was a great affront this spring given to y[e]
> imperor of those indyans a very subtle fellow and one who
> bears the greatest command and keepes his indyans in y[e]
> greatst aw in this part of ye worlde.

Could this "subtle fellow" have been the Tentackan noted by Lindeström twenty-two years before? The description of these people coming to the Horekill for a month or two certainly suggests that the Ciconicins were still there, but that by 1676 they were not tending the large plantations which they had kept in 1654 and may have shifted to a foraging lifestyle. Evidence for the continuity of these people derives from the discussion of the murder of David Williams in 1677. At a Council held at New Town on 23 March 1677 the name of a native named Krawacom was presented as the possible killer. Krawacom was said to be an inhabitant of "Checonesseck, A towne upon the Horekills, that last summer he came among them to trade,...some Mannanoses w[ch] he sold for Peake...." Note is made that he "did not belong to the Wiccomeese..." nor to the Nanticoke (Md. Archives 15:142-6). The conclusion was that the murderers were Krawacom, from Checonesseck and Papomco (Md. Archives 15:147), but the cultural affiliation of the latter is not specified.[6]

What became of the inhabitants of the town of "Checonesseck" after 1677 is unknown. Not one of the names of the grantors of 1659 reappears in the literature. Since the Ciconicins were not Lenape we would not expect to find any of the former noted in Lenape land grants.[7] At least some of the Ciconicins continued to occupy their ancestral lands as late as 1677. Others may have moved across the peninsula to the Chesapeake Bay or up into the Susquehanna Valley. Still others may have merged with the colonial population beginning to spread into the peninsula. The fate of these people, like that of the Lenape, may have had many facets, but for now they appear to have led an existence very different from that of the Lenape, operating with a cultural system, as might be expected, intermediate between that of the Lenape and that of the peoples in the Virginias.

The conclusion that the Ciconicin-Lenape boundary being at Duck Creek is consistant with all of the available evidence. Only one set of data is not comprehensible within the "history" presented above: the relationship between the Ciconicins of Cape Henlopen and the Little Siconese of the Jerseys. The existence of a group called Siconese in New Jersey during the early 17th century is "established" in the literature (Goddard 1978:215). A search of the original data suggests that they may have been an apochryphal group mislocated "to the Jerseys" in the early accounts. Examination of the evidence indicates that there never existed a band known as Siconese (Ciconisin) in the Jerseys.

The first appearance of a reference to the Siconysyn being in New Jersey comes from John de Laet's publication of 1625. De Laet made no first hand observation but recorded various earlier voyages into the Delaware River and produced a synthesis of these accounts. Weslager (1954:3) offers a transcription of a relevant section of De Laet's work regarding the peoples on the Delaware Bay: "On a smaller stream that flows into the bay a little below the mouth of the large river dwell the Sewapoos; immediately above on the right hand are the Siconysy; and on the left the Minquasy."

Since the Minquas (Susquehannock) were known to be on the west or left shore of the Delaware River in the early 1600's, the "Siconysy" have been assumed to be placed correctly on the east shore in the Jerseys. The source of De Laet's information is unknown, but his account appears to be the basis for all subsequent accounts. Since other data in De Laet is garbled one may assume that this is only one of many errors.

Robert Evelyn's account dating from about 1640 also notes the presence of the "Sikonesses" in southern Jersey (Force 1836:21-23), but this appears to derive from De Laet's identification. Accepting Evelyn's account, which gives population figures very much similar to those given by Smith for the Virginias (see Smith 1965), Weslager (1954:1,5) suggests that these "Sikonesses" inhabited the area around the Oldmans Creek. The "location" is a surmise derived from the premise that these people actually existed in this area. The "New Netherland map" described by Dunlap and Weslager (1958:1-3) appears to date to the period 1629-1639. Among the villages and other names appears "Groote Sironese Aende Hoerenkil." This appears to be a correct identification of the Ciconicins who are well documented from other sources (see above). Since this map also has the information "kl. Siconese" (presumably for "kleyne Siconese") in the area of Oldman's Creek the map is taken as evidence that there were two groups of "Siconese," one on either side of the Delaware (Dunlap and Weslager 1958:10-11).

The references on this map, like that in Evelyn's account, could be taken from an earlier and erroneous reference.[8] No evidence for an eyewitness account exists, nor do the Jersey Siconese ever appear again. By the time traders and settlers began to inhabit this part of the New World they found no trace of this group and I believe that they did not exist.

The Ciconicins, a small population occupying the area immediately south of Duck Creek, were neighbours of the Lenape. The border at Duck Creek roughly demarcated their northernmost extent, and appears to mark the most northerly extent of the chiefdoms so well known along the Potomac and

Chesapeake Bay. Their lifestyle and political organization, apparently more dependant on maize than that of the Lenape, may be important in reconstructing their earlier culture history. The retreat which Griffith documents after 1350 A.D. may have resulted from increasingly cold weather as the world moved towards a little ice age. The longer, colder winters which ended the thriving Norse communities on Greenland also may have caused the Ciconicins to withdraw their focal point or base camp further south toward Cape Henlopen. The extent of their hunting territory remained over much of the area which formerly they had used more intensively.

For our study of the Lenape border this information is very important. Possibly the Lenape expansion after 1500 is a result of extending their foraging range into areas abandoned by the southerly movement of the Ciconicins. The apex of this expansion, reached about 1600 A.D., brought the Lenape into conflict with the Susquehannock, where this brief history had begun.

FOOTNOTES

1. Note must be made of the proximity of the area of Cape Henlopen to the
    upper reaches of the Nanticoke River, home of the Nanticoke (Conoy)
    people. The Nanticoke, like the Choptank, Assateague, Pocomoke,
    Monoponson, Matapeake and others, were separate peoples (cultures?) each
    treated as a distinct political unit by the Maryland provincial
    government.

    The Nanticoke occupied only the drainage of the Nanticoke River and its
    tributaries, with the "Emperor" resident at a town called Chicacoan on
    the Nanticoke River. In later years the Maryland government granted the
    Nanticoke two reservations along the river of the same name: one in 1698
    and a second in 1711. The second was on Broad Creek, an upstream
    tributary of the Nanticoke River. Laurel, Delaware, was founded years
    later on the site of the latter of these reservations, long after the
    Nanticoke had abandoned the area and moved north into Pennsylvania.

    When occupied by the Nanticoke this land was part of the Maryland colony,
    but the settlement of the boundary dispute between the heirs of William
    Penn and the Calverts placed the region in modern Delaware. There is no
    evidence that any Nanticoke ever occupied the shores of Delaware Bay or
    any part of the Delaware River (see Feest 1978).

    Feest's data suggest the existence of two important aspects of Nanticoke
    life. The Nanticoke, and other groups of natives in Maryland, appear to
    have been relatively sedentary as compared to the Lenape and had larger
    populations. If the southerly groups in Maryland operated in foraging
    bands, these bands were larger in population than those of the Lenape.
    The area occupied by each independent culture in Maryland noted above is
    larger than that occupied by each Lenape band. This could provide a
    basis for larger populations. However, given the ecological differences,
    the Maryland peoples may have relied more on maize, other cultigens and
    fish resources than did the Lenape bands.

    Second, the second reservation allotted the Nanticoke in 1711 may reflect
    their movement upstream and away from colonial settlement. This expected
    pattern parallels that documented for the Lenape bands (see Becker 1976,
    1980) and suggests that the Nanticoke also were foragers.

    The confusion in Nanticoke "village" names resulting from shifting the
    entire settlement from one place to another, and using a distinct name at
    each location, has been noted by Feest (1978:240). This problem has
    confused numerous researchers working with documents relating to various
    native peoples along the Atlantic coast. Only careful work in that area,
    as in the Lenape area, will clarify some of these problems.

2. The term "Siconese" or its variations reflect the orthographic convention
   in which "S" and "Ch" appear to be equivalents (see Marye 1939:53). The
   Siconese appear to take their name from some feature in the area which
   they inhabited. The name, however, appears with considerable
   orthographic variation. The term "Sickoneysincks," with a locative
   ending, refers specifically to the geographic area (possibly spelled
   Checonesseck as well), along the Hoerenkil. Present Lewes, Delaware, is
   in this area.

3. The south bastion of the Dutch pallisaded fort erected at Swanendael
   (Lewes, Delaware) has been located and excavated. The plan, which
   conforms to DeVries' sketch of 1632, is that of a diamond over 250 ft.
   from North to South and with rectangular bastions (about 12 by 15 feet)
   at each of these two ends (Bonine 1964). A building (house?) was inside
   the pallisade, and another outside was associated with 3 Indian lodges
   (Bonine 1956). This external house was of brick.

   The second colony on the Hoerenkil (Sekonnessick) dates from some time
   around 1659, possibly having begun as early as 1657 (Fernow 1877:522).
   Governor Calvert of Maryland in 1673 ordered this Dutch colony, whose
   citizens had become "naturalized" English subjects, exterminated. In
   December of that year the town was burned, the inhabitants surviving
   largely through the efforts of their native allies. This attack, plus
   the destruction of the Susquehannock the following year, appears to have
   been part of Calvert's efforts to claim the Lenape realm by right of
   conquest (see Jennings 1982).

4. Seventeen native grantors are mentioned in the text but only 16 affix
   their marks (see Appendix). This deed of 1659 (Weslager 1949) notes that
   "the Hoerekil (Called in the Indian Lingo Siconece)" is the property of
   Neckosmus and his kin. Although the name of this land area is not noted,
   several other "Land" areas sold are noted: Quistin, Peskamohot,
   [K]wickenesse, and Seckatackomeck. None of these include a locative
   ending (such as the Lenape ing) nor do they seem to relate to
   Plantagenet's Cui Achomoca (Force 1836:17). Possibly Plantagenet had an
   eastern shore informant provide a name for the area rather than using the
   Ciconisin term. Note that one of the 8 July 1654 deeds lists "Tamakongh"
   (the area of Sandhock), which has the ongh variant locative ending.

   Another term used by the natives of the Lewes, Del. area about 1630 was
   "racontyn marenit," which de Vries translates as "a firm peace" (in Myers
   1912:16). Weslager's (1949:8) transcription spells this native term as
   "racontyn mareuit." Weslager (1949 fn. 11, also fn. 9) lists the earlier
   translations of de Vries' Korte Historiael, q.v.

   C. A. Weslager asked Nora Thompson Dean to "translate" the meaning of the
   term "Siconese" or variations thereof, assuming that the word may be
   Lenape or Lenape related. Mrs. Dean suggested that it might be broken
   into "Chick-hawn-ness-sing" which could be translated as "A place where
   there is a sound like waves splashing on the shore."

5. Marye (1938:151) believes the Wiccomiss were one of the three or four
   most important people inhabiting the East Shore. The major groups must
   have included the Nanticoke and Choptank. John Smith's account of 1608
   locates the Massowomeks on the west shore between the Bush and Gunpowder
   rivers, and describes them as enemies of the Susquehannock and the
   Tockwogh. Smith places the Tockwogh on the Sassafras River (infering
   that the two terms are synonymous). Smith said that the Tockwogh can
   muster 100 men and that the Ozines, also on the Sassafras River, can
   muster 60. Marye's (1938, 1939) location or identification of the
   Wiccomiss, in the light of Smith's data, is uncertain. Smith also said
   that the Susquehannock could muster 600 men. Susquehannock power must
   have been great by 1608 and seems to have continued to expand through
   1634 (see Gifford and Tinling 1958; Thorogood 1974).

6. "Mannanoses" appear to be soft-shelled clams. "Peake" is wampum (see
   Becker 1980b). A reference from 1697 (Md. Archives 19:519) notes that
   Captain John Hance Tillman (Johan Hans Stelman?) went to the head of the
   Bay and visited the Susquehannock, Delaware, and "Chanhannan" (possibly
   Shawnee). Tillman reported on the numbers and locations of various
   populations including the Shevanor (Shevanoes), who remain unidentified.
   Indian affairs in general are treated on these pages (519-523).

7. The elder of the Brandywine band of Lenape, Checochonicon, who was active
   in the early 1700's, has a name similar to that of "Ciconicin" but the
   similarity in names must derive from linguistic similarities between the
   Lenape and the Ciconicin.

8. This practice of accepting vague statements made by earlier authors as
   documentation continued well into the 20th century. Amandus Johnson (in
   Lindeström 1925:154 fn.) suggests that the "Sironesack" may be "a branch
   of the Shawnee ... (or a branch of) the Sarapinagh (Soraphanigh), of
   Smith and Purchas. Cf. Nelson, Indians, 100." No reference to
   "Sarapinagh" has been found in Smith (1965) and Nelson's (1894:100)
   reference to the "Sikonesses" is accepted from Robert Evelin's letter, as
   it appeared in Smith's New Jersey, p. 29.

APPENDIX

Signatories of the Deed of 7 June 1659

Area "Owned"	Name in Text	Marks made (in order)
Owners of the "Hoerekil (Called in the Indian Lingo Siconece) and the land than aboud,"	"Neckosmus or Teotacken"	Neckakosmus
	Meoppitas (his brother)	Meoppitas
	Meas (his brother)	Meas
"	Kocketoteka	Koketotoka
Quistin?	Mocktowekon	Mocktotockas
"?	Sawappone	Sawappone
"?	Mettomemeckas	Mettomemeckas
Quistin	Katenacku	Katenagka
"	Esippens	Esipens
"	Sappeton	Sappataon
Land Next Unto	Pochocton	Pochoeton
Boempies Hook	Queogkamen	Quegkamen
"	Hohatagkon	Hoatagkony
Of "Tarackus ther Land is Called Peskamohot"	Mameckus	Mameckus
	Honkarkus	Hockarus
[K]wickenesse	Hemmagkomeck	–
Seckatackomeck	Matapugsickan	Matapagsikan

ACKNOWLEDGEMENTS

Preliminary investigations of this subject were supported by a grant from the American Philosophical Society (Penrose Fund), supplemented by a grant from West Chester State College. The general research which completed this study was supported by a grant from the National Endowment for the Humanities (Research Grant RS-20091-80-2094).

My sincere thanks are due W. A. Hunter for his continued encouragement in matters concerning the Lenape and for his aid in many aspects of this research. Thanks also are due D. S. P. Dechert for suggestions regarding format, L. Mitchell for aid in the preparation of this manuscript, and to the many archivists and librarians who provided knowledgeable, gracious, and wonderfully efficient cooperation throughout this research. The ideas and opinions presented herein as well as any errors of fact or interpretations are the responsibility of the author alone.

REFERENCES

Becker, Marshall Joseph
    1976   The Okehocking: A Remnant Band of Delaware Indians in Chester
              County, Pennsylvania during the Colonial Period. Pennsylvania
              Archaeologist 46 (September) 25-63.

    1980a   Lenape Archaeology: Archaeological and Ethnohistorical
              Considerations in Light of Recent Excavation. Pennsylvania
              Archaeologist 50(4):19-30.

    1980b   Wampum: The Development of an Early American Currency.
              Bulletin, The Archaeological Society of New Jersey 36:1-11.

    In   The Boundary Between the Lenape and Munsee: Indications that
    Press   the Forks of Delaware was a Buffer Zone During the Early
              Historic Period. Man in the Northeast.

Bonine, Chesleigh A.
    1956   The Archeolog 8(3).

    1964   The South Bastion of the DeVries Palisade of 1631 (7S-D-11):
              Lewes, Delaware, 1964. The Archeolog 16(2): cover, 13-19.

Custer, Jay E.
    1982   A Reconsideration of the Middle Woodland Cultures of the Upper
              Delmarva Peninsula. In Practicing Environmental Archaeology:
              Methods and Interpretations. Edited by R. Moeller. Occasional
              Paper No. 3: American Indian Archaeological Institute,
              Washington, Conn.

Dunlap, A. R. and C. A. Weslager
    1958   Toponymy of the Delaware Valley as Revealed by an Early
              Seventeenth-century Dutch Map. Bulletin of the Archaeological
              Society of New Jersey, 15-16:1-13.

Feest, Christian F.
    1978   Nanticoke and Neighboring Tribes. Handbook of North American
              Indians, Volume 15: Northeast. Edited by Bruce Trigger.
              Smithsonian Institution: Washington. pp. 240-252.

Fernow, B. (translator)
1877   Documents Relating to the History of the Dutch and Swedish
        Settlements on the Delaware River. Vol. XII, New York Colonial
        Documents. Albany: Argus.

Force, Peter (compiler)
1836   Tracts and Other Papers Relating Principally to the Origin,
        Settlement, and Progress of the Colonies in North America,...
        Gloucester, Mass: Peter Smith (1963 Facsimile). Volume 2,
        No. VII: A Description of the Province of New Albion.

Gifford, George E. Jr. and Marion Tinling
1958   A Relation of a Voyage to the Head of the Baye. The
        Historian. pp. 347-351.

Griffith, Daniel R.
1980   Townsend Ceramics and the Late Woodland of Southern Delaware.
        Maryland Historical Magazine 75(1):23-41.

1983   Late Woodland in Southern Delaware: A Case Study. Paper
        presented at the annual meeting of the Middle Atlantic
        Archaeological Conference (9 April). Rehoboth Beach, Md.

Jennings, Francis
1982   Indians and Frontiers in Seventeenth-century Maryland. In Early
        Maryland in a Wider World. Edited by David B. Quinn. Detroit:
        Wayne State University. pp. 216-241.

Johnson, Amandus
1911   The Swedish Settlements on the Delaware: 1638-1664. New York:
        D. Appleton.

Juricek, John T.
1966   American Usage of the Word "Frontier" from Colonial Times to
        Frederick Jackson Turner. Proceedings of the American
        Philosophical Society, 110 (1):10-34.

Lewis, Clifford M. and Albert J. Loomie
1953   The Spanish Jesuit Mission in Virginia, 1570-1572. Chapel Hill:
        University of North Carolina Press.

Lindeström, Peter
1925   Geographia Americae: (1654-1656). Trans. Amandus Johnson. The
        Swedish Colonial Society: Philadelphia.

Marye, William B.
1938 The Wiccomiss Indians of Maryland. <u>American Antiquity</u> 4
(2):146-152.

1939 The Wiccomiss Indians of Maryland, Part II. <u>American Antiquity</u>
5 (1):51-55.

McNamara, Joseph M.
1982 Summary of 1981 Excavations at the Conowingo Site, 18-CE-14.
<u>Maryland Geological Survey, Division of Archeology File Report
172.</u>

1983 Summary of the 1982 Excavations at the Conowingo Site,
18-CE-14. <u>Maryland Geological Survey, Division of Archeology
File Report 176.</u>

In Excavations at Conowingo: A Late Archaic Through Late Woodland
Press Manifestation in the Piedmont Floodplain of the Lower
Susquehanna River Valley. <u>Maryland Archeology.</u>

n.d. The effects of mid Post-glacial Changes at Conowingo: A
stratified Late Archaic through Late Woodland Site in the
Piedmont Floodplain of the Lower Susquehanna River Valley.
Paper, Middle Atlantic Archaeological Conference April 1983,
Rehoboth Beach, Del.

Nelson, William
1894 <u>The Indians of New Jersey: Their Origin and Development</u>
Paterson, New Jersey: Press Printing and Publishing Company.

O'Callaghan, E. B. ed.
1858 <u>Documents Relating to the Colonial History of the State of New
York.</u> Volume II. Albany: Weed Parsons.

Smith, John
1965 The description of Virginia (1607). In, <u>Hakluytus Posthumus or
Purchas His Pilgrimes</u>, by Samuel Purchas. Volume XVII.
New York: AMS Press Inc., pp. 420-458. Also, "Occurrents in
Virginia (1606-1610), pp. 459-540.

Stewart, R. Michael, Chris Hummer, and Jay Custer
1983 Late Woodland Cultures of the Middle and Lower Delaware River
Valley and the Upper Delmarva Peninsula. Paper, Annual Meeting
of the Middle Atlantic Archaeological Conference, 9 April.
Rehoboth Beach, Delaware. Copy, Anthropology Section, West
Chester University, Pennsylvania.

Thorogood, Cyprian
    1974   "A Relation of a Voyage to the Head of the Baye" (1634).   In
            Cecil County, Maryland, 1608-1850. Comp. G. E. Gifford.
            Calvert Elementary School: Maryland. pp. 11-13.

Weslager, C. A.
    1949   The Indians of Lewes, Delaware and an Unpublished Indian Deed
            dated June 7, 1659. Bulletin, Archaeological Society of
            Delaware 4(5):6-14.

    1954   Robert Evelyn's Indian Tribes and Place-names of New Albion.
            Bulletin of the Archaeological Society of New Jersey 9:1-14.

    1972   The Delaware Indians: A History. New Brunswick, New Jersey:
            Rutgers University Press.

PREACHERS, PRIESTS AND PAGANS:
Catholic and Protestant Missions in Colonial North America

by

James Axtell

ABSTRACT

   Christian missions to the Indians of colonial North America have not
received a favourable press, either from contemporaries or historians close
to the scene, much less those of a secular bent in our own day. Whatever
their particular complaints against the missions, most assessments share four
characteristics. First, they admit - however grudgingly - that the major
missionary efforts did enjoy <u>some</u> success, however slight. Second, they
ignore any appraisal of the mission's effect on the Indians as individuals or
societies. Third, they tend to judge the missions by their long range or
"permanent" effects; the farther the critic stands from the seventeenth
century, the more likely he is to find the missions wanting. Finally, with
the single exception of the Jesuits, the missionary strategy was grounded
upon the assumption that the Indians had to be "civilized" before they could
be converted. This paper re-examines early colonial Protestant and Catholic
missions. It considers what the various Christian denominations sought to do
to or for the Indians, how much they accomplished, and which missionaries
succeeded best and why.

PREACHERS, PRIESTS, AND PAGANS:
CATHOLIC AND PROTESTANT MISSIONS IN COLONIAL NORTH AMERICA

James Axtell

The Christian missions to the Indians of colonial North America have not
received a favourable press from either contemporaries or historians close to
the scene, much less those of a more secular bent in our own way.

We might expect lay observers to be somewhat skeptical of the inflated
appraisals of the missionaries themselves, but the consistently low marks
given to both Protestant and Catholic efforts come as something of a
surprise. What is perhaps equally surprising is that while marks are freely
handed out, the various missions are seldom distinguished from one another
and the standards of judgement are never made explicit. The historiography
of missions resembles nothing so much as a single report card given
corporately to a whole class of hard-working students who neither know what
subject they were supposed to have mastered or why their earnest efforts did
not earn them more than a "D."

One obvious reason for such negative appraisals is that many of those
passing judgement were avowed or situational opponents of the missionaries
under scrutiny. New England Puritans sought to puncture the Catholics'
record in New France by ridiculing their alleged propensity for baptizing
natives sunk in pagan ignorance or on their deathbeds--the thick and the
dead.[1] Jesuits fired a double salvo by suggesting that Protestant
"depravity" made such a mockery of the labors of the Recollects that in the
friars' first ten-year stint in Canada "almost no progress" was made.[2] To
which the Recollects--or hired pens--retorted that even the English and the
Dutch were doing better than the Jesuits, who, since they replaced the
Recollects in 1625, had propagated "scarcely any Christianity among the
Indians, except some individuals in very small number...."[3] And to top it
off, an anticlerical Canadian officer thought that both orders had
"lavish[ed] away all their Divinity and Patience to no purpose" because they
refused to recognize "the (almost) invincible Aversion of the Indians to the
Truths of Christianity."[4]

Another category of unflattering judgements belongs to missionaries and
their countrymen who found their own labors barren. The English were
especially prone to this mode of self-scourging for having neglected the
conversion of the natives until colonial land hunger, injustice, and
"civilized" vices had "unpeople[d] them."[5] The 18th-century editor of an
optimistic 17th-century description of New England believed that "the
christianizing of the Indians scarcely affords a probability of success. As
every attempt to civilize them since the first settlement of this country
hath proved abortive...it will rather appear a Utopian amusement than a
probable pursuit."[6] In 1772 Samuel Kirkland, arguably the most effective

67

Protestant missionary to the Iroquois, confessed that "religion is very low with us in the wilderness" and prospects "are very small, or rather none at all." After long experience, he had concluded against his fondest hopes that the Indians were "in a peculiar sense and manner under the curse of Heaven" and "as a people or Nation" would never he called to God at the millenium.[7] A visit to Kirkland's Oneida some years later persuaded the Reverend Jeremy Belknap that conversion of Indians was indeed "a hopeless business." "The numbers who have been converted from Paganism to the rational worship of the Deity, and a regular practice of morality," he lamented, "is not by far equal to those who have either retained their native Superstitions, or changed them for some more glittering and refined"--by which he meant Catholicism.[8] But the English were not alone in their pessimism. Even the Catholic bishop of Canada told the Vatican in 1788 that "there is little that can be done for the salvation of these barbarians...I was myself a missionary among them several years and I saw how little one can expect from them."[9]

The most critical assessments of the colonial missions, however, were made by two early 19th-century historians--a Frenchman in America and an Englishman in Canada. After extensive travel in the United States, Alexis De Tocqueville concluded that "the Europeans have not been able to change the character of the Indians; and though they have had power to destroy, they have never been able to subdue and civilize them."[10] In 1825 John Halkett, a director of the Hudson's Bay Company and a champion of the Red River colony, published a damning critique of the major missions in North America, Protestant and Catholic alike. Believing that it was "far easier" to civilize than to convert Indians, he declared after an extensive review of the sources that the Jesuits had effected little, the Puritans even less. Neither group had left behind any "permanent trace of the real conversion" of the natives, he said, for "while the Romish and the Protestant missionaries reviled each other, the Indian lent a deaf ear to both."[11]

Whatever their particular complaints against the missions, most of these assessments shared four characteristics. First, they admitted--however grudgingly--that the major missionary efforts did enjoy some success, however slight. Second, they ignored any appraisal of the missions' effects on the Indians as individuals or societies. Third, they tended to judge the missions by their long-range or "permanent" effects; the farther the critic stood from the 17th-century, the more likely he was to find the missions wanting. Finally, with a single exception, they were grounded upon the assumption that the Indians had to be "civilized" before they could be converted. The exception was the Jesuits, who, after 1640, abandoned that policy as impossible and undesirable to concentrate on converting the natives to Roman Catholicism. For this they were roundly criticized by the Recollects, who before 1625 and after 1670 pursued the former goal with a marked lack of success. In 1691 a Recollect spokesman in France complained that none of the Jesuits' native converts "are seen living among French Europeans, but only in neighbouring villages, cut off from intercourse, living in the Indian way, incompatible with real Christianity"--that qualifier again--"giving no signs of religion but the chant of hymns and prayers, or some exterior and very equivocal ceremonies."[12]

The Recollects notwithstanding, the Jesuits consistently received the highest marks from the critics for effort if not effect. Recognized by all as "indefatigable," the Black Robes won points for their adaptations to native life, their well-regulated reserves, their positive outlook on native ability, and their political and pedagogical skills. Baron de Lahontan, no admirer of the priesthood, noted that the Recollects branded the Indians as "stupid, gross and rustick Persons, incapable of Thought or Reflection," while the Jesuits entitled them to "good Sense, to a tenacious Memory, and to a quick Apprehension season'd with a solid Judgment."[13] Large and flourishing Jesuit missions, small and languishing Recollect missions were the result. Perhaps the Jesuits were respected most by English Protestants who suffered from their effectiveness. Dr. Belknap of New Hampshire prescribed the Jesuit reductions in Paraguay as a cure for English missionary ineptitude, and commended the Jesuits for conforming to the natives' manners and "follow[ing] them in their peregrinations through the wilderness...."[14] Jonathan Edwards, recently posted to the frontier mission of Stockbridge in western Massachusetts, credited his Jesuit adversaries not only with zealous pursuit of their religious goals but with using "all the arts and subtle management" of the Roman Church to win the political allegiance of most of New England's Indian neighbours.[15] For better or worse, the Jesuit missions appeared to contemporaries of all persuasions to be the most successful.

From a European perspective, they were undoubtedly right. The English missions, which were all based on a "civilize-first" philosophy, were confined effectively--in the 17th century, exclusively--to southern New England. There, by 1674, John Eliot, the Mayhews, and a number of colleagues had gathered nearly 2300 "Souls yielding obedience to the gospel" from local tribes which had been battered by disease, frightened by English power, and increasingly deprived of their land by fair means and foul. A sizeable minority of these "praying Indians" had been baptized or admitted to full membership in highly selective Indian churches, having been nurtured on the Bible and other devotional works translated into a Massachusetts dialect. By the American Revolution, there had been at various times in New England 22 Indian churches, 91 praying towns or reservations, 72 white missionaries, and 133 native preachers and teachers. In the 18th century many of the natives dressed in English clothes, lived in English houses, followed English trades or farming, and lived under English laws. Most spoke English, which some acquired in English schools. At least 600 Indians had clearly crossed the cultural divide to become Anglicized Christians in all but color and perhaps memory.[16]

The other colonies fell far short of the Puritan standard for both conversion and civilization. Neglecting to send ministers to the natives, the Virginia Company concocted a grandiose scheme for an Indian college and collected a great deal of money toward it, but the Powhatan uprising in 1622 blasted any hopes of implementing it. Early in the 18th century Governor Spotswood briefly sponsored a school at a frontier fort, but that too collapsed with the fur trade there. In 1724 William and Mary raised a handsome building for Indian students, but the few who attended came too late, left too early, and died or took sick in an urban setting, much like the handful of Indians at Harvard in the 17th century.[17] In Pennsylvania the Quakers did not believe in proselyting except by quiet example, but the Moravians, a German sect, met some success in converting Delawares and

Mahicans and gathering them in Europeanized towns to farm and to pray. Not coincidentally, many of their missionary methods resembled those of the Jesuits.[18]

Partly to halt further Jesuit inroads upon the Iroquois and partly to keep New England Congregationalism at bay, the Society for the Propagation of the Gospel maintained a broken series of Anglican missionaries at British forts in Mohawk country throughout much of the 18th century. Anglican prayer books and Scripture were translated into Mohawk, and Queen Anne handsomely endowed a chapel for the converts, but the New Yorkers did little more than hold a portion of the Mohawks in the British alliance; nearly half the tribe had moved to Sault Saint-Louis opposite Montreal in the last two decades of the 17th century to become Catholics.[19] In South Carolina the SPG confined its few priests to the coastal settlements where only a few Indian stragglers were ministered to among the whites and black slaves.[20] David Brainerd had a moment of spiritual success in New Jersey during the Great Awakening, but he died at twenty-nine and his brother John never caught fire in the same way, although he oversaw a dwindling congregation until the Revolution. When another missionary visited him in 1773, he "mourn[ed] the little success of his labours among them"--which might well serve as an appropriate epitaph for the fitful efforts of most of their Protestant colleagues in the 18th century.[21]

But even the Puritan performance was not as solid as its statistics seem to suggest. Several tribes in Connecticut and Rhode Island stoutly resisted Christian blandishments well into the 18th century. Schools failed notoriously to turn Indian children into English adults. Even Eleazar Wheelock's famous Indian school in Connecticut enjoyed a success rate in the short run of less than 30% during its sixteen-year life; most of its students dropped out prematurely or apostasized soon after graduation.[22] The great majority of praying towns were also short-lived and soon lost to the Indians because of white land pressure, debts, and ineffective white overseers. The land base of Mashpee on Cape Cod was unique in being inalienable except by unanimous consent of its native inhabitants, a provision inserted by its missionary progenitor that preserved the town in Indian hands until 1870.[23] By contrast, Natick, the centerpiece of Eliot's enterprise, had been overrun by white settlers by the mid-18th century. Likewise, most Indian churches died by the 19th century as native populations melted away; only Mashpee (which became solidly Baptist by 1830) and Gay Head on Martha's Vineyard survive today.

Moreover, most of New England's Indian converts had no viable alternative. Surrounded by native enemies and proliferating English settlements, and decimated by inexplicable diseases, they were quickly thrown into political, social, and religious disarray. Eliot's colonial equivalent of the Marshall Plan seemed to many to offer the best or the only hope for demographic survival and cultural regeneration. And finally, the Puritans' goal of complete "civilization" before conversion inevitably entailed a high rate of failure, even among putative "converts." Native social values, dress, housing, work patterns, language, and religious rituals survived and even flourished in many "praying towns." While traditional families of "the blood" assumed leadership of the new communities, surrounding English ethnocentrism and later racism helped the natives to maintain enclaves of

Indian identity which may have _looked_ English but continued in many respects to _feel_, _think_, and _believe_ Indian.[24]

In marked contrast to the lacklustre Protestant performance among predominantly small, weakened coastal groups, the Jesuits enjoyed remarkable success with large, powerful, sedentary groups around the Great Lakes and with mobile hunting bands all over New France. Having abandoned early a mission policy that sought to "civilize" the natives by settling them among the French and transforming every aspect of traditional culture, the Jesuits poured their considerable resources and energies solely into the Indians' religious conversion and the moral reform of those native practices that contravened essential tenets of Catholic dogma, such as polygamy and divorce. Rather than demanding that the Indians move to French territory, where they would inevitably fall from grace at the invitation of French brandy-sellers, fornicators, and gamblers, the priests travelled to Indian country to learn enough language and adopt enough customs to become accepted by the natives as one of them. Their ultimate goal was to replace the native shamans, to lead whole tribes and villages to Christianity, and to establish Catholic churches for the sustenance of their new neophytes. If that proved impossible, the alternative was to draw Christian factions away from their "pagan" kinsmen to settle morally guarded _reserves_ along the St. Lawrence, though at arm's length from the major French towns.

By the beginning of the 18th century, 115 Jesuit fathers and numerous lay brothers had established some 30 missions across New France, from Nova Scotia through Maine, Quebec, Ontario, and New York to Michigan, Wisconsin, and Illinois. In succeeding decades, with the addition of another hundred priests, the Society planted the cross in Louisiana and the Ohio valley.[25] It is impossible to calculate the number of Indians they converted in this enormous effort. Some idea of its magnitude may be gained from the number of baptisms seriously underrecorded in the _Jesuit Relations_ between 1632 and 1672: a careful Jesuit historian counted 16,014 souls who received the rite, about a third of them on their deathbeds. But in 1653 Father Bressani testified from personal knowledge that some 12,000 Hurons alone had been baptized, most of whom had succumbed to epidemics or Iroquois war parties. Whatever the number of moribund baptisms, we are left with an impressive sum of more than 10,000 natives, mostly adults, who chose to become Christians after long and painstaking instruction by the priests.[26] For the Jesuits, consciously avoiding the mass baptisms of the Spanish friars, feared that the natives "would soon show a contempt for [their] holy Mysteries, if they had only a slight knowledge of them."[27] Apostasy was worse than paganism.

Another measure of the Jesuits' success is the number and fidelity of _reserves_ established along the St. Lawrence. Excluding the first, Sillery, all seven _reserves_ were populated by Indians who had exiled themselves from their kinsmen and communities, many of whom had been or still were deadly hostile to the French. Many converts, particularly Abenakis and Iroquois, were potential English allies and stood to gain economically by turning south. Instead they willingly sacrificed material advantage for the Black Robes' religion, at the same time serving as military counterweights to the imperial designs of the more numerous English. When Montcalm's army assembled in 1757 for the attack on New York's northern forts, 820 warriors from the _reserves_ and three of their priests fell in, including 363 Iroquois into whose former country the army was headed. In another war a missionary had correctly observed that "nothing else than religion retains the Indians in their fidelity to the French." Montcalm's aide-de-camp agreed. Of his native troops he said, "all real control is ecclesiastical."[28]

Indian converts not only left their homelands to embrace Catholicism, but after the fall of New France the vast majority remained in the Faith, at times with no priests to guide them. The Micmacs of Nova Scotia and New Brunswick were typical. After Jesuits had introduced them to Christianity in the 17th century, other priests who had thoroughly adopted the Jesuits' time-tested methods completed their conversion in the 18th. When these political priests could not stem the English tide, the French were expelled and the Micmacs were subjected to a determined campaign of "decath-olicization" by the transplanted New England Company, which had spearheaded Eliot's missionary thrust and its successors. By conserving Catholic prayers, hymns, and catechisms in homemade "books" written in the Micmac hieroglyphic, faithfully celebrating the feast of their patron saint, and baptizing infants with a special formula designed by the missionaries, the Micmacs preserved their identity as Catholics, which they have maintained ever since.[29] By the same token, the former Laurentian reserves are still Catholic, more than two centuries after the British Conquest.

How can we account for the Jesuits' pronounced superiority in the mission field? The answer, I think, lies in three areas: French colonial settlement, Roman Catholicism, and the Jesuit order itself.

Unlike the swarm of English farmers, the few French colonists in the St. Lawrence valley and elsewhere did not settle on occupied Indian lands and proceed to alienate the natives by their insatiable demand for more. Although the Jesuits had to contend with the pernicious example of French traders and soldiers, the Indians were not deprived of their homelands by the miscreants. Moreover, the dependence of New France's small and sexually imbalanced population on Indian trappers, porters, and mercenaries fostered a greater tolerance of native culture. The French readiness to marry Indians stood in marked contrast to the ethnocentric disdain of the more balanced English population for such "mongrel" matches.

Another advantage was the nature of Catholicism. The contrast between Catholic and Protestant was not a distinction between emotion and intellect, for both religions were at bottom devotional movements, rooted in religious experience and aimed at the heart as well as the head. Both were, in that sense, "popular" religions, with a common source in Scripture and medieval Catholic practice. Despite the similarity of methods, however, Catholicism posited a "divine spark" that survived the Fall and remained unblemished by Original Sin. While Protestants denied that man could do anything to achieve his own salvation, Catholics encouraged him to elect God, to seek salvation through good works, right living, and faithful worship.[30] Although the Indians originally entertained no well-defined idea of heaven or salvation in an afterlife, they found more sense in the possibility of earning their future condition than in having it given or denied them regardless of a lifetime of intentions and actions.

Catholicism was also highly liturgical, appealing to all the senses as
well as to reason. In native hands the Jesuit priest put attractive medals,
rings, crucifixes, and rosaries as mnemonic devices to recall his oral
message. To their noses he introduced the mysterious fragrance of incense,
which resembled their own tobacco offerings to the Great Spirit. To their
lips he lifted holy wafers. To their eyes he offered huge wooden crosses,
candle-lit altars rich with silk and silver, long brocaded chasubles, and
pictorial images of the major acts in the historical drama of Christianity.
And into their ears he poured sonorous hymns and chants, tinkling bells, and
a steady stream of Indian words. Although Christianity was a prophetic
religion that put a premium on the faithful adhesion of will to a theology,
Catholicism over the centuries had become more like a religion of tradition
in which practice is paramount. Indians who practiced their own tolerant
traditional religions found it easier to advance to understanding of the
Christian creed through affective Catholic rituals than through formal
Protestant "harrangues" of "abstract truth."[31]

A third Catholic advantage was the Church's attitude toward women. With
the Virgin cult and several indispensable communities of nuns in Canada, the
Church had role models to attract the women of native tribes, in many of
which women enjoyed more status than in European societies and the founding
culture heroes were nurturing women.[32] It may also be that Indian women who
suffered from a lack of men, particularly in the war-torn 17th century, found
in virginity a practical as well as a spiritual solution.

As important as the character of French settlement and Roman Catholicism
were, the major credit for the Jesuit successes must go to the Jesuits
themselves. Personally created by the pope and answerable directly to him,
the Society of Jesus was blessed with mobility, discipline, and wealth.
Although its members took a vow of poverty, the order itself enjoyed
substantial revenues from testamentary bequests, lands in France and Canada,
and royal subventions. This freed its numerous personnel from parish work to
pursue heresy and paganism wherever in the world they flourished; Puritan
ministers, who were tied to a congregation for ecclesiastical validation, had
to rely on the uncertain support of lay societies of English benefactors if
they wished to undertake Indian missions in their spare time. And while the
Society was a collection of distinct, often strong-willed, individuals, they
were bound by a vow of unquestioning obedience to their superiors, which gave
their teachings more consistency than Protestants could obtain from their
atomistic encounters with the Bible. The catechism heard by an Indian in
Sault Sainte-Marie would not be contradicted by that taught in Quebec City.

The individual preparation of the Jesuits was also superior. When they
arrived in Canada at an average age of thirty-four, they had been educated in
the finest schools and colleges of Europe--their own. Most had taken seven
years of philosophy and theology beyond the B.A. in classical humanities, and
virtually all had taught in Jesuit colleges for some years to sharpen their
pedagogical skills for the task ahead. Their linguistic and rhetorical
training in the learned languages of Greece, Rome, and France, while it was
limited in some technical areas, prepared them well for acquiring the native
languages of North America.[33] By contrast, the Harvard graduates who devoted

any time to Indian missions were typically in their mid-twenties with only home study in theology after the B.A. to their credit. Socially and intellectually, they had ranked in the bottom third of their classes.[34]

The Jesuits' final and perhaps most important advantage was their attitude toward native culture. Unlike the Dominicans and Franciscans within their own church and the Puritans and Anglicans without, the Jesuits articulated and practiced a brand of cultural relativism, without, however, succumbing to ethical neutrality. While they, like all missionaries, sought to replace the Indians' cosmology and religion with their own, they were more willing than their Christian counterparts to adopt the external life-style of the Indians until their goal could be realized. Rather than immediately condemn and destroy what they found, they carefully studied native beliefs and practices and tried to reshape and reorient them in order to establish a common ground on which to begin conversion. In large measure, whatever success the Jesuits enjoyed was gained not by expecting less of their converts, as the English accused, but by accepting more.

Thus far we have focused on the missions solely from a European viewpoint. We have asked what the various Christian denominations sought to do to or for the Indians, how much they accomplished, which missionaries succeeded best and why.

What we have not asked is why did the Indians convert to any new religion, and what were the effects of conversion on native societies and individuals. For better or worse, those are subjects for Laurier III.

FOOTNOTES

1. See, for example, Roger Williams, Christenings make not Christians
(London, 1645), in Complete Writings of Roger Williams, 7 vols.
(New York, 1963), 7:36; Collections of the Rhode-Island Historical
Society, 4 (1838), 138; John Wolfe Lydekker, The Faithful Mohawks
(Cambridge, 1938), 36.

2. Father François Du Creux, The History of Canada or New France [Paris,
1664], ed. James B. Conacher, trans. Percy J. Robinson, 2 vols.
(Toronto: The Champlain Society, 1951-52), 1:19.

3. Father Christian Le Clercq, First Establishment of the Faith in New
France [Paris, 1691], ed. and trans. John Gilmary Shea, 2 vols.
(New York, 1881), 1:255. See also Rapport de l'Archiviste de la
Province de Québec (1939-40), 216 (1671). For the authors of First
Establishment, see Raphael N. Hamilton, "Who Wrote Premier Établissement
de la Foy dans la Nouvelle France?" Canadian Historical Review, 57
(1976), 265-88.

4. Baron de Lahontan, New Voyages to North-America [The Hague, 1703], ed.
Reuben Gold Thwaites, 2 vols. (New York, 1905), 1:146, 329, 2:413-14,
438.

5. Gideon Hawley to the Commissioners of the Scottish Society, Feb. 8, 1762
(draft), Hawley Manuscripts, Congregational Library, Boston.

6. William Wood, New England's Prospect [London, 1634], ed. Nathaniel
Rogers (Boston, 1764), 94.

7. Samuel Kirkland to the Rev. Rodgers, June 20, 1772 (draft), Kirkland
Manuscripts, Hamilton College Library, Clinton, N.Y.

8. Gideon Hawley to Jonathan Walter Edwards, Feb. 18, 1801, Yale University
Library; [Jeremy Belknap], "Has the Discovery of America Been Useful or
Hurtful to Mankind?" The Boston Magazine (May 1784), 281-85 at 283.

9. Bishop Hubert to Cardinal Antonelli, 1788, quoted in Cornelius J.
Jaenen, The Role of the Church in New France (Toronto, 1976), 36.

10. Alexis De Tocqueville, Democracy in America [Paris, 1835-40], ed.
Phillips Bradley, 2 vols. (New York, 1945), 1:334.

75

11. John Halkett, Historical Notes Respecting the Indians of North America with Remarks on the Attempts Made to Convert and Civilize Them (London, 1825), 256, 293, 354.

12. Le Clercq, First Establishment of the Faith, 1:256.

13. Lahontan, New Voyages to North-America, 2:413.

14. The Boston Magazine (May 1784), 283.

15. Jonathan Edwards to Joshua Paice, Feb. 24, 1752 (transcript), Andover-Newton Edwards Collection, file folder 1752B, Yale University Library.

16. Frederick L. Weis, "The New England Company of 1649 and its Missionary Enterprises," Publications of the Colonial Society of Massachusetts, Transactions, 38 (1947-51), 134-218; William Kellaway, The New England Company, 1649-1776; Missionary Society to the American Indians (London, 1961); Alden T. Vaughan and Daniel K. Richter, "Crossing the Cultural Divide: Indians and New Englanders, 1605-1763," Proceedings of the American Antiquarian Society, 90 (1980), 23-99.

17. W. Stitt Robinson, Jr., "Indian Education and Missions in Colonial Virginia," Journal of Southern History, 18 (1952), 152-68; Jerome W. Jones, "The Established Virginia Church and the Conversion of Negroes and Indians, 1620-1760," Journal of Negro History, 46 (1961), 12-23.

18. Elma E. Gray and Leslie Robb Gray, Wilderness Christians: The Moravian Mission to the Delaware Indians (Ithaca, 1956); Kenneth G. Hamilton, "Cultural Contributions to Moravian Missions among the Indians," Pennsylvania History, 18 (1951), 1-15; Thomas F. McHugh, "The Moravian Mission to the American Indians: Early American Peace Corps," ibid. 33 (1966), 412-31.

19. Lydekker, The Faithful Mohawks; Frank J. Klingberg, Anglican Humanitarianism in Colonial New York (Philadelphia, 1940); Gerald J. Goodwin, "Christianity, Civilization, and the Savage: The Anglican Mission to the American Indian," Historical Magazine of the Protestant Episcopal Church, 42 (1973), 93-110.

20. Klingberg, ed. The Carolina Chronicle of Dr. Francis Le Jau, 1706-1717,
     University of California Publications in History 53 (Berkeley and
     Los Angeles, 1956); Klingberg, "Early Attempts at Indian Education in
     South Carolina: A Documentary," South Carolina Historical Magazine, 61
     (1960), 1-10; Klingberg, "The Indian Frontier in South Carolina As Seen
     by the S.P.G. Missionary," Journal of Southern History, 5 (1939),
     479-500.

21. Diary of David McClure, Doctor of Divinity, 1748-1820, ed. Franklin B.
     Dexter (New York, 1899), 132.

22. James Axtell, The European and the Indian: Essays in the Ethnohistory
     of Colonial North America (New York, 1981), ch. 4, "Dr. Wheelock's
     Little Red School."

23. Francis G. Hutchins, Mashpee: The Story of Cape Cod's Indian Town (West
     Franklin, N.H., 1979).

24. Axtell, "Some Thoughts on the Ethnohistory of Missions," Ethnohistory
     (forthcoming); James P. Ronda, "Generations of Faith: The Christian
     Indians of Martha's Vineyard," William and Mary Quarterly, 38 (1981),
     369-94; Kathleen Bragdon, "American Indian Christianity in
     Eighteenth-Century Massachusetts: Ritual as Cultural Reaffirmation,"
     Paper delivered at the 2nd Laurier Conference on Ethnohistory and
     Ethnology, London, Ontario, May 13, 1983.

25. [Arthur Melançon], Liste des Missionnaires-Jesuites, Nouvelle-France et
     Louisiane, 1611-1800 (Montreal, 1929).

26. Léon Pouliot, Étude sur les Relations des Jésuites de la Nouvelle-France
     (1632-1672) (Montreal and Paris, 1940), 223-24; Reuben Gold Thwaites,
     ed. The Jesuit Relations and Allied Documents, 73 vols. (Cleveland,
     1897-1901), 39:143. Hereafter cited as JR.

27. JR 7:275.

28. JR 66:173; Adventure in the Wilderness: The American Journals of Louis
     Antoine de Bougainville, 1756-1760, ed. and trans. Edward P. Hamilton
     (Norman, 1964), 17, 150-53.

29. L.F.S. Upton, Micmacs and Colonists: Indian-White Relations in the Maritimes, 1713-1867 (Vancouver, 1979), chs. 2-5, 11; Harold Franklin McGee, Jr., Ethnic Boundaries and Strategies of Ethnic Interaction: A History of Micmac-White Relations in Nova Scotia (Ph.D. dissertation, Southern Illinois University [Anthropology], 1974), chs. 3-7.

30. Charles E. Hambrick-Stowe, The Practice of Piety: Puritan Devotional Disciplines in Seventeenth-Century New England (Chapel Hill, 1982), esp. ch. 2.

31. The Boston Magazine (May 1784), 283; A.D. Nock, Conversion: The Old and the New in Religion from Alexander the Great to Augustine of Hippo (London, 1933), chs. 1, 13.

32. Adrien Pouliot, Aux Origines de Notre Dévotion à l'Immaculée-Conception, La Société Historique de Québec, Cahiers d'Histoire, N°. 8 (Québec, 1956); Hector Bibeau, "Le climat marial en Nouvelle-France à l'arrivée de Mgr. de Saint-Vallier," Revue d'Histoire de l'Amérique Française, 22 (1968), 415-28.

33. Axtell, The Invasion Within: The Contest of Cultures in Colonial North America (forthcoming), ch. 2, "When in Rome."

34. Based on a sample of 29 missionaries who graduated between 1693 and 1731. John L. Sibley and Clifford K. Shipton, Sketches of Those Who Attended Harvard College (Cambridge, Mass., 1873), 4-9.

MISCEGENATION IN EIGHTEENTH CENTURY NEW FRANCE

by

Cornelius J. Jaenen

ABSTRACT

Métissage is an acknowledged fact of French-Native relations in the seventeenth and eighteenth centuries. However, the origins of the mixed-blood population prior to the emergence of Métis communities in the Great Lakes basin, as traced by Jacqueline Peterson in The New Peoples, has not been fully documented hitherto. Much confusion, even misinformation, exists about French policies concerning racial inter-marriage. It is a mistake to assume that there existed during the French régime a consistent policy on the part of either the church or the state. Both the ecclesiastical and secular powers made decisions in response to immediate and specific problems or challenges. This paper examines, therefore, many cases and decisions over a significant time span to determine the general trends and attitudes. Neither the Native peoples nor the French - be they clergy, military officers, civil officials - enunciated a widely supported or consistent "policy." What does emerge is that métissage was never favoured as much as most historians have asserted. While it is true that the terminology during the French régime was not pejorative, nevertheless the concept of racial inter-breeding aroused some speculation about degeneration of the colonizing stock and served to consolidate nascent racist theory.

MISCEGENATION IN EIGHTEENTH CENTURY NEW FRANCE

Cornelius J. Jaenen

Miscegenation, or métissage, has been defined as racial interbreeding, or the mixing of supposedly different "racial" groups to produce a hybrid métis offspring. The proper nouns Métis and Métisse do not appear in the reports, journals and official correspondence of New France and came into common usage after the Conquest. Under the French régime, and even under the British occupation of Nova Scotia from 1710 to 1760, all the native peoples, whether "full blooded" natives or "mixed blood" natives, were accounted part of the Amerindian "nations" without distinction. In other words, there is little basis in French colonial practice for a distinction between Amerindians and Métis. Certainly, the Amerindians at the time made no distinctions and they even accepted adopted European members as full-fledged kin. The term "half-breed" seems to have originated in the Carolinas and did not come into usage in the Canadian area until the early 1800s.

Nevertheless, the French were very much aware of métissage and whether one "passed" as a native or a Frenchman depended more on one's life-style or culture than on skin pigmentation or ancestry. Cornelius de Pauw employed the term Métis in 1770 in his Recherches philosophiques, stating categorically that they were superior to the native inhabitants. Julien Raymond, in 1791, used the term to describe the offspring of a fourth degree of intermarriage between a tierçon (i.e. the offspring of a union between a white person and a quarteron, or child of a mulatto) and a European. De Pauw generalized whereas Raymond seems to have had the West Indies in particular in mind, and Negroes more often than Amerindians. The latter traced the rise of racial prejudice in the French colonies to approximately 1744, when relatively large numbers of European women and children emigrated to the New World, and racial discrimination to the order in 1768 that mixed blood militia officers were to be deprived of their commissions.[1] Prejudice and discrimination, as described by Raymond, were manifestations of a new concept in France which hitherto had known only simple patriotism and ethnocentric notions. Racism, as distinct from ethnocentrism and patriotism, rested on two basic assumptions: firstly, that humanity is made up of superior and inferior stocks; secondly, that there is a correlation between physical characteristics and moral qualities. The intrusion of Amerindians and America into the European consciousness aroused Occidental self-awareness at a time when the Reformation had stirred new and antagonstic local allegiances, militant parochialism and intolerance. The nationalism of the age of discoveries easily became chauvinism, and in the eighteenth century chauvinism with the support of new scientific ideas rapidly became racism. Any consideration of miscegenation in the eighteenth century must of necessity, therefore, take into account evolving racial concepts.

Generally, in the context of New France, miscegenation referred to the unions of Frenchmen with Amerindian women, and more rarely to those of French women with Amerindian men. Of course, it could be applied also to the increasing inter-marriage across tribal lines, which was a result of French contact and influence: Laterrière reported in 1766, in observing the gathering of Iroquois, Micmacs, Montagnais and Abénakis at Pointe Lévis for the annual distribution of the King's presents, that "it happens almost every year that such a meeting produces many marriages between the different tribes."[2]

Before considering the frequency and distribution of miscegenation in 18th century New France, and official support for or opposition to racial mixing, it will be necessary to examine the circumstances in which it occurred, the stated motives for such inter-marriage, and the prevailing scientific views according to which it was judged.

Miscegenation may be said to have begun at first European contact with the New World inhabitants either in the violent context of kidnapping and rape or the consenting context of what many Europeans, especially the clergy and civil officials responsible for imposing social controls, termed illicit sexual relations. The differences between Amerindian and French sexual standards, for example, were a source of deep and continuing misunderstanding. The Roman Catholic clergy and pious laity considered the pre-marital Algonkian and Iroquoian freedom nothing other than gross immorality and promiscuity, whereas many French traders and soldiers were more apt to condone (and take advantage of) native customary practices. However, Amerindians were not infrequently shocked by what, according to their standards, were French indecency and lack of restraint, and they lodged complaints with the missionaries, commanding officers and even governors. Enforcement of Amerindian standards of marital fidelity, and its concomitant punishment of adultery, was probably more severe than the enforcement of the Roman Catholic moral code on the colonists.[3]

Miscegenation cannot be limited to inter-racial marriage as defined by church and state. There were such marriages blessed "before the church," as contemporaries said, but many others were long-lasting, stable and productive of numerous offspring without benefit of clergy. These mariages à la façon du pays were sometimes blessed later, and as far as the church was concerned both the unions and their resulting offspring were legitimized. Father P.F.X. Charlevoix in his travels from Michilimackinac to New Orléans met with Frenchmen who were living in what we now call "a common law relationship" with Amerindian women and who had not been visited by a missionary for more than five years. He recorded:

> The first proposal made to me was to marry, in the face of
> the church, those inhabitants, who by virtue of a civil
> contract, executed in the presence of the commandant and
> principal clerk of the place, had cohabited together with-
> out any scruple, alleging, for excuse, along with those
> who had authorized this concubinage, the necessity there
> was of peopling the country, and the impossibility of

procuring a priest.... In short, the evil being done, the
question was only how to remedy it, which I did.[4]

Many of the unions, on the other hand, were of a more casual or
temporary nature, such as encounters between French soldiers, Canadian
militiamen, voyageurs and coureurs-de-bois with Amerindian girls and women.
The children thus procreated were raised by their Amerindian mothers in the
Amerindian environment and culture. These casual unions fitted well into the
general native pattern of pre-marital sexual behaviour and the child-rearing
process whereby the children belonged to the mother. There was no concept of
illegitimacy in Amerindian cultures, and little account taken of paternity,
so that even Charlevoix with the insight of a Jesuit had to admit that
illegitimacy was a concept tied in French law to property and inheritance.
He wrote that even among the Huron Catholics there were offspring of
"concubines" but "their children were on the same footing with the others,
which occasioned no sort of inconvenience in the country where there was
nothing to inherit."[5]

These were the situations in which miscegenation occurred.

What made métissage attractive? One report, dated 1723, asserted that
the Amerindians were quite pleased "if some French have children with their
young women because these children grow up strong, well-built and warlike."[6]
A French report from Louisbourg in 1756 concurred and added that from the
European viewpoint it "is a circumstance that draws the ties of alliance
closer" and that "the children produced by these are generally hardy, inured
to the fatigues of the chase and war, and turn out very serviceable subjects
in their way."[7] These assessments were utilitarian evaluations and did not
touch on the question of acculturation.

Miscegenation was rooted not only in the desire of Frenchmen who found
themselves somewhat isolated in North America for female companionship and
sexual partners, but also in the very practical role played by Amerindian
women in supporting their male companions in domestic duties not only at
home, but in travels, on the hunt and in war parties. The Jesuit Relations
refer to these women in less flattering terms:

They are all the prostitutes of Montreal, who are alternately
brought here and taken back; and they are all the prostitutes
of this place, who are carried in the same way from here to
Montreal, and from Montreal here. At present this is the
usual manner in which their journeys are carried on; and
voyages are no longer performed without a continual flow and
ebb of that tide of prostitutes....[8]

An English trader, on the other hand, thought that the French had excelled in
establishing relationships with what in Carolina were called "trading girls"
because many benefits ensued. Among those he enumerated were:

> ...whereby they soon learn the Indian tongue, keep a Friendship
> with the Savages; and, besides the satisfaction of a
> She-Bed-Fellow, they find these Indian Girls very serviceable
> to them, an Account of dressing their Victuals, and
> instructing'em in the Affairs and Customs of the Country.
> Moreover, such a Man gets a great Trade with the Savages; for
> when a Person that lives amongst them, is reserv'd from the
> Conversation of their Women, 'tis impossible for him ever to
> accomplish his Designs amongst that People.[9]

Some metropolitan writers tended to see miscegenation as a concession to
greater European sexual vigour. Amerindian males were frequently
represented, in contrast to lusty and lascivious Negroes, as deficient in
ardour and virility. Buffon in his historic Histoire naturelle (1749)
depicted Amerindians in these terms:

> In the savage, the organs of generation are small and feeble.
> He has no hair, no beard, no ardour for the female. Though
> nimbler than the European, because more accustomed to running,
> his strength is not so great. His sensations are less
> acute....[10]

Chastellux described a Métis informant whom he had met in America as
continuing to live among the Iroquois for twenty years "more out of
licentious ways than for any other motive."[11] Volney said that too many
Canadians wasted their time "in love affairs with sauvagesses, girls who were
more coquettish and much more wasteful than whites," and unlike the
Anglo-Americans they relished such unions as "the daintiness of dissolute
ways." Obviously, he added, such Canadians were "poor subjects, lazy, of
violent temper, and limited intelligence." They persisted in this demeaning
practice for civilized white Europeans because "the kind of esteem they
acquire from the savages flatters their self-image, at the same time as a
licentious life among the sqauws and sauvagesses beguiles the dominant
passion of their ardent youth." He was certain, however, that when they grew
older and "are reduced to extreme misery, they scarcely ever fail to return
home, deploring too late their waywardness."[12] The less enduring
short-term unions he dismissed with a memorable phrase: "In travel appetite
sometimes gives rise to taste for dishes which would otherwise be found
insipid." The Duke of Liancourt opined "what a dispicable race is this
creole race, there always being a few exceptions, as everywhere."[13] Such was
the most commonly expressed view in Europe.

Anglo-Americans were convinced that in this domain they were different
from the French colonists, and observers of native affairs often deplored the
fact that "the inclinations of our people are not the same with those of that
Nation."[14] Consequently they were less well entrenched in the New World.
One official report speculated that "their new Empire may in time be Peopled
without draining France of its Inhabitants" because of the encouragement
given miscegenation.[15]

There were Canadians also who, like their metropolitan counterparts,
decried the custom of racial mixture. Jean-Baptiste Le Moyne de Bienville,
when left in command in Louisiana, disputed the claims of any beneficial

results from these unions and saw in addition to a barbarization process the endangering of harmony between native communities and Europeans.[16] Father Pierre Marest saw inter-marriage as leading not to the founding of a "new nation" loyal to France, which had been the hope of the early assimilationists in the early seventeenth century, but merely a means by which coureurs-de-bois and garrison troops debauched Amerindian women for their own self-serving purposes and which reaped no long-term benefits for either the Roman Catholic missions or the French state.[17] François Le Maire objected to the Europocentric bias in favour of marriages with Amerindian girls from western Louisiana who were supposedly "whiter than the others usually are." He thundered:

> Every native woman is always a native woman, that is to say
> fickle, and very difficult to turn about once they get into
> evil ways. One must however leave to the judgment of the
> missionaries to sometimes perform these sorts of marriages,
> when they cannot by any other means bring an end to some
> scandal which will distress their missions; but the Court
> must not base itself on these pretended expedients.[18]

These views passed into French Canadian historiography, of course, so that métissage was represented as a contamination of the pure and superior French racial stock, and "to go native" was the surest means of assuring moral, spiritual and physical decadence.[19]

Miscegenation and its consequences were of scientific interest in 18th century France. There was as yet no thoroughly developed and widely disseminated scientific explanation of "generation" of organisms. Scientific confusion in this domain did not help to establish any clear views about miscegenation and human hybrids. Europeans were still uncertain about the nature of procreation. There were two main theories which held the field: the preformism view which assumed that the father fashioned the embryo within the seminal fluid; and the pre-existence view, sometimes called the Chinese box theory, which assumed that Adam carried in his loins all of humanity and that the embryo had been created "in the beginning." Father Joseph François Lafitau, for example, resorted to the latter theory and the popular belief in the influence of the mother's thoughts and imaginations on the unborn child to explain that the redness of many Amerindians had come about through women seeing their husbands painted red. Voltaire attacked both concepts of generation, asserting that they failed to explain the production of monsters, of hybrids of animals of various species, and they did not take into account the likeness of progeny to both parents. He concluded that "men still do not know how to make either babies or ideas!"

Yet Voltaire, who was influenced by the school of the anatomists, by Malpighi and Ruysch in particular, declared in 1734 that humanity was divided into quite different races. Race was a word which had appeared first in Tant's Thesor de la Langue Françoise (1616) and was used especially by breeders to denote families of plants or animals. So Voltaire could say that Amerindians were as different from Europeans as spaniels were from terriers. Linnaeus' classification of human beings helped to entrench such views. The

Amerindians, in Voltaire's scheme of things, were among the "beardless nations" and quite distinct from Europeans. Just as a supposed reticulum mucosum accounted for the blackness of Negroid skin so a similar mucuous membrance in Amerindians, were these dissected, would explain their reddish or copper colour. He held a very mechanical view of the universe, so Nature invariably followed the same rules everywhere and at all times. Hence, Amerindians would produce only their own kind wherever they lived, regardless of climate or environment.[20]

Chambon challenged Voltaire to demonstrate the falsity of the proposition that the union of a "red person" with a black or white one, "or of whatever other colour you will be pleased to invent" would produce "an offspring which is not mulish and will perpetuate itself without any impediment." The Comte de Buffon also opposed Voltaire's ideas of the singularités of fixed racial groups, asserting that it was necessary to distinguish between accidental alterations or nuances in various white, yellow and brown peoples and hereditary characteristics which may have originated as accidental alterations. Races were, according to Buffon, variétés de l'espèce, the characteristics of which had become hereditary by constant and prolonged action of the causes at the origin of the individual variations. The question of whether races had one origin or several was more than support for or opposition to earlier pre-Adamite theories. The partisans of the monogenetic view were more apt to see the equality of all human beings, whereas the partisans of the polygenic or multiple origins position were more likely to believe that races created separately were inherently unequal. Julien-Joseph Vireu asked in his Histoire naturelle du genre humain what would the world be without the Europeans, whose arts and science civilized the world:

> The European, called by his high destiny to rule the world,
> which he knows how to illuminate with his intelligence and
> subdue with his courage, is the highest expression of man and
> stands at the head of the human race. The others, a wretched
> horde of barbarians, are, so to say, no more than its
> embryo....[21]

Europeans had never questioned the humanity of the Chinese, Hindus, or Arabs, yet it seems that man's relationship to the animal world, the bestial level, was raised in connection with Negroes and Amerindians. Pope Paul III's declaration of 1537 had consecrated Amerindians as veri homines, but while "truly men" they were still inferior beings. European superiority could be assumed on the basis of their evangelizing mission, their technological superiority, their arts and science, and especially their military power. At the popular level a scale of social gradations by "race," based primarily on colour of skin, evolved until one can speak of a virtual pigmentocratie. The general concept had long associated the tropics with black skins, and cold and white skins with the northern regions. Amerindians seemed to be at an intermediary stage. In De Orbe Novo (1516), Pietro d'Anghiera had contrasted "white" Amerindians with "black" Ethiopians. George Hornius, professor at Leyden and disciple of Hugo Grotius, in Arca Noae, sive historia imperiorum et regnorum (1666) divided humanity according to Noah's posterity, a concept which has enjoyed considerable longevity, according to which the Japhethites became whites, Semites became yellow, and

Hamites became black. In 1684, François Bernier, a physician who was interested in human differences, proposed a new classification of races defined according to facial lineaments and bodily conformations, rather than by the traditional countries or climatic regions inhabited. Then, in 1733, a Jesuit wrote an article entitled "Mémoire sur l'origine des nègres et des américains" in the Mémoires de Trévoux, in which he claimed that blackness was a curse which God placed on Cain, from whom all Negroes descended; Amerindians were descendants of Lamech; while the rest of mankind descended from the three sons of Noah. Not all these hypotheses were widely accepted, although all seem to have contributed something to the development of the "scientific opinion" of the Enlightenment. Buffon, as a naturalist, for example, continued to regard climate as the main determinant of race, and he was certain that the white race was the norm and all other races in the pigmentocratie were but exotic variations.[21]

Governor Vaudreuil in Louisiana in 1744 called the Amerindians "red men," but Morénos Dictionnaire (1760) insisted that "they are born white, but the open air and the grease with which they rub themselves gives them their ruddy colour, albeit by degrees...." Towards the close of the eighteenth century, the Comte de Maulevrier defended the same thesis. Their traits resembled those of Frenchmen, he observed, but "their coppery colour derives, I believe, entirely from being exposed to the sun and from the custom they have of rubbing themselves with bear grease, the property of which is to darken things, and their mania for painting themselves with red or black." He concluded with the assertion that "different people have assured me of having seen natives who were absolutely white." Amerindians, in other words, were not as far removed from Europeans as Negroes.[23]

It became evident that Amerindians from the sub-Arctic forests to the equator did not vary from white to black but rather all maintained, as the Almanach américain (1784) stated, "an astonishing resemblance." Le Cat in his Traité de la couleur de la peau humaine (1765) had attacked the belief that bile was responsible for skin coloration and theorized instead that a substance he called ethiops (today known as melanin) determined coloration. He noted that Europeans who lived in Africa did not become Negroes, nor did those who lived in America become Amerindians. The tradition remained, nevertheless, that all other races sprang from the whites. This emboldened the Comte de Volney, following a visit to the Mississippi valley, to observe that some Amerindians referred to themselves as hommes rouges, esteeming themselves as red men to be superior to the pallid Europeans. He did not question the widespread notion that their children were born white nor the theory that it was wind, sun and the environment which had altered skin coloration. "People of colour" implied, for him, no inherent biological or moral inferiority, merely a distinguishing characteristic which could be accounted for by environmental factors. Buffon, on the empirical evidence of different races producing fertile offspring, concluded that all peoples must belong to the same species. Many of his contemporaries were content to accept his monogenetic thesis that although all were once one, the different races originated through subsequent diversification under differing environmental conditions.[24]

The debate was then resumed about the environmental influence of America. Cornelius de Pauw argued that just as European plants and animals tended to degenerate when introduced into North America, so Europeans in the colonies were subject to dégénéresence. French institutions also degenerated along with the transplanted human stock, in the opinion of many clerical, bureaucratic and military leaders. On the other hand, it might be argued that miscegenation could raise the Amerindians to better levels. De Pauw went farther and added that interbreeding accelerated the decline of the European race in the colonial environment. He wrote:

> The Métis, inferior to the Créoles, nevertheless surpass
> by far the natural peoples of America whose blood has not
> been mixed with that of Europeans; from which it may inferred
> that the latter barely merit the title of reasonable men.[25]

The opposite view was argued by Vandermonde in 1756. In his essay on "the means of perfecting the human species" he argued:

> It is up to us to awaken nature and to raise up its work by
> perfecting the form of individuals; it is necessary to
> transport grains and flowers, to change climates for animals,
> to give them foreign males, or females from another country,
> to mix, to cross the races; by this means to entertain a sort
> of general commerce between all the creatures of the universe.

Humans were as subject to these observations as the animals, according to Vandermonde. Therefore there was a "necessity to cross the human races in order to prevent them from degenerating," and those who wanted "children of handsome and strong constitution" should "seek a union with foreign women, or avoid unions with those of one's own town."[26]

The contention, likewise, that miscegenation had equally laudable social and political effects was taken up by some missionaries and political observers. Father Gabriel Marest, who expressed negative feelings, nevertheless saw benefits in his Illinois mission field. He wrote:

> The Illinois are much less barbarous than the other Indians.
> Christianity and their intercourse with the French have by
> degrees somewhat civilized them. This is particularly
> remarked in our village, of which the inhabitants are almost
> all Christians, and has brought many French to establish
> themselves here, three of whom we have recently married to
> Illinois women.[27]

Miscegenation aided the implantation of Catholicism, he argued, which in turn "softened their savage customs," and this had induced more French "to take their daughters in marriage." So it was that Thomas Mante, a discerning observer of the tenacity of the French hold on North America and its native peoples in the protracted imperial struggle with Britain, concluded as follows:

The French court encouraged marriages between its subjects
and Indian women; and this not only proved a great means of
civilizing the nations to which the latter belonged, but
effectively served to procure the former admission into their
councils and thereby a thorough knowledge of all their most
secret designs, from the formation of them; and this procedure
so entirely won their affections that to this very hour, the
savages say the French and they are one people.[28]

This was an eloquent testimonial to the success of miscegenation, but it was
not necessarily an accurate representation of all the facts as we now
perceive them.

In this ferment of ideas and scientific theories, four main views
propounded during the Enlightenment stand out as relevant to the study of
miscegenation. First, it had been suggested that the intellectual activity
and mentality of Amerindians was quite different from that of Europeans. The
eighteenth century was a period when different races and nations were
attributed distinctive qualities of character, temperament and mentality.
Secondly, it was held that the natural condition of humanity was that of
whiteness, but because of environmental factors and degeneracy some groups
had lost their whiteness, and some perhaps their humanity. Thirdly, it was
postulated that some beings looked human but were not really so. They were
lower than the humans on the great chain of being and represented a link
between man and the higher animals. Finally, it was assumed that there
possibly had been separate or concurrent creations of human beings, in which
case white Europeans were the superior beings, while others, including some
hypothetical pre-Adamites, never contained "the stuff of genuine men."[29]

What do we know about the frequency and distribution of miscegenation?
The short answer is relatively little. By virtue of the fact that the Métis
population was incorporated or assimilated into the various bands and tribes,
until the mid-eighteenth century, no estimates or statistics (such as
obtainable from parish records and censuses) exist in sufficient quantity for
significant periods to guide us.

We do have some indicators, nevertheless, that miscegenation was neither
universally despised nor widely espoused in the colony. The parish registers
for the island of Montreal for the period 1642-1715 record only seven such
marriages. French farmers and artisans presumably did not find an Amerindian
bride well suited for life in the riverine colony. Yet, on the seigneury of
Boucherville, whose founder had taken a native wife, there were three
marriages of Amerindian men to French women celebrated between 1703 and
1710. This appears to have been an exceptional case. On most seigneuries
there would have been limited and infrequent contact between the two
groups.[30]

Slavery was an institution which brought a number of Amerindians into
French settlements. Marcel Trudel calculated that of 921 Amerindian women
slaves he was able to identify who bore children, 158 (or 17.2%) were unwed.
Several slaves were pregnant by the time they reached Montreal from the

interior, and at the upper country posts like Detroit several slaves gave birth to a number of illegitimate children. Labutte's slave gave him six children, Lamothe and Courtier's slaves each bore their masters five children, and Cabassie's slave bore him four children. The greatest number of such children were not found where there was the greatest concentration of domestic slaves (i.e. in Montreal and Quebec) but rather were found at the interior military posts. Of 255 identified illegitimate Métis children born to Amerindian slaves, 167 were recorded in Detroit and 31 at Michilimackinac.[31]

Captivity in the colonial wars accounted for further cases of inter-marriage. In May 1710, for example, eighty English prisoners of war were given letters of naturalization at Quebec and some chose to remain on the Amerindian reserves where they had first been brought as captives. It is virtually certain that those who so remained, converted and married. Pastor John Williams, captured along with ten others at Deerfield in 1704, saw his daughter Eunice marry an Iroquois of the Sault St. Louis reserve. The resident missionary had refused to marry them "but the two young people protested that with or without the service they would live together" so he performed the ceremony. Another case, that of Isaac Peck, indicates that he was married to an Abenakis woman of the St. François reserve "and has no desire to come home" to New Hampshire.[32]

Indeed, inter-marriage was more common on the reserves than in the parishes. Peter Kalm who botanized near the Lorette reserve was assigned a guide by the Marquis de La Galissonière who was "an Englishman by birth, taken by the Indians thirty years ago when he was a boy and adopted by them...married [to] an Indian woman." This caused Kalm to reflect on the fate of such prisoners. He wrote sympathetically:

> In the wars between the French and English in this country,
> the French Indians made many prisoners of both sexes in the
> English plantations, adopted them afterwards, and married
> them to people of the Indian nations. Hence the Indian blood
> in Canada is very much mixed with European blood, and a large
> number of the Indians now living owe their origin to Europe.
> It is also remarkable that a great number of the people they
> had taken during the war and incorporated with their nations,
> especially the young people, did not choose to return to their
> native country, though their parents and nearest relations came
> to them and endeavoured to persuade them to, and though it was
> in their power to do so.[33]

Kalm went on to speculate about the attraction of native life for these assimilated Anglo-Americans. It was clear to him that "the free life led by the Indians pleased them better than that of their European relations" in Puritan country, that externally they dressed and acted like the natives, and therefore it was difficult, in his words, "to distinguish them, except by their color, which is somewhat whiter than that of the Indians." He found similar examples of Frenchman "going amongst the Indians and following their mode of life." If miscegenation were a means of assimilation, it was evident to Kalm that the flow was in the direction of and in favour of the native communities and not the European societies.

What Kalm saw at Lorette was not unique for the engineer Louis Franquet observed that at Sault St. Louis (Caughnawaga) "there are among them several French bastards and many English children taken prisoner during the last war which have been adopted." Franquet said they grew up with all the native ways and temperament and so enjoyed the free and libertine way of life that they never wanted to leave their adopted homes. The interpreter, paid from the royal purse, at this reserve was "a bastard born of a Frenchman and a native woman who speaks good French and even all the native languages of the closest nations."[34]

Jean-François Martin De Lino, royal attorney of the provost and admiralty courts at Quebec, had complained as early as 1717 that illegitimate children were being placed at the Lorette reservation by French unwed mothers. In addition to circumventing the community moral code, this action ignored the fact that "the intention of His Majesty has always been to francize the natives and accustom them to our manners and not the French to the native customs," condoned the "vice of the girls and debauchery of the young men," and threatened to spread to other reserves. De Lino concluded, as a conscientious Gallican Law enforcement official, that "religion itself is interested in this matter because it is certain that the Whites who are raised among the natives are more drunken and more addicted to all other sorts of vices than the savages themselves." These negative judgements notwithstanding, a French military officer noted in 1755 that Lorette reserve contained "the most francised and the best Catholics" and that consequently "two or three of their number have married Canadian women."[35]

Miscegenation also occurred outside the towns and reserves. Peter Kalm recorded what seemed to him to be the two chief occasions for racial mixing:

> But it is to be observed that it is difficult to judge the
> true complexion of the Canadian Indians, their blood being
> mixed with the European, either by the adopted prisoners of
> both sexes or by the Frenchmen who travel in the country and
> often contribute their share towards the increase of the
> Indian families, to which the women, it is said, have no
> serious objection.[36]

His observations about the "increase of Indian families" and the mothers' acceptance of the care of Métis children confirm the belief that the children were usually raised as Amerindians. Some French military officers not only became adopted members of various tribes but also entered into liaisons with the women. Even the Comte de Bougainville was reported to have had a Métis son who rose to the position of a chief at Oswego. Philippe Joncaire was reportedly influential among the traditionally English-oriented Seneca in 1755 because his father had been adopted by them in 1721 and he himself "was one of them and had children among them."[37] Individuals of inferior social standing also inter-married. The church register at Fort Frontenac records a marriage between a French labourer and a Sioux woman and the subsequent baptism of their children.[38] These are examples of the métissage which lay behind the statement in the official report on the boundaries of Canada (1755) which said:

> Several French families are even intermarried with the
> Iroquois and have lived with them throughout the course of
> the last war, during which the Five Nations have observed
> the strictest neutrality.[39]

At every French post there seem to have been Métis. At Michilimackinac,
Charles Hamelin married a Saulteaux woman in 1738 who had already borne him
four children. In 1746, a year after he was widowed, he took another
Saulteaux companion "after the fashion of the country" who bore him another
natural son. One of his sons, Louis, had five children by his Saulteaux
partner before the local missionary married them.[40] Even in the Far West
métissage occurred during the French régime. Blonde women were reported
among the Cree as early as 1719, and twenty years later La Vérendrye went in
search of rumoured "tribe of whites" and an even more bizarre tribe of "mixed
bloods, white and black" whose women were proverbially beautiful
"particularly the light coloured ones; they have an abundance of fair
hair."[40] The first identified Prairie Métis was Fleurimond, born around 1735
of a Sioux mother, who was sent by his father to Montreal to be educated and
who later returned to live in the Dakota region.[41] In their contacts with
the Sioux, the French soon learned that to refuse a husband who offered his
wife in hospitality was a grave insult, however to seek her favours
thereafter without his offer and consent was to invite assassination.[42]

After the British conquest, most of the French in the upper country
elected to remain in the West and intermarriage with the various tribes
increased. The Potawatami in the St. Joseph river area remained attached to
the French in this way.[43] In the upper Missouri region the traders all seem
to have taken Mandan, Hidatsa and Arikara women. Menard, René Jesseaume,
Joseph Garreau and Toussaint Charbonneau (whose wife Sacajawea was the
Shoshoni interpreter of the Lewis and Clark expedition) owed much of their
trading success to their marriages.[44]

At Kaskaskia, founded in 1703, in the Illinois country, the story of
miscegenation began with the trader Michel Accault, who accompanied La Salle
in 1679, and to whom chief Rouensa insisted his 17-year old daughter Marie be
married. Father Jacques Gravier reported:

> Many struggles were needed before she could be induced to
> consent to the marriage for she had resolved never to marry,
> in order that she might belong wholly to Jesus Christ. She
> answered her father and mother, when they brought her to me
> in company with the Frenchman whom they wished to have for a
> son-in-law, that she did not wish to marry....[45]

Nevertheless, the Jesuit, sensing no doubt the advantages to be gained both
for trade and missionary work, sacrificed a candidate for the convent to
marriage with a trader he acknowledged was "famous in all this Illinois
country for all his debaucheries." Marie seems to have reformed her husband
somewhat, bore him two children (one of whom was sent to be educated at
Quebec), then after Accault's death she married the trader Michel Philippe, a
militia captain, and bore him six children.

At Kaskaskia, Jacques Bourdon, Louis Delaunis, Jean Laviolette, Pierre Chabot and Nicolas Migneret all married Amerindians "before the church." Father Julien Binneteau said that these Illinois mothers would have served as good examples of Catholicism "in the best disciplined houses of France."[46] Others did not enter into formal marriages but nevertheless produced a number of Métis offspring, either through illicit alliances in the native village or cohabitation with their domestic slaves who were usually Missouri women. On at least two occasions, troops were sent up from Louisiana to "restore order" among the traders when the priests accused them of corrupting their Amerindian converts and spreading dissension.[47] The children seem to have been largely Métis at Cahokia mission, at Fort de Chartres, and at the villages of St. Philippe, Prairie du Rocher and Ste. Genevière in the 1730s, but by 1750 the French population was everywhere in the majority. The parish record at Fort de Chartres (Ste. Anne) for 1725-26, for example, indicates seven baptisms of children of French fathers and Amerindian mothers, of which in three cases the identity of the father is French but otherwise unknown.[48]

In Louisiana the developments were much the same. At first there was a shortage of white women so métissage was common and accepted. Then "King's daughters" were sent out as brides for the colonists but the results were not always happy. In 1713, for example, of twelve girls sent to Bayou La Fourche only two were married and the others were rejected as being too ugly and misshapen. The naval commissary Duclos sent a stinging commentary to Versailles:

> M. de Clairambault should pay attention rather to the figure than to virtue, the Canadians and especially the voyageurs of whom we have found here a considerable number are all well-built people, are not very scrupulous about the kind of conduct the girls have had before they marry them... instead they have all gone away assuring us that they still preferred the native women with whom they marry, especially in the Illinois country....[49]

This was not the only strange occurrence in the lower Mississippi region. The abbé Jean-François Buisson de Saint-Cosme, who stigmatized throughout his correspondence and in his public utterances the debauchery of the French and the depravity of the natives, was himself the lover of the Natchez ruler, Great Sun, by whom he had a son who directed, it was said, the 1729 massacre of the French by his tribe.[50]

The region where the greatest degree of racial admixture occurred was Acadia. It too had its unusual incidents. The Métis Petitpas, whose father Claude Petitpas was French and mother Micmac, was sent to Boston by his father to be educated for the Protestant ministry. But Governor St. Ovide successfully lured him away and sent him to Quebec to be trained at the Seminary for the priesthood. He ended up studying navigation instead, but the Governor and Intendant doubted his loyalty and sent him to France to pursue his career.[51]

Other cases of miscegenation in Acadia had more auspicious outcomes. Several of the leading families, among them the Denys, the d'Entremonts, and the Saint-Castins intermarried with the Abenakis, Micmacs and Malecites.

Several of the Métis sons of these families became capitaines des sauvages, that is to say the official interpreters and intermediaries in all inter-racial dealings, especially the important distribution of presents. Indeed, the Saint-Castins founded a dynasty of Métis chiefs in Acadia who were revered by the French, the British and the Amerindians. In 1755, a French officer met third generation Saint-Castins of whom he said:

> They possessed nothing more outstanding than the other
> natives. I danced with their daughters in the native
> fashion. All the men and women felt honoured to
> descend from a French nobleman and called me their cousin.[52]

The pattern of behaviour relative to métissage seems to have been very similar in Acadia to that in the Illinois country, at least in the early days of French penetration into the area south of the Great Lakes. Robert Challes never forgot, or forgave, the spectacle he had witnessed when the English attacked the fort at Chedabouctou and the commanding officer and his peers were caught by surprise:

> He was caught in his bed, sleeping between native girls or
> women, and that without firing a single pistol shot. The
> other officers, wise imitators of such judicious conduct,
> were all captured as he was, the gates of the fort being wide
> open....[53]

The Acadians relocated at Louisbourg were seen as a very mixed community. M. de la Varenne described them (1756) in these terms:

> They are a mixed breed, that is to say, most of them proceed
> from marriages, or concubinage of the savage women with the
> first settlers, who were of various nations, but chiefly
> French, the others were English, Scots, Swiss, Dutch, etc.
> The Protestants among whom, and especially their children
> were, in process of time, brought over to a conformity of
> faith with ours.[54]

The abbé Pierre Maillard, in considering this heterogeneity and miscegenation, wrote in 1753 that racial mixing had become so prevalent with the Micmacs and Malecites that within fifty years "they will be seen to be so mixed up with the French colonists that it will be impossible to distinguish them apart."[55] The extent of intermingling probably explains the great fear expressed by the Acadians in 1744-45 "that all who had any Indian blood in them would be treated as Enemys" by the British administration and garrison.[56]

All indications point to marriage between French and Amerindians being not uncommon when and where white women were not available, less frequent once French women arrived in a settlement. More illusive, and seemingly more productive of numerous Métis offspring who ultimately represented a gain for Amerindian societies rather than French Canadian society, were the casual and sometimes sustained non-sanctioned relationships. In the riverine Laurentian area of settlement, roughly equated with the seigneurial tract, the encounters were infrequent except in the vicinity of the reserves. Acadia was the area where there was the greatest degree of miscegenation to the point that not only many Algonkian peoples of the region could claim some "French Blood" but also the Acadians could lay claim to Amerindian parentage.

It has long been assumed that the missionary clergy and Gallican officials, unlike their counterparts in the Anglo-American colonies, consistently encouraged racial intermarriage. The tradition of official sanction and encouragement of métissage finds its origins in the assimilationist policies of Champlain, article xvii of the Charter of the Company of New France, the inter-racial marriages promoted by the Jesuits in the 1660s, and the permissive utterances of Louis XIV who had been influenced by the populationist Ministers Colbert and Seignelay and by the Canadian hero d'Iberville. Louis XIV's tacit approval, which was in effect at the beginning of the 18th century, has often been cited as representative of "policy" throughout the Ancien régime:

> His Majesty has examined the proposal made by the Sieur
> d'Iberville, namely, to allow the French who will settle in
> this country to marry Indian girls. His Majesty sees no
> inconvenience in this, provided they be Christians, in which
> case His Majesty approves of it. His Majesty welcomes the
> opportunity to let him know with regard to this matter that
> his intention is that he should apply himself to prevent
> debauchery and all disorderly conduct, that he should protect
> the missionaries and that his principal aim should be to
> establish the Christian Religion.[57]

Even at an early date, some reservations had been expressed concerning the wisdom of permitting or encouraging such alliances. The suggestion that a marriage between a Frenchman and an Amerindian, in addition to the usual publication of banns, required the express approval of the Bishop and colonial Governor, as well as the consent of the parents, indicates that inter-marriage was not a usual occurrence universally approved.[58] By 1685, the Jesuits and the Sulpician secular priests were convinced that the reserves near Quebec and Montreal should be removed farther from the French settlements and that gradual francisation would be pursued best through segregationist rather than integrationist practices. Governor Denonville added his voice to the expressions of disappointment at the limited success of earlier programmes of assimilation and evangelization:

> It was believed for a very long time that domiciling the
> native people near our settlements was a very effective means
> of teaching these people to live like us and to become
> instructed in our religion. I notice, Monseigneur, that the
> very opposite has taken place because instead of familiarizing
> them with our laws, I assure you that they communicate very
> much to us all they have that is the very worst, and they take
> on likewise all that is evil and vicious in us....[59]

In this climate of opinion, at least at an official level, métissage was not likely to be held in high esteem either.

It would be a mistake to assume, as has been said, that there existed a consistent policy on the part of either the church or the state. Policy is often the creation of historians who seek to impose a rational pattern and orderly and progressive sequence on historical events in order to render human actions explicable. The issue of miscegenation illustrates well the absence of a fixed and continuous "policy" adhered to by all concerned. What did exist, in fact, on the part of both the ecclesiastical and the secular powers were a number of decisions made in response to immediate and specific problems or challenges. Both the temporal and spiritual powers operated within historic and more or less permanent parameters, to be sure, yet both demonstrated a certain flexibility of action and of interpretation in individual cases. If there was a policy, either static or dynamic, it can only be confirmed through the study of cases distributed over a significant time span.

Canon law forbade the marriage of Roman Catholics with pagans. That was the reason that in 1648 a Jesuit missionary had asked for a papal dispensation to permit an unbaptized Amerindian woman, or one barely instructed in the Roman Catholic religion, to marry a Frenchman. The church's position did not change – disparitas cultus remained an impediment. Nevertheless, the missionaries kept insisting that in the hinterland, particularly in the Illinois and Mississippi regions, traders and Amerincian women lived in "concubinage." Was it not preferable to regularize such unions, even if it meant accepting a lesser evil? Jesuits had less difficulty with such a rationalized approach, it would appear, than did many of the civil officials and the King. The civil power sometimes adopted a more uncompromising and doctrinaire position than did the missionaries in the field who were much influenced by practical and environmental considerations, as well as intellectual approach, to defend decisions which seemed to denote a degree of cultural relativism.

La Mothe Cadillac's plan in founding Detroit in 1701 was to settle Europeans and natives together so that they would intermarry and "form one people," to echo Champlain's phrase. He assumed that in this way the natives would be francised and the French would become permanently entrenched in the pays d'en haut. To Maurepas, the Minister of the Marine, he wrote:

> It is certain that there are no native women who by I know
> not what inclination do not prefer to marry a mediocre
> Frenchman rather than the greatest of her own nation, and all
> the natives feel honoured by these kinds of marriages, so much
> so that the children who will result therefrom will speak only
> French and will have an aversion for the native language, as
> experience shows daily in Canada.[60]

Of course, the Canadian experience, if anything, had demonstrated the very opposite results. The Amerindians did not learn French or take on European ways, while the Métis offspring were normally raised by their native mothers in her culture.

Cadillac's proposal might recommend itself to metropolitan officials because it supposedly avoided depopulating the Laurentian seigneuries, or calling upon extensive immigration from France, in order to populate the upper country. It was, therefore, in line with Louis XIV's "compact colony" view enunciated in 1674. Cadillac observed:

> It would be absolutely necessary also to allow the soldiers
> and Canadians to marry the savage maidens when they have been
> instructed in religion and know the French language which they
> will learn all the more eagerly (provided we labor carefully
> to that end) because they always prefer a Frenchman for a
> husband to any savage whatever, though I know no other reason
> for it than the most ordinary one, namely that strangers are
> preferred, or, it were better to say, it is a secret of the
> Almighty Power.[61]

The economic attractions for both partners were not mentioned, but these would have been known to the bureaucrats in the Ministry of Marine and Colonies who filtered out the despatches from overseas for the Minister and King. Detroit was to be a military post, mission station and trading centre, therefore it was not inappropriate to underscore the advantages to be reaped from sanctioned métissage for both the military and the missions:

> Marriages of this kind will strengthen the friendship of
> these tribes, as the alliances of the Romans perpetuated
> peace with the Sabines through the intervention of the women
> whom the former had taken from the others.[62]

The classical allusion might invite thoughts of forcible integration, or it might simply reinforce the image of the Amerindians as barbarians to be subdued. To rally the support of the ecclesiastics, it was pointed out that inter-marriage would assist in converting the Amerindians and would result in "the deplorable sacrifices which they offer to Baal being entirely abolished."

The argument presented was not entirely convincing for the Jesuits opposed Cadillac's plan. They said that it would result in a decline in civilized standards, in the demoralization of both peoples in contact with each other, and in uninhibited brandy trafficking - all of which would ultimately undermine the work of the missions. Cadillac replied that the Jesuits were attempting to undermine his plan in order to maintain their dominance in the interior country, and he showed his displeasure by proceeding to remove Father Claude Aveneau from the Miami mission and replacing him with a more tractable Recollet, but Governor Philippe de Rigaud de Vaudreuil intervened (keeping his own interests in mind) on behalf of the Jesuits and the Miamis.[63] Furthermore, in June 1706, he ordered Cadillac, who as commandant at Fort Pontchartrain at Detroit had to give his permission to any soldier under his command who wished to marry, to hold in abeyance his authorization:

> ...enjoining him to cause the soldiers and habitants to live
> in such good discipline that we shall receive no complaints
> whatever, preventing them from having any scandalous inter-
> course with the native women, and permitting no Frenchman
> whatever, either soldier or otherwise, to marry them until
> such time as we have received orders from the Court on this
> matter.[64]

The King, when informed of this chicane, commented in July 1709 despatches on what seemed like "the great utility of marriages which were proposed for Frenchmen established at Detroit with the daughters of the natives," and the fact that Cadillac had counted heavily on such marriage alliances "to establish on a solid basis" this interior post. But Louis XIV stopped short of rendering a clear-cut decision on the merits of métissage in general, or even in the case of this particular military post. The royal communication said: "(His Majesty) wishes him to examine the reasons which he had to issue this prohibition, if they still hold true, and if he is still of the same opinion."[65] Governor Vaudreuil, was being upheld in his stand against Cadillac at least until more convincing evidence could be produced in favour of métissage.

Vaudreuil replied to the Court by the return vessels in November 1709, justifying his actions and adding his own assessment of the consequences of racial inter-marriage:

> I am persuaded that one must never mix bad blood with good.
> The experience we have had in this country, that all the
> French who have married native women have been licentious,
> lazy and insufferably independent, and that the children they
> have had have been as lazy as the natives themselves, must
> prevent any allowing of any such kinds of marriages.[66]

The king finally approved Vaudreuil's prohibitory order to LaMothe Cadillac, who by this time had been sent to Louisiana, on 17 July 1711.

In the meantime, the Court had been informed of another dispute in the lower Mississippi region. On the one hand, Governor Bienville, who had been ordered by Versailles to forbid Amerindian servant or slave girls to cohabit with Canadian traders and French officers at Fort Louis (Mobile), was greatly displeased when many Canadians as a consequence of this order removed themselves and went to cohabit with women and girls in the village of the nearby Tomeh and Pascagoula. Some also went to live among the Natchez, Biloxi and Tunica. He protested vehemently:

> I do not think it proper for the good of the colony that any
> such marriage should be performed, and those thus contracted
> will not be approved until the Court has made known what is
> to be done. All the coureurs de bois should be gathered in
> Mobile or in the other French posts and should not live as
> libertines in the Indian villages under the pretext that they
> are married with Indian women. Those marriages should be
> pronounced null if the Prince does not approve of them.[67]

The Minister of Marine apparently stood behind such sentiments. On the other hand, the abbé Henri Roulleaux de La Vente saw the problem in a moral and religious light. Cohabitation was living in sin, therefore it would be preferable to promote marriages between the Canadian sinners and their native partners than to tolerate "concubinage" which seemed to insure that the children of such unions would not receive any religious instruction or guidance. Bienville was setting a bad example by not stopping debauchery and by his own notorious involvement with an unmarried woman. The missionary argued that inter-marriage might eliminate concubinage and eventually, it could be hoped, there would be numerous baptisms and Christianity would slowly be extended in the native villages. To the general objections voiced at Court, bordering on racism, that miscegenation weakened the colonizing stock, he responded in terms meant to reassure his brethren of the Foreign Missions at Quebec and Paris: "We do not see that the blood of the natives will have any ill effect on the blood of the French...in certain cases, the whiteness of the offspring is equal to that of the French themselves."[68] The Seminary priests were involved at the time in an acrimonious theological debate with the Jesuits, accused of compromising orthodox doctrine and practice in the Chinese rites question. The Jesuits in Louisiana were befriended by Bienville, so the colonial confrontation had wider ramifications.

La Vente saw the natives as victims of French abuse and oppression. He confided:

> Among these nations, as crude as they are, and full of the
> baleful traits of sin...it seems to me that there still
> remains something of a fine Natural Law which God has graven
> in the heart of a people in the state of innocence.... Our
> religion while being professed by persons more enlightened
> than they, is a true subject of confusion among them in that
> the French, it turns out, are actually less Christian than the
> very natives who have no knowledge of Jesus Christ.[69]

He persisted therefore in performing such marriages and in baptizing the children of such unions. As a Vicar General of the Bishop of Quebec, La Vente felt authorized to order the missionary among the Tunica to marry a Frenchman to a native woman and to perform three other such marriages among the Natchez. Bienville objected that among the Natchez "there is no Christian nor any adult who wants to become one" and they had been little instructed "during the seven years that the missionary has been among them" because, in his opinion, "so greatly does their lubricity separate them from Christianity."[70] This was an important clarification because in the eyes of the church and of the French Court, in spite of Bienville's assertions to the contrary, mixed marriages could be considered valid provided both partners were Catholic. If the missionary could be shown to be either delinquent in enforcing the canonical requirements or defiant of the secular power, his defence of inter-racial marriages might be discredited.

Bienville first took up the offensive on the latter grounds. He informed Pontchartrain of his conduct in the affair:

> I had written to these missionaries that the intention of the
> King was that no Frenchman be married to a native girl in the
> villages of this new colony (I do not know by what reasoning
> the Sieur de Vente was not satisfied with what I had told
> him); that I did not think it fit for the good of the colony
> that there should be any such marriages, and that those who
> performed them would not be upheld until it should be
> explained to the court that the coureurs-de-bois should all be
> concentrated in Mobile and in French dwellings and not be

dispersed among the savage villages to live like libertines
and under no authority, under the pretext that they have
married among the savages. These sorts of marriages should be
declared null. If the court does not permit them, it seems to
me that the Sieur de La Vente and all his confrères should have
more respect for that which a commandant who is in the King's
service tells them.[71]

On the former charges of failure to observe the canonical requirements, the
abbé La Vente fell into a trap. A Canadian carpenter and trader at Mobile
asked La Vente to marry him to a local Amerindian woman. La Vente seemed to
ignore her reputation as a prostitute, frequented on numerous occasions by
the prospective groom's own brothers. Sensing that there was opposition to
such a marriage yet desirous of restraining debauchery, the missionary
unadvisedly resorted to performing a hasty pre-dawn ceremony in a makeshift
chapel without publishing the required banns.[72] Bienville brought severe
accusations to bear against him and La Vente defended himself by saying that
he was being persecuted and had been forced to act secretly. Moreover,
La Vente argued that the Jesuits in the Illinois country performed similar
marriages. Pontchartrain did not react as Bienville had hoped he would
because the news of the murder of a Frenchman by an abused concubine upset
him more than did the report of La Vente's behaviour.[73] The illicit
cohabitation of which both the Governor and the Seminary priest had
complained, albeit for different reasons and from different perspectives, was
perceived at Versailles as tending to undermine French authority, as drawing
off manpower from the settlements, and inciting incidents which could be
injurious to the peace and tranquillity of the colony.

The Council of the Marine was of the opinion that "marriages of this
sort must be prevented as much as possible," consequently French women would
be sent to Louisiana. The missionary François Le Maire was in general
agreement with this point of view, nevertheless because of what he called
"the inconstancy of the natives," not to speak of that of the French and
Canadians, "it should be left to the prudence of the missionaries to allow
them at times, that is, when there is no other means to prevent scandal in
their missions."[74] Simply stated, miscegenation was preferable to
concubinage. Bishop Saint-Vallier, who frequently despaired of the moral
standards of his far-flung flock, issued a pastoral letter on 19 July 1721,
addressed to the missionaries and populace of the lower Mississippi region,
warning against concubinage and fornication as well as against public
defiance of the church's teachings on marriage. He decreed that public
penance be imposed for public sins, as required by the discipline of the
Council of Trent, against scandalous persons who "inspite of all the
prohibitions directed at them wish to keep seeing each other and even live
together."[75]

In 1725 the commissaire ordonnateur Jean Baptiste Duclos, who had been
commissioned to prepare a full report on the question of mixed marriages,
rendered a largely unfavourable assessment. First of all, he contended, few
Amerindian women were really willing to marry Frenchmen and take on French
ways. They usually returned to their traditional life-style, sooner or
later, and their French husbands sometimes followed them into savagery.
Secondly, few Frenchmen were willing to enter into sacramentally binding

marriages with Amerindian women. Thirdly, there was a practical hurdle at
Mobile in as much as the missionaries did not speak the Amerindian languages,
therefore it would take at least four or five years for the native women to
learn French, and neither the French nor Amerindians would wait that long
before contracting marriages. Duclos' final argument turned on the danger of
degeneration of white society through miscegenation. His report said:

> The fourth is the adulteration that such marriages will cause
> in the whiteness of the blood of the children, for whatever
> M. de la Vente may say, experience shows every day that the
> children that come of such marriages are of an extremely dark
> complexion; so that in the course of time, if no Frenchmen
> come to Louisiana, the colony would become a colony of half-
> breeds who are naturally idlers, libertines and even greater
> rascals, as those of Peru, Mexico and the other
> Spanish colonies give evidence.[76]

An unusual legal dispute erupted in the Illinois country in 1728 which
did much to illuminate both the popular views of inter-marriage and the
official position on the matter. A certain Guillaume Poitier suspected that
his Amerindian wife, Marie Achipicourata, had been unfaithful and that the
child she was carrying had been fathered by another. He declared his
intention to disinherit mother and child; however, he died before the child
was born. It was the Jesuit missionary at Kaskaskia, Father Boullenger who
took legal action against the widow Achipicourata, saying one ought "to
regard her as a woman of ill repute and incapable of holding the property."
He capped his argument with what seemed to him to be a decisive factor - "she
is after all a Native Woman."[77] The Superior Council at New Orleans was
asked to make a ruling; it rendered its decision on 18 December 1728.
According to the Custom of Paris which was the law applicable in New France,
if a French husband left a property as a "donation" to his widow she
inherited it all, but if not she was entitled to one-half the property.
However, in this case, the Council decreed the widow could not dispose of any
of the real property because "the native woman, always holding to the love of
her country and its native manners carries off in her lifetime to her own
nation all that she can after the decease of her husband."[78] The inheritance
was to revert to the Company of the Indies which "as a curator of the
children of such a widow will be required to pay her an annual pension equal
to one-third of the revenues of the property remaining after the decease of
her husband." This arrangement was to be valid only "so long as this native
woman will remain among the French, whether she remarries or not, and that it
shall cease forthwith if she shall return among the natives to live according
to their manners."[79]

What was the legal basis for such a decision whereby the succession fell
to the domain of the Company of the Indies? Was this racial discrimination?
The Superior Council agreed that the "King moreover grants them only his
protection and not the same privileges as his other subjects...in article 23
of the letters patent of the month of August 1717, these Natives not being
included therein, they cannot be so deemed and must not enjoy the same
benefits."[80] The Council did acknowledge that the child born to Marie
Achipicourata was legitimate, born in wedlock, and therefore according to the
terms of the Custom of Paris should have been able to inherit as well. The

Council decreed that the remaining two-thirds of the revenues of the property, administered by the attorney for unclaimed goods and vacant lands, should belong to the children and heirs. The decree concluded with a stern prohibition addressed to "all Frenchmen and other white subjects of the King to enter into marriages with Native women until it please His Majesty to make his will known."[81]

The commissaire ordonnateur, Jacques de La Chaise, notified the Company of the Indies of the proceedings but admitted that the decision went contrary to the provisions of the Custom of Paris. "I thought," he wrote, "that there was a regulation forbidding such marriages. All we found was a few letters, where it is said that they should be prevented as much as possible. But this is not enough, for the Church never takes any notice."[82] Therefore, on 8 October 1735, an edict was promulgated forbidding all marriages between French and Amerindians without the prior consent of either the Governor, Intendant, commissary, or commandant of the post of the Illinois. The abbé Jacques de Brisacier, one of the directors of the Seminary of Foreign Missions in Paris, was informed that the missionaries in the Illinois country had been too lax in permitting mixed marriages. Besides the fact that such alliances were "dishonourable for the nation," they tended to lead to social unrest because "the children thus begotten are more libertine than the savages themselves."[83] Father Joseph François Lafitau, who was procurator for the Jesuit missions, received a similar message from Maurepas, who had been informed by Governor Bienville and the commissaire ordonnateur Edme Salmon in Louisiana, that "the missionaries lend themselves too easily to these marriages and even encourage them." He instructed as follows:

> His Majesty has commanded me to tell you that he wishes you
> to explain to the Jesuits who are in the Illinois country and
> in the other parts of Louisiana, that they should not so
> easily marry Frenchmen with native women, and His Majesty
> wants no such marriage to be performed without the consent of
> the Governor and of the commissaire ordonnateur of the colony
> and that of the commandant of the post.[84]

The Jesuit missionaries in the Illinois country found this ruling inappropriate. Father René Tartarin, stationed at Kaskaskia, protested that only by sanctioning inter-marriage could the whole problem of illegitimacy and social disorder be overcome. He replied:

> The missionaries, very respectful of the slightest directions
> emanating from the Court, are conforming themselves thereto
> without waiting for precise orders and positive prohibitions.
> But could not the missionaries submit a few considerations on
> this subject without lacking in the respect they owe to the
> least wishes of the Court?

Tartarin affirmed that children born of marriages sanctified by the church, by virtue of a French upbringing and the inheritance they would receive from their European fathers, would be more French than Amerindian. In his experience, in twenty years, only one child of such a mixed marriage (a possible reference to Michael Accault) had "returned to the wilderness." On the other hand, he said, bastards were left without education and any hope of inheritance and these were the ones responsible for social disorders. As for the young Europeans who lived in concubinage with native domestics and slaves "to the scandal of the community," they should obviously be forced to marry.[85]

The missionaries had decided early in their mission work in the Illinois country, frequented by traders and later by soldiers and settlers, to perform such marriages to avoid "a scandal intolerable to all; a scandal directly opposed to the establishment of Religion." Tartarin argued:

> But His Majesty is zealous of the establishment of Religion; it is for that reason that he maintains missionaries in the country. The natives can only judge poorly of Religion when they see the French live in such disorder. To remedy such disorders disagreeable to the Court and of which the missionaries have the same opinion as the Court, these marriages are performed.

It was not a question whether there would be Métis in the community, according to the Jesuits, but whether they would be respectable and honourable Métis accepted as equals, i.e. Métis who wished to be considered as "real French creoles," or outcast and illegitimate Métis more likely to be troublemakers.

The orders of 1735 were never revoked, it would appear, but the Jesuits remained convinced of the wisdom of their view. Father Sébastien-Louis Meurin would admit years later that only a few marriages between Europeans and Amerindians had been performed thereafter and these only with the consent of the commandant. Unsanctified relationships continued to exist and there were always a number of Métis children at the posts and settlements of the upper country. The secular authorities, rather than the missionaries, placed obstacles in the way of inter-marriage.[86]

The official position remained one of opposition, and it became more entrenched in administrative policy. The Marquis de la Galissonière, commandant general of New France, explained to the Bishop of Quebec in 1749 that the prohibitions which had been issued in Louisiana should be applied officially in the upper country of Canada. He wrote to Bishop Pontbriand:

> You will see from the letter enclosed from Father Du Jaunay (St. Ignace) that he did not receive yours of last autumn on the question of marriages of Frenchmen to native women. I am more persuaded than I was then that they are pernicious for the state and at least useless so far as concerns Religion. It would be easy to obtain a prohibition from the Court similar to the one it issued for the Government of Louisiana, but I would rather follow the natural course of events and that it were you who ordered the Missionaries to perform the least number possible of such marriages and especially never to perform any without the very express consent of the commandants of the place....[87]

The Marquis de Vaudreuil's instructions to M. de Macarty, who was being sent to the Illinois country in 1751, were explicit on the matter and reflected the viewpoint expressed by La Galissonière:

> An essential point of public order which directly concerns solely M. de Macarty is to prevent the marriages which the French have hitherto contracted with the native women. This union is shameful and of dangerous consequences because of the familiarity which it encourages between the natives and the French, and because of the bad race which it produces.[88]

There was no doubt whatever in the Louisiana Governor's mind that miscegenation produced a mauvaise race, an inferior and degenerated Métis people. This was not what the Anglo-Americans imagined to be the French point of view, nor that matter what most historians have believed to have been their views. The problem of interpretation has been obscured somewhat by the fact that when dealing with the advantages the French enhoyed in fur trade rivalry or in continental warfare the close relationship with the Amerindians is invariably cited as a contributing factor. The French, in other words, in appreciating the benefits of their relationship with the Amerindians in the economic and military spheres did not extend that favourable judgement to the cultural sphere. Miscegenation might be good for trade and military alliances but it was deemed detrimental to their social development, their civilizing mission and the perpetuation of the French racial stock in the New World.

Were La Galissonière's and Vaudreuil's views acted upon in the pays d'en haut? Marquis Duquesne associated the evils of miscegenation with those of running the woods. The third article of the Regulation of 6 July 1755 was aimed at voyageurs who, without official leave, went to establish themselves in the hinterland "to carry on trade furtively from one post to another, or again out of dissoluteness with the native women" and ordered officers to send them back to the colony to be tried.[89]

On Isle Royale more radical measures had been taken indicating that the policy although proclaimed only in Louisiana may unofficially have been applied throughout New France. An ensign who disobeyed a direct order from his commanding officer and proceeded to marry Marguerite Guedy, a Métisse of Acadian and Micmac parentage living at Baie des Espagnols, who arrested. His marriage was annulled and the young officer and the priest who had performed the ceremony were sent back to France in disgrace.[90] The case may have been exceptional, but the punishment was exemplary.

Contrary to widely held views, official policy in New France by the end of the French régime seems to have been steadfastly opposed to sanctioning racial inter-marriage. The problems seem to have persisted after the British conquest for we find Bishop Briand, in 1767, sending a pastoral letter to the inhabitants of Kaskaskia ordering them to obey their Grand Vicar and condemning those who "have the temerity to marry without having their marriages blessed by the priest."[91] It is possible that some of the inhabitants were resorting to mariages à la gaumine, which had been denounced in the Laurentian colony, but it is also possible that they were simply cohabiting with Amerindian women. Bishop Briand also found it necessary to warn a curate in Beauce that "the mariage of French with natives is not authorized by the government; I permit you, however, to celebrate the one of which you speak."[92] Non-authorization was tantamount to prohibition. In any case, the practice was not regular and therefore it required a specific dispensation.

The role and importance of miscegenation in New France has not always been correctly and adequately treated. Too frequently there has been an uncritical acceptance of some contemporary and subjective judgements that métissage was actively promoted by church and state, eagerly entered into by both groups in contact, and invariably produced results which favoured French commercial and military interests in the upper country and benefitted both Catholic missions and French colonization. Misinterpretation of the complexity of the issue may be traced to selectivity of sources on which a judgement is based, and restriction, all too frequently, to sources of the early seventeenth century or the "heroic age" of New France on the assumption that this period is representative of society of the Ancien régime. Therefore, we have chosen to concentrate on the eighteenth century when the colony was more populous, transplanted peoples and institutions had had opportunity to take root in the New World, and the French had spread themselves out over a vast expanse of North America and had come into contact with a great number of Amerindian bands and tribes.

Louise Dechêne, more than any other historian of the French régime, has put miscegenation into its proper demographic and cultural perspective for the period and region she studied. Charles O'Neill has warned against two historiographic exaggerations: one, "to maintain that the French had none of the racial prejudices of the English or of the Indians;" the other, "to project upon French rulers and officials of the early eighteenth century a race mentality such as that found in nineteenth-century Louisiana." For French Canadian nationalist historians the question of miscegenation touched a raw nerve and became taboo. The abbé Lionel Groulx, chief exponent of a conservative, racist and theocratic nationalism, abhorred any suggestion of the pure and select French stock which formed the embryonic nation in America having been contaminated through métissage. It was sufficient evil that Frenchmen should have "gone native" as coureurs de bois, without adding to their "crime" and Quebec's humiliation the "mixing of blood." Groulx claimed there had been only 94 marriages between French and Amerindians over a period of two centuries. In his words, "it was sufficient for our pride to have in our veins only the blood of France and to have none other." As for miscegenation having benefitted the Amerindians, Groulx conceded that it "could be an element of progress between superior races," but "it always constitutes an element of degeneration when these races, even superior ones, are too different." "To cross two peoples is to change in one stroke," he argued, "their physical being as well as their mental being." He concluded that "it is therefore with reason that all peoples who have reached a high degree of civilization have studiously avoided mixing with foreigners." Many historians, of course, have simply ignored the question when dealing with New France, or they have assumed it is unimportant and have relegated it to the North-West Company fur trade era after the Conquest.[93]

The question of miscegenation, as has been argued, was complex and controversial. It never gave rise to a clearly enunciated and widely supported "policy" with which all parties concerned - Frenchmen, Amerindians, clergy, military officers and civil officials - could identify. Although the terminology was not pejorative - unlike the term mulatto which suggested unnatural union and sterile progeny - the concept of racial interbreeding aroused some speculation about degeneration of the colonizing stock and served to consolidate nascent racist theory.

The French, in general, appear rarely to have doubted the superiority of their culture and technology compared to the primitiveness of Amerindian societies. Marriage, as the institution upon which the family as the basic unit of society, was founded, implied more than a social contract and residential arrangements. The future of an entire society - its manners, morals, mentality and material success - depended upon its qualities. Not surprisingly, ecclesiastical and secular leaders had reservations about the appropriateness of inter-racial unions for both the European colonizers and the native peoples.

However, there were compelling arguments in favour of such unions, ranging from dreams of conversion to hopes of increased trade profits and assurances of military support. In fact, miscegenation usually occurred for less prosaic reasons and in less romantic circumstances. It was particularly attractive to early settlers deprived of European spouses, to voyageurs who travelled the difficult water routes, to traders and soldiers who were isolated in the upper country. Miscegenation took on four distinct forms: sanctified life-long unions, or sacramental marriages, between French and Amerindians; customary unions à la façon du pays which might eventually be regularized "before the church" or terminated if the European partner returned to the main French settlements; "concubinage" or cohabitation with domestics and slaves; casual encounters or promiscuous behaviour. All four types of unions produced Métis progeny and these, with few exceptions, were raised by their Amerindian mothers and thus grew up naturally in native society. Amerindian societies were able to assimilate these children without traumatic effects, given their lack of concept of illegitimacy and their matrilocal and matrilineal social organization.

The French were not too different from other Western European peoples in their basic attitudes to native peoples. The circumstances of contact, notably in the upper country where a small minority (largely male) of French traders, voyageurs, soldiers, settlers and missionaries lived in Amerindian territory at the good pleasure of the native population, were different from the experiences of most Anglo-American seaboard colonists, or St. Lawrence valley settlers. The Acadians did not share the same experiences or views as their riverine Laurentian cousins. Each social group involved in contact brought its own motives and attitudes to bear, so that Amerindian women had their reasons for entering into alliances with Frenchmen, just as young Frenchmen had their motives for preferring Amerindian girls, missionaries had their objectives for wanting to regularize these unions, and administrators had their rationalizations for wishing to limit or eliminate them.

The social and natural sciences associated with the Enlightenment did little to clarify the issue of métissage. Instead, they injected a note of racism into the debate and New France was to feel keenly the anti-colonialism of the philosophes. New France in the seventeenth century seemed to have embarked on state subsidized métissage, a programme of educating native girls in the convents and on reserves to prepare them for a sedentary life in the colony, inspired by the rhetoric that shortly Amerindians and French would form "but one people." As the eighteenth century began, miscegenation was permissable but not necessarily recommended, and by the end of the French régime it was by and large out of favour, and suspect when not outrightly denounced.

It would be inaccurate to suggest that there was a persistent and constant move away from promotion of métissage by the civil and clerical powers towards strict control and eventual prohibition of miscegenation. The movement was uneven, with some sectors of society resisting change. It would be equally inaccurate to suggest that there was unanimity in colonial society either in favour of miscegenation in the early seventeenth century or in opposition to it in the mid-eighteenth century. Nevertheless, the general movement of ideas, and consequently of official directives, was away from a favourable assessment of miscegenation and its consequences in the early years of French colonization toward a less favourable assessment in the closing years of the Ancien régime. In this matter, as in others, New France seemed to be moving closer to the social attitudes and organization of traditional and conservative Old France, at a time when these were themselves coming under serious criticism in the metropole.

FOOTNOTES

(Abbreviations: A.A.Q. - Archives de l'Archevêché de Québec;
A.C. - Archives des Colonies; A.R.S.I. - Archivum Romanum Societatis Jesu;
A.S.Q. - Archives du Séminaire de Québec; B.N. - Bibliothèque Nationale,
Paris; B.R.H. - Bulletin de Recherches historiques; C.H.R. - Canadian
Historical Review; D.C.B. - Dictionary of Canadian Biography; P.A.C. - Public
Archives of Canada; R.A.P.Q. - Rapport de l'Archiviste de la Province de
Québec).

1. Corneille de Pauw, Recherches philosophiques sur les Américains; ou
    Mémoires intéressants pour servir à l'Histoire de l'espèce humaine
    (Londres, 1770), II, 168; Julien Raymond, Observations sur l'origine et
    le progrès du préjugé des colons blancs (Paris, 1791), 5-7, 9, 16;
    Marcel Giraud, Le Métis canadien. Son rôle dans l'histoire des
    provinces de l'Ouest (Paris, 1945), 312-333, 429-473, in discussing the
    origins of the Western Métis population does not deal with the
    terminology. The writings of Jennifer Brown, John Foster, Jacqueline
    Peterson, Fritz Pannekoek and Sylvia Van Kirk shed little light on the
    question. For an analysis of "the conjunction of certain historical
    developments" which serve "not only to account for the rise of racism
    but to set it off from the earlier ethnocentric notions and simple
    patriotism" see Dante A. Puzzo, "Racism and the Western Tradition,"
    Journal of the History of Ideas, XXV, 4 (October-December 1964),
    579-586.

2. Pierre Favre dit Laterrière, Mémoires de Pierre de Sales Laterrière et
    de ses Traverses (Ottawa, 1980), 55.

3. Louise Dechêne, Habitants et Marchands de Montréal au XVIIe siècle
    (Paris, 1974), 41 cites a case in 1701 at LaMontagne reserve near
    Montreal. For the sixteenth and seventeenth century background to
    miscegenation see my Friend and Foe. Aspects of French-Amerindian
    Cultural Contact in the Sixteenth and Seventeenth Centuries (New York,
    1976), 107-109, 161-175, 183-185; "Problems of Assimilation in New
    France, 1603-1645," French Historical Studies, IV, 3 (Spring, 1966),
    265-289; "Amerindian Views of French Culture in the Seventeenth
    Century," C.H.R., LV, 3 (September 1974), 272-2, 279; "French Attitudes
    toward Native Society," in Carol M. Judd and Arthur J. Ray, eds., Old
    Trails and New Directions: Papers of the Third North American Fur Trade
    Conference (Toronto, 1979), 59-72.

4. Charles E. O'Neill, ed., Charlevoix's Louisiana (Baton Rouge, 1977),
    158-159. The Canadian Courts upheld the legality of mariages à la façon
    du pays (country marriages) and the legitimacy of their offspring in the
    famous case of Connolly V. Woolrich, Superior Court, 9 July 1867, Lower
    Canada Jurist, XI, 228.

5. Pierre-François-Xavier de Charlevoix, Journal of a Voyage to North-America (Ann Arbor, 1966), II, 116.

6. P.A.C., MG1, Series C^{11}A, Vol. 45, "Relation de la vie et moeurs des Sauvages," 1723, 152-153.

7. Ken Donavon, ed., "A Letter from Louisbourg, 1756," Acadiensis, X. 1 (Autumn 1980), M. de la Varenne to a friend in La Rochelle, 8 May 1756, 119.

8. R.G. Thwaites, ed., The Jesuit Relations and Allied Documents (New York, 1959), LXV, 241.

9. Hugh T. Lefler, ed., John Lawson: A New Voyage to Carolina (Chapel Hill, 1967), Letter of 1709, 192.

10. G. Richard, ed., Comte de Buffon: Oeuvres complètes (Paris, 1828), XV, 445-456.

11. Marquis François-Jean de Chastellux, Voyages de M. le Marquis de Chastellux dans l'Amérique septentrionale dans les années 1780, 1781 et 1782 (Paris, 1786), I, 331.

12. F.C. Constantin, Comte de Volney, Oeuvres de C.F. Volney (Paris, 1826), X, 353, 395.

13. Jean Marchand, ed., Duc de Liancourt: Journal de Voyage en Amérique (Baltimore, 1940), 98.

14. Howard Peckham and Charles Gibson, eds., Attitudes of Colonial Powers Toward the American Indian (Salt Lake City, 1969), 92, citing Spotswood to Board of Trade, 5 April 1717.

15. General Report on the Plantations, 8 September 1721, cited in Honorius Provost, "Mariages entre Canadiens et Sauvages," B.R.H., LIV (1948), 53.

16. Bienville to Minister, 28 July 1706 and 10 October 1706 cited in Jay Higginbotham, Old Mobile (Mobile, 1977), 282.

17. Natalie M. Belting, Kaskaskia under the French Régime (New Orleans, 1975), 12-13.

18. P.A.C., MG7, I, A-2, Fonds français Ms 12105, "Mémoire sur la Louisiane, 1717," 72. I have translated sauvage, an adjective, as "native" rather than "savage" when no obvious pejorative reference is made to the state of savagery, and have translated the collective noun sauvages as "native peoples."

19. Lionel Groulx, Notre maître, le passé (Montréal, 1937), 258; L'Appel de la Race (Montréal, 1956), 131. Groulx cited a Dr. Gustave Le Bon as his authority on the degenerating effects of racial intermarriage.

20. Georges-Louis Leclerc, Comte de Buffon, Histoire naturelle, générale et particulière (Paris, 1753), IV, 387-389; Philip R. Sloan, "The Idea of Racial Degeneracy in Buffon's Histoire Naturelle, "in Harold E. Pagliaro, ed., Racism in the Eighteenth Century (Cleveland, 1973), 294; On the question of eighteenth century concepts of human origins, races and hybridization the following are invaluable: A. Owen Aldridge, "Feijoo and the Problem of Ethiopian Color," pp. 263-277 and Richard H. Popkin," The Philosophical Basis of Eighteenth Century Racism," pp. 245-262, in Harold E. Pagliaro, ed., Racism in the Eighteenth Century (Cleveland, 1973); Arnold H. Rowbothamn" Jesuit Figurists and Eighteenth Century Religion," Journal of the History of Ideas, XVII, 4 (October 1956), 384-483); Dante A. Puzzo, Racism and the Western Tradition," Journal of the History of Ideas, XXV, 4 (October-December 1964), 579-586; Leonard Lieberman and Larry T. Reynolds, "The Debate over Race Revisted: An Empirical Investigation," Phylon, XXXIX, 4 (December 1978). 333-343.

21. C. Chambon, Traité général du commerce de l'Amérique contenant l'histoire des découvertes des Européens dans cette partie du Monde, son étendue, ses productions (Amsterdam, 1783), II, 470-472; Julien-Joseph Virey, Histoire naturelle du genre humain, ou Recherches sur ses principaux fondements physiques et moraux au siècle des Lumières (Paris, 1800), I, 146-147. See also Michèle Duchet, Anthropologie et histoire au siècle des Lumières (Paris, 1971), 270-273, 281-284; Jean Meyer, Les Européens et les autres (Paris, 1975), 308-311.

22. François Bernier, "Nouvelle Division de la Terre, par les différents Espèces ou Races d'hommes qui l'habitent, envoyée par un fameux Voyageur à M. L'Abbé de la *** à peu près en ces termes," Journal des Scavans (24 avril 1684), 85-89, 133-140; Père Auguste, "Mémoire sur l'origine des nègres et des américains," Mémoires de Trévoux (novembre 1733) cited in Aldridge, "Feijoo and the problem of Ethiopian Color," 266, 276; Georges-Louis Leclerc, Comte de Buffon, Natural History, General and Particular (London, 1791), III, 151-153, 201-204; VII, 34-35. The theories of Amerindian origins and their implications are laid out in Lee Eldridge Huddleston, Origins of the American Indians, European Concepts, 1492-1729 (Austin, 1967) and to a more limited extent in Diamond Jenness, ed., The American Aborigines: Their Origin and Antiquity. A Collection of Papers (Toronto, 1933). The concept of a westward movement of civility and true religion is found in Cartier's report on Canada (1534) and the idea that some ancient Hebrews had once journeyed to America is discussed in Lescarbot's Nova Francia (1609). The 1733 assertion that Amerindians were descendants of Lamech was but one theory among many current in Western European speculation of links between ancient Israel and America. The heliotropic idea, Jewish messianism, Christian millenarianism and American nationalism all began to come together in Elias Boudinot, A Star in the West, or, A humble attempt to discover the long lost Ten Tribes (Trenton, N.J., 1816), Ethan Smith, View of the Hebrews, or, The Tribes of Israel in America (Poultney, Vt., 1825), Joseph Priest, A View of the Expected Christian Millennium (Albany, 1828), which nourished and culminated in Joseph Smith, The Book of Mormon, An Account by the Hand of Mormon upon plates taken from the plates of Nephi (Palmyra, N.Y., 1830), the basis of the

Mormon religion. Cf. Gustav H. Blanke, "Early Theories about the Nature and Origin of the Indians, and the Advent of Mormonism," <u>Amerika Studien/American Studies</u>, 25, 3 (1980), 243-268.

23. Mariane Bienvenue, a captive among the Chickasaws, is cited as referring to Amerindians as <u>hommes rouges</u>, and Vaudreuil repeated the phrase in 1744. The term <u>Peaux rouges</u> seems to have been a 19th century appellation. François Morénas, <u>Dictionnaire Portatif, Comprenant la géographie et l'histoire universelle, la chronologie, la mythologie...</u> (Avignon, 1760-62), III, 30; E.C.V. Colbert, Comte de Maulevrier, <u>Voyage dans l'Intérieur des États-Unis et au Canada</u> (Baltimore, 1935), 50-51; <u>Huntington Library</u>, Vaudreuil Papers, Letterbook I, Vaudreuil to Maurepas, 25 September 1743, Fol. 17; <u>ibid</u>., Vaudreuil to Maurepas, 12 February 1744, fol. 17v.

24. Poncelin de LaRoche-Tilhac, <u>Almanach américain, ou Etat physique, politique, ecclésiastique et militaire de l'Amérique</u> (Paris, 1784), 18-19; Claude-Nicolas Le Cat, <u>Traité de la couleur de la peau humaine en général, de celle des nègres en particulier et de la métamorphose d'une de ces couleurs en l'autre</u> (Amsterdam, 1765), 4-6; C. Constantin, Comte de Volney, <u>Tableau du climat et du sol des États-Unis d'Amérique</u> (Paris, 1803), II, 434-436; Buffon, <u>Histoire naturelle</u>, IV, 387-389.

25. de Pauw, <u>Recherches philosophiques</u>, II, 168.

26. M. Vandermonde, <u>Essai sur la manière de perfectionner l'espèce humaine</u> (Paris, 1756), I, 100, 106, 109, 113, 118.

27. Gabriel Marest to Louis Germain, 9 November 1712, in W. I. Kip, ed., <u>The Early Jesuit Missions in North America</u> (New York, 1846), 199, 204. The missionaries tended to attribute positive qualities to tribes receptive to the Gospel and negative qualities to pagan resistors. The images of the Hurons and Iroquois in the seventeenth century are the best known examples of such prejudicial stereotyping. Hurons were frequently described as docile and relatively humane compared to bellicose and excessively cruel Iroquois although both confederacies shared the Iroquoian cultural practices of scalping, platform torture, ritual cannibalism and blood feud.

28. Thomas Mante, <u>The History of the Late War in North-America</u> (London, 1772), 479-480.

29. Popkin, "The Philosophical Basis of Eighteenth Century Racism," 247. Cf. Cornelius J. Jaenen, "Les Sauvages amériquains: Persistence into the XVIIIth Century of Traditional French concepts and constructs for comprehending Amerindians," <u>Canadian Journal of Native Education</u>, 10, 4 (Summer 1983), forthcoming.

30. Dechêne, <u>Habitants et Marchands</u>, 39. For a Sulpician opinion see <u>P.A.C.</u>, MG17, A7, 2-1, Vol. I, Tronson to Seignelay, 1682, 140-143. Armand Martineau, "La Seigneurie de Boucherville du temps de Pierre Boucher (1672-1717)," Unpublished manuscript, 247.

31. Marcel Trudel, L'Esclavage au Canada français (Québec, 1960), 257-261.

32. P.A.C., MG1, Series C^{11}A, Vol. 34, Vaudreuil to Minister, 14 April 1714, 334; T. Charland, Histoire de Saint-François-du Lac (Ottawa, 1942), 100; J. Norman Heard, White into Red (Metuchen, 1973), 20; "Journal of Capt. Phineas Stevens to and from Canada, 1749," Collections of the New Hampshire Historical Society (Concord, 1837), V, 203.

33. Adolph B. Benson, ed., Peter Kalm's Travels in North America (New York, 1966), II, 456-457.

34. P.A.C., MG18, K-5, Franquet Papers, Vol. II, Voyage de Québec, 1752, 47-51, also Voyages et Mémoires sur le Canada (Québec, 1889), 38.

35. P.A.C., MG1, Series C^{11}A, Vol. 38, De Linto to Council of Marine, 1717, 210-211; Charles Coste, ed., Aventures Militaires au XVIIIe siècle d'après les mémoires de Jean-Baptiste d'Aleyrac (Paris, 1935), 27.

36. Benson, Peter Kalm's Travels, II, 472.

37. André Chagny, François Picquet, "Le Canadien" (Paris, 1913), 135; Charles H. McIlwain, ed., An Abridgment of the Indian Affairs...Transacted from the year 1678 to the year 1751 by Peter Wraxall (New York, 1968), 243.

38. Richard A. Preston and Leopold Lamontagne, eds., Royal Fort Frontenac (Toronto, 1958), 241-243.

39. P.A.C., MG5, B1, Vol. 24, "Discussion sur les limites du Canada," 9 May 1755, 354.

40. P.A.C., MG1, Series C^{11}A, "Mémoire sur les Sioux et Nadouessis," 1719, 22; Laurence J. Burpee, ed., Journals and Letters of Pierre Gaultier de Varennes de La Vérendrye and his sons (Toronto, 1927), 340.

41. A.G. Morice, La Race métisse. Étude critique (Winnipeg, 1938), 13; Bruce Sealy and Antoine S. Lussier, The Métis. Canada's Forgotten People (Winnipeg, 1975), 7. Arthur Dobbs, for example, got nearly all his information from the Métis trader Joseph La France.

42. P.A.C., MG1, Series C^{11}A, Vol. 122, "Mémoire sur les Sioux and Nadouessis," 1719, 7.

43. James A. Clifton, The Prairie People (Lawrence, 1919), 134.

44. John C. Ewers, Indian Life in the Upper Missouri (Norman, 1968), 58-59.

45. Thwaites, Jesuit Relations, LXIV, 193-195.

46. Relation de la Mission du Mississippi du Séminaire de Québec en 1700 (Nouvelle York, 1961), 31; F. Emile Audet, Les Premiers Établissements des Français au Pays des Illinois (Paris, 1938), 43-45.

47. Natalie M. Belting, Kaskaskia under the French Régime (New Orleans, 1975), 74-76.

48. Margaret Kimball Brown and Laurie Cena Dean, eds., The Village of Chartres in Colonial Illinois, 1720-1765 (New Orleans, 1977), 5-20.

49. P.A.C., MG1, Series F^3, Vol. 24, pt. 1, Memorandum of Duclos, 1713, 184-185.

50. B.N., Nouvelles acquisitions françaises Ms. 2550, fol. 115. The correspondence of Saint-Cosme is A.S.Q., Lettres R, Nos. 26-40. Cf. DCB, II, 109-110.

51. E.B. O'Callaghan, ed., Documents relative to the Colonial History of the State of New York (Albany, 1855), IX, Vaudreuil and Bégon to Council of Marine, 17 October 1777, 912.

52. Coste, Aventures militaires d'Aleyrac, 29; Journal des Campagnes du Canada de Malartic (Dijon, 1890), 220; Kip, Early Jesuit Missions, Sebastien Rasle to nephew, 15 October 1722, 13-14; P.A.C., MG1, Series B, Vol. 29 (1), Minister to Vaudreuil, 30 June 1707, 167.

53. Frédéric Deloffre and Mélâhat Menemencioglu, eds., Journal d'un voyage fait aux Indes orientales (1690-1691) par Robert Challe, écrivain du roi (Paris, 1979), 215.

54. Donavon, "Letter from Louisbourg," 8 May 1756, 122.

55. Gaston de Bosq de Beaumont, Les Derniers Jours de l'Acadie (Paris, 1899), Maillard to Surlaville, 21 February 1753, 85.

56. D.B. Ferguson, ed., Minutes of His Majesty's Council at Annapolis Royal, 1736-1749 (Halifax, 1967), 55-56.

57. W.L. Grant, ed., Voyages of Samuel de Champlain, 1604-1618 (New York, 1917), I, 323; Edict du Roy pour l'établissement de la Compagnie de la Nouvelle France (Paris, 1657), article xvii, 13; Le Journal des Jésuites (Montréal, 1892), 312; A.S.Q., Lettres N, No. 27, Colbert to Laval, 7 March 1668; A.R.S.I., Gallia 110, Vol. III, fols. 356-357; A.C., Series B, Vol. 20, Instructions to Iberville, 22 September 1699, fols. 279-280.

58. Thwaites, Jesuit Relations, XLV, 148.

59. P.A.C., MG1, Series C^{11}A, Vol. VII, Denonville to Minister, 13 November 1685, 46-47.

60. Pierre Margry, ed., Découvertes et Établissements des Français dans l'ouest et dans le sud de l'Amérique septentrionale, 1614-1754: Mémoires et documents inédits (Paris, 1879-1888), V, Memorandum to Maurepas, n.d., 146.

61. Ernest J. Lajeunesse, ed., <u>The Windsor Border Region</u>. Canada's Southernmost Frontier. <u>A Collection of Documents</u> (Toronto, 1960), Cadillac to Governor, 18 October 1700, 15.

62. <u>Ibid</u>., 16.

63. Margry, <u>Découvertes</u>, V, 239; Thwaites, <u>Jesuit Relations</u>, LXIII, 302; Georges Paré, <u>The Catholic Church in Detroit, 1701-1888</u> (Detroit, 1951), 78-140.

64. <u>P.A.C.</u>, MG1, Series F^3, Vol. 9, pt. 1, Vaudreuil to Cadillac, 20 June 1706, 7.

65. <u>P.A.C.</u>, MG1, Series B, Vol. 30 (2), King to Vaudreuil and Raudot, 6 July 1709, 344-345, 359.

66. <u>R.A.P.Q.</u>, 1942-43, Vaudreuil and Raudot to Minister, 14 November 1709, 420.

67. <u>P.A.C.</u>, MG1, Series C^{13}B, Vol. 1, Bienville to Pontchartrain, 10 October 1706; also Jean Delanglez, <u>The French Jesuits in Lower Louisiana (1700-1763)</u> (Washington, 1935), 395-396; Higginbottam, <u>Old Mobile</u>, 283.

68. <u>A.S.Q.</u>, Lettres R, No. 83, La Vente to Brisacier, 4 July 1708.

69. <u>A.S.Q.</u>, Lettres R, No. 79, La Vente to Brisacier, 4 March 1708.

70. <u>P.A.C.</u>, MG1, Series C^{13}B, Vol. I, Bienville to Minister, 10 October 1706.

71. <u>Ibid</u>., as cited in Higgenbottam, <u>Old Mobile</u>, 283.

72. <u>A.C.</u>, Series C^{13}A, Vol. 2, Bienville to Minister, 20 August 1709, f. 413.

73. <u>A.C.</u>, Series B, Vol. 32, Minister to Bienville, 10 May 1710, Fols. 39-39v.

74. <u>B.N.</u>, Fonds français Ms. 12105, "Mémoire sur la Louisiane," 17-18.

75. H. Têtu and C.O. Gagnon, eds., <u>Mandements, Lettres pastorales et circulaires des Evêques du Québec</u> (Québec, 1887), I, Pastoral letter of 19 July 1721, 503.

76. <u>A.C.</u>, Series C^{13}A, Vol. 3, Duclos to Pontchartrain, 25 December 1725, as cited in Delanglez, <u>French Jesuits</u>, 397-398.

77. <u>P.A.C.</u>, MB1, Series F^3, Vol. XI, pt. 2, Decree of Superior Council, 18 December 1728, 292-296.

78. <u>Ibid</u>., 286.

115

79. Ibid., 292.

80. Ibid., 288-289.

81. Ibid., 291.

82. Delanglez, French Jesuits, 398-400; Clarence W. Alvord, The Illinois Country, 1673-1818 (Chicago, 1965), 219-220.

83. Provost, "Mariages," 50.

84. A.C., Series B, Vol. 62, Maurepas to Lafitau, 1735, f. 88v.

85. A.C., Series C^{13}A, Vol. 23, Memorandum of 1738, fols. 241-243v.

86. Belting, Kaskaskia, 74-76.

87. A.A.Q., Registre G, Vol. III, La Galissonière to Pontbriand, 14 May 1749, 102.

88. Huntington Library, Vaudreuil Papers, No. 325, Vaudreuil to Macarty, 8 August 1751, 8.

89. H.R. Casgrain, ed., Extraits des Archives des Ministères de la Marine et de la Guerre à Paris (Québec, 1890), Regulation of 6 July 1755, 27-28.

90. A.N., Series G^2, Vol. 189, Dossier of Jules Caesar Foelix de la Noue, 1754-55, fols. 270-360; Gaston Du Bosq, Derniers Jours de l'Acadie, 112-113.

91. Têtu and Gagnon, Mandements, II, Pastoral Letter of 7 August 1767, 205.

92. Provost, "Mariages," Briand to abbé Jean-Marie Verreau, 24 January 1774, 53.

93. Dechêne, Habitants et Marchands, 39-42; Charles Edwards O'Neill, Church and State in French Colonial Louisiana. Policy and Politics to 1732 (New Haven, 1966), 248; Groulx, Notre Maître, le passé, 258, L'Appel de la Race, 131.

NATIVE CHRISTIANITY IN EIGHTEENTH CENTURY MASSACHUSETTS:
Ritual as Cultural Reaffirmation

by

Kathleen J. Bragdon

ABSTRACT

    The lives of the Massachusett speakers of southeastern New England were
severely impacted by the colonization of the region by English settlers in
the seventeenth century. Many of the Massachusett became Christian converts,
acquired literacy in their own language, and formed settled, self-governing
communities. This paper discusses the ways in which native Christian ritual
as described in contemporary English sources and native language texts
mediated and interpreted change in other domains of Massachusett experience,
in a way which allowed the reaffirmation of traditional beliefs and values.

NATIVE CHRISTIANITY IN 18TH CENTURY MASSACHUSETTS: RITUAL AS CULTURAL REAFFIRMATION[1]

Kathleen J. Bragdon

The meaning and efficacy of ritual, whether newly adopted, or traditional, depends upon its ability to reconcile the incongruity between social action, and the framework of beliefs, symbols, and values in terms of which individuals define their world (Geertz 1957:33;53).[2] In at least some southern New England native communities, Christian ritual newly adopted in the late 17th and 18th centuries was successful in mediating and interpreting social change in ways which were meaningful both in terms of adopted Christian beliefs and symbols, and of traditional values. The native church services were expressive of these new beliefs, and of the native interpretation of present circumstances, using traditional forms and values.

At the time of contact with English settlers and missionaries in the seventeenth century, the Massachusett, like other Algonquian-speaking peoples of the eastern woodlands, recognized and characterized as manitou many "beings other than human" (Tooker 1979:28) interpreted by the English as a multiplicity of "gods" and "devils" (e.g. Thomas Mayhew 1834:201-202). Access to the power and favor of these beings was achieved through dreams and visions, and the recipient of such power was designated by the term powwaw. The powwaw or shaman, acted principally as a curer and diviner, and sometimes performed acts of witchcraft or sorcery against enemies of himself or his community (Mayhew ibid:204).

The relationship of the individual powwaw to supernatural beings determined his or her power, and the exclusiveness of that relationship may explain the ambivalent feelings of the natives towards the powwaw. For the source of Massachusett moral or ethical standards did not reside with the supernatural beings who communicated with the shamans, but rather in kin and community. Moreover, as with other Algonquian-speaking peoples, morality was not necessarily connected with religiosity (Tooker 1979:69). Membership within the traditional sachemships was defined by family ties as well as by willingness to "defend" the community. Failure to faithfully carry out the wishes of one's ancestors, or acting in a manner detrimental to future community members, could result in the expulsion of the individual from the community, and a loss of the rights of community members (Goddard and Bragdon n.d. docs. no. 22, 35). The community itself was thus the "locus of morality" (Wantanabe 1984) for the Massachusett.

Conversion of the Massachusett to Christianity took place after the native population had been greatly diminished through disease, and overwhelmed by the influx of English settlers into the Massachusetts Bay and Plymouth colonies in the mid-seventeenth century. Perhaps more significantly, as William Simmons has argued, conversion occurred as a result of the conviction on the part of the Massachusett, that the religious power of their shamans was not equal to that of the English (1979a:218). Although this conversion has been seen as primarily destructive in its effects on the native cultures of the mainland (Salisbury 1974), recent analyses of native Christian communities on Martha Vineyard, Nantucket, and Cape Cod suggest that Christianity played a positive role in the maintenance of distinct native communities in the eighteenth century (Ronda 1981; Bragdon 1981). Massachusett Christian religious ritual, as practiced in these communities, illustrates the way in which newly adopted beliefs integrated with traditional ways of looking at the world, promoted a successful reinterpretation of native society, and daily experiences.

The practice of Christianity among the Massachusett included both attendance at public worship and the performance of private devotions. The participants in the public meeting (moeonk), constituted an "assembly" in the sense of a gathered "church" (Goddard and Bragdon n.d. doc. no. 50). On the island of Martha's Vineyard, and in the native communities of Mashpee, Plymouth, Nauset, and Herring Pond, the native service was attended by men, women, and children, who were seated in separate sections of the meetinghouse (Goddard and Bragdon n.d. doc. no. 50). Meetings were occasionally held at the homes of the faithful (Cotton 1733-1748). Although church membership tended to follow family lines (Ronda 1981), not all members of individual families attended service, or became church members. Some even joined rival Baptist congregations (Backus 1969:I:346-7).

The service itself, although not standardized in either Indian or English communities in the late 17th or early 18th century had a more or less established form. In Natick, and the other native christian communities under John Eliot's ministry, for example, the service consisted of an opening prayer, scriptural reading and exegesis, the singing of psalms, the sermon, another psalm, and a final prayer. The celebration of the Lord's Supper was often part of the morning service, along with catechism, while the conduct of church business, baptism, and "any act of publick discipline" took place in the afternoon of the same day (Eliot 1926:9). Samuel Sewell described a morning service similar to Natick's at Gay Head on Martha's Vineyard in 1703 (1973:II:432). By the mid 18th century, yearly meetings, held jointly by Indians from several communities, particularly Gay Head and Mashpee, also followed this format (Anon 1815:13; Goddard and Bragdon n.d. doc. no. 140).

The native service was conducted by both native and non-native ministers and preachers, although fluency in Massachusett was a requirement in most native churches until the mid-eighteenth century. The native ministers were generally literate in both Massachusett and English, and served a number of functions within the native community; teacher, scribe, messenger and community representative (Goddard and Bragdon n.d. docs. no. 49,50). These men seem to have been accorded authority because of their knowledge and rhetorical skill, rather than as a result of their direct communication with God, as the traditional shaman would have been.

Little is known about the content of sermons preached by native ministers. As most English observers did not understand Massachusett, they note only that the Indian preachers were serious and deliberate (e.g. Anon. 1815:13). Several sermons preached by English ministers fluent in

Massachusett at native services survive, however, which gave some indication
of the subject matter. One sermon by Josiah Cotton, is concerned with family
love and with the importance of family worship (Cotton 1728). Others stress
the importance of good behaviour on earth to ensure eternal life (Cotton
1711-1728; Forbes (?) 1710; Treat (?) 1705). All are studded with references
to scriptural passages. Common to all is the continual reference to the
brotherhood of Christians, using generalized Massachusett kinship terminology
such as nemat ("brother, friend").

Exhortation, characteristic of traditional eastern Woodland moral
teaching (Tooker 1979:70), also appears to have been common in native
Christian religious practice, both in the form of scriptural exegesis, and
in "lessons" delivered by native preachers and ministers. Copies of
native-owned Massachusett bibles often contain examples of such exhor-
tations. In one bible, containing the signatures of several natives of
Plymouth, is found the enjoinder in Massachusett "My brothers, remember love
for God, and all people, always," (Goddard and Bragdon n.d. doc. no. 246).

An important part of Christian religious ritual, both public and
private, was prayer. The Massachusett referred to religion itself as
"praying" (peantamonk), and to a Christian as a "praying man." In
traditional Massachusett oratory, petition, wherein the speakers
characterized themselves as powerless and pitiful was a common rhetorical
theme (Goddard and Bragdon n.d. docs. no. 49,50,65), and seems to have
survived in Christian prayer. Several of the annotated Massachusett bibles
contain such references written in the native language, such as "poor people
(are) we. It is not good. Always falsehood is heard about us," and "I am
always a p[o]or person in the world. I am not able clearly to read this
book," (Goddard and Bragdon doc. no. 245).

Music, particularly the singing of psalms, was also part of both public
and private religious devotion among the Christian Indians. The structure
and cadence of traditional Massachusett music is difficult to reconstruct,
but something of its nature can be inferred from more recent studies of
related eastern native peoples. The eastern U.S. from Labrador to Florida,
can be considered one musical area (Nettl 1954:33). The main characteristics
of the eastern native musical tradition are an undulating melodic movement,
relatively short songs, the use of forms which consist of several short
sections with iterative and reverting relationships, relative simplicity and
asymmetry in the rhythmic organization, and, perhaps most distinctively,
antiphonal and responsorial passages with some rudimentary polyphony
including imitation and canon. (Ibid:33).

The Calvinist musical repertoire consisted mainly of the Old Testament
Psalms, translated into vernacular, metrical poetry, and set to a limited
number of prescribed tunes (Inserra and Hitchcock 1981:1). The psalter
brought by the Pilgrims to Plymouth in 1620 was probably that of Henry
Ainsworth, published in Amsterdam in 1612. John Eliot, best known for his
missionary work among the Massachusett, also collaborated in the translation
of another psalter, the Bay Psalm Book of 1636, which was the first work
published in North America, and succeeded the Ainsworth psalter in common
use.

Psalms were meant to be sung in unison, without accompaniment, and were meant to be led by men's voices, since the melodies were set for tenor (Pratt 1921:17). The melodies used in the Ainsworth psalter were not generally set in uniform notes and were probably sung with the variety and vigor of a glee or part-song. At least 45 distinct line-rhythms have been noted for these tunes, which seem to have been similar to folk-songs with great freedom of inner structure (ibid. 16). It is this style of music which Samuel Sewell heard performed in a Gay Head service in 1703 (1973:II:432). The Indians, like the English, did employ a tune setter, who sang each line, which was then repeated by the congregation. Later writers, in particular Experience Mayhew of Martha's Vineyard, note psalm singing in the context of the native church service, as well as by solitary individuals, and in family worship (e.g. Mayhew 1727:99). The success of Protestant psalm-singing among the Massachusett may have been partially attributable to this musical style, which resembled traditional native music in brevity, simplicity of rhythmic organization, frequent lack of musical accompaniment, and especially in the responsorial format. Such a style would have been suitable even among those native congregations where few were literate, and psalms were sung as semi-meaningful strings of words and syllables, learned by rote. Descriptions of native services in the mid-eighteenth century indicate that the Indians were not involved in the singing controversy of the 1720's and 1730's (Becker 1982), but continued to sing in the "Old Way" probably until the late eighteenth century reforms of the Great Awakening swept through the Indian congregations of southern New England (Simmons 1979b).

The structure and content of the native Christian service was similar in most respects to that of the English, with two exceptions: the use of Massachusett, the native language, for most or all of the service, and the possible ritual use of tobacco. Literacy among the Christian Indians was not in English, but in Massachusett, the first language of the Martha's Vineyard Indians until at least 1750. However, as many of the religious works were translated by non-native speakers, and were in any case difficult to obtain, it seems more probable that instruction in Christian dogma was received aurally, and that many lessons were learned by rote.

Other aspects of the Christian Indian service reflect the oral nature of native culture. Familiarity and respect for long orations such as sermons, the frequency of verbal instruction, the importance of recitation, chanting, and singing are some examples, and attest to the strength of oral tradition and oral literature in spite of relatively widespread native language literacy.

The use of Massachusett as the language of the native church service had several important implications, especially in the eighteenth century. The Indians had always undergone pressure to adopt the English language, and were aware that their language was considered inferior to English, particularly in the expression of religious concepts. The deliberate, continued use of Massachusett in the native church service served to reinforce the cultural distinctiveness of the Indians. The role of the use of Massachusett in the religious service in preserving native traditions was explicitly recognized in anecdote concerning the native minister Zachary Howwoswee. (Howwoswee's identity was probably collapsed with that of a former minister Zachary Hossueit who died in 1782.) According to the story, Howwoswee, who presided at the Gayhead "Presbyterian" church until his death in 1872, was the last to preach in Massachusett. When asked why he did so, he replied, "Why, to keep up my nation" (Burgess 1926:22). The continued use of Massachusett among the Indians until the late eighteenth century was one characteristic which served to distinguish native communities during that period from those of the English. At the same time, the public use of Massachusett in a religious context provided a basis for, and continually reinforced, a sense of common identity among the Indians.

In addition, what transpired in Massachusett during the church services was less vulnerable to criticism since the natives' language was understood by relatively few Englishmen. The use of Massachusett in a religious context, even when Englishmen were present, may have been an instance of ritualized "code-switching." Gay Headers remembered that when Howwoswee "wanted to say something that was not for all to hear, he would talk to them very solemnly in the Indian tongue, and they would cry, and he would cry" (Burgess 1926:22).

Zaccheus Macy, resident of Nantucket, and semi-fluent speaker of Massachusett, described native Christian services he had witnesses in a letter written in 1792, and noted:

> and when the meeting was done, they would take their
> tinder-box and strike fire and light their pipes, and, may
> be, would draw three or four whiffs and swallow the smoke,
> and then blow it out of their noses, and so hand their pipes
> to their next neighbor. And one pipe of tobacco would serve
> ten or a dozen of them.... It seemed to be done in a way of
> kindness of each other (in Macy 1835:257-258).

That pipe-passing remained a part of native Christian ritual reflects its continuity with traditional council meetings and documents the continuing ritual use of tobacco among the Indians of the northeast (Tooker 1979). Pipe-sharing as a symbolic reaffirmation of concord and group solidarity, served, like the use of spoken Massachusett in the religious service, to underscore both the shared values of native life, as well as their cultural distinctiveness.

The significance of the native Christian service and of native Christianity lies beyond its role in maintaining group solidarity. Moreover, it was not only the overt continuities between traditional and Christian practice that ensured the success of Christianity among the Massachusett. It was through the Christian service that traditional notions of family unity and continuity with past and future were made relevant to new Christian beliefs concerning the brotherhood of man and of eternal life after death. Traditional family functions, such as those of moral teaching, also became the responsibility of the church brotherhood. Old reliance on direct contact with the spiritual world gave way to new respect for learning and literacy.

Finally, traditional loyalty to the wider kin group and the sachemship community came to rest with the Christian community, the community which included all Christian natives in southern New England. These changing loyalties, and structures of order, redefined through Christian belief and practice, served in turn to justify and explain everyday experience, and continuing social change for the natives of eighteenth century Massachusetts, in a way which seemed inevitably connected both with tradition, and with the new order.

FOOTNOTES

1. This paper is essentially the same as given in 1983 with the exception of the section concerning church music, and the updated bibliography.

2. I would like to thank the research department of Plimoth Plantation for information concerning Separatist religious practice, and Dr. Ives Goddard for advice and assistance in translating and interpreting the Massachusett texts.

REFERENCES

Anonymous. 1815. [1767]. Report of a Committee on the State of the Indians in Mashpee and parts Adjacent. Collections of the Massachusetts Historical Society. 2s:3:12-17.

Bakus, Isaac. 1969. [1796]. A History of New England, with particular reference to the Baptists. New York: Arno Press.

Becker, Laura. 1982. Ministers vs. Laymen: The Singing Controversy in Puritan New England, 1720-1740. New England Quarterly. March: 79-95.

Bragdon, Kathleen. 1981. 'Another Tongue Brought In:' An Ethnohistorical Study of Native Texts in Massachusett. Ph.D. Thesis. Department of Anthropology, Brown University.

Burgess, Edward. 1926. The Old South Road of Gay Head. Dukes County Intelligencer. 12:1:1-35.

Cotton, Josiah. 1711-1728. Sermons. Manuscript in the collections of the American Antiquarian Society.

Cotton, Josiah. 1728. Sermon. Manuscript in the collections of the Massachusetts Historical Society.

Cotton, Josiah. 1733-1748. Diary. Manuscript in the collections of the Pilgrim Society, Plymouth, Massachusetts.

Eliot, John. 1926 [1684]. John Eliot to The Honorable Robert Boyle. Old South Leaflets. Boston: Old South Association. 1:21:9-11.

Forbes, Eli (?). 1710-1729. Sermons. Manuscript in the collections of the American Antiquarian Society.

Geertz, Clifford. 1957. Ritual and Social Change: A Javanese Example. American Anthropologist. 59:32-54.

Goddard, Ives and Kathleen Bragdon. n.d. The Massachusett Texts. American Philosophical Society. In press.

Inserra, Lorraine and H. Wiley and Hitchcock. 1981. The Music of Henry Ainsworth's Psalter. Brooklyn College Institute for Studies in American Music #15.

Macy, Obed. 1835. History of Nantucket. Mansfield: Macy and Pratt.

Mayhew, Experience. 1727. Indian Converts, or Some Account of the Lives and Dying Speeches of a Considerable Number of Christianized Indians of Martha's Vineyard. London: J. Osborn and T. Longman.

Nettl, Bruno. 1954. North American Indian Musical Styles. Philadelphia: American Folklore Society.

Pratt, Waldo Selden. 1971. [1921]. The Music of the Pilgrims; A description of the Psalm-book brought to Plymouth in 1620. New York: Russell and Russell [1971].

Ronda, James. 1981. Generations of Faith: The Christian Indians of Massachusetts. William and Mary Quarterly. 38:3:369-394.

Salisbury, Neal. 1974. Red Puritans, the Praying Indians of Massachusetts Bay and John Eliot. William and Mary Quarterly. 3s:31:27-54.

Sewell, Samuel. 1973. The Diary of Samuel Sewell 1674-1729. M. Halsey Thomas ed. 2 Vols. New York: Farrar, Straus, and Giroux.

Simmons, William. 1979a. Conversion from Indian to Puritan. New England Quarterly. 52:2:197-218.

Simmons, William. 1979b. The Great Awakening and Indian Conversion in Southern New England. Papers of the Tenth Algonquian Conference. William Cowan ed. Ottawa: Carleton University Press. 25-36.

Tooker, Elizabeth. 1979. ed. Native North American Spirituality of the Eastern Woodlands. New York: Paulist Press.

Treat, Samuel (?). 1705. Sermon. Manuscript in the collections of the Massachusetts Historical Society.

Wantanabe, John. 1984. "We Who Are Here:" The Cultural Conventions of Ethnic Identity in a Guatemalan Indian Village 1937-1980. University Microfilms.

Whitfield, Henry. 1834 [1651]. The Light Appearing more and more towards the perfect Day. Or, a farther discovery of the present state of the Indians in New-England, concerning the progress of the Gospel amongst them, manifested by letters from such as preached to them. Collections of the Massachusetts Historical Society. 3s:4:100-147.

RUSSIAN ORTHODOX MISSIONARIES AND THE TLINGIT OF ALASKA,
1880-1900

by

Sergei Kan

ABSTRACT

While the Tlingit Indians began to be baptized in the Russian Orthodox Church prior to the sale of Alaska to the United States in 1867, their voluntary massive conversion did not begin until the 1880s. The Russian Church's success is surprising, since at that time it was experiencing severe shortages of funds and manpower and had to compete with a well-financed Presbyterian mission, which enjoyed the local American authorities' support. The paper explores the cultural and sociopolitical causes of this phenomenon, utilizing historical materials and ethnographic data collected in southeastern Alaska in 1979-1980.

RUSSIAN ORTHODOX MISSIONARIES
AND THE TLINGIT INDIANS OF ALASKA, 1880-1900

Sergei Kan

The first serious attempt to Christianize the Tlingit was made in the 1830's by a Russian Orthodox priest, Fr. Ivan Veniaminov (Bishop Innokentii; St. Innocent, Apostle to America), when he was assigned to Novo-Arkhangel'sk, the capital of Russian America.[1] For over sixty years this town existed side by side with Sitka, one of the major communities of southeastern Alaska Natives. Despite the existence of a heavily guarded stockade around Novo-Arkhangel'sk, symbolizing Russian fear and distrust, considerable amount of trading between the two populations did occur. While providing the Russians with furs and vital food supplies, the Indians eagerly sought European tools, clothing, and other artifacts. Their interest was stimulated not only by the recognition of the superiority of some of those objects (e.g., steel axes, guns), but by the indigenous emphasis on the accumulation of wealth (especially exotic artifacts from distant tribes), which increased individual and collective prestige, and indicated that their owners possessed spiritual power (laxeitl, 'luck,' 'blessing'). Many European gods, such as cloth and blankets, found their way into the Tlingit system of ceremonial exchange and feasting, i.e., the potlatch. For their own use, the aristocrats, controlling much of the trading, sought military uniforms and other items associated with Russian leaders and perceived as similar to the indigenous ceremonial garments of lineage and clan heads, decorated with crest designs.

In addition to the exchange of goods, Tlingit leadership highly valued occasional gifts, feasts, and permissions to visit Novo-Arkhangel'sk, granted to them by the Russian-American Company. At the same time, the Tlingit maintained total independence and resisted even the slightest attempts to change their social order and customary behaviour (e.g., elimination of slavery). Several times hostilities erupted and gunfire was exchanged, but on the whole the Natives seemed to tolerate the presence of the White Man in the heart of their territory. Thus, prior to the sale of Alaska in 1867, Tlingit relationships with Europeans were structured by the same principles of mutual "respect" and exchange, combined with maintaining a distance and non-interference, that characterized their interaction with other powerful neighbours, such as the Haida or the Tsimshian.[2]

Tlingit independence as well as the limited amount of contact between the two groups did not favour mass conversion. In fact, Veniaminov himself attributed even his limited success to the devastating effects of the 1835-1837 smallpox epidemic and the inability of the native healers (or shamans) to prevent it from destroying almost half of Sitka's Natives (Veniaminov 1886 [1840]:641-645). Despite the fact that by 1860 the Russian church could boast 427 Tlingit members (about one half of Sitka's population), most contemporary observers agreed that the Native understanding of and commitment to Orthodoxy was rather superficial. The "exchange model" that characterized Tlingit relationships with secular Russian authorities seemed also to influence their attitudes towards the Russian church. Writing in 1863, a Russian inspector of the colony characterized Tlingit Christianity in the following way:

> Of all the newly converted Native peoples, the Tlingit can be placed on the lowest level.... One cannot see in them any inclination towards accepting Christianity. Those who have converted are hardly converts at all.

> They do not go to church, despite the fact that a special church was built for them near the village.[3] They are not inclined to fulfill Christian obligations. A Tlingit is ready to go to church, confess, and have communion, only if he hopes to receive a gift or be treated with dinner and wine afterwards (Doklad...1863:115).

With the sale of Alaska the Russian church was deprived of a large segment of its parish, since only about one hundred Russians and two hundred Creoles (persons of European-Native origin) remained; financial support provided by the Russian-American Company also ended. Most importantly, the town was now under the American jurisdiction. The next two decades brought a number of Americans to Sitka, including numerous fortune-seeking "frontier types," as well as military personnel, businessmen, bureaucrats, and Presbyterian missionaries (see Hinckley 1972). The latter posed the most serious threat to Orthodox evangelizing activities among the Tlingit. In the 1860's-1870's the Sitka Natives' attendance of the Russian church came almost to a standstill. Reports written by Orthodox clergy during that period (e.g., Bishop Paul's 1869 report quoted in DRHA, Vol. I, p. 151) repeat the earlier negative assessments of Native religious conditions, lamenting Tlingit indifference to Orthodoxy and commitment to "heathen beliefs and practices."

From 1878 on, Presbyterian missionaries led a vigorous and well-financed campaign to Christianize, educate, and civilize the Tlingit (cf. Berkhofer 1965; Ronda and Axtell 1978; Bowden 1981:164-198). For a time they were able to attract large numbers of Natives in Sitka and several other Tlingit villages. In 1880-1881 they started a boarding trade school for Indian children, and in 1884 the Presbyterian Church of Sitka was formally organized, with the majority of members being Tlingit students and their Sitka relatives.

Despite the resumption of financial support from Russia, the Orthodox church could not compete with the Presbyterian wealth or manpower. It also lacked the political connections in Washington, cultivated by the Presbyterian missionary leader Sheldon Jackson, or the support of the

American military and civil authorities in Alaska. After 1867 it was an
alien church operating among the Indians who for decades showed little
interest in it.[4]

In light of these facts, one can imagine the astonishment of Sitka's
Orthodox clergy, when, in the early 1880's, local Natives began appealing to
them to be baptized and expressed a strong desire to have a missionary priest
sent to Sitka with the special task of administering to their needs (DRHA,
Vol. II, p. 247). The priest who came to Sitka in 1886 to carry out those
duties later wrote: "Since 1883, without any appeal made to them, the
Tlingit began asking the Orthodox priest to accept them into the church.
Their wish was willingly granted by the Sitka parish priest, but no special
effort was made to keep them in the faith or to attract new members" (Donskoi
1893:861). Parish records of Sitka's St. Michael Cathedral indicate clearly
the beginning of a new stage in Tlingit-Orthodox relations. Thus, in 1881,
80 persons, mainly young people and children, were baptized "from paganism."
In the next few years about 50 to 60 more Tlingit joined the Russian church,
but the really dramatic breakthrough occurred in 1886 when 176 Natives were
baptized, including the heads of the two leading clans of the Raven and the
Eagle moieties (ibid.). A year later another 291 Natives joined them and by
the early 1890's the majority of Sitka Indians (between 2/3 and 3/4) became
Orthodox. In addition, large segments of several major Tlingit villages were
also converted, with churches built in some of them.

More important than the mere numbers was the fact that baptism was
voluntarily and eagerly sought and that during this period of Orthodox
beliefs and ritual practices became an essential part of Tlingit culture. As
historic and ethnographic data indicate, this was the time when the
foundation of Tlingit Orthodoxy—an important aspect of the
twentieth-century Tlingit life—was firmly established (see Kan 1982b; 1982c).

The purpose of this paper is to explain the timing and the various
causes of this "small miracle," as the current Orthodox bishop of Alaska has
called it (Afonsky 1977:80). I am particularly interested in the Tlingit
choice of Christian denominations (Orthodox vs. Presbyterian) as well as
their interpretation of Orthodoxy and relationships with the Russian clergy.
My approach is to interpret specific events by relating them to the histories
and ideologies of missionary activities as well as particular characteristics
of Tlingit culture.

AMERICAN RULE AND THE PRESBYTERIAN MISSION

To comprehend the sudden shift in Tlingit attitudes towards Orthodoxy
one has to examine, at least briefly, the drastic changes that occurred in
their relationships with the White Man since the establishment of the U.S.
rule on Alaska. In the first years of American military occupation, the
Tlingit tried to maintain the same type of interaction with the people they
called "Boston Men" as they had established earlier with the Russians.
Initially contacts with the newcomers seemed to offer greater advantages than
ever before: more numerous and less expensive goods of better quality, eased
restrictions on visiting the Euro-American settlement in Sitka (former
Novo-Arkhangel'sk), greater opportunities to earn extra money (for buying new

goods and potlatching) by working for the Army, the Navy, the canneries or the mines. The Indians did not shy away from contacts with the Americans, since possessing their goods, eating store-bought food, wearing European clothing, or taking part in American social activities were perceived as signs of equality with the powerful strangers or what the Tlingit usually describe as "mutual respect."

What they resented, however, was the occupation of their ancestral lands, interference with salmon runs and other essential sources of food, which began in the 1870's and intensified in the 1880's, as well as the attempts to punish them for applying indigenous system of justice to the Whites. Very soon the Tlingit learned that the Americans had their own definite ideas about justice and the place of Indians in their new social order. Thus, when the Tlingit murdered a White Man or held him hostage for a similar crime committed against their own clan relatives by another American, the U.S. men-of-war retaliated by bombarding whole villages. They also engaged in arresting other Indian "offenders," including shamans and those who persecuted witches (Hinckley 1982). The awesome power and military superiority of the newcomers had to be recognized.

Native behaviour and a number of public statements made during the 1870's indicated ambivalence about this power, i.e., fear and acceptance mixed with fascination and a strong desire to gain access to this new laxeitl (see p. 1 above). Tlingit aristocratic leadership as well as commoners began to recognize that the new power had something to do with knowledge and possibly with the White Man's ability to read and write, since written documents seemed to play such an important role in his life. This would explain the desire of many young Natives to learn to speak, read, and write English and the consent of many Tlingit leaders to have schools built in their villages. The latter wish was expressed in several meetings between Tlingit leaders and American officials and missionaries in 1878-1880. What the Tlingit "chiefs" resented was the change in the basic values of their culture and the principle patterns of the indigenous social life. One of those leaders, chief "Shustack" of Wrangel, expressed the Tlingit position clearly, in a meeting with Reverend Lindsay of the Oregon Presbytery who visited his village in 1879 and offered to build a school and a church there:

> I want my people to learn the new ways to make them
> strong, and to keep the old dances and ceremonies, because
> we...have always practiced them. White people have their
> ways—so have Tlinkets [sic]; and it is not seemly for
> Indians to give up their practices and adopt other
> peoples'. But you tell us that we must change some
> things, and I begin to believe I shall consider what you
> have said. You will teach the children many things and I
> will not oppose it. ... But I want to observe the
> ancient rites and customs. We want our children and their
> children to stay in this land, as long as the tide flows
> and the sun shines. (Lindsay 1965[1881]:20).

It appears that the initial enthusiasm of many Tlingit about the establishment of Presbyterian missions in their villages could be explained by the attractiveness of the new type of knowledge (schools) and material assistance (clothing for children, medical help, gifts) that they offered. The school for Natives started by two Presbyterian missionaries in Sitka in 1878 had 103 students, while the prayer meetings they conducted were also quite popular and well-attended. The desire expressed by several Sitka teenagers (some of whom belonged to high-ranking Tlingit families) to remain in the school overnight, justified the establishment in 1880-1881 of a Presbyterian boarding school named "Sitka Industrial School," which soon began admitting boys and girls from all of southeastern Alaska Tlingit communities (Austin 1892; Hinckley 1966). Those students and some of their Sitka relatives formed the core of the Sitka Presbyterian Church organized in 1884.

It is also possible that the spiritual dimension of the White Man's power began to attract the Tlingit, who were probably associating the hymns and prayers of the Presbyterians as well as their "Holy Book" with the practical knowledge, skills, wealth, and influence that the American missionaries seemed to possess. While Presbyterian sermons were difficult for the Natives to comprehend, religious hymns were popular, since singing played an important role in traditional Native ceremonies. Medical services provided by the Presbyterian mission--the power to fight the devastating new diseases that the shaman (ixt) failed to eliminate--must have been an important factor in gaining Indian converts (cf. Russian Orthodox success during the 1835-1837 smallpox epidemic, p. 2).[5] Even in the pre-1867 era, the Tlingit were occasionally appealing to the Christian God for help, health, and good fortune, and used sacred Orthodox objects and substances (e.g., holy water), in their own magical and healing rites (see, e.g., Emmons n.d., Shukoff's Account, p. 4).[6] Appeals to the Great Spirit, whose name the missionaries translated into Tlingit as "Chief/Rich Man of the Above" (Dikée Aankáawu), did not challenge the indigenous cosmology, which included a multitude of spirits and possibly a vaguely defined supreme one (see de Laguna 1972:812-816).

Despite these initial ideological innovations, the Tlingit continued to perceive their relationships with the Presbyterians as an exchange, in which they volunteered to participate in the new ceremonies and allowed their children to attend classes rather than help their parents in daily chores and subsistence activities; in return they expected goods, services, and "respect." An example of this Tlingit pragmatism was the behaviour of the Presbyterian converts in the village of Klukwaan in the early 1880's, reported by German explorer Krause (1970 [1885]:229-230): "after they had gone to [the Presbyterian] church for half a year and sent their children to school, the Chilkats went to the missionary and complained that they had not been rewarded for their virtue and had not received boards to build their houses as the Tsimshian did." Two decades later Russian missionaries were still complaining about the Tlingit being "spoiled" by the Presbyterians and making excessive demands to the Orthodox Church. Thus a Juneau priest, who reported a great movement towards Orthodoxy in a nearby village of Hoonah, complained that the collection of money among the Indians for the construction of the church was going very slowly, "not because the Indians are poor, but because they have been spoiled by the Presbyterian mission, which builds churches, schools and orphanages for them without charge. That is why they are demanding everything for free, but we cannot compete with the wealty Presbyterians" (Juneau Parish Records, 1904, report of Fr. A. Yaroshevich).

The Tlingit were greatly disappointed when it became clear that the Presbyterians had quite a different view of the nature of their relationships with the Natives. They demanded loyalty and, in Sitka, they relied on the Navy to force Tlingit children to attend the mission school, when their parents' enthusiasm began to decline. The major method of maintaining a high level of attendance was to force the parents who tried to prevent their children from going to school to pay fines or stay in jail (Glass 1890). With the establishment of the missionary boarding school, Tlingit parents began to lose control over their offspring: removing Native children from the "evil and corruption" of the "heathen hovels" that could not even be called "homes" was one of the chief goals of the Presbyterians, who saw Tlingit family life as being characterized by promiscuity, violence, drinking, and "heathen feasts." In the boarding school the use of the Tlingit language was strictly prohibited and resulted in punishment. Along with practical knowledge of the White Man's skills and religious instruction, the children were indoctrinated with negative stereotypes of their own parents' social life and culture. Beginning in 1888, Native graduates were encouraged to marry their schoolmates (sometimes disregarding the fundamental Tlingit law of moiety exogamy) and to set up independent nuclear families in "Boston-style" cottages built on mission-owned land, away from the "uncivilized" Sitka village (labelled "Ranch" by the White Sitkans) (see Austin 1892; Hinckley 1972; Dauenhauer 1980).

Paradoxically, the increased participation of the Natives, particularly the Industrial School graduates, in some of the activities of the Euro-American population of Sitka (e.g., Fourth of July celebrations) and their imitation of American fashions, house styles, and even holidays (Christmas parties and gift-giving were particularly popular) did not eliminate anti-Tlingit prejudice. At the same time, military and civil authorities, which replaced the former in 1884, continued their attacks on shamanism, potlatching, cremation, and other indigenous practices. While the Presbyterian missionaries defended the rights of the "Alaskan Natives" whom they perceived as more civilized than the reservation "Indians" of the Western states, they were actively promoting their own version of proper life for the Tlingit, surpassing other Euro-Americans in their attacks on the traditional Tlingit culture. They also maintained two congregations—one White and one Native—arguing that language difficulties were the reason for that, although it is more likely that they had to satisfy the wishes of some of their American members who refused to pray together with the "Siwashes."

With the growth of Tlingit membership in their church, Presbyterian missionaries began to demand abstention from potlatches, memorial feasts, dancing, and other essential Native ceremonial activities. Christian marriage was strictly enforced, and so was the prohibition on drinking and participation in American dances. As Ronda and Axtell (1978:31) point out:

> Nineteenth-century missionaries, products of an intensely
> nationalistic culture, defined civilization as a mixture
> of sedentary agriculture, individualism, capitalism, and
> routine labor. Earlier missionaries had expressed their
> strong personal preference for changes in dress, hair
> style, language, and sexual behaviour. In the nineteenth

century those changes were elevated to matters of faith and dogma. <u>Missionaries set higher standards of conduct for their Indian converts than for their fellow Americans</u>.

Finally, some of the Presbyterian missionaries and their allies in the civil government, both of whom spoke out against abuses of the Tlingit committed by miners, liquor merchants and others, felt no guilt when they took over portions of Indian land in and around the Sitka village (see, e.g., Hinckley 1982 for the discussion of such activities of the Presbyterian missionary-merchant-judge and future governor of Alaska, John Brady) (Kamenskii 1985:132-136).

Presbyterian attacks on Native customs were often combined with harsh criticism of the Russian Church, especially its emphasis on holidays (too many for the hard-working Presbyterians!), elaborate "Catholic" rituals, and lack of any "civilizing" influence on the Natives. While medical and educational services were initially granted to all Tlingit, the Presbyterian mission soon began to demand that those who still maintained some affiliation with the Russian Church had to renounce it. The Tlingit who never fully understood why one could not benefit from the "power" available in the Presbyterian church, while also utilizing other sources of <u>laxeitl</u>, including the Russian Church, were very disappointed.[7]

As a result of all these developments, the mid-1880's were marked by increased tension between the White and the Native communities in Sitka, including attempts by many Tlingit parents to remove their children from the Industrial Training School and the general decline of their enthusiasm about the Presbyterian church.[8] The price of the White Man's "power" and "knowledge" was the loss of independence and self-determination, decline of inter-generational continuity, and, ultimately, cultural extinction. For some of the more ambitious or Americanized Tlingit the benefits of being affiliated with the Presbyterian church outweighed the costs. Others tried to walk a tightrope between acting as good Protestants and continuing their participation in traditional feasts and ceremonies. Reports of frequent suspension and reprimanding of Tlingit members, which fill the pages of the "session records" of the Sitka Presbyterian Church, indicate the difficulty of their situation.

THE 1880'S CONVERSION TO ORTHODOXY AND ITS MEANING

ORTHODOX MISSIONARY THEORY AND PRACTICE

In his own attempt to explain the sudden surge of Tlingit interest in Orthodoxy, Fr. Vladimir Donskoi (1893), who himself played an important role in Tlingit christianization in the late 1880s-early 1890s, emphasized such factors as the Native disappointment in the intolerance and heavy-handedness of the Presbyterians as well as the revival of the Orthodox missionary activities. Conservative, nationalistic government of Tsar Alexander III, and particularly the Ober-procurator of the Holy Synod, were sympathetic towards Russian missionary efforts in Alaska and increased its financial support (Kan in Kamenskii 1985:5-12).

Undoubtedly, Donskoi's announcement to the Tlingit that he had come specifically to be their missionary and the personal attention he gave to them, contributed to the Tlingit change of heart. Among the new activities that Donskoi and his predecessor Vechtomov introduced in 1886 were the following: weekly religious instruction and "friendly discussions" with the Native parish members, conducted in the church and their own homes through a knowledgeable interpreter, opening a school for Tlingit children, frequent visits to their communities with participation in memorial feasts, and attempts to defend them from Presbyterian excesses, e.g., forced school attendance (Ushin n.d.; Donskoi 1893; Afonsky 1977).

In their work among the Tlingit, Donskoi and other priests were following the basic principles of Orthodox missionary theory and practice, developed much earlier and introduced in Southeast Alaska by Fr. Ivan Veniaminov (see above; see also Smith 1980). Compared to most Protestant missionaries, the Orthodox showed greater tolerance of native culture, especially those aspects that did not radically contradict Orthodox dogma and ritual practices. The early Orthodox theologians and the more enlightened Russian missionaries in Siberia and Alaska did not necessarily equate Christianization with Westernization or even Russification (see Dauenhauer 1979; 1980; Smith 1980).

First and foremost, the Orthodox Church emphasized that the word of God had to be preached in the native language and, similar to Catholicism, invested considerable time and effort in translating major prayers, liturgy, and the New Testament itself into various native Alaskan languages.[9] In the Russian seminary operating in Sitka at various times before and after the sale of Alaska, Tlingit, Aleut, and other native languages were taught to prospective missionaries.

Donskoi followed this tradition, translating and reprinting Orthodox materials in the Tlingit language (Donskoi 1895; 1901; Nadezhdin 1896). These translated prayers became very popular among the newly-converted Tlingit, and, in 1891, services in the Sitka cathedral were conducted with the participation of two choirs—a Russian and a Tlingit one (The Alaskan, Jan. 10, 1891, p. 3). Tlingit converts also learned numerous prayers in Church Slavonic and gladly seized the opportunity to become active participants rather than spectators in the Orthodox service.

In contrast to this approach, the Alaska Presbyterian Church has done relatively little in translating Christian hymns and prayers into Tlingit. While also relying on interpreters in its services involving adult Natives and translating a few popular hymns, the Presbyterians tended to view the "primitive" language of the Tlingit as an obstacle to civilization (i.e., Americanization) and Christianization of the Indians, and totally forbade its use in the Industrial Training School (Dauenhauer 1980:20-21, footnote 7; Kan 1979-1984).

Speaking of schools, one must point out that, while the Orthodox parish schools in Southeast Alaska lacked funding and manpower and could not offer such as an extensive program in general and trade instruction as the Presbyterian ones, they did attract a large number of Tlingit children and introduced a curriculum that included the teaching of Russian, English,

Church Slavonic, and Tlingit languages. The Orthodox seminary trained Tlingit deacons, song-leaders, interpreters, and other lay workers who were bi- or even trilingual and carried out active missionary work among their own people, helping to maintain Orthodox parishes in those villages that for years lacked a resident priest.

This emphasis on utilizing native languages in missionization was combined with considerable interest in indigenous customs and beliefs, exemplified in several ethnographic studies of the Tlingit (Veniaminov 1886 [1840]; Kamenskii 1985). Even those Russian priests that were ignorant of or indifferent to Tlingit culture showed less hostility towards it than the Presbyterian missionaries convinced that they knew everything there was to know about "Indian heathenism and superstition."[10]

Nevertheless, tolerant and sensitive attitudes towards Tlingit beliefs and practices were not uniformly shared by all Orthodox priests laboring in Southeast Alaska in the 1880's-1900's. As a matter of fact, Donskoi himself as well as his successor Fr. Anatolii Kamenskii made frequent negative comments about Tlingit "paganism" in their published works addressed to Orthodox readers (1901; 1985). Not all Russian missionaries followed Bishop Innokentii's advice "not to show open contempt for the natives' manner of living, customs, etc., no matter how these may appear deserving of it..." (quoted in Afonsky 1977:45).

Despite such attitudes, Orthodox missionaries were less persistent in their efforts to stamp out "heathenism" than their Presbyterian adversaries. More importantly, their own cultural background and unique position in American Alaska made them somewhat ambivalent about Tlingit Westernization in general, and Americanization in particular. Their major emphasis was on administering the sacraments, and maintaining a certain degree of temperance and peace in Native villages. Their mixed reaction to the surrounding American society, apprehension of rapid Americanization of some of their Russian-Creole parishioners, and idealization of the traditional life-style of the majority of their countrymen back home, led Russian missionaries to defend indigenous Tlingit subsistence practices from American exploitation and make fewer demands on the Native family life, appearance, etc. (Kamenskii 1901). The clergymen and their Russian-Creole parishioners were themselves occasionally victims of mistreatment or bitter criticism by American authorities and ordinary citizens (Kamenskii 1985:123-131). Finally, the fact that Russification of Natives, carried out in some parts of the Russian Empire in the late nineteenth century, was not possible in this foreign country, should also be taken into consideration in evaluating Orthodox missionary practices in Alaska.

Even their condemnation of Tlingit "heathenism and superstition" was not uniform, so that while some priests referred to the potlatch as a "heathen feast for the dead," others compared it to the "memorial feasts of the ancient Slavs" or simply labelled it a "national Tlingit celebration." Orthodox missionaries often ignored Native practices or preferred to look the other way, especially when they lacked power to interfere. This approach was undoubtedly influenced by the Russian Church's experience with Russian peasants whose folk Orthodoxy incorporated many ancient pre-Christian beliefs and observances.

This approach was exemplified by their practice of baptizing illegitimate children of Native women-members of their church or consent to marry very young brides, which was strongly objected to by Presbyterian ministers.[11] Russian church records continued to list Tlingit members under their Christian as well as native names for a much longer period of time than for Presbyterian, the latter indicating an early preference for giving a newly-baptized Indian a Christian (English) first name and an American last name.

Punishments imposed upon disloyal or wavering members, who "slid back into heathenism," by the two churches were also quite different. Russian missionaries preferred to admonish and lecture their Native parish members, carefully trying not to offend them too much with their criticism. In most extreme cases a guilty individual might be denied communion or told to stand outside the church on the porch during the service, but it was next to impossible to "suspend" an Orthodox Indian from membership as was frequently done in the Presbyterian church, which functioned more like an organization (see Session Records of the Sitka Presbyterian Church; also Billman Archives, Sheldon Jackson College Library; Kan 1979-1984).

ORTHODOX ACCOMPLISHMENTS IN THE 1880'S

One of the major obstacles in Christianizing the Tlingit that priests Vechtomov and Donskoi had to overcome in 1886, was the existence of some anti-Tlingit prejudice among many Russian-Creole members of the parish. These hostile feelings were weaker than among the American Sitkans, since the Creoles and the poor Russians constituted a separate class in the town's social hierarchy—above the Indians but below the "White" Americans. Since the early 1880's, when the Tlingit began accepting Orthodox baptism, several Creole men married their women, thus bridging the gap that was not particularly wide in the first place. Nevertheless, Tlingit insistence on having an equal status in the church and the fact that in 1886 Orthodox Tlingit already outnumbered the Russians and the Creoles gave the latter reasons for anxiety.[12] Thus Ushin, a Russian resident of Sitka, reported Russian resentment against the special attention paid by the new priests to Native parishioners (Ushin MS, 1887). Despite such feelings, Vechtomov and Donskoi insisted that the Tlingit had the same rights as the rest of the church members. Orthodox emphasis on sacraments and liturgy rather than sermon and reading the Gospel undoubtedly facilitated the survival of a single congregation divided by cultural and linguistic differences (cf. the separation of the Presbyterian congregation mentioned above, p. 11).

Conversion to Orthodoxy clearly eased Tlingit access to social and religious activities of the Russian-Creole Sitka. They were particularly fond of Orthodox Christmas celebrations (with the accompanying caroling, visitations, and masquerades of Christmas-tide) (Kamenskii 1985:141-145) and Easter (with its religious processions, blessing of houses, and so forth). Membership in the church gave them a legitimate right to enter the homes of the Russian-Creole population and to receive food and presents. Special relationships were established between individual Natives and their Russian godparents; whether they liked it or not, the latter were obligated to treat their godchildren with food and presents. Such behaviour confirmed to the indigenous model of "respectful" behaviour between allies of different ethnic background, described above (p. 2). It is not surprising then, that since the pre-1867 times the Tlingit demanded to have high-ranking godparents with recognized prestige and influence in the Euro-American community. In the 1880's this role was often played by the clergymen themselves or by several respectable members of the Russian community sympathetic to the Natives, such as merchant and U.S. Government interpreter, George Kostromitinov. In return, the latter were feasted by the Tlingit and invited to attend "White Man's style" banquets in the Native village which usually followed baptisms and marriages of high-ranking Indians.

Through this interaction with their Russian godparents, the Tlingit incorporated a number of Russian religious folk customs even before learning some of the fundamentals of Orthodox dogma from the priests. Mutual feasting and visiting during Orthodox holidays also occurred within the Tlingit community itself, which undoubtedly strengthened inter-clan relations and village solidarity, essential in this period of increased American pressure and internal conflicts. Here is how Ushin (MS, 1887) described Easter celebrations in 1887:

> Tlingits of both sexes, dressed up for the occasion, visit
> the homes of their godparents and offer their congratu-
> lations, for which they receive eggs, pieces of kulich
> [Easter bread] and paskha [rich mixture of sweetened
> curds, butter, and raisins], or simply bread. They like
> the customs of the Orthodox people and are introducing
> them in their own homes. Their own tables are now
> decorated with holiday food. Visitors are offered tea and
> coffee with milk. Today they are visiting themselves,
> tomorrow they are expecting visitors, including priest
> V. Donskoi and the deacon.

Orthodox holidays, especially Christmas, fitted well into the Tlingit annual cycle, since winter was the time for inter-village visits, feasts, and potlatches. In Sitka in the late 1880's, Tlingit and Christian feasts were celebrated during the same period of time, with "White Man's food" consumed in some Native feasts, and with some Western goods (cloth, blankets) distributed as Christmas as well as potlatch gifts. One might add that the Tlingit participation in Orthodox holiday processions during Christmas, Easter, and Annunciation Day increased their prestige somewhat in the eyes of the Euro-American population, while also being interpreted by the Natives themselves as evidence of their new power and "respect" given to them by the Russian church.

Among the Russian missionaries' major accomplishments of 1886-1887, repeatedly stressed in their ecclesiastical reports and publications, was the baptism of several Tlingit "chiefs" (heads of the major clans), especially Annahootz of the Kaagwaantaan clan and Katlian of the Kiks.adi clan, performed with great pomp in the spring of 1886 (Archives of the Diocese of Alaska, Sitka, Alaska). As the missionaries themselves realized, the two leaders brought their numerous lineage and clan relatives with them and gave the Russian church a new image in the eyes of the whole Native community. It is not surprising that within the next year several other leading aristocrats and heads of important matrilineal groups from Sitka and other villages also converted.

Sitka parish records indicate that prior to 1886 most converts were younger people, some of whom had attended Russian religious schools, spoke English and some Russian, or even had some Russian-Creole ancestry.[13] On the other hand, converts of the late 1880's were generally older, more conservative, Natives, many of whom were high-ranking aristocrats and their immediate kin. The recognition of their power and influence and the special "respect" shown to them by the Russian missionaries distinguished the Orthodox church from the Presbyterian and became an important factor in its greater popularity among the more traditionalist Natives--the majority of Sitka's Tlingit population.

The practice of rewarding Indian aristocratic converts with gifts, ceremonial regalia, and letters or certificates of praise went back to the pre-1867 era, when several heads of Sitka clans were baptized (e.g. Kamenskii 1985:108-110). Unlike the more democratic American Presbyterians, Russian clergymen, belonging to a highly stratified society where nobility was still the ruling class, treated Tlingit aristocrats in accordance with their rank and relied on them in their interaction with the rest of the Natives. Baptisms, marriages, and especially funerals of Tlingit aristocrats (see below) were always conducted with greater pomp and ceremony than those of ordinary people. All available sacred objects and additional ritual forms were utilized to honor the "chiefs" as the Russians referred to them, e.g., participation of the bishop, large funeral processions carrying icons and banners, longer services, ringing of the church bells, etc.

At the time when the power of the traditional Tlingit leadership was beginning to be challenged by American authorities, Presbyterian missionaries, and American-educated and American-employed younger Natives, this special treatment by the Russian Church helped maintain some of the aristocracy's prestige in the eyes of the White community as well as their own. Not surprisingly, icons and certificates presented to Native leaders have always been treated as valuable sacred possessions and passed on to their matrilineal descendants, not unlike ceremonial crest objects and other traditional valuables.

While some American authorities in Sitka (e.g., U.S. Navy Captain Beardslee) recognized the influence held by the Native "chiefs" and tried to win their support by using them as "Indian policemen" (Hinckley 1982:87-88; 269-271), Presbyterian missionaries did their best to undermine the role of Tlingit aristocracy in the Native social and ceremonial life. For example, whenever a student of the Industrial School became an heir to a deceased chief and had to assume his responsibilities, Presbyterians strongly discouraged and occasionally physically prevented him from doing that (Kan 1979-1984).

So far I have discussed primarily the socio-political gains made by the Tlingit who converted to Orthodoxy in the 1880's. However, to understand the persistence of their commitment to the Russian church one has to examine some of the major aspects of Orthodoxy compatible with the indigenous Tlingit culture and present at least a general outline of the Native interpretation of Orthodox dogma and ritual.

ORTHODOXY AND SPIRITUAL POWER--THE TLINGIT VIEW

In a recent discussion of the advantages that Catholicism had over Protestantism in gaining Indian converts, Ronda and Axtell (1978:8) emphasized "the Catholic use of ceremony--processions, pictures, colourful vestments, impressive rites, and mysterious symbols" as well as "sacramentalism" that "gave Catholic missions an entrance into the Indian mental world and a functional purpose in the Indian daily world denied to Protestants." This observation may be applied to Russian Orthodoxy as well. In the Tlingit religious system, magical objects containing superhuman power could be used to obtain health, wealth, and general well-being (laxeitl, 'luck'), if approached by human beings in a state of physical and spiritual purity, and handled with "great respect." Historical data as well as my own recent ethnographic research indicate that reverent attitudes towards sacred Orthodox artifacts (icons, crosses, vestments) and especially holy (blessed) water and communion have been strongly influenced by these traditional beliefs (Kan 1979-1984).

Unlike the Presbyterian church, which offered primarily hymns, prayers, and other sacred utterances, Orthodoxy provided a supply of potent substances blessed by the priest (a person with extra power), which could be distributed among the parishioners and even brought to their homes. Hence an extreme popularity of such Orthodox practices as the blessing of Native houses and fishing boats. The latter was performed as a collective rite preceding Tlingit departure for summer fishing and other subsistence activities. The sacrament of extreme unction administered to the sick and dying, as well as the "holy water" believed to possess healing and protective powers were also in demand among Indian converts. As I have mentioned earlier, these substances were occasionally used as protection against witchcraft and in traditional magical practices. This Native approach also explains careful preparation for communion and Lenten observances which, since the 1880's, have always been carried out with strict adherence to such Orthodox rules as fasting, meatless diet, temperance, abstention from sex, etc.

While some Russian missionaries complained that the Tlingit interpretation of the Orthodox dogma and ritual was far from the canonical, these opportunities for Native rethinking of Christianity and synthesis of Orthodox and indigenous beliefs helped strengthen Tlingit commitment to the Russian church. Orthodoxy was thus made accessible and understandable even to those older monolingual converts who were only slowly learning about the new religion through Native interpreters.

In some instances, conversion to Orthodoxy not only led to the development of syncretism, but reinforced some of the indigenous beliefs that were being challenged by Presbyterian missionaries and American authorities. Thus, for example, a fundamental opposition between purity and pollution that structured many of the traditional Tlingit religious ideas and practices, most importantly attitudes towards menstrual blood, was actually strengthened

Blessing of the Tlingit fishing fleet by an Orthodox priest. Sitka, ca. 1900-
1920. Photograph by Elbridge W. Merrill. Stratton Memorial Library, Sheldon
Jackson College, Sitka, Alaska.

by the Orthodox rule of excluding menstruating and post-parturient women from the church until they had been purified and blessed by the priest. Similarly, the taboo on sexual relations prior to receiving communion reinforced the indigenous practice of abstention as part of the man's preparation for hunting. As de Laguna's (1972:362–365) informant suggested:

> It's like the rule in the Bible. We used to live like God created us. Hunters stay[ed] away from their wives four months before hunting.... They stay away from everything. <u>They keep clean. It's like the Christian life.</u>

Orthodox rituals, with their use of sacred objects and the leading role played by the priest dressed in rich vestments, paralleled Tlingit ceremonies conducted in a large lineage-owned house, under the direction of aristocratic leaders dressed in ancestral costumes representing their matrilineal crests. The basic structure of space inside the church and the way it was utilized corresponded to that of the Tlingit lineage house, e.g., with the rear being the most sacred area where lineage treasures and regalia were kept by the head of the house, paralleling the use of the altar by the priest in the Orthodox church. Various categories of the Native social order, e.g., aristocrats vs. commoners, old vs. young, men vs. women, could be mapped more easily on the Orthodox than the Presbyterian church's space.

The allocation of such tasks as carrying sacred artifacts during religious processions or distributing candles in the course of the liturgy to outstanding laymen was utilized by the Tlingit aristocracy to maintain its traditional prestige. Thus, even today, during the midnight procession around the church on Easter Sunday, the clergy is followed by the heads of the major clans carrying icons and other sacred objects. This annual ritual also reinforced moiety reciprocity, the fundamental principle of the Tlingit sociocultural order, since the honorable task was equally divided between members of the Raven and the Eagle moieties[14] (Kan 1979–1984). Finally, while both Protestantism and Orthodoxy presented the Tlingit with a model of the universe governed by a single omnipotent God, the Russian church populated it with saints, angels, and demons, thus making it more compatible with the Tlingit cosmology that included a vague notion of the "Spirit Above" as well as a multitude of other powerful beings.[15]

These examples clearly demonstrate that the Tlingit approach to Orthodoxy was "creative, incorporative, and synthesizing" (Brown 1982:62). This conclusion can be further supported by their resistance to or rejection of some of those Orthodox beliefs and practices that totally contradicted the fundamental categories of the indigenous culture. Thus the idea of Hell as a place "down below" (<u>Diyée</u>, as the missionaries called it), where the sinners were being burned and tortured made little sense for the Tlingit. In their own cosmology no emphasis was placed on the underground, while suffering of the deceased was caused by aimless drifting in the sky, away from the "village of the dead" (Kan 1979–1984). Satan—"Chief of the Above" (<u>Diyée Aankáawu</u>)—did not figure prominently in the Native cosmology of that period either.

While enthusiastically accepting Christian baptism, perceived as protection against evil and acquisition of physical and spiritual power, and reacting positively to Orthodox mortuary rituals (see below), Tlingit converts of the 1880's-1890's were reluctant to accept the sacrament of marriage, despite the repeated admonitions of the missionaries. What prevented them was the fear that some of the more Americanized children of such marriages could claim their fathers' property and use the support of the civil and religious authorities, who did not understand or approve of the Tlingit rule of matrilineal descent.

The "synthesizing" Native approach to Orthodoxy and the dynamics of Tlingit relations with the Russian church are best exemplified by the continuity and change in the Tlingit death-related rituals since the mass conversion of the 1880's. The crucial role of Orthodox mortuary rituals in attracting Tlingit converts and keeping them loyal to the church has been frequently pointed out by Orthodox clergy and was also confirmed by Native testimony that I obtained in 1979-1980. This suggests that the topic requires special attention.

ORTHODOXY AND THE TLINGIT WAY OF DEATH

The central role played by death-related rituals—from the funeral to the final memorial feast or potlatch—in the Tlingit sociocultural order has been noted by anthropologists, missionaries, and other observers since the time of Fr. Ivan Veniaminov (1886[1840]; see also Kan 1982a; 1986). Cremation was practiced so as to separate the unclean flesh from the relatively pure bones and several immortal spiritual attributes of the deceased. Prior to cremation, a four-day wake took place, during which the corpse was displayed in the lineage house of the deceased. It was dressed in ceremonial regalia that represented the lineage and clan of the departed. The matrikin of the deceased, whose grief was expressed through a series of taboos imposed upon them, were encouraged to "show their respect" to the deceased by bringing gifts to his house, later to be distributed to members of the opposite moiety who performed crucial practical tasks as well as comforted the mourners. During the wake and the subsequent memorial feasts, social ties between the living were reiterated and solidarity strenghtened. Mourners' singing of ancestral songs was seen not only as the expression of their sorrow but as a way of helping the spirit of the deceased reach the "village of the dead" located in a distant region on top of the mountains. Another "village of the dead" (i.e., the cemetery) was located behind that of the living. There the cremated remains were stored in gravehouses and mortuary poles representing the deceased's crests. Matrilineal relatives of the dead were obligated to feed and warm their departed ancestors by burning food and clothing in the fire, which released the spiritual essences of those objects and sent them to the "village of the dead."

The final memorial feast, which took place about a year after cremation, served to put an end to mourning and recycle the various attributes of the social identity of the deceased, e.g., his ceremonial name, festive clothing and even his spirit which was believed to return through the body of a newborn infant of the same matrilineal group. Another essential function of the potlatch was for the mourners/hosts to express their gratitude to their affines/guests for the mortuary services the latter had earlier performed; feasting and gift-giving was also aimed at strengthening intermoiety ties. The performance of this final memorial feast was essential for the perpetuation of the social order, since without it the heir of the deceased could not assume his role, the widow/widower could not remarry, and proper "respect" was not shown to the dead as well as members of the opposite moiety. Status of each member of society was determined by his/her role in the ritual.

Thus death-related rituals reiterated the fundamental values and underlying principles of the whole Tlingit sociocultural order. At the same time, they became the major arenas for negotiating and establishing alliances between major social units and their members, while also confirming the current status of each individual and matrilineal group involved. These rituals can be seen as periodic impositions of order upon the flow of social life, as temporary agreements between members of society on the distribution of power and prestige. Today, death-related rituals, and especially the potlatch, remain the most conservative aspect of Tlingit culture, modified but not eliminated by one hundred years of Christianization and American influence.

In their initial encounters with Christian missionaries, the Tlingit quickly accepted those mortuary practices that they perceived as "showing respect" to the deceased and emphasizing new dimensions of his social identity. At the same time, they refused to abandon cremation, wondering why the Europeans were willing to let their dead remain in the cold and wet earth. From the point of view of Tlingit eschatology, the White Man's afterlife must have appeared quite miserable. As one observer reported, the Tlingit thought that "White people are plentyful [in the afterworld], but occupy a very inferior position. They wander about in cotton sheets or their sleazy night-gowns and are cold and hungry all the time" (Knapp and Childe 1896:161).

Thus the funeral of a Native chief, who was a member of the Orthodox church, that took place in the late 1860s included a number of innovations, while retaining the fundamental traditional patterns. During the first day of the wake, the chief's membership in the church and his ties with the European community were emphasized:

> In the back of the hut there was a catafalque covered with
> a black cloth which contained the body of the deceased,
> and around the dead were the lighted wax candles. A
> general's cocked hat and a Russian sword were laid on the
> coffin together with some ornaments, chiefly beads and
> brass chains. At the foot of the catafalque knelt a
> Russian acolyte...who was saying the Prayers for the
> Dead. (Teichmann 1963 [1925]:234-243)

Next day a totally different scene was observed by Teichmann:

> At the back of the house near the body, which today was
> not surrounded by Christian elements, but was simply
> covered with skins and blankets, a kind of platform has
> been erected a few feet above the ground. On it there was
> an Indian dressed in skins, with a hideous mask over his
> face, and his head decked with feathers, who executed a
> series of wild leaps and bounds...(ibid.)

The wake was followed by an elaborate Orthodox funeral conducted by the
bishop himself. The Tlingit accepted various forms of "respect" from the
church and buried the chief with artifacts representing his ties with the
European society—an umbrella, a walking stick, and a bottle of wine. A few
hours later, however, after the Russians had departed, the body was exhumed
and cremated. Since the arrival of the U.S. Army and Navy and the
establishment of a National cemetery, the Sitka Tlingit were able to observe
the honors bestowed by the military on their dead. The Indians were clearly
impressed and often demanded the participation of a military guard and a
salute when a high-ranking member of their community was put to rest (see
e.g., The Alaskan. December 12, 1885, p. 3).

From the Tlingit point of view, Orthodox mortuary practices offered a
great deal of additional "respect" to the deceased, if compared to those of
the Presbyterian mission. By means of communion given to the dying and
special prayers said at the time of death, the spirit was "strengthened" and
given protection during its dangerous journey to the "village of the dead."
The practice of having lit candles near the body until the time of the
funeral was also quickly accepted, since it corresponded to the indigenous
vigil aimed at guarding the deceased against the attacks of witches. While
the Tlingit provided their dead with warm clothing and weapons to fight evil
creatures along the road to the land of the dead, the Russian church placed a
small picture of a saint inside the coffin for protection.

The funeral service of the Orthodox, with its use of incense, solemn
hymns and prayers, and a general emphasis on showing love to the deceased by
decorating the coffin and the church itself, appealed to the Tlingit. Both
cultures rejected the idea of an egalitarian funeral and provided a more
elaborate ceremony for persons of high rank. Thus, when a recently-baptized
chief Annahootz died in 1890, he was "buried with all the honors that the
church could bestow upon him" (The Alaskan, February 22, 1890, p. 2). Since
that time funerals of aristocrats and Native leaders have always involved a
large procession of Indians led by the clergy, with the body being carried
from the Sitka village to the cathedral and later to the cemetery. Finally,
neither Orthodox nor Tlingit mortuary practices restricted expressions of
sorrow, while Presbyterian missionaries strongly discouraged the Natives from
loud wailing and other "uncivilized" forms of behaviour.

The compatibility between the Tlingit and the Orthodox mortuary
practices went beyond the funeral itself: both included a memorial meal or
feast immediately after the disposal of the body as well as some time later.
In the Orthodox tradition, the latter feast took place on the fortieth day
after death when a special memorial service was performed and the soul of the
deceased was believed to have finally reached its destination. The Tlingit,
on the other hand, conducted several memorial feasts between the funeral and

the final memorial potlatch. The fact that Fr. Vladimir Donskoi began attending such memorial feasts (which the Russians called 'pominki'), suggests that he saw nothing offensive in them from the Christian point of view. It is also possible that the Natives, who were very pleased by his participation, modified their ceremony somewhat, eliminating those practices that were particularly difficult for the missionary to accept (Ushin, MS, 1887). One might also add that the speeches made during those feasts were delivered in Tlingit, so that the priest probably missed numerous statements alluding to traditional ("pagan") cosmology and eschatology. His own words of comforting and a prayer, with which he opened the ceremony, were probably accepted with gratitude as a show of sympathy and respect to the deceased and the mourners (see Kan 1982b).

Gradually the banquet held on the fortieth day after death became the major Tlingit memorial feast between the funeral and the potlatch. The Orthodox concept that the soul of the deceased remained in limbo for forty days and needed help from the living (prayers, lighting candles, etc.) was also incorporated into the Tlingit way of death soon after the mass conversion of the 1880's. Even a special dish of rice, prepared by the relatives of the deceased to be blessed in the church during the memorial service on the fortieth day and later to be shared at the beginning of the banquet, was easily interpreted as "feeding the dead," since the food eaten by the living during a traditional Tlingit memorial feast was believed to be shared by the spirit of the deceased.[16]

The Orthodox emphasis on remembering the dead by invoking their names in the liturgy throughout the year and especially during Lent and Easter also appealed to the Tlingit. The two cultures shared the view that the living and the dead constituted a community and that the former could help the latter by their actions. This was totally unacceptable to the Presbyterians, who frequently criticized the Tlingit for "worrying about the dead while one should care for the living." Prayers for the dead were rarely offered in that church and the Presbyterian funeral itself, with its modesty and brevity did not appeal to the Tlingit.

While the incorporation of Orthodox practices into the Tlingit mortuary ritual began in the 1880's, if not earlier, Native resistance against certain basic Christian mortuary customs continued for several decades. One issue on which Presbyterian and Russian missionaries were in agreement was the rejection of the Tlingit practice of cremation. In the 1880's in Sitka, Governor Swineford himself allegedly interfered with it, threatening to put down the fire and arrest the participants (Wells n.d.). Cremation was much more difficult to hide in communities with mixed population, whereas in smaller villages it persisted into the early 1900's. Nevertheless, even in Sitka cremations still occurred in secret in the late 1880's. There was a great deal of anxiety among the Natives with regard to the shift from burning the bodies in warm fire to burying them in wet and cold ground. For years members of the same community would vacillate between the two practices. For example, in 1889 in the village of Chilkat, where the Presbyterian missionary insisted on Christian burial, bad weather was attributed to this new custom, so that when a child had been buried instead of being burned on the funeral pyre, "The mother became alarmed and felt that her life was in jeopardy for permitting the child to be buried, so she kindled a fire over the grave in order to appease the gods[?] and bring good weather" (The North Star, 1891, Vol. 2, No. 6, p. 1). According to Ushin (MS, 1883), in the early 1880's some recent converts left the Russian church because, as they put it, "the dead were not warmed there."

Gradually a compromise was worked out: the dead were buried but their graves were lined with lumber; sometimes an additional coffin or several sets of clothing for the corpse were used to keep the deceased warm. A fire might also be built on top of the grave as a compromise between the old and the new practices. The coffin itself was filled with various objects believed to be necessary for the spirit of the deceased in the other world--water containers, household objects, guns, etc. The traditional practice, of course, was to burn those objects with the body. Although both denominations discouraged such practices, the Russian missionaries were much more tolerant and were satisfied with the general shift to burial among members of their church. One of the first Orthodox burials in the village of Chilkat was performed in the following manner:

> ...the baby had been laid out and placed in a small chest
> with a picture of the Madonna on its breast...while the
> family knelt in silent prayer in their corner. The next
> day came the simple burial; the family and a few others
> gathered around the dead and I saw the weeping mother lift
> the blanket and slip some little keepsake into the baby's
> hand, then the lid was closed and fastened down.... A
> small grave had been dug into which the little chest was
> lowered, covered with a new blanket and then a wooden box
> was placed over it; the mother then placed the little
> one's clothing and cradle on the box and each dropped in a
> handful of earth and then the men filled the grave (Alaska
> Searchlight, Vol. II, No. 2, January 11, 1896).

In their reports and probably sermons as well, Orthodox missionaries condemned cremation and a number of other "heathen" mortuary practices of the Tlingit, such as the depiction of the clan crest of the deceased on the gravestone. However, when it came to enforcing what they preached, the priests were rarely too persistent. In some cases they lost the battle altogether, as in the famous controversy over a marble bear which the Sitka Tlingit planned to erect on the grave of a member of the Bear clan in the 1910's. When the priest insisted that the act was against Orthodox principles and ideas, relatives of the deceased chose to bury the man in front of his own house and proudly placed the controversial gravestone there (Russian Orthodox American Messenger, 1911, Vol. 5, No. 6, p. 278).

Other examples of mortuary practices that contradicted what the missionaries considered appropriate was the display of the body in the coffin surrounded by Christian artifacts (candles, decorated covers, etc.) as well as ancestral heirlooms of the deceased and his matrilineal group. Such displays must have been either ignored by the Russian priests or were so important for the Tlingit that they refused to abandon them (see fig. 1, p. 36). Missionary journals indicate frequent cases of non-interference into Native mortuary observances, e.g., a Juneau clergyman commented on the plans of his colleague to eliminate Tlingit grave monuments "contrary to the

149

Orthodox spirit" by writing that "these gravestones are not numerous and
eliminating them would cause too much trouble" (Juneau, Records of
St. Nicholas Russian Orthodox Church, 1911). Russian clergymen were most
likely unaware of the persistence of moiety reciprocity in mortuary rituals
and the compensation of the pallbearers through the traditional potlatch.
Neither did they understand fully the extent of the "indigenization" of the
forty-day memorial banquet, which has even spread to those Native communities
that have never had an Orthodox church. Under the name "forty-day party"
this ritual persists today and is considered by the younger generations to be
an "Indian custom" (Kan 1982b).

     Tlingit approach to Orthodox mortuary rituals is typical of their
general relationship with the Russian Church. While allowing the Church to
perform its role and conduct the funeral according to the religious dogma,
the Tlingit have quietly kept some of the fundamental elements and patterns
of the indigenous mortuary ritual underneath the Christian surface. They
have also continued certain practices in private, taking advantage of the
Russian missionaries' relative tolerance or indifference. Finally, they
often maintain their own interpretations of Orthodox death-related beliefs
and practices. As a result of this, contemporary Tlingit way of death,
undoubtedly formed in the end of the nineteenth century, begins with a
Christian funeral, followed by a syncretistic "forty-day party," and ends
with a traditional potlatch, which, except for an occasional prayer, has
little to do with Christianity (ibid.).

     Such opportunities for a creative approach to Christianity did not exist
for those Tlingit who had joined the Presbyterian Church. There missionary
control over Native mortuary practices was much stronger and so was the
condemnation of the "heathen practices." Consequently, while some
Presbyterian Indians had to abandon traditional observances, others performed
them in great secrecy, risking to be suspended or expelled from the church.
The missionaries themselves tried to perform most of the necessary services,
so as to eliminate the traditional expenses and the need for a lavish feast
for compensating the opposite moiety which usually performed the mortuary
tasks. Presbyterian opposition to potlatches was total and uncompromising,
because it was perceived by the missionaries as both a "devil worship" and a
"wasteful practice"--the major obstacle to Tlingit progress.

CONCLUSION

     In this paper, Tlingit conversion to Orthodoxy has been examined in the
context of the discussion of complex economic, social, political, and
cultural conflicts and changes that occurred in southeastern Alaska in the
1870's-1880's. The history and the nature of the European and American
presence in this area, as well as particular characteristics of Tlingit
culture have been analyzed to suggest the main reasons for the Native
accommodation to the newcomers, including gradual acceptance of their
religion. Since 1867, the Tlingit tried to benefit from the White Man's
wealth and spiritual power, but were unable to maintain their independence
and protect the integrity of the traditional sociocultural order as they had
managed to do during the Russian era.

The body of a chief of the L'uknaxadi (Coho Salmon) clan lying in state in his lineage house in Sitka. His widow is sitting next to the body. Clan regalia of the deceased are displayed. The house was used for the prayer meeting of the St. Michael Brotherhood of Temperance and Mutual Aid. Attributes of the Orthodox funeral are also visible. Ca. 1900-1910. Photograph by Elbridge W. Merrill, Stratton Memorial Library, Sheldon Jackson College, Sitka, Alaska.

Aside from a few small-scale violent confrontations, no organized armed resistance to the intruders was offered. Neither was there a nativistic movement of the sort that swept through the Plains in the end of the nineteenth century. The Tlingit approach was different--to learn as much as possible about the new ways of the Euro-Americans and to take advantage of some of their material and intellectual resources, while trying to maintain the fundamental patterns and principles of the traditional culture and social order. Of course, changes in the economy and the power structure in the region eventually affected many aspects of Native belief and social life. The process of change, however, was more gradual than among many other American Indian cultures, resulting in the persistence of many essential aspects of the pre-Christian Tlingit way of life and world view well into the twentieth century.

In their attempt to adjust to Euro-Americans the Tlingit were presented with several alternative models. The Presbyterian one promised greater material benefits and faster assimilation into the new social order. Young Tlingit graduates of the Sitka Industrial School were better equipped for survival in the White Man's world than other Natives, provided they were not discriminated against once they tried to enter it. Not surprisingly, many Presbyterian Tlingit became Native political leaders who fought for Indian citizenship, civil rights, and the land claims. The price of progress, however, was some degree of estrangement from the rest of the Native society, which found Presbyterian missionaries too domineering and their form of Christianity unsatisfying--culturally, socially, and emotionally.

Russian Orthodoxy, on the other hand, offered an alternative model, which allowed for a great deal of compromise between indigenous and exogenous ideas, values, and social forms. Membership in that church enabled the more traditionalist, less Americanized Natives to gain some "respect" from the Euro-American and Russian-Creole communities, while maintaining considerable independence from the missionaries. The Orthodox version of Christianity provided much greater opportunities for Native reinterpretation and synthesis. Certain of its aspects even helped to preserve some important elements of the traditional Tlingit sociocultural order, which have persisted in an Orthodox disguise until the present. The Russian Church, with its somewhat negative attitudes towards the Americanization of Alaska, provided an alternative institution that gave the Tlingit some protection and provided a context for the development of a distinct Native version of Christianity. The latter, however, took place independent or even in spite of the missionary activities and indoctrination.

In the late 1880's, early 1890's, the first step was made towards a large-scale acceptance of Orthodoxy and the development of Orthodox-Tlingit syncretism, especially in Sitka. During the next decade, Orthodoxy spread to most northern and central Tlingit communities, from Yakutat to Atlin in the Yukon Territory. Tlingit interest in Orthodoxy was remarkable, considering the lack of manpower and funds, which prevented the church from providing many of the villages with regular pastoral care.

In those communities where Orthodoxy maintained a stronger, more permanent base, the most important development of the 1890's-1900's was the creation of Native religious brotherhoods of temperance and mutual aid. (Kan 1985). Originally they were designed by the missionaries, primarily to fight against drinking and the "tribal mode of life," and especially "feasts for the dead," shamanism, etc. This program did not attract the majority of the Orthodox Natives who assumed the same wait-and-see attitude as they did a decade earlier when their younger kinsmen began joining the Russian Church.

A few years later, however, leadership in the new organizations was taken over by the aristocracy, including heads of several important lineages and clans, who utilized their new position to maintain or even increase their power and prestige challenged by the process of social change. While the priests' influence over the affairs of the brotherhoods weakened, the new organizations were joined by the majority of the adult population and became one of the leading forces behind various religious and social activities in Sitka and other Tlingit communities.

Among their most popular activities were holiday banquets where the Russian clergy and the whole Native community were guests, with brotherhood presidents and other officers playing the honourable role of the potlatch hosts. Several times a week, brotherhood members met in the village (sometimes in a special meeting house), for "testimonial" or "prayer" meetings, where instruction in Orthodox dogma and liturgical singing took place. The priests attended some of the meetings, but the major part of the instruction was conducted in the Tlingit language by Native lay workers and interpreters, who often presented Orthodox ideas in a unique Tlingitized form, thus encouraging Orthodox-Tlingit syncretism. Since oratory had always been essential in Tlingit ceremonial life, brotherhoods added Protestant-style "testimonials" to these Orthodox prayer meetings, creating a unique Native religious form. Dressed in special uniforms, brotherhood "marshals" monitored and enforced proper behaviour during services and strict observance of Lenten rules; occasionally they also acted as peace-maker and mediators in disputes between members of the parish (Kan 1979-1984).

Thus, these semi-independent Native religious organizations not only reinforced the traditional social order but helped to strengthen solidarity in the Native community through collective rituals and mutual aid. With a gradual decline of clan unity, the increased role of the nuclear family, and the growth of tensions between some of the members of the community, brotherhoods became a crucial factor in Tlingit social life.[17]

While Native church brotherhoods no longer exist, Tlingit Orthodoxy has survived many upheavals of the twentieth century. In the last two decades, when a Native "cultural revival" took place in Alaska and when many of the more Americanized Tlingit and their children tried to rediscover the indigenous cultural values and ceremonies, it was often the elderly Orthodox leadership that became the major source of traditional knowledge (cf. Dauenhauer 1979:18). Today the Orthodox Church is perceived by many younger Tlingit, especially in Sitka, as a "Tlingit (Indian) Church," while the Presbyterian one is harshly criticized for the intolerance and ethnocentrism of the past era.

FOOTNOTES

1. This paper is based on archival and library research conducted in
   1979-1983, as well as thirteen months of ethnographic fieldwork in
   several Tlingit communities in 1979-1980. Part of the funding for the
   study was provided by the Melville and Elizabeth Jacobs Fund of the
   Whatcom Museum of History and Art. The author wishes to acknowledge the
   helpful cooperation of several church officials who provided access to
   parish records: His Grace the Right Reverend Gregory, Bishop of Sitka
   and All Alaska, Fr. Eugene Bourdukofsky of St. Michael Cathedral of
   Sitka, Archimandrite Fr. Innocent of St. Nicholas Russian Orthodox
   Church of Juneau, Fr. Michael Williams of Hoonah and Angoon, and Rev.
   Neil Munro of the Presbyterian Church of Sitka. Valuable archival
   materials were also discovered with the help of the friendly staff of
   the Alaska State Historical Library and Stratton Memorial Library of the
   Sheldon Jackson College.

2. Such relations did not exclude warfare, when other peoples showed
   weakness or dared to insult the Tlingit.

3. In 1849 the Church of the Holy Trinity was built for the Sitka Natives
   outside the Russian town. Tlingit language was used during its
   services. However, the Tlingit seemed to resent having a segregated
   place of worship and preferred occasional visits to the Cathedral of
   St. Michael, with its decorative splendor and the presence of the
   Russians and the Creoles. In 1855, the "Native" church became the
   object of a Tlingit attack following a confrontation with the Russian
   military men guarding Novo-Arkhangel'sk. During the attack, the Tlingit
   destroyed religious artifacts, which indicated the weakness of their
   commitment to the new religion. In 1872, the church was ordered to be
   demolished by the Russian bishop, since it was rarely attended by the
   Natives who were now free to enter the cathedral whenever they wished.

4. In an 1878 report to the Alaska Ecclesiastical Consistory, an Orthodox
   priest complained about Tlingit acts of theft and vandalism against the
   church property (DRHA, Vol. III, p. 126).

5. Both the Russian and the Presbyterian missionaries tried to combine
   medical assistance with prayers, correctly assuming that this would make
   a strong impression on the Natives. (Wilbur n.d.)

6. Emmons' informant Shukoff reported that in the 1860's-1870's many
   Tlingits already knew the Lord's Prayer (most likely in the Orthodox
   version) and were appealing to God for luck and success in hunting,
   trade, and even gambling.

7. A Russian missionary who visited the village of Hoonah reported that the Presbyterian Tlingit continued "showing respect," as they put it, to him and his church by praying with the Orthodox Natives for a few minutes and then going to their own church. (See Russian Orthodox American Messenger, 1903, Vol. 7, No. 4, pp. 55-56). This practice persists today in small villages, while in larger communities Tlingit "ecumenism" is not tolerated by the clergy.

8. Native membership of the Presbyterian church continued to grow due largely to a large number of the Industrial School children who automatically became its members. However, by 1910 it dropped to 200—the same number the church claimed in 1888.

9. Veniaminov himself was a talented linguist who translated Orthodox materials into Aleut and created Aleut literacy with the help of talented Native interpreters (see Black 1977; Dauenhauer 1979).

10. Most of the articles on Tlingit customs and beliefs published in the local and national Presbyterian publications (The North Star, The Assembly Herald, etc.), were filled with mistakes and distortions.

11. Many of those so-called "illegitimate" children were probably quite legitimate from the Native point of view, i.e., their parents lived together as Tlingit husbands and wives, but refused to "legitimize" their marriage in the church. Cf. the case of one of the elders of the Presbyterian church who was reported in the church's records to have taken a young woman to his house "as his wife according to heathen custom and without legal marriage, and had lived with her for two or three days before they were legally married." For his offense the elder was suspended from membership indefinitely. (Session records of the Sitka Presbyterian Church, 1905).

12. In 1885 there were 192 Russians and Creoles in the Orthodox church and only 128 Tlingit; but in 1886 the proportion changed to 215 Russians and Creoles versus 320 or 330 Tlingit.

13. A few of those younger converts were of aristocratic background and later became important leaders in the Russian church as well as the Tlingit community.

14. One of the most frequent positive comments made by Tlingit today about the Orthodox ritual in comparison to the Presbyterian is that the former is "longer, more orderly, and more beautyful" (Kan 1979-1984).

15. For a discussion of the Tlingit-Orthodox syncretism see Kamenskii (1985:70), e.g., the confusion between the Mother of God and the indigenous wealth-bringing mythological women, Tl'anaxéedakw. Numerous accounts of miracles, visions, and dreams that I recorded in 1979-1980 indicate how thoroughly Tlingit and Orthodox ideas, beliefs, and symbols have been synthesized (Kan 1979-1984).

16. I have obtained several accounts describing dying non-Orthodox Tlingit being afraid that they would not be able to eat rice in the land of the dead and asking to be admitted into the Russian church (Kan 1979-1984).

17. Temperance societies and other Christian organizations also existed among the Presbyterian Tlingit during this period. However, because of the firmer control of the missionary leadership they never achieved the status of the semi-independent Native religious institutions, as did the Orthodox brotherhoods.

REFERENCES

INDIVIDUAL WORKS

Afonsky, Gregory, Bishop
    1977   A History of the Orthodox Church in Alaska. Kodiak, Alaska:
              St. Herman's Theological Seminary.

Austin, Alonzo E.
    1892   History of the Mission. The North Star 5(12):1-4.

Berkhofer, Robert F., Jr.
    1965   Salvation and the Savage: An Analysis of Protestant Missions
              and American Indian Response, 1787-1862. Lexington: University
              of Kentucky Press.

Bowden, Henry Warner
    1981   American Indians and Christian Missions. Chicago: The
              University of Chicago Press.

Brown, Jennifer S.H.
    1982   The Track to Heaven: the Hudson Bay Cree Religious Movement of
              1842-1843. Papers of the Thirteenth Algonquian Conference.
              Edited by William Cowan. Ottawa: Carleton University.

Dauenhauer, Richard
    1979   The Spiritual Epiphany of Aleut. Orthodox Alaska 8(1):13-42.

    1980   Conflicting Visions in Alaskan Education. Unpublished
              Manuscript.

Doklad komiteta ob ustroistve Russkikh Amerikanskikh kolonii
    1863   [Report of the Committee on the Organization of the
              Russian-American Colonies]. 2 vols. St. Petersburg.

Documents Relative to the History of Alaska. Unpublished manuscript,
    1936-38   University of Alaska, Fairbanks.

Donskoi, Vladimir, Fr.
1893 Sitkha i Koloshi [Sitka and the Tlingit]. Tserkovnye Vedomosti 22:822-828; 23:856-862.

1895 Molitvy na Koloshinskom Narechii [Prayers in the Tlingit Language]. Sitka, Alaska: n.p.

1901 Kratkaya Istoriia Vetkhogo i Novogo Zaveta...[A Short History of the Old and the New Testament...in Tlingit and Russian]. New York: Russian Orthodox American Messenger.

Emmons, George T.
n.d. Unpublished manuscript on Tlingit Ethnography. Archives, American Museum of Natural History, New York.

Glass, Henry
1890 Naval Administration in Alaska. The Proceedings of the United States Naval Institute, Vol. XVI, No. 1, Whole No. 52.

Hinckley, Ted, C.
1966 The Presbyterian Leadership in Pioneer Alaska. The Journal of American History 52(4):742-756.

1972 The Americanization of Alaska, 1867-1897. Palo Alto, California: Pacific Books Publishers.

1982 Alaskan John G. Brady, Missionary, Businessman, Judge, and Governor, 1878-1918. Ohio State University Press.

Kamenskii, Anatolii, Archimandrite
1901 Liagushinyi Protsess. [The Frog Case]. Russian Orthodox American Messenger 5(11):233-234.

1985 Tlingit Indians of Alaska. Translated by S. Kan [Originally published in Russian in 1906]. Fairbanks: University of Alaska Press.

Kan, Sergei
1979-84 Ethnographic Notes from 14 Months of Fieldwork among the Tlingit Indians. Unpublished Manuscript in Author's Possession.

1982a Wrap Your Father's Brothers in Kind Words: An Analysis of the Nineteenth-Century Tlingit Mortuary and Memorial Rituals. Unpublished Ph.D. Thesis. University of Chicago.

1982b   The "Forty-day Party": Russian Orthodox Christianity and the
         Death Rituals of the Tlingit Indians. Paper presented at the
         22nd Annual Meeting of the Northeastern Anthropological
         Association. Princeton, New Jersey.

1985   Orthodox Church Brotherhoods of the Tlingit Indians,
         1896-1940's. Paper presented at the 81st Annual Meeting of the
         American Anthropological Association. Washington, D.C.

1986   "The Nineteenth-century Tlingit Potlatch: a new Perspective."
         American Ethnologist 13(2):191-212.

Knapp, F. and Childe, R.L.
    1896   The Thlinkets of Southeast Alaska. Chicago.

Krause, Aurel
    1956
    [1885]   The Tlingit Indians. Translated from German by Erna Gunther.
             Seattle: University of Washington Press.

de Laguna, F.
    1973   Under Mount Saint Elias: the History and Culture of the Yakutat
             Tlingit. Smithsonian Contributions to Anthropology.
             Washington, D.C.: Smithsonian Institution Press.

Lindsay, Aaron L., Rev.
    1965
    [1881]   Sketches of an Excursion of Southern Alaska. Seattle: The
             Shorey Bookstore.

Nadezhdin, Ivan
    1896   Sbornik Tserkovnykh Pesnopenii na Koloshinskom Narechii [A
             Collection of Church Songs and Hymns in Tlingit]. San
             Francisco.

Ronda, James and Axtell, James
    1978   Indian Missions. A Critical Bibliography. Bloomington:
             Indiana University Press.

Smith, Barbara S.
    1980   "Orthodoxy and Native Americans: the Alaskan Mission."
             Orthodox Church in America, Department of History and Archives,
             Historical Society, Occasional Papers, No. 1, Syosett, New York:
             St. Vladimir's Press.

Teichmann, Emil
1963
[1925]   A Journey to Alaska in the Year 1868: Being a Diary of the Late
         Emil Teichmann. New York: Argosy-Antiquarian Ltd.

Ushin, Stepan
n.d.   Unpublished Manuscript. (Diary kept in Sitka, 1874-1895).
         Library of Congress. The Alaska Church Collection.

Veniaminov, Ivan (Bishop Innokentii; St. Innocent)
1886
[1840]   Tvoreniia [Collected Works], Vol. 3:26-154. Edited by Ivan
         Barsukov. Moscow: Synodal Press. Reprint of the Notes on the
         Islands of the Unalaska District, originally published in 1840.

Wells, William
n.d.   Unpublished Papers. Billman Collection. Archives, Stratton
         Memorial Library, Sheldon Jackson College, Sitka, Alaska.

Wilbur, Bertrand K.
n.d.   "JAM [Just About Me]: Medical Missionary to Sitka, Alaska,
         1894-1901." Unpublished Manuscript. Archives, Sitka Historical
         Society, Sitka, Alaska.

PERIODICALS

The Alaska Searchlight, 1895-1896.

The Alaskan, 1885-1907.

The Assembly Herald, 1908-1914.

North Star, 1889-1898.

Russian Orthodox American Messenger, 1896-1939.

Thlinget, 1908-1912.

MANUSCRIPT COLLECTIONS

Juneau, Alaska. Archives of St. Nicholas Russian Orthodox Church. Records of the Russian Orthodox Church, Juneau, Hoonah, and Killisnoo Parishes, 1894-1911.

Sitka, Alaska. Archives. Stratton Memorial Library, Sheldon Jackson College. Billman Collection.

Sitka, Alaska. Archives of the Diocese of Alaska, Orthodox Church in America. Records of the Russian Orthodox Church, Sitka and Other Parishes of Southeastern Alaska, 1866-1980.

Sitka, Alaska. Archives. Presbyterian Church of Sitka, 1884-1941.

Washington, D.C. Library of Congress, Manuscript Division. Alaska Church Collection.

FROM SOREL TO LAKE WINNIPEG:
George Nelson as an Ethnohistorical Source

by

Jennifer S.H. Brown

ABSTRACT

Fur trader George Nelson stands out among early-nineteenth-century Canadians for his interest in the lives and ways of the natives he encountered. His writings testify to his willingness to listen seriously to what his Indian associates had to tell him, and to his thirst for detail and accuracy. He was successively in the employ of the XY Company, the North West Company, and the Hudson's Bay Company, from 1802 to 1823. His manuscripts are an invaluable source on all the parties involved in the fur trade social sphere, and particularly on the Indians.

His manuscripts comprise both letters and journals written on the spot, and reflective reminiscences written over a lengthy period some years after his retirement. They show his knowledge of the Ojibwa and Cree communities he met and his ability in their languages, especially Ojibwa. They also demonstrate the extent to which he appreciated native customs and belief systems, not just as curious and interesting but as highly adaptive, functional, and understandable means of surviving in their northern hunting-based environment.

FROM SOREL TO LAKE WINNIPEG: GEORGE NELSON AS AN
ETHNOHISTORICAL SOURCE

Jennifer S. H. Brown

Among Anglo-Canadian fur trade writers of the early nineteenth century,
George Nelson stands out for his interest in the lives and ways of the
natives he encountered, his willingness to listen seriously and with a
relatively open mind to what they had to tell him, and his eagerness for
accuracy and detail. Always at the rank of clerk, he served the XY Company
(Sir Alexander Mackenzie and Company) in 1802-04, the North West Company from
1804 to 1816 and again from 1818 to 1821, and the Hudson's Bay Company from
the time of its merger with the North West Company until 1823. Yet, while
attending to their business in a seemingly competent manner, he also became a
good observer and recorder of both the native and non-native people around
him. His manuscripts are an invaluable resource on all the parties involved
in his fur trade social spheres—and particularly on the Indians.

Nelson's papers consist of two major groups of materials: the
manuscripts written during his fur trade service, and a body of reminiscences
set down between 1825 and about 1851, two to twenty-eight or more years after
he left the northwest. Only two Nelson documents have appeared in print.
The first was a post-retirement reminiscence of his 1802-03 winter in the
St. Croix River valley in northwestern Wisconsin (Bardon and Nute 1947). The
second, his Lac la Ronge letter-journal of 1823, which deals with Cree and
Ojibwa religion and traditions and stands out as an ethnological contribution
of high quality, was published recently (Brown and Brightman 1988).

NELSON'S FAMILY AND CHILDHOOD

Nelson grew up in a loyalist community in Sorel, Lower Canada (now
Quebec), about fifty miles down the St. Lawrence River from Montreal. His
parents, William, a schoolmaster originally from northern England, and Jane
Dies, were married in Sorel (or William Henry as it was then known) on
24 May 1785. Both had been among the many New York residents who came to the
Sorel area to escape the American Revolution. George, their eldest child,
was born on 4 June 1786. He was followed by at least eight other children.
The only two who found fame—or notoriety—in their lifetimes were Wolfred
and Robert, conspicuous for their roles in the Papineau uprising of 1837
(Van Kirk and Brown 1985, Brown and Brightman 1988:4).

George received, and evidently absorbed with success, a sound basic education; the Lac la Ronge and other texts demonstrate considerable literacy and some familiarity with classical mythology and European intellectual currents. But in February of 1802, his father and the local notary set him upon a new course, drawing up a five-year contract with the partnership of Parker, Gerrard, and Ogilvy to engage him in the fur trade as an apprentice clerk (Van Kirk and Brown 1985:653). He thus entered the service of their affiliate, the XY Company (Sir Alexander Mackenzie and Company), the firm which from the late 1790s to 1804 so vigorously challenged the North West Company for the fur trade beyond the Great Lakes. There were probably two reasons that William Nelson allowed George to take up this career at so early an age. First, George himself, infected by the examples of many other local youths who took up this adventurous life for what seemed a liberal salary, "was seized with the delirium" of their enthusiasm and compaigned to go (Bardon and Nute 1947:5-6). Second, the fact that George as the eldest son had by that time six younger brothers and sisters in need of support probably swayed his father's views.

THE WISCONSIN YEARS (1802-04)

On 3 May 1802, George left Lachine, the fur traders' take-off point near Montreal, in a brigade of six canoes to travel to the depot of Grand Portage on the southwestern shore of Lake Superior; then on 13 September, he left that place with three men to winter in northern Wisconsin (Bardon and Nute 1947:6, 144). Nothing in his previous experience had prepared him for life in the fur trade and among the Indians, and he poignantly recorded his early homesickness and the trials of adjusting to so foreign a setting. Yet he remained open to contact with and involvement in his new world, gaining the Indians' acceptance and support, and even a tie of kinship. As he later recalled, "a mere stripling—how they laughed at, and pitied me alternately. A lad about a year older than myself, took a fancy for me, and treated me as a friend indeed: his father was well pleased, and adopted me in his family" (Brown 1984; see also Bardon and Nute 1947:150).

In 1803, after a summer visit to Grand Portage, Nelson returned inland in mid-August, to winter in the Lac du Flambeau and Rivière des Sauteux (Chippewa River) areas of northern Wisconsin. Much travelling was necessary during this difficult winter, partly to avoid encounters with hostile Sioux, and partly because of food shortages. While under these stresses, Nelson had three memorable experiences with Wisconsin Chippewa variants of the Northern Algonkian practice of conjuring as a means of seeking information and securing game, although use of the shaking tent, which he later found so common in more northerly areas, was absent in these instances. It is interesting that on all three occasions, Nelson and his men fostered or even initiated these activities, in empathy, it seems, with the Indians' sense that conjuring was, in the circumstances, as good and useful a coping strategy as any, and more satisfying than most.

The Wisconsin years made an indelible impression on Nelson's mind. He was at that time between the ages of sixteen and eighteen—sensitive and quick to learn. His progress toward eventual fluency in the Ojibwa language certainly began in this period. In remote inland settings where white companions were few and not necessarily congenial, and where Indian attentions and support were essential to his trade, Nelson found that his Indian ties were of great practical and personal value. Having an observant and inquiring disposition, he began also to learn about native ways, which he found understandable and adaptive in light on the conditions of northern life, or at least, as he sometimes hastened to add, in view of the natives' lack of exposure to Christianity. Dreaming and conjuring had their place as means of coping with the uncertainties of subsistence and survival. As Nelson expressed the point in the Lac la Ronge text, "Their [the Indians'] wants indeed are also few, but they are arbitrary and cannot be dispensed with, at least for any time; it is therefore very natural that they should employ their whole thoughts and most of their time in procuring means to warding [off] or averting their dangers" (Brown and Brightman 1988:83).

THE LAKE WINNIPEG PERIOD (1804-12)

The Lake Winnipeg phase of Nelson's career put him on familiar terms with the "Sauteux" or Ojibwa of that area (cf. Steinbring 1981), and later acquainted him with the more northerly "Mashkiegons" or Swampy Cree (perhaps a somewhat misleading term) as they began to seek out the North West Company's trade. (On synonymy and variants of terms for these Indians of the York Factory area and inland, see Pentland in Honigmann 1981:227; Bishop 1981:159.) No journal survives for the 1804-05 season, spent at the mouth of the Red River, or for 1806-07; and that for 1805-06, spent at Lac du Bonnet on the Winnipeg River, is incomplete. Reminiscences written in the 1830s, however, help to fill the gaps, recounting some of the best-remembered occurrences of those years.

The 1805-06 journal, running from late August to early March, gives a good overview of seasonal activities and interactions with Ojibwa of the Lac du Bonnet area. Nelson once again became a kinsman of the Indians; his reminiscences note that sometime before November 1805, "The Red Breast a very good and sensible man, had adopted me as his Son." On various occasions, Nelson visited both Red Breast and his brother ("uncle" to the young trader) in their lodges. In all, thirteen Indians and their families were named at one time or another as having trade ties with Lac du Bonnet in 1805-06 (Brown and Brightman 1988:11).

Nelson moved to the western Lake Winnipeg area in the fall of 1807 and remained there until 1812, developing some close personal acquaintance with the natives. His move was linked with increasing North West Company efforts in that region. As of 1805-06, six NWC posts ringed the Lake Winnipeg basin: at Cross Lake to the north, Pike (Head) River (also known as Jack Head or Tête au Brochet) on the west shore, and Lake Folle Avoine (Rice Lake), Pigeon River, and Broken River on the east side, all subordinate to Bas de la Rivière (Fort Alexander) at the mouth of the Winnipeg River (Nelson 1805-06:

8 January 1806; Lytwyn 1986:fig. 20). The Nor'Westers placed their posts
well; HBC man William Brown admitted in 1820 that they had been "settled with
much more judgement than ours, in regard to the Indians hunting grounds,"
thanks to the Nor'Westers' greater experience in the area (HBCA B. 122/e/1,
fo. 10). Nelson's new post lay just west and north of Jack Head on the River
Dauphine (sometimes called the Little Saskatchewan), the waterway to the Fort
Dauphine area and the outlet for Lake St. Martin and other Lakes to the
southwest.

Nelson's voyage to this place was marked by near disaster, and by the
founding of a new and valued Indian tie. On 13 September 1807, while
encamped at Tête au Chien, Lake Winnipeg, he was severely burned by the
explosion of a keg of gunpowder. Immediate immersion in cold water and
subsequent treatments with native remedies made from swamp tea and larch pine
(tamarack) aided his recovery, as, perhaps, did the advice of Ayagon, the
local Ojibwa leader in whose area Nelson was to be stationed. Ayagon urged
Nelson to take a purgative to help remove the smoke particles and poisons
from his system, and impressed the young clerk at the time by his "sound
rational remarks" (1825 ff.:194).

As a man of some seniority and influence both among his countrymen and
in the fur trade, Ayagon became an important figure during Nelson's years on
the west side of Lake Winnipeg. Although sometimes difficult to deal with,
he became a surrogate father (e.g., Nelson's journal of 2 August 1810) and a
friend. Nelson appreciated in him the distinctive qualities of northern
Algonquian leadership patterns:

> He would only speak when there was occasion, but always to
> the purpose and expressed his ideas with ease and fluency;
> and when he had occasion to use his authority, which, by the
> by, was very limited out of his family he would do so in such
> a manner as to convince all of what he was able...yet without
> giving offense (Brown 1984:226).

SAUTEUX, MASHKIEGONS, AND OTHERS

Although analysis of Nelson's Manitoba journals and reminiscences is not
yet completed, his data on these years, combined with HBC archival materials,
is beginning to provide a good view of fur trade and native life around
central Lake Winnipeg in the period before 1820. For the years 1807-11,
during which Nelson was almost constantly in charge of his post either at
River Dauphine or at Jack Head and was keeping good records, considerable
details on Indian interactional patterns may be gleaned from the journals.
In 1807-08, most contact was with the Sauteux Ayagon and two associates
closely connected by marriage—Cu-fessé, Ayagon's father-in-law, and
La Bezette, who was married to another daughter of Cu-fessé. These three
Sauteux and their families formed the core of Nelson's identifiable Sauteux
trade ties throughout the four years in question, augmented only by Tête
Grise, the father of another wife of Ayagon, in the 1808-09 season, and by
Cou-fort, the son of a Lac la Pluie Sauteux, in the years 1808-10.

Despite the smallness of his visible following, Ayagon was evidently a force to be reckoned with in the trade of central Lake Winnipeg, that area being so sparsely populated (one native inhabitant or less per 25 square miles, according to Peter Fidler in 1820--HBCA B. 51/e/1, fos, 3, 16). His affection or disaffection was a matter of concern to Nelson and also to his bourgeois and fellow Nor'Wester, Duncan Cameron, who took pains to show him high regard whenever they met. Ayagon's North West Company attachment persisted for several years after Nelson left the region. Peter Fidler, in his Manitoba District report for the HBC in 1820, recorded that "Iahcoo," although a brother to a chief named Blue Coat who was an HBC ally, "generally trades with the Nor West Company--and resides in general about the Partridge Cross and the vicinity [upper River Dauphine] he is a good fur hunter quiet but a confounded beggar--he is generally clothed every year gratis by the NW Company and has about six or eight followers." He was, Fidler added, "the most staunch Indian the NW have" (HBCA B. 51/e/1, fos. 16, 19).

Nelson's first Mashkiegon contacts occurred in 1807-08, when two men known as Old Brochet and Cu-levé appeared on the scene at River Dauphine. The next year, they were joined by five of their countrymen and families from what Nelson called the north side of the lake, evidently the northeastern quarter (1825 ff.:228). Belly (Le Ventre), Le Gendre (son-in-law to a Canadian named Lorrin), Nez Corbin and one of his sons, and Petites Couilles (some of these French names probably reflect both Indian and Canadian French broad humor) and established themselves as regular traders at Nelson's post through 1810-11. Several other natives who seemed affiliated with them yet were not explicitly classed as Mashkiegon also began to appear on the scene at this time; I shall return to them later.

Numerically, the Mashkiegons surely came to match or at times surpassed Ayagon's little band. But politically and economically they appeared to play a lesser role, for in that area and to the south, the Sauteux had the upper hand. Nelson's writings attest the often close ties of the Sauteux bands to the Nor'Westers, and HBC man Peter Fidler, who had many years' knowledge of the region, recorded that numbers of the Lake Winnipeg Sauteux owed their contemporary residency patterns to the Nor'Westers, having been led in their trade with that company to move westward from western Lake Superior and Rainy Lake beginning in the late 1790s (HBCA B. 51/e/1, fo. 16). As the Nor'Westers' longterm associates, they maintained a certain precedence with them, despite the Mashkiegons' sometimes greater trade productivity and cooperativeness.

The Sauteux also had access to more varied resources for subsistence and for the trade. They carried on maple sugaring in the region just south of Nelson's post, and they also harvested some wild rice there in favourable seasons, (ibid., fos. 4, 5, 10). Some distinguished themselves over the other natives for their knowledge of cures and medicinal plants; as seen earlier, Ayagon impressed Nelson with his capacities in that line on their first meeting in 1807. Peter Fidler noted that "a select few" of them knew the virtues of "a great variety of different medicinal roots." Having "the reputation amongst their neighbours to be the most skilled in the healing art," they were well paid for their advice and prescriptions, thereby holding considerable influence (ibid., fos. 5, 17).

The central and southern Lake Winnipeg Saulteaux also appeared to have a more heightened pride and sense of their own political identity than the Mashkiegons. The documentary sources of the time and region do not appear to raise questions about who the Saulteaux were as a group, whereas they do raise them, directly and indirectly, about the Mashkiegons and others who arrived from the northeast. Nelson never called the Mashkiegons Crees, but simply noted, "they were called Mashkiegons, from the word mash-kieg, signifying a Swamp. Their language nearer the Cris than the Sauteux" (1825 ff.:228).

During 1808-11, the period of their best documented trade with Nelson, the Mashkiegons also had some links with other natives whom Nelson did not label by that term or any other. Gagnon (perhaps Métis), Mangeekiejeck, Morpion and his sons, Muffle d'Orignialle and his sons, Old Nanjobe, and Tête de Loup-cervier probably also came from the northeastern shores of Lake Winnipeg. Each of these traded with Nelson for at least two of the seasons between 1808 and 1811, while a few others of their compatriots turned up for occasional visits.

Contemporary HBC writers shared Nelson's hesitancy to lump these people together as one homogeneous group. The 1815 HBC "Report on the Eastern Coast of Lake Winnipeg" stated that in this area the "Southward or Knisteneaux Indians" consisted of four principal tribes who had tended to move across Lake Winnipeg in its very narrow central portions. These were the Pelicans who were the most numerous and widely scattered, the Moose, the Suckers, and the Kingfishers (HBCA B. 16/e/1, fo. 6). Peter Fidler in 1820 described some of them more bluntly. "There are," he wrote, "a small Band of Indians a bastard Crees who generally reside on the Borders of Lake Winnipeg about the Jack head and the Fisher rivers...sometimes these Indians winter on the East side of the Lake about Berens and Pidgeon rivers (HBCA B. 51/e/1, fo. 18). There was, then, no clear European consensus on their identity, a fact that helps to justify the emphasis that Edward and Mary Black Rogers have placed on the region east of Lake Winnipeg as the home of a variety of locally separable rather than tribal (Cree or Ojibwa) groups.

In their personalities as in their political ways, these visitors varied from the Sauteux. George Nelson in his reminiscences of his Mashkiegon and non-Sauteux native associates offered a descriptive portrait of how their character and behaviour compared to that of Ayagon and his band, and of relations between the two groups. The former, he observed, were "a very peaceable and harmless set, extremely hospitable, social and gay, always singing, dancing, laughing and playing. They are so light hearted that in their greatest distresses and Starvation they cannot, it would seem, refrain from 'cracking their jokes' on each other. Of course they were good natured, and always wished to please, and very seldom offended or wronged, maliciously." Nelson was nervous about how the Sauteux would behave with them, for, as he recorded, "My old indians, the Sauteux had a contempt for them because they were too frivolous, and 'had never faced an enemy.' Yet they treated them kindly, carefully avoiding every word or gesture that might convey even a hint of disparagement. Still, the grave and solemn silence or taciturnity, yet quick penetrating eye and dignified demeanor of the Sauteux's, were of themselves sufficient to mortify these good people. I was afraid of a clashing, and warned the Sauteux's how much I should be

ADULT MEN TRADING WITH GEORGE NELSON 1807-11,
RIVER DAUPHINE AND JACK HEAD, LAKE WINNIPEG

(Source: Nelson 1807-11)

Sauteux

	1807-08	1808-09	1809-10	1810-11
Ayagon (Cu-fessé's and Tête Grise's son-in-law)	x	x	x	x
La Bezette (Cu-fessé's son-in-law)	x	x	x	x
Cou-fort (son of Bras Court, an Indian at Lac la Pluie)		x	x	
Cu-fessé (Ayagon's and La Bezette's father-in-law)	x	x	x	x
Tête Grise (Ayagon's father-in-law)		x		

Mashkiegons

	1807-08	1808-09	1809-10	1810-11
Belly (Le Ventre)		x	x	x
Le Beson (Nez Corbin's son) (twin) (same as Kiewaykoakow, also N.C.'s son?)		x	x	x
Old Brochet	x	x	x	x
Cu-levé	x	x	x	x
Le Gendre (Lorrin's son-in-law)		x	x	x
Nez Corbin (father of Le Beson [Kiewaykoakow?])		x	x	x
Petites Couilles		x	x	x

Affiliations Mashkiegon or Unspecified

	1807-08	1808-09	1809-10	1810-11
Gagnon (Métis?)				
Mangee Kiejeck		x	x	x
Morpion (Weaga) and sons			x	x
Muffle d'Orignialle and sons	x		x	x
Old Nanjobe		x		x
Tête de Loup-cervier		x	x	

displeased if they attempted to insult them. 'Man-nay-nag in-nung-gay 'replied they, i.e., 'surely we will not be so indiscreet'--showing in that single expression how much they thought of themselves" (1825 ff.:228).

NELSON'S CAREER, PERSPECTIVES, AND WRITINGS: SOME COMPARISONS

The Nelson journals and reminiscences will yield much further information on a variety of topics relating to the Indians, the fur trade, and native-white interactions of early-nineteenth-century Lake Winnipeg; this paper serves simply to introduce some facets of their content and contributions. I would like to conclude with some comments on Nelson himself, placing him in juxtaposition to certain other fur-trader-writers of the early 1800s who already have the high regard of ethnohistorians.

In his character, perceptions, relations with the natives, and ultimate fate as a retired trader, Nelson compares perhaps most closely with the explorer David Thompson (first a Hudson's Bay man and later a Nor'Wester) and old Hudson's Bay surveyor Peter Fidler whose Manitoba district reports so usefully complement Nelson's Lake Winnipeg journals. All three were of English origins. All used their considerable literacy to great advantage, recording far more about the fur trade country and its inhabitants than their employers required, and clearly finding such an enterprise personally rewarding (none of the three was to find it financially so). None attained membership in the increasingly Scottish-dominated elite circles of their firms, or recognition of their services and accomplishments in their lifetimes. Nor'Westers Thompson and Nelson retired in 1812 and 1823 respectively to live out many penurious years in eastern Canada (Thompson died there in 1857; Nelson in 1859). Fidler and Nelson were both victims of the HBC/NWC coalition of 1821. Fidler, after making pleas to remain in the new concern, died in 1822. Nelson, after serving out the coalition year at Cumberland House and the 1822-23 season at Lac la Ronge, found himself abruptly declared redundant; his last appearance in the company books is with the statement, "Good Clerk and Trader no place for him" (Brown and Brightman 1988:20).

All three men, perhaps in part since they lacked congenial lasting ties with most of their company superiors, seemed to enjoy or even prefer the companionship of native trading associates--Thompson with Saukamappee and Nelson with Ayagon, for example. But their native ties went still deeper than these friendships. All had large families by native women to whom they were permanently attached. Thompson married the half-Cree Charlotte Small "according to the custom of the country" in the 1790s, and later in the St. Gabriel Street Presbyterian Church in Montreal in 1812--a step almost universally shunned by other British Nor'Westers with native families. (Those who belonged to that church would baptize native children there but the mothers were usually absent, unnamed, and unwed by Christian rite--Brown 1982). Peter Fidler married an Indian named Mary according to fur trade custom and later by Anglican rite at Norway House (Manitoba) on 14 August 1821, and kept a detailed record of the birth times, dates and places of their fourteen children, born between 1795 and 1820 (Brown 1980: pl. 15).

Nelson in 1808 married Mary Ann of the Ojibwa Loon clan from the north shore of Lake Superior; she was the cousin of the Indian wife of Duncan Cameron, Nelson's bourgeois at the time. Nelson brought her and their family to Sorel, Lower Canada. Their eight children were baptized there, and he and Mary Ann were married in the Sorel Anglican church in 1825. The family was beset by tragedy; by late 1831 Mary Ann and all her children except for one daughter had died (Brown 1984). Nelson, depressed and economically troubled in his later years, seemed to find his greatest pleasure in setting down his recollections of his fur trade days.

It is no accident, then, that Nelson, Fidler, and Thompson should have produced some of the most detailed, voluminous, and most importantly, perspective and sympathetic, documentation of the native inhabitants of the Canadian northwest, for they all became, more than most trader Europeans, closely affiliated with and respectful of native people as their kin, friends, and often, teachers. In part because Nelson made no great journeys of exploration and left no great maps or scientific surveys, his contributions have been slower than Thompson's or Fidler's to gain attention. But in their quieter way, these texts as a group are comparable in their value to the best efforts of any contemporary fur trade writer, and they will prove to be worthy companions to those of Thompson and Fidler.

REFERENCES

Bardon, Richard, and Grace Lee Nute
    1947   A Winter in the St. Croix Valley, 1802-1803. <u>Minnesota History</u>
                28:1-14, 142-59, 225-40.

Bishop, Charles A.
    1981   Territorial Groups before 1821: Cree and Ojibwa. Handbook of
                North <u>American Indians</u>; Vol. 6, <u>Subarctic</u>, edited by June Helm,
                158-68. Washington, D.C.: Smithsonian Institution.

Brown, Jennifer S.H.
    1980   <u>Strangers in Blood: Fur Trade Company Families in Indian</u>
                <u>Country</u>. Vancouver: University of British Columbia Press.

    1982   Children of the Early Fur Trades. <u>Childhood and Family in</u>
                <u>Canadian History</u>, edited by Joy Parr, 44-68. Toronto:
                McClelland and Stewart.

    1984   "Man in his Natural State": The Indian Worlds of George
                Nelson. <u>Rendez vous: Selected Papers of the Fourth North</u>
                <u>American Fur Trade Conference, 1981</u>, edited by Thomas C.
                Buckley. St. Paul: North American Fur Trade Conference.

Brown, Jennifer S.H., and Robert Brightman
    1988   "The Orders of the Dreamed": George Nelson on Cree and Northern
                Ojibwa Religion and Myth, 1823. Winnipeg: University of
                Manitoba Press/St. Paul: Minnesota Historical Society Press.

Honigmann, John J.
    1981   West Main Cree. <u>Handbook of North American Indians</u>, Vol. 6,
                <u>Subarctic</u>, edited by June Helm, 217-30. Washington, D.C.:
                Smithsonian Institution.

Hudson's Bay Company Archives, Provincial Archives of Manitoba
B.16/e/1.   Report on the Eastern Coast of Lake Winnipeg.

B.51/e/1.   General Report of the Manitoba District for 1820, Peter Fidler.

B.122/e/1.   Report of the Manitoba District 1818 and 1819, William Brown.

Lytwyn, Victor P.
1986   The Fur Trade of the Little North: Indians, Pedlars, and
         Englishmen East of Lake Winnipeg, 1760-1821. Winnipeg:
         Rupert's Land Research Centre, University of Winnipeg.

Nelson, George
1805-06 Lac du Bon[n]et Journal. Nelson Papers, Metropolitan Public
         Library of Toronto.

1807-11 Lake Winnipeg Journals (Tête au Brochet, River Dauphine). Ibid.

1825-ff Reminiscences. Nelson Papers, Metropolitan Public Library of
         Toronto.

Steinbring, Jack H.
1981   Saulteaux of Lake Winnipeg. Handbook of North American Indians,
         Vol. 6, Subarctic, edited by June Helm, 244-55. Washington,
         D.C.: Smithsonian Institution.

Van Kirk, Sylvia, and Jennifer S.H. Brown
1985   George Nelson. Dictionary of Canadian Biography 8:652-54.
         Toronto: University of Toronto Press.

"THE GREAT MART OF ALL THIS COUNTRY":
Lewis and Clark and Western Trade Networks

by

James P. Ronda

ABSTRACT

When the Lewis and Clark Expedition (1804-1806) ventured into the trans-Mississippi West, it was the first exploring party funded by the United States. As planned by President Thomas Jefferson, the expedition had a complex set of duties ranging from botany to diplomacy. Central to the enterprise was trade with native people. Jefferson's vision of the West was a commercial one and Lewis and Clark were instructed to lure Indians away from Anglo-Canadian traders and into the grasp of St. Louis merchants. Directed by the president, Lewis and Clark became students of native exchange systems. Although the explorers consistently imposed their Euro-American values on Indian economies, the descriptions of the Middle Missouri and Pacific-Plateau systems were remarkably accurate. Expedition journals are filled with notes about trade routes, merchant fairs, and desirable merchandise. That information provides vital clues for the understanding of reciprocal trade arrangements that brought native people together to barter, sing, and court.

'THE GREAT MART OF ALL THIS COUNTRY':
LEWIS AND CLARK AND WESTERN TRADE NETWORKS

James P. Ronda

On a miserable, rainy morning in late May, 1806 a small detachment from
the Lewis and Clark expedition made its way to the junction of the Salmon and
Snake Rivers in present-day Idaho. Sergeant John Ordway and his men were in
search of fish for hungry explorers camped back along the Clearwater River.
At one of the many Nez Perce fishing stations that dotted the Salmon, Robert
Frazer - a private in Ordway's party - encountered a Nez Perce woman. The
two soon struck up a trade bargain. Frazer offered an old broken razor in
return for two Spanish mill dollars.[1] Although Ordway and Frazer did not
realize it at the time, they had stumbled upon a clue to part of a vast trade
system that stretched from the Middle Missouri to Pacific margins and far
into the Southwest. But it was not the first time that the Corps of
Discovery had seen such traces. Among the Mandans and Hidatsas there were
North West Company trade guns, fancy leather clothing of Cheyenne
manufacture, and mules sporting Spanish brands. When the expedition crossed
the Great Divide and spent time with Lemhi Shoshonis, those Indians proudly
displayed Spanish riding tack. Along the Columbia, especially at The Dalles,
Lewis and Clark saw mountains of dried salmon and heaps of goods ready for
exchange. And there was one last clue. Early in May, 1806 the expedition
stopped briefly at a Nez Perce village along the Potlach River. There in the
growing darkness several Nez Perce men were busy gambling for buffalo robes
and weapons. At second look those weapons proved to be war axes made by the
explorers themselves as trade items during the 1804-1805 winter at Fort
Mandan.[2] Like the Spanish dollars, those axes had travelled far and passed
through many hands. What all those traces and clues reveal is a set of
exchange networks first fully described in the records of the Lewis and Clark
expedition.

The exploring venture created by Thomas Jefferson and commanded by
Captains Meriwether Lewis and William Clark did not have ethnography as its
primary mission. Uncovering the web of personal and trade relations that
bound Arikara farmers, Teton Sioux hunters, and Cheyenne leather tailors to
the lives of Columbia fishers and canny Chinook traders did not have highest
priority for the Corps of Discovery. Yet, piecing together and understanding
such systems was not far from Jefferson's mind. If the expedition's primary
task was to locate "the direct water communication from sea to sea," then the
creation of a commercial empire to rival that being forged by Hudson's Bay
Company and North West Company agents was equally important.[3] An American
trade empire, anchored at St. Louis and reaching up the Missouri and toward
the Rocky Mountains, depended on making connections with native systems
already in operation. Jefferson's vision, more commercial than colonial,
demanded at least a rudimentary understanding of Indian trade networks.

Lewis and Clark encountered their first western trade network during the summer of 1804. Struggling up the Missouri, the explorers began to see both the material and political consequences of the Middle Missouri system. The character of that system became plain when the Corps of Discovery spent several tension-filled days with the Brulé Teton Sioux opposite what is now Pierre, South Dakota. The Brulés and their village farmer neighbours the Arikaras were at the heart of the lower focus in the Middle Missouri system. As Lewis and Clark gradually learned, Tetons of the Brulé, Oglala, and Miniconjou bands travelled each year to a trade fair known as the Dakota Rendezvous, held on the James River in east central South Dakota. There they met Sisseton and Yankton Sioux who had obtained manufactured goods from North West Company posts on the Des Moines and St. Peters (Minnesota) Rivers. The Tetons used those goods and buffalo robes in their agricultural trade with Arikara farmers. With Teton population growing, a secure food supply was essential. So long as the Tetons could control the flow of goods to the earth lodge village people, the Sioux position would be reasonably strong. But if the villagers gained easy direct access to St. Louis traders, the Teton role as brokers and middlemen would be lost. Demographic and commercial considerations required the Tetons to at most blockade the Missouri River or at least exact considerable tribute from traders coming up river. The well-armed Lewis and Clark expedition, representing St. Louis interests and determined to make direct contact with Arikara, Mandan, and Hidatsa villages, was an intrusion that could not be ignored. And for several anxious September days Lewis and Clark engaged in some nasty thrust and parry with Brulé headmen the likes of Black Buffalo, the Partisan, and Buffalo Medicine.[4]

Lewis and Clark left their Teton confrontation convinced that American policy needed to forge a military, political, and economic alliance of village farmers against the predatory nomads. Labouring under a woefully inadequate notion of the Middle Missouri system, the diplomats in buckskin had already picked villains and victims. The Tetons were cast as "the vilest miscreants of the savage race, the pirates of the Missouri" while village farmers were depicted as innocent sufferers under Sioux colonial oppression.[5] Such were the myths. As Lewis and Clark edged toward the Grand River Arikara villages they were about to face reality. Reality was a complex set of trade relations blending equal measures of cooperation, exchange, and intimidation.

From St. Louis sources it was known that the Arikara farmers were an integral part of the Middle Missouri system. The three earth lodge Arikara villages provided the southern focal point for the system while the Mandan and Hidatsa towns on the Knife River served as the upper exchange center. The villagers supplied the agricultural needs of the nomads. Lewis and Clark aptly described the Arikara role by calling them the "gardners for the Soues."[6] Arikara gardeners grew corn, raised horses, and processed hides in return for a wide variety of merchandise and foodstuffs brought by their western and southwestern customers. William Clark noted that those patrons included Arapahoes, Comanches, Kiowas, and Osages. But the most important Arikara customers were Sioux and Cheyennes.[7]

Trapped by their own political and economic preconceptions, Lewis and
Clark never understood that the often-troubled relationship between Arikaras
and Tetons was an uneasy symbiosis. From a Teton perspective, some sort of
control had to be maintained over the Arikaras. Teton expansion beyond the
Missouri was fuelled by Arikara corn and horses. Each August Tetons flocked
to the Arikara towns bringing meat, fat, and hides from the Plains and metal
goods from the Dakota Rendezvous. Lewis and Clark, like other non-Indian
observers, misinterpreted the character of those late summer transactions.
Already disposed to portray the Tetons as "that lawless, savage, and
rapacious race," the explorers viewed the relationship as naked
exploitation. Clark believed that this economic link meant Teton political
domination of the Arikaras. As he explained it, the Tetons maintained "great
influence over the Rickeres, poison their minds and keep them in perpetial
dread."[8] In both their written records and diplomatic behaviour, Lewis and
Clark argued that a disruption of the Arikara-Sioux alliance would free
village farmers from tyranny and might even wean Tetons away from John Bull
and into the ledgers of Uncle Sam.

But this harsh view of the trade system and its politics was not shared
by the Arikaras themselves. They saw many benefits in the Teton connection
not quickly evident to outsiders. Those advantages included a predictable
source of manufactured goods, especially guns, and a reliable market for corn
and horses. Lewis and Clark, conditioned by an economic system that stressed
intense competition, tended to overestimate the violence and intimidation
present in Arikara-Sioux dealings. There was, in fact, far more cooperation
in times of war and friendship in times of peace. Much of the hostility the
Corps of Discovery encountered between Arikaras and Mandans stemmed from
raids carried out by joint Arikara-Sioux war parties against the Knife River
villagers. The Arikaras knew well the military power of the Tetons but they
were equally aware how important their corn was to Sioux survival. Missouri
River trader and explorer Jean Baptiste Truteau was closer to the mark when
he wrote in 1795 that "the Ricaras and this Sioux nation live together
peacefully. The former receive them in order to obtain guns, clothes, hats,
kettles, etc. which are given them in exchange for their horses."[9]

If the explorers and the Arikaras had very different perceptions of the
Tetons, both agreed that Cheyennes were far more acceptable and less
troublesome customers. The Cheyennes, who had abandoned woodland ways to
become a Plains people, depended heavily on the Middle Missouri trade system
for foodstuffs and tobacco. Each summer many Cheyennes journeyed to the
Arikara villages to trade and renew old friendships. Some advance parties
came in mid-June while larger groups arrived later in July. Lewis and Clark
found that some Cheyennes lingered well into the fall and a handful lived
year round in Arikara and Mandan households. Cheyenne traders brought a
variety of meat products as well as exquisite skin clothing made by their
women. Arikaras especially valued "shirts of antelope skin, ornamented and
worked with different coloured quills of the porcupine." Much of what the
Cheyennes offered might be classed as luxury goods but there was one
commodity that Arikaras were very anxious to possess. Cheyenne horses and an
occasional Spanish mule were essential to fill out herds in preparation for
the Sioux trading days. The Arikaras were so desperate for horses that they
were willing to trade precious guns, powder, and shot for them. During the
Lewis and Clark era the exchange rate was one gun, one hundred rounds of

ammunition, and a knife for a single horse. The result of this trade, however, was that Sioux-Cheyenne relations were often tense. Tetons resented seeing Arikara corn in Cheyenne mouths and English trade guns in Cheyenne hands.[10]

Because they arrived in October, Lewis and Clark did not see the festive trading days of August and September. Some fifteen to sixteen hundred people thronged to the fair, described by Pierre Antoine Tabeau as "this great gathering of different nations." While there was always the threat of violence, especially between the competitive Sioux and Cheyennes, the trading days were occasions to make bargains, visit old friends, and learn a new song or story. "Times are lively," recalled American Fur Company trader Edwin Denig, "Feasting and dancing goes on constantly, both in the village and camp—horse racing, gambling in many ways. Bucks and belles dressed in their best and tricked out in all the gaudy colours of cloth, paints, and porcupine quills may be seen mingled in the dance or exchanging their professions of love in more solitary places. The old men smoke and eat without intermission. The middle aged exchange horses and other property. The soldiers gamble. And the young warriors spend both day and night in attempts at seduction of the young women in both camps. Strange scenes are witnessed here, much that would be interesting, much more that would be indescribable."[11]

Lewis and Clark never took part in those indescribable scenes but they could not escape the Middle Missouri system. Wintering at the Mandan and Hidatsa towns, the expedition was surrounded by an Indian world conditioned by that network. The five traditional Mandan and Hidatsa towns have been aptly described as "the central market place of the Northern Plains" and "the keystone of the upper Missouri region."[12] The towns were a great Missouri River country store. What was transacted at this crossroads of goods and cultures touched the lives of people far from central North Dakota and in turn conditioned Mandan and Hidatsa relations with all outsiders. At that market one could find horses and mules brought by Cheyennes destined for Assiniboin herds, fancy Cheyenne leather clothing for Mandan dandies, English trade guns and ammunition, and the ever-present baskets of corn, beans, squash, and tobacco. The Mandans and Hidatsas served as brokers in an international economic and cultural network that faced in three directions and stretched over thousands of miles.

Like their Arikara neighbours, Mandans and Hidatsas shared an important western connection with Cheyennes, Crows, and Arapahoes. These Plains people brought a variety of meat products as well as luxury leather goods. But in the eyes of all villagers, the most valuable commodity brought from the West and Southwest were horses and mules. Just as the Arikaras sought those animals to supply Sioux needs, so did Mandan and Hidatsa traders bargain for horses to satisfy the requirements of their Assiniboin and Cree customers. Reaching to the Southeast, the Knife River brokers also did some trading with Tetons. However, the close trade ties between Tetons and Arikaras and the frequent raids that alliance launched against Mandan and Hidatsa towns made the Sioux connection somewhat chancy.

Because Teton intermedaries could not be relied on the bring European goods to the Knife River villages as they did to the Grand River towns, Mandans and Hidatsas had to find another and more reliable source of supply. The third face of the Mandan-Hidatsa system looked north to Crees and Assiniboins. Long before Lewis and Clark, these Indians had been carrying French and English goods to the Missouri in exchange for produce, tobacco, and horses. When La Vérendrye visited the Mandans on the Heart River in 1738, he saw the trade in full swing. The French explorer, impressed with Mandan business skill, wrote that the villagers "knew well how to profit by it in selling their grains, tobacco, skins, and coloured plumes which they knew the Assiniboins prize highly." As testimony to the penetration of European goods on the northern Plains well before mid-century, La Vérendrye observed that the most sought-after merchandise brought by the Assiniboins were "guns, axes, kettles, powder, bullets, knives, [and] awls."[13]

Whenever Lewis and Clark analyzed an Indian trade system, they always thought in terms of the distribution of political power in that network and the possible future competition with American merchants. The explorers' understanding of the Middle Missouri system was based on the belief that the Teton Sioux needed to be weaned away from North West Company traders and brought into an emerging St. Louis system. Beyond that, Lewis and Clark were always eager to cast the Sioux as colonial masters exercising undue influence over innocent and vulnerable villagers. The message was simple. Teton power must be broken and honest villagers freed to participate in an American trade network.

Lewis and Clark attempted to impose the same simplistic model on the Mandan and Hidatsa trade with Assiniboins and Crees. Those northern middlemen provided manufactured goods from Canadian sources that might be instead supplied by American merchants. Knowing that there was often tension between the villagers and their northern trading partners, Lewis and Clark used such incidents as a pretext to lecture Mandan headmen on the reasons for abandoning Assiniboins and Crees in favour of Chouteaus and Lisas. What the captains did not understand was that the merchandise exchanged between the villagers and the northern peoples—food and horses—did not in the least interest Americans increasingly obsessed with peltry. Despite this, William Clark still told Mandans "you know yourselves that you are compelled to put up with little insults from the Christinoes [Crees] and Ossinaboins because if you go to war with those people, they will prevent the traders from the North from bringing you guns, powder, and ball and by that means distress you very much."[14] Clark was determined to cast Mandans and Hidatsas in the same role as the Arikaras with the new oppressors as Assiniboins and Crees. If the Sioux were the masters lower down the river, Lewis and Clark seemed prepared to brand Assiniboins as "great rogues" from the north.[15] As the explorers had misunderstood Arikara-Sioux relations, so they failed to appreciate both the ability of the villagers to cope with the northern nomads and the essential equality of the trade arrangement. Because he saw actual bargains made, La Vérendrye better understood the operation of the system. "The Mandans." he wrote, "are much more crafty than the Assiniboins in their commerce and in everything, and always dupe them."[16]

Throughout the summer of 1805 the Corps of Discovery travelled the river road across Montana and passed over the Continental Divide at Lemhi Pass. These lands were at the western margin of the Middle Missouri system. As Lewis and Clark struggled over the Lolo Trail in northern Idaho and met the Nez Perce Indians the explorers were now beyond buffalo and corn economics and edging into a Pacific-Plateau system.

On October 20, 1805 the expedition saw its first piece of European clothing--a "salors jacket"--on a Columbia River Indian. Even more European goods were in evidence when the explorers visited the upper Memaloose Islands. Located above present-day Dalles City and known as the "place of the departed," the islands contained many large burial vaults filled not only with human and equine remains but all sorts of trade goods of European manufacture. That those grave offerings were fully part of river daily life was verified when the explorers stopped at Indian camps and found "some articles which showed that white people had been here or not far distant." By the time Lewis and Clark were around the John Day River, non-Indian clothing and implements were everywhere.[17]

Sailors' overalls, brass bracelets, tea kettles, scarlet blankets, and salty phrases like "sun of a pitch" all pointed to the presence of a vast trade network centered at The Dalles of the Columbia. While Lewis and Clark did not know it in September, 1805, they were about to encounter that center and cross a fundamental cultural and linguistic boundary. Just as the Middle Missouri network and the people involved in it attracted expedition attention, so did the Pacific-Plateau system demand thoughtful consideration.

Taken on the broadest level, the Pacific-Plateau system as seen by Lewis and Clark involved exchanging huge quantities of dried salmon for other food and trade goods. What corn, squash, and buffalo were to the Missouri villagers, pounded fish was to the Wishram and Wasco merchants at The Dalles. Stretching from the Pacific coast to Nez Perce territories and linked to the Middle Missouri system by way of the Shoshoni Rendezvous and the journeys of Crow traders, the network joined Chinookan and Sahaptin-speaking peoples in an intricate set of personal and economic relations. Through the system flowed not only fish, wappato roots, buffalo robes, and European goods but also games, songs, rituals, and stories. Preserving the system served not only the needs of The Dalles middlemen but also their more distant Chinookan and Sahaptin trading partners.

Geography, in the form of a dramatic narrowing of the Columbia at The Dalles and the creation of ideal fishing stations, conspired with dry warm winds blowing up the gorge to make the Indian villages around the Long and Short Narrows a place William Clark properly described as "the great mart of trade."[18] Wishrams lived on the north bank at The Dalles; Wascos occupied sites on the south side of the Columbia. While Lewis and Clark knew that fishing and trading took place from Celilo Falls down to The Dalles, the most intense bargaining was focused at the main Wishram village of Nixluidix. That village, whose name meant "trading place," was located at the head of the Long Narrows. When Lewis and Clark visited the settlement on October 24, 1805 they found twenty large plank houses. Each house held three Wishram families. Asked by the explorers who they were, the Wishrams replied "i'tcxluit," meaning "I am Ita xluit." The phrase sounded like echeloot to American ears, hence expedition maps and journals always referred to the Wishrams as Echeloots.[19]

The towering stacks of dried salmon at Nixluidix, estimated by Clark at about 10,000 pounds, pointed up the vast quantities of goods exchanged in the Pacific-Plateau system. Trading took place from spring through fall with the most intense activity reserved for the fall season. It was during September and October that dried fish and roots were freshly prepared and in abundant supply. To The Dalles trade fair came nearby Sahaptins like the Yakimas and Teninos as well as more distant Umatillas, Walulas, and Nez Perces. Local Sahaptins making the trip carried food products including meat, roots, and berries. At the trading places Wishram middlemen exchanged those goods for dried salmon and European cloth and ironware. Distant Sahaptins, especially the Nez Perces who had access to the Plains, brought skin clothing, horses, and buffalo meat. Less interested in fish, Plateau Sahaptins were drawn to The Dalles in search of European goods, especially metal and beads.

Centered at The Dalles and with one arm stretching east, the Pacific-Plateau system also extended west down the Columbia to the coastal Chinookans. Those Pacific peoples brought to the trade system a variety of European goods obtained in the maritime fur trade as well as indigenous crops. Among the manufactured objects carried by lower Chinookans and eagerly sought by Dalles merchants were guns, blankets, clothing, and the prized blue beads. Coming upriver in their graceful shovel-nose canoes, the lower Chinookans also carried wappato roots to be pounded and made into a bread that even the explorers found tasty. Once at The Dalles, lower Chinookans obtained dried salmon, buffalo meat, and valuable bear grass used in making cooking baskets and the distinctive Northwest coast hats.[20]

While Lewis and Clark observed and recorded much about the Pacific-Plateau network and the kinds of goods that passed around the system, they arrived too late in the season to witness the full flavour of a Dalles rendezvous. Although the smell of dead fish still hung in the air and clouds of fleas hovered everywhere, the real trading days were over by mid-October. The explorers grasped something of the economic significance of The Dalles because they could see physical signs of the trade. What they did not understand were the cultural and political aspects of the fair. The Astorian Alexander Ross, who had extensive Columbia River experience just after Lewis and Clark, caught the personal side of Dalles trading before it was swept away by the great fur companies. Ross estimated that at peak trading times some three thousand Indians gathered at the villages for bargaining. But Ross also knew that the trading days involved more than acts of object exchange. Here Indians met old friends, made new ones, and heard the latest news. Gambling with the hand game, socializing, and sporting for the opposite sex were all essential features of The Dalles fair. "The Long Narrows," Ross put it simply, "is the great emporium or mart of the Columbia and the general theatre of gambling and roguery."[21]

What escaped the analysis of Lewis and Clark as well as later outsiders was the political significance of upper Chinookan control at The Dalles. In the Middle Missouri system it was essential for Tetons to dominate both the flow of goods up the river and access to crops produced by village farmers.

While Lewis and Clark consistently misconstrued the nature of the
relationship between nomads and villagers, they at least sensed that trade
and politics were allied along the Missouri. The captains were much less
aware of the balance of power down the Columbia. Upper Chinookans such as
the Skilloots did not have the military power possessed by Teton bands, but
they were willing to resort to force in order to protect their place as
middlemen in the trade. Just how far Indians from The Dalles to the Cascades
would go to defend the network was revealed in 1812 and 1814 when fur traders
Robert Stuart, Alexander Stuart, and James Keith fought pitched battles with
river Indians for passage on the Columbia. While Lewis and Clark never drew
such a violent response from river folks, it is worth recalling that the only
real trouble the expedition had on the river was with the Skilloots, a people
very jealous of their trading role.[22]

At Fort Clatsop as at Fort Mandan, ethnography was never an end in
itself but always intented for the service of government policy and
commercial expansion. When Jefferson instructed Lewis to learn about the
"ordinary occupations" of native people, he had in mind the ways that Indian
economic patterns might fit in an American trade system. Knowing that an
essential part of their mission was to lay the foundations for future
"commercial intercourse," the explorers continued to pay special attention to
Indian trade routes and the kinds of goods that passed along them. By the
time Lewis and Clark reached the Pacific, they were reasonably experienced in
analyzing trade networks and their potential for the eager merchants of St.
Louis. Had Lewis and Clark been further north, they might have had a closer
look at the maritime fur trade. However, their location on the Netul River
south of the Columbia did provide a good place to watch a stream of brass tea
kettles, blue beads, wappato roots, and pelts pass around a circle of Indian
and white hands.

Despite the fact that more than one hundred ships of United States
registry were engaged in the Northwest coast fur trade operations between
1788 and 1803, Meriwether Lewis evidently knew very little about either the
organization or the schedule of that trade. When Lewis gathered his notes
and began writing about coastal trade, he did not know whether traders who
visited the Columbia came from Nootka Sound or made the river their first
stop on voyages direct from England or the United States. Lewis was equally
unsure about the possible presence of a trading post somewhere on the Pacific
coast south of the Columbia. Strangely enough, the explorer did not even
appear aware of the role of Hawaii as an important re-supply point, although
he speculated that "some island in the Pacific ocean" was perhaps being used
in the trade. From lower Chinookans Lewis learned that traders came to the
Columbia in April, anchored in Bakers Bay, and stayed some six or seven
months. More important, he was able to discover what sorts of goods native
people were anxious to obtain. Those goods ranged from high quality two and
three point blankets and coarse cloth to sheet copper and brassware. Also in
demand were knives, fish hooks, pots, kettles, and guns. Chinookans enjoyed
sporting European fashions, making cast-off sailors clothing an important
item for exchange. Of course there was always a market for blue beads, known
in the Chinook trade jargon as tyee-kamosuk or "chief beads." In return, the
maritime traders obtained dressed and undressed elk skins, sea otter and
beaver pelts, and so Lewis thought, dried salmon. Lewis knew that vast
quantities of pounded fish came down from The Dalles market but he frankly

could not understand why white traders wanted it. Only later did he discover that he had misinterpreted Indian information. The salmon was not meant for the sailors but was part of a large domestic trade system of which the tall ships were only a small part.[23]

That extensive coastal trade network also got expedition attention. Lewis already knew about the role of The Dalles as "the great mart for all the country." After further investigation he better understood the flow of dried salmon and European goods up and down the river. Typical of the exchanges Lewis was able to trace involved a variety of products from blubber and whale oil to wappato roots and coloured beads. On one day in January, 1806 Lewis watched Cathlamet canoes loaded with upriver wappato destined for the Clatsop towns. At those towns the wappato would be traded for blubber and oil, items the Clatsops obtained from their southern neighbours the Tillamooks. Clatsops, rich in European trade goods, paid for the whale products with beads, clothing, and metal. "In this manner," explained Lewis, "is a trade continually carried on by the natives of the river each trading some article or other with their neighbors above and below them; and thus articles which are vended by the whites at the enterence of this river, find their way to the most distant nations enhabiting its waters."[24]

Despite political preconceptions and cultural confusions, Lewis and Clark made a major contribution to understanding western trade systems. In their journals and maps one finds a catalogue of the goods, services, and practices involved in the Middle Missouri and Pacific-Plateau systems. But the explorers knew that these networks meant more than the exchange of fish and buffalo for guns and tea kettles. Even though they often misinterpreted what they observed, Lewis and Clark did make the connection between trade and power. Recent studies of the balance of power on the Plains and along the Columbia are all based on evidence in the Lewis and Clark record. And finally it was as William Clark had said. Up the Missouri and down the Columbia the Corps of Discovery had seen and recorded "the great mart of all this Country."[25]

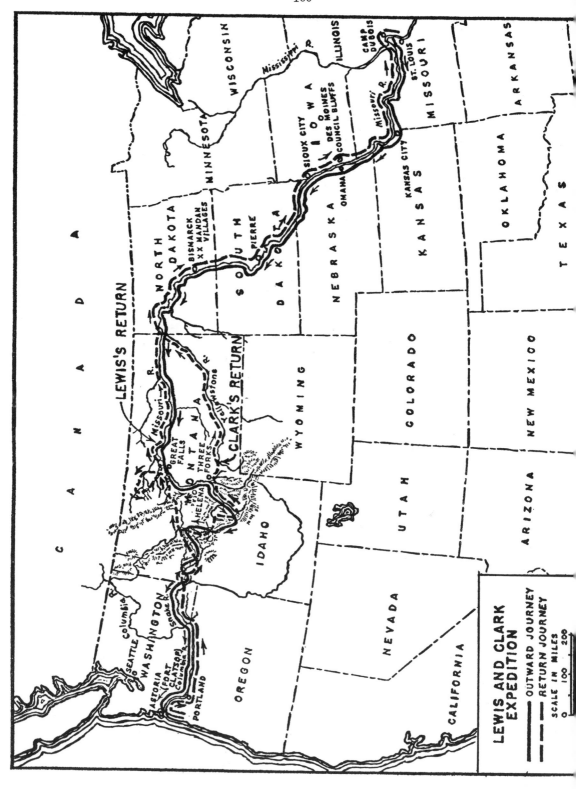

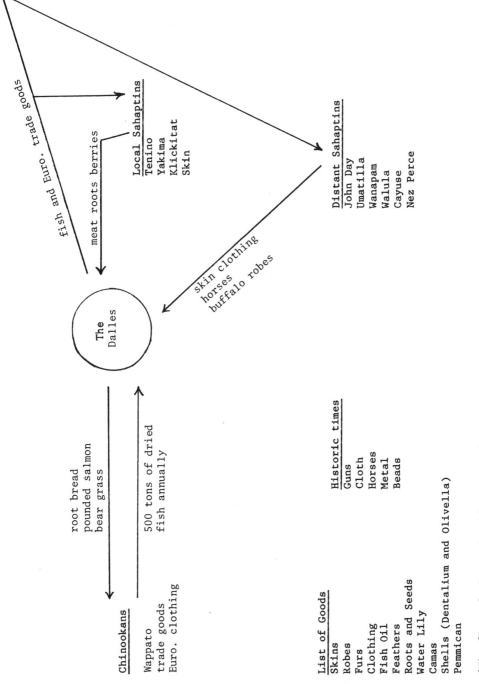

List of Goods
Skins
Robes
Furs
Clothing
Fish Oil
Feathers
Roots and Seeds
Water Lily
Camas
Shells (Dentalium and Olivella)
Pemmican

*The flow of slaves in this system is uncertain.

FOOTNOTES

1. Milo M. Quaife, ed., The Journals of Captain Meriwether Lewis and
   Sergeant John Ordway (Madison, 1916), p. 361; Patrick Gass, A Journal of
   the Voyages and Travels of a Corps of Discovery (Pittsburgh, 1807;
   reprint, Minneapolis, 1958), p. 267. See also James P. Ronda, "Frazer's
   Razor: The Ethnohistory of a Common Object," We Proceeded On, 7 (August
   1981):12-13.

2. Quaife, ed., Journals of Lewis and Ordway, p. 353.

3. Donald Jackson, ed., Letters of the Lewis and Clark Expedition with
   Related Documents, 1783-1854, 2 vols. Revised Ed. (Urbana, 1978), 1:137.

4. For a detailed treatment of the Teton confrontation see James P. Ronda,
   Lewis and Clark Among the Indians (Lincoln, Nebraska, 1984), ch. 2.

5. Jackson, ed., Letters, 1:178.

6. Reuben G. Thwaites, ed., The Original Journals of the Lewis and Clark
   Expedition, 1803-1806, 8 vols. (New York, 1904-05), 6:89.

7. Thwaites, ed., Original Journals, 1:190.

8. Thwaites, ed., Original Journals, 1:189. See also Annie H. Abel, ed.,
   Tabeau's Narrative of Loisel's Expedition to the Upper Missouri (Norman,
   1939), pp. 130-131.

9. Jean Baptiste Truteau, "Missouri River Journal," A. P. Nasatir, ed.,
   Before Lewis and Clark: Documents Illustrating the History of the
   Missouri, 1785-1804, 2 vols. (St. Louis, 1952), 1:310.

10. These aspects of the Middle Missouri system are analyzed in John C.
    Ewers, "The Indian Trade of the Upper Missouri before Lewis and Clark,"
    Bulletin of the Missouri Historical Society, 10 (1954):429-446;
    W. Raymond Wood, "Contrastive Features of Native North American Trade
    Systems," University of Oregon Anthropological Papers, 4 (1972):153-169;
    W. Raymond Wood, "Northern Plains Village Cultures: Internal Stability
    and External Relationships," Journal of Anthropological Research, 30
    (1974):1-16; Gary A. Wright, "Some Aspects of Early and Mid-Seventeenth
    Century Exchange Networks in the Western Great Lakes," Michigan
    Archeologist, 13 (1967):181-196. For an alternative view of the entire
    Middle Missouri system, see Donald J. Blakeslee, "The Plains Interband
    Trade System: An Ethnohistoric and Archeological Investigation."
    Ph.D. dissertation, University of Wisconsin-Milwaukee, 1975, passim, but
    esp. ch. 15.

11. Edwin T. Denig, Five Indian Tribes of the Upper Missouri John C. Ewers, ed. (Norman, 1961), p. 47; Abel, ed., Tabeau's Narrative, p. 162.

12. John L. Allen, Passage through the Garden: Lewis and Clark and the Image of the American Northwest (Urbana, 1975), p. 207; E. M. Bruner, "Mandan," Edward H. Spicer, ed., Perspectives in American Indian Culture Change (Chicago, 1961), p. 199.

13. John A. Alwin, "Pelts, Provisions, and Perceptions: The Hudson's Bay Company Mandan Indian Trade, 1795-1812," Montana, The Magazine of Western History, 29 (1979):16-27; Joseph Jablow, The Cheyenne in Plains Indian Trade Relations, 1795-1840 (Seattle, 1950), pp. 39-50; L. J. Burpee, ed., Journals and Letters of Pierre Gaultier de Varennes De La Vérendrye and His Sons (Toronto, 1927), pp. 323-324; Truteau, "Narrative," Nasatir, ed., Before Lewis and Clark, 1:381.

14. Thwaites, ed., Original Journals, 1:231.

15. Thwaites, ed., Original Journals, 1:251.

16. Burpee, ed., Journals and Letters of Vérendrye, pp. 324, 332-333.

17. Gass, Journal, p. 183; Thwaites, ed., Original Journals, 3:138, 140, 143.

18. Jackson, ed., Letters, 2:527.

19. Leslie Spier and Edward Sapir, Wishram Ethnography (Seattle, 1930), p. 164.

20. Ronda, Lewis and Clark, ch. 7.

21. Alexander Ross, Adventures of the First Settlers on the Oregon or Columbia River (London, 1849; reprint, Chicago, 1923), pp. 127-128.

22. David French, "Wasco-Wishram," Spicer, ed., Perspectives in American Indian Culture Change, pp. 337-430.

23. Ronda, Lewis and Clark, ch. 8; Thwaites, ed., Original Journals, 3:327-328.

24. Thwaites, ed., Original Journals, 3:338, 343.

25. Thwaites, ed., Original Journals, 4:289.

INDIAN AND NON-INDIAN FISHERIES FOR KLAMATH RIVER SALMON:
Environment and Cultural Change on the Northwestern California Frontier

by

Arthur F. McEvoy

ABSTRACT

Three Indian groups of radically different cultural and linguistic
backgrounds, the Yurok, the Hupa, and the Karok, shared control of the Klamath
River basin in what is now northwestern California. Each pursued a highly
specialized fishing economy based on that watershed's productive salmon
resource. Despite the great diversity of their cultural roots, these groups
developed in common an elaborate world-renewal religion, one of whose
functions was apparently to allocate access to salmon between them. Their
unique cultural adaptation to the ecology of the Klamath River basin enabled
them actively to manage their resources so as to sustain from them harvests
superior to any achieved by the commercial fisheries which superseded them.
It also enabled them to resist non-Indian expropriation of their lands and
economies to a degree unprecedented among California Indian groups. Although
the world-renewal religion had mostly died out by the first decades of the
twentieth century, these groups, alone among California Indians, managed to
retain control of their traditional resources until federal courts reaffirmed
their title to them in the 1960s and 1970s. This paper, part of a larger
study of the history of fisheries use and fisheries management in California,
analyzes the ongoing conflict between northwestern California Indians and
other resource users, with particular emphasis on the relationship between the
Indian culture and the conservation of the fishery resource. It finds a
functional relationship of an ecological nature between the two and suggests
that the integrity of tribal government and culture may be an essential
precondition for the successful management of this valuable, but endangered,
fishery.

INDIAN AND NON-INDIAN FISHERIES FOR KLAMATH RIVER SALMON:
ENVIRONMENT AND CULTURE CHANGE ON THE NORTHWESTERN CALIFORNIA FRONTIER

Arthur F. McEvoy

What follows is a brief summary of work completed for the first third of a book on the history of fisheries use and fisheries management in California from aboriginal times to the passage of the Fisheries Conservation and Management Act of 1976. Human beings have harvested fish in California under three overlapping but very different cultural regimes. The first of these was that of the original inhabitants, especially those in the northwestern corner of the state who based their economy primarily on the harvest of Pacific salmon. The second was that of the motley assortment of immigrant groups which came to California in the second half of the nineteenth century and established exclusive rights to use and manage particular fisheries according to their own, widely disparate traditions. The third, finally, is the modern, legal-industrial system under which twentieth-century Californians have tried, with mixed results, to husband many of the same resources which their predecessors used. The book concerns itself with the interaction between the ecology of the fisheries, economic development, and the social or cultural processes by which people regulate their use of resources. The Yurok, Hupa, and Karok Indian tribes of the Klamath River basin in northwestern California are of special interest in the study, first, because of the remarkable elegance and success with which they managed their salmon fishery and because their retention in the late twentieth century of preferential rights to the fishery brings the differences between Indian and industrial cultures with respect to resource use into sharp contrast.[1]

The book concludes that resource ecology, economic development, and social control over resource use constitute a functionally-interrelated, interdependent whole. Each possesses its own dynamism; each, moreover, both generates and responds to changes in the other two. The extent to which a harvesting community's strategies for managing its use of fishery resources take into account the systematic interaction between these three elements, ecology, economy, and social process, is the extent to which they do or do not "work," whether one measures the success of such a strategy in terms of efficiency, equity, or the conservation of productive potential in the environment.[2]

The "culture" of a harvesting community, be it an Indian tribe, an immigrant group, or a modern industry overseen by government bureaucracy, is the context within which it articulates its relationship with its environment and regulates its members' use of resources. It is, as Clifford Geertz put it, "a set of control mechanisms--plans, recipes, rules, instructions (what computer engineers call 'programs')--for the governing of behaviour."[3] Its ecological function, or its "adaptive significance" for the community, is to synthesize information about the group's environment, its strategies for

193

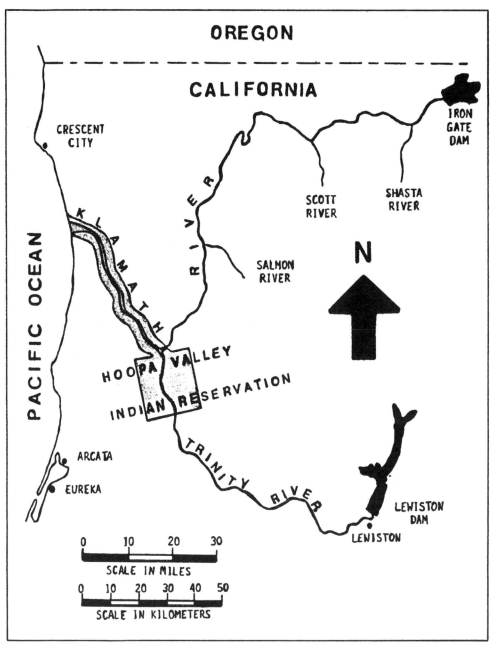

Klamath River Basin, showing outlines of Hoopa Valley Indian Reservation.
Map courtesy of USFWS, Arcata Field Station.

subsistence, and its collective decisionmaking processes and to translate that information into effective controls on resource use so as to preserve the long-term stability and well-being of the group.[4] Competition between Indians and non-Indians for Klamath River salmon, then, has meant not only a struggle for access to scarce resources but also a struggle between very different strategies for monitoring and adjusting the relationship between society and environment. The competition between cultures in northwestern California not only highlights the inherent characteristics of each but, insofar as it has disrupted the orderly adjustment of that relationship, has itself been an important cause for the near-extinction of Klamath River salmon stocks. Indeed, although the Klamath Basin Indians by the late twentieth century had adopted the language and tactics of modern Anglo-American law in the defense of their rights to the fishery, the integrity of what remained of Indian society and Indian culture in the basin remained, as it had been in aboriginal times, key to the ecological well-being of the salmon resource.

INDIAN CULTURE AND THE KLAMATH BASIN ENVIRONMENT

The Yurok, Hupa, and Karok tribes of the lower Klamath River basin represented the southernmost extension of aboriginal Pacific Northwest culture, whose principal subsistence base consisted of fish. The tribes' known universe consisted of the narrow, rocky, and densely-forested canyons through which passed the Klamath and its principal tributary, the Trinity. Into this universe, twice a year, surged hordes of running salmon on their way to their spawning beds in the system's tributaries, passing first through the forty miles of Yurok country between the ocean and the Klamath-Trinity confluence and on through Karok territory farther up the Klamath and Hupa territory on the lower Trinity. The fall run, especially, was of the greatest cosmic significance to the tribes because it was the most spectacular natural event of the year and because the Indians depended primarily on it to provision them for winter in the otherwise relatively barren canyons. While Erik Erikson may have drawn some rather fanciful inferences about Yurok psychology and sexual mores from the peculiar life cycle of the Pacific salmon, he was nonetheless correct in observing that the tribes' utter dependence on the fish for subsistence made the harvest of the fall run an event of the utmost economic, cultural, and spiritual importance for them.[5]

At the heart of northwestern California social and cultural organization was a stable and lucrative adaptation to the salmon resource upon which it rested. The three groups were themselves originally from very different cultural origins: the Yurok language stemmed from a Ritwan stock, the Hupa Athapaskan, and the Karok Hokan.[6] Nonetheless, when Westerners first began to interact with them on any scale in the early 1850s, they had retained their linguistic distinctiveness but had developed material and spiritual cultures that were indistinguishable from one another.[7] Richard A. Gould's "principle of negative determinism" is a conservative enough theoretical approach to the relationship between environment and culture and suffices to explain the remarkable uniformity of the three groups. "Ecological requirements," he wrote,

> do not necessarily determine the specific characteristics
> of the cultural response...but they do limit the options
> open to people in any given habitat and they do mean that
> prolonged lack of cultural conformity to these
> requirements will not occur.[8]

In the Klamath basin those requirements were so constraining that the Yurok the Hupa, and the Karok developed identical material cultures. The fact that they had to share the salmon runs, which passed through their territories serially, encouraged them to develop in common a world-renewal religion that articulated their interdependence with one another and with the salmon. Even Jorgensen, who was loath to ascribe any primacy to environment over inheritance in the shaping of aboriginal culture, admitted that in northwestern California Indian culture represented an adaptation to a peculiar environment that took place "independent of adaptations and influences from northern tribes" to which they were related.[9]

It was also a stable and highly lucrative adaptation. By combining his own estimates of per-capita Indian consumption of salmon and Kroeber's estimates of tribal populations, Gordon Hewes calculated that harvests of salmon by all Indian groups in the Klamath-Trinity watershed reached 3.5 million pounds per year.[10] In 1912, by contrast, the "greatest run of salmon known to white men" at the mouth of the Klamath produced only 1.4 million pounds of fish.[11] Hewes derived his estimates of consumption from observations of more northerly groups, so they may not be altogether reliable. He did, however, use Kroeber's figures for population, which come only to 69% of Cook's later and more reliable estimates.[12] We have no way of knowing what the maximum sustainable yield of Klamath River salmon was in aboriginal times or if the Indian harvests approached it, although Baumhoff found that most other California Indian groups lived at or near the long-term carrying capacity of their habitats.[13] It is reasonable to conclude, however, that Indian fishing on the Klamath reached intensities at least comparable and perhaps superior to those applied by commercial fisheries after 1850. What is more important is that the Indians managed their fishery deliberately and that they sustained such intensive harvests for centuries.

It is easy enough, as modern fishers have learned, to deplete a salmon stock. Early commercial fishers in Alaska, for example, simply blocked their streams by felling logs into them and gathered up entire races of salmon in the season, obliterating them in the process.[14] The Yurok and their immediate neighbours, though, took far fewer fish than they could have. Baumhoff found that, unlike other California tribes, linear functions of resource productivity significantly underpredicted the populations of the three groups in the lower Klamath basin. Unable to find other Malthusian limits on population in the basin, Baumhoff concluded that overt, social or political controls held down the harvest.[15]

The Indians, like most historical and contemporary hunter-gatherers, apparently took steps to limit their population and hence their demand for fish.[16] More directly, though, they elaborated over time a complex and highly individuated system of private rights to fishing spots, a system more thoroughly atomized than anywhere else in western North America and resembling in significant aspects the Anglo-American concept of private property.[17] Although owners generally shared access and proceeds with all comers, especially in times of need, they defended their rights strenuously against interlopers. They did so, moreover, entirely on individual initiative, without benefit of the merest trace of an organized political or legal system. As a result then, as individuals and as communities, the Yurok, the Hupa, and the Karok learned to be avaricious, suspicious of strangers, and litigious in the extreme. One Indian Affairs Agent described the Yurok, significantly, as having "the model idea of an American life."[18]

A belief in active, watchful, and potentially vengeful animal spirits, according to Driver, was "probably universal" among North American Indians.[19] For them, proper treatment of game animals and strict observance of ritual in their use was essential to the continued productivity of those resources. Suffusing the whole of Indian economy and society in the Klamath basin, then, was a world-renewal religion whose ostensible function was to propitiate the game, especially the salmon, for their sacrifice, to thank them for keeping everybody alive and prosperous, and to pray for their return in future seasons.[20] Its practical effect was twofold: it articulated in spiritual terms the functional relationship between society and its natural resources that modern ecologists express in the language of science, and it allocated access to the harvest among the various communities along the river while allowing enough fish to escape harvest to spawn new recruits for future seasons.

As the fall run moved upstream, each community staged a first-fruits ritual in which a local shaman let the first of the run pass on and ceremonially killed the group's first fish, reciting the while the mythical history of the fishery and the rules which people were to observe in catching and using the salmon. All of the communities in the basin, as well as some in outlying areas, shared the religion, attended each other's ceremonies, and observed each other's taboos.[21] As individuals and communities along the rivers observed each other's rights to access and the strictures of the religion, enough salmon passed through the territory of each to reach others farther upstream and, ultimately, their spawning gravels to ensure both an equitable distribution of fish and a prudent share left unharvested to spawn.

The most significant observance of the world-renewal religion, indeed probably the most elaborate technological and ceremonial undertaking in aboriginal California, was the annual construction in the fall of a communal salmon weir at Kepel, a Yurok village that lay a few miles below the Trinity confluence at the eastern edge of the coastal redwood belt. Here, in a round of ceremonies that may have lasted some fifty to sixty days in all, the Yurok and their neighbours gathered and dried a good share of their winter's provisions. Kepel was probably the best site in the basin to harvest large quantities of salmon. It lay far enough up the river that the fish, who do not feed once they enter fresh water, had by the time they reached the site had enough time to burn off some of the excess water in their flesh but had not yet begun the destructive ascent over the rocks and rapids that began just upstream. The ceremony, which had its mythical origins in a conflict between neighbouring villages over rights to erect fish dams in the river, involved the careful, ritual construction of the weir, communal harvests and celebrations, and the ritual dismantling of the edifice after it had stood for precisely ten days. The ceremony drew participants from many widely-scattered villages in all three tribal territories, as well as some from more outlying groups.[22]

George Gibbs, who visited the Klamath on a treaty-making expedition in 1851, described the practical effect of such ceremonies. Salmon weirs, he observed,

> form[ed] a frequent cause of quarrel among the bands inhabiting different parts of the rivers. Some understanding, however, seems to exist as to opening portions of them at times, to allow the passage of fish for the supply of those above.[23]

This balance of power between competing individuals and groups, then, maintained by individual initiative and given force and coherence by the world-renewal religion, worked to sustain both peace and prosperity in the basin and the long-term stability of the salmon fishery. The restraint which the Yurok, the Hupa, and the Karok people practiced in their fishery in normal times, moreover, as well as the peculiar characteristics of the culture they built up around their fishing economy, contributed significantly to their relative success in the late nineteenth-century confrontation with non-Indian peoples.

ENVIRONMENT AND CULTURE CHANGE

Normal times came to a close much later for the Klamath basin tribes than it did for other California Indians: until as late as 1850 non-Indians shunned the area, finding the coast difficult of access and the natives something short of cordial to strangers.[24] When gold and timber brought the outsiders in, though, the conflict was sudden, thorough, and ferocious. "They were," wrote Stephen Powers in 1871, "burst into the air.... Let a tribe complain that the miners muddied their salmon-streams, or steal a few pack-mules, and in twenty days there might not be a soul of them left living."[25]

The Klamath basin tribes faced the same travail that other California groups did, then, but theirs took place over the space of little more than a generation. Strikingly, though, the Yurok, the Hupa, and the Karok fared much better in the conflict than did any of their neighbours. The Yurok and the Hupa reached the turn of the twentieth century with legal title to reservations in their aboriginal territories. Losses of population to disease and warfare, though severe, were much milder than the norm for California Indian groups: while by the turn of the century their neighbours had fallen to the approximately 5% of aboriginal numbers that seems to have been typical for North American Indians, residuals among the three tribes in the lower Klamath basin were much higher, perhaps on the order of 20-30%.[26] In 1943

Erikson described the Yurok as the "picture of relative historical and economic health."[27] In the late twentieth century these groups were the wealthiest and most powerful Indians in California. Their income per capita compared quite favourably with that of non-Indians in the northwestern corner of the state.[28] Most importantly, they retained significant, if ill-defined, legal rights to the salmon fishery of the Klamath River. The key to their success was the nature of the Klamath basin environment and the resilience of the Indians' adaptation to it.

One reason why the three groups fared so well was, simply, that the lower Klamath basin was not much good for anything besides fishing. "Nature seems to have done her best to fashion a perfect paradise for these Indians," wrote an Indian Affairs agent in 1885, "and to repel the approach of the white men."[29] Miners invaded Karok country for a few years in the early fifties, but by the time the Whitney party of 1860-1864 arrived they had left and the Karok drifted back to their old homes.[30] The Army abandoned its fort at the mouth of the river after floods washed away buildings and topsoil in the winter of 1861-1862, but the Yurok under its supervision simply waited out the water on high ground and returned to their old homes in the spring.[31] Not to be discounted, however, was the Indians' own active and skillful military defense. Both the Yurok in the 1850s and the Hupa a decade later fought fiercely and successfully with troops and militia. At the conclusion of each struggle the defending tribe secured substantial reservations in their home territories from the federal government.[32] Even though disease, war, and harassment from settlers shattered their economy, the Indians had so limited their draft on the Klamath's abundant salmon that there seem to have remained enough fish in the river relative to their numbers that the Indians did not have to deal with the famine, the inconstancy of federal provisions, and the reprisals for stockraiding that contributed so mightily to the final demise of other California Indian groups. Though the salmon were "not so plentiful as in former times," wrote the agent at Hoopa Valley Reservation, on the lower Trinity, in 1871, "yet...[the Indians] manage to have plenty."[33]

Also working on the Indians' behalf was the striking, if superficial, similarity between their culture and that of the invaders. This disposed the latter more favourably toward these Indians than toward others and enabled the Indians better to deal with settlers and bureaucrats on familiar terms. Indian Affairs agents generally left them alone because they formed such a "respectable peasantry," living in nuclear families and subsisting without much government aid on fish, rather than on such less "civilized" foods as wild grasses, rodents, and acorns.[34] They had a good idea of what private property was all about and understood the cash value of things. George Gibbs reported in 1851 that a Karok "chief" had managed to smooth over tensions raised by the theft of a miner's rifle by collecting a tax of fifty cents in US silver on every sale of a fish by an Indian to a miner until the aggrieved miner got his due.[35] Powers was surprised at the facility and initiative with which the Yurok took up wage-paying jobs on the outside.[36] The agent at Hoopa Valley noted that the Hupa were disinclined to work on communal projects at the reservation but would "work industriously if left to do so on their own account."[37] Erikson, finally, could not miss the key fact about intergroup relations on the Klamath: "Yurok and white man each understands too well what the other wants, namely, possessions."[38] The acquisitiveness, competitiveness, and litigiousness that had developed to quicken the Indians' management of their salmon fishery, then, served them well in their dealings with their new neighbours.[39]

Commercial fishing for salmon on the Klamath began in 1876, on terms carefully worked out between the natives, Indian Affairs, and commercial packers from the outside.[40] The Indians had managed to hold on to their lands long enough that when serious competition for their resources arose the federal government was ready in a small way to protect their interests. The uncertain legal status of the lower stretch of the river, which had been a reservation but abandoned by the Army in 1861-1862, led to conflict between Indians and interlopers especially. The Army nonetheless evicted squatters from the land below the Trinity confluence in 1877. In 1891, after a commercial packer got the federal courts to declare that the lower river no longer constituted "Indian country" and that he could pack fish there without license from the Indians, President Benjamin Harrison formally attached the lower forty miles of the river to the twelve-mile square Hoopa Valley reservation, which Congress had established by statute in 1864.[41] Although the world-renewal religion died out during the first decade or two of the new century, the Indians retained some preferential interest in the fishery, although the precise nature of their title would remain unclear for many years to come.[42]

Indian rights to the resources of the basin thereafter remained key to the continued productivity of the salmon fishery, although after 1891 the natives articulated their bond with the fish in legal rather than spiritual terms. The relationship between Indian security and conservation was not lost upon some nineteenth-century observers: a federal biologist at the headwaters of the Sacramento River, to the south, recognized in the 1870s and 1880s that the survival of that watershed's valuable salmon fishery depended on the continued well-being of the Indians on the McCloud River, in the upper reaches of the system. "The supply of the Sacramento salmon has a singular natural protection," he reported, "arising from the fact that the McCloud River, containing the great spawning grounds of these fish, is held entirely by Indians:"

> the appearance of the white men, on the American and Feather Rivers, two great forks of the Sacramento, has been followed by the total destruction of the spawning beds of these once prolific streams, and the spoiling of the water, so that not a single salmon ever enters these rivers now where once they used to swarm by the millions.... It would be an inhuman outrage to drive this superior and inoffensive race from the river, and I believe that the best policy to use with them is to let them be where they are, and if necessary, to protect them from the encroachments of the white men.[43]

His policy failed on the Sacramento because the Indians had no legal control over activities on the river below them, where overfishing and pollution crippled the salmon fishery in the mid-1880s. The Eel River salmon fishery, just a few miles to the south of the Klamath, likewise enjoyed no insulation from the destructive effects of unregulated commercial use and collapsed at the same time.[44] The Klamath River salmon did not suffer the same fate, however, because Indians held the river all the way to the ocean as well as a good share of its spawning areas. In 1893 another federal biologist suggested that the government set the Klamath aside as a nursery to protect the long-term health of the Pacific salmon industry generally, reasoning that the river was already a government reservation and thus required no special legislation to keep developers out.[45] Although the government never acted on the proposal, Indian title to the reservation and, in the 1920s, a well-organized sportfishing lobby, accomplished the same purpose.[46]

INDIAN RIGHTS, INDIAN CULTURE, AND THE MODERN FISHERY

The Klamath basin Indians retained much of their traditional economy, supplemented by wage work on the outside, until the 1940s.[47] As the twentieth century progressed, though, new technology brought new competition for the resources of the basin and new threats to the survival of the salmon fishery. As one of the last unspoiled rivers on the Pacific Coast of the United States, the Klamath drew increasing numbers of sportfishers to compete with the Indians for its salmon. Electricity and internal combustion engines enabled miners and loggers to devastate the headwaters of the system, both on the Hoopa Valley Reservation and in the mountains to the east. In the 1960s the Central Valley Project began drawing up to 80% of the Trinity River away from the basin for agricultural use in the south. By the 1970s, finally, motorized, oceangoing trollers took as much as 80% of the dwindling stock of Klamath River salmon before it ever reached the mouth of the river.[48] Although the Indians continued through the early 1960s to fish the river commercially under informal agreements with the California Department of Fish and Game, by then there were so few fish left that the state began moving to regulate the Indian fishery more closely. The Indians, determined to retain what remained in their view and in the eyes of the law a traditional livelihood, took to the courts to reaffirm in modern terms the close relationship between their culture and the health of the fishery.

They took as their inspiration the success of salmon fishing tribes in the Pacific Northwest, who won an impressive series of victories in the federal courts guaranteeing them their treaty rights to fish "at all usual and accustomed places in common with" other US citizens.[49] The leading case was US v. Washington, decided in district court for western Washington in 1974, in which Judge George Boldt decreed that "in common with" meant, among other things, that treaty Indians were entitled to up to 50% of the entire inshore commercial harvest. Tribes which demonstrated their ability to regulate their own fishing, moreover, were completely exempt from state regulation.[50] The same court went farther in US v. Washington (Phase II) in 1980, when it declared that the tribes' rights to the fish included a right "to have the fishery habitat protected from man-made despoliation" inshore by timber companies, hydropower projects, and the like.[51] One legal commentator described the Phase II decision as potentially the most important Indian fishing rights decision in seventy-five years and one "critically important for the preservation of Indian culture and livelihood, and for the preservation of decimated salmon runs."[52] Because the salmon in question spawn in rivers that reach into the remotest corners of three states, the Phase II decision, if it survives appeal, will place Indian rights squarely in the middle of environmental policymaking for the entire region.

The legal ground on which the Klamath basin tribes stood was less certain than that of Indians to the north because the former held their reservation not under a federal treaty but by dint of statute and executive order. Nonetheless, a parallel line of decisions dealing with reservation Indians' rights to water flowing through their lands suggests that the distinction may not count for much. The leading case here is US v. Winters, a 1908 decision in which the US Supreme Court enjoined the diversion of water from the Milk River in Montana, upstream from an Indian reservation, so as to reserve enough to the Indians to fulfill the purposes of their reservation.[53] In Arizona v. California, a 1963 decision, the Court ruled that the Winters doctrine applied to all Indian reservations, whether established by treaty or other means.[54] Although Indian rights is one of the most chaotic areas in US law, well-settled "reservation purposes" include traditional hunting and fishing,[55] the devotion of reservation resources to the permanence and well-being of the Indian community,[56] and to allow the Indians as much as possible to "make their own laws and be ruled by them."[57] In northwestern California, there was "little question," in the view of the Interior Department, "that the prevailing motive for setting apart the reservation was to secure to the Indians the fishing privileges of the Klamath River."[58]

In the 1960s and 1970s Yurok litigants won decisions in state and federal courts that immunized them against state fishing regulations by virtue of their community's status as an Indian reservation.[59] In the early 1980s, as a result, government management of the Klamath River salmon lay in chaos, the fishery itself in grave danger of extinction. In the regulatory vacuum left by the Indians' victories, a group of some 100 of the 3,800 Yuroks on the reservation intensified their commercial fishing to harvest 34% of the fish that made it into the river between 1978 and 1981. Sportfishers continued, as before, to take about 5% of the runs, while local outfitters and civic authorities demanded that Congress abolish the reservation and put the Indians out of business. Offshore fishers, meanwhile, continued to take 70-80% of the entire stock, essentially unregulated by any authority.[60] In 1982 the reservation Indians filed suit against the US Commerce Department in federal district court in San Francisco, alleging that the Department's plan for managing the ocean fishery subjected it to no meaningful control and thereby failed to protect their preferential rights to the salmon.[61] The case is potentially of extreme significance, not only for the management of the Pacific salmon industry but for other Indians with non-treaty reservations as well.[62]

In California, as in the Pacific Northwest, the conflict between Indians and non-Indians over rights to salmon has itself been a significant cause of the serious decline in the resource over the past few decades. Without clearly-defined legal ground on which to work, government authorities can do little to protect the salmon from competing users who probably have the technological capacity to take every last fish out of the ocean.[63] For the Klamath Basin Indians, the salient issue in the conflict was the preservation of a traditional livelihood that was vital to the survival of what remained of their traditional culture and of their right as a community to regulate their members' activities in their own way. The Indians expressed willingness to cooperate with federal authorities in controlling the inshore fishery, but steadfastly refused to delegate power to police the fishery to non-Indian authorities.[64] Interior Department efforts to enforce an emergency ban on fishing in the river during the drought of 1976-1977 led to serious outbreaks of violence on the reservation. A special Court of Indian Offenses set up to try fishing violations failed to function because Indians refused either to give testimony or to serve as jurors.[65] Tribal government on the reservation, meanwhile, was in disarray because of a long-standing dispute between Yuroks and Hupas over the distribution of revenues from timber harvesting on the reservation, a dispute which some Indian witnesses accused the Bureau of Indian Affairs of abetting.[66] The California Supreme Court, meanwhile, pointed to the "frequent recognized reversals of federal policy regarding...the encouragement of tribal independence and self-government" as an important cause of the disorder in tribal affairs.[67]

CONCLUSION: A COMMENT ON KEEPERS OF THE GAME

The integrity of tribal society and culture in the Klamath basin, then, remained in the 1980s as it had been before 1850, entwined with the conservation of the salmon resource from which they drew life. Like it or not, history had thrust the Indians into the maelstrom of American commercial society and forced them to compete for rights and resources on its terms. All in all, the Indians had done quite well, in significant measure because the Klamath basin environment and the culture which the Indians had developed in order to sustain life in it left them better prepared than other Indians to meet the onslaught. Although their aboriginal approach to managing the fishery would not suffice in the modern world, that did not mean that Indian culture itself was dead or that the tribes as tribes had adopted the non-Indian view that the fish were, in Annette Hamilton's words, "disposable items of wealth free of social constraints and moral obligations."[68] Indian culture, as Bushnell found, was alive and well on the Hoopa Valley Reservation, despite the Indians' new wealth from their timber resources and their ready adoption of many of the appurtenances of the outside culture.[69] Given that the thrust of the recent Indian fishing rights decisions has been to dismantle non-Indian authority to police Indian activity on the reservations, the best hope for conserving the Klamath River salmon may lie in allowing the Indians to strengthen their communities by securing their ability to regulate the fishery themselves with the help of state and federal scientists, if not peace officers.

"Americans," noted Barsh and Henderson at the conclusion of their study of the Indians' place in the history of US law, "persist in denying the existence of tribalism."[70] Tribal culture, though, had important ecological functions in aboriginal times, even though many historians join in the general denial of tribalism by asserting that pre-Contact Indians lacked only the tools and the markets, not the will or the acquisitiveness, to abuse their natural resources.[71] It may prove to be a valuable, if yet untapped, resource for government to use in promoting good relations between people and between people and salmon in the Klamath basin. Putting it to use, however, would require that the law first protect the Indians from off-reservation depredation of their resources and then erect reasonable safeguards for their political liberty and self-determination.[72]

The minority of Yuroks who fished the Klamath River salmon in the 1970s without regard for the future of the stocks bear a strong resemblance to the fur-trapping Indians of Calvin Martin's controversial study, Keepers of the Game: Indian-Animal Relationships and the Fur Trade.[73] Martin asserted that the Indians of what is now eastern Canada maintained before Contact a spiritually-articulated, contractual relationship with the beaver and other animals they harvested, in which the Indians agreed to use the animals conservatively so that the animal spirits would sustain the well-being of Indian society. Indians became active abusers of the beaver when Europeans arrived, Martin claimed, not because Western trade held any inherent attraction for them but because they perceived their overwhelming losses to Western disease as evidence that the animal spirits had broken their end of the contract. They apostasized from their religion, then, and took vengeance on their former allies, the game.

The first half of Martin's thesis, that Indians managed their resource use through religious sanctions and rituals, is not very controversial; it is the second half that has aroused a great deal of contention. Martin, though, need not have resorted to apostasy to explain the change in the Indians' behaviour or to buttress his conception of the fundamentally non-destructive, non-capitalist nature of Indian society. Human culture, as Geertz explained, organizes and transmits information about life in the world in such a way as to compel people to behave in certain ways toward each other and toward their environment.[74] One of the "most fundamental ecological functions" of a benign human culture, in Mildred Dickeman's words, is to integrate individuals' perceptions of their personal interest with the long-term interests of their communities.[75] One such interest, presumably, is the sustenance of yields from renewable resources.

That Martin's subjects depleted their game animals wantonly, or that a minority of Yuroks overfished Klamath River salmon in defiance of the law and the wishes of their people, then, is evidence neither of apostasy nor of any inherent human tendency to pursue profit at the expense of community and environment, but only of the historical disintegration of the social and cultural controls that formerly would have restrained them. The Indians no longer honoured their commitments to the game because disease and colonialism dissolved the culture which articulated and compelled adherence to those commitments. The human being, as Geertz noted, "is precisely the animal most desperately dependent on such extragenetic, outside-the-skin control mechanisms, such cultural programs, for ordering his [sic] behaviour.... Culture, the accumulated totality of such patterns, is not just an ornament of human existence, but...an essential precondition for it."[76] Although Bushnell concluded that the Hupa were "unequivocally members of the dominant American culture," they nonetheless retained a sense of their own, distinctive identity and a profound determination to preserve it.[77] On the Klamath, recognizing the functional relationship between that determination and the conservation of Indian resources, even today, would in the long run serve not only justice for the Indians, but the public interest in the salmon fishery, as well.

ABBREVIATIONS USED IN THE FOOTNOTES

AR–CIA   Annual Report, US Commissioner of Indian Affairs
AR–DOI   Annual Report, US Department of the Interior
CFG   California Department of Fish and Game
Ct. Cl.   United States Court of Claims
LD   Decisions of the General Land Office, US Department of the Interior
NMFS   US National Marine Fisheries Service
NOAA   US Department of Commerce, National Oceanic and Atmospheric
            Administration
UCAR   University of California Anthropological Records
UC–PAAE   University of California Publications in American Archaeology and
            Ethnology
USBF   United States Bureau of Fisheries
USFC   United States Fish Commission
USFWS   United States Fish and Wildlife Service

FOOTNOTES

1. See James Axtell, The European and the Indian: Essays in the Ethnohistory of Colonial North America (Oxford, 1981), 6-7.

2. On measuring the efficacy of environmental policy, see S.V. Ciriacy-Wantrup, Resource Conservation: Economics and Policies, 3d (Berkeley, 1968), 48-51, 251-254; Robert B. Haveman, "Efficiency and Equity in Natural Resource and Environmental Policy," American Journal of Agricultural Economics, 55 (1973):868-878; Ciriacy-Wantrup, "The Economics of Environmental Policy," Land Economics, 47 (1971):37-45.

3. Clifford Geertz, The Interpretation of Cultures: Selected Essays (New York, 1973), 44.

4. See William H. Durham, "The Adaptive Significance of Cultural Behavior," Human Ecology, 4 (1976):89-121; Roy A. Rappaport, "The Sacred in Human Evolution," Annual Review of Ecology and Systematics, 2 (1971):23-44; id., "Ritual, Sanctity, and Cybernetics," American Anthropologist, 73 (1971):59-76. Appended to Durham's piece in Human Ecology is an illuminating discussion of his ideas.

5. Erik H. Erikson, "Observations on the Yurok: Childhood and World Image," UC-PAAE, 35 (1943):277-279.

6. Harold E. Driver, Indians of North America, 2d. (Chicago, 1969), 49.

7. Id.; for an introduction to California Indian ethnology, see William C. Sturtevant, ed., Handbook of North American Indians, 8: California (Vol. ed. Robert F. Heizer) (Washington, 1978); older and now dated, though nonetheless valuable as contemporary observation, is A.L. Kroeber, "Handbook of the Indians of California," Bureau of American Ethnology, Bulletin, 78 (1925: repr. ed. New York, 1976). A very thorough taxonomic work on western Indian cultures is Joseph G. Jorgensen, Western Indians: Comparative Environments, Languages, and Cultures of 172 Western American Indian Tribes (San Francisco, 1980).

8. R. A. Gould, "Ecology and Adaptive Response Among the Tolowa Indians of Northwestern California," in Native Californians: A Theoretical Perspective, ed. Lowell J. Bean and Thomas C. Blackburn (Ramona, California, 1976), 53.

9. Jorgensen, supra, note 7, 262.

10. Gordon W. Hewes, "Indian Fisheries Productivity in Pre-Contact Times in the Pacific Salmon Area," Northwest Anthropological Research Notes, 7 (1973):137-138.

11. John O. Snyder, "Salmon of the Klamath River, California," CFG, Fish Bulletin, 34 (1931):87.

12. Sherburne F. Cook, "The Aboriginal Population of the North Coast of California," UCAR, 16 (1956); cf. id., The Population of the California Indians, 1769-1970 (Berkeley and Los Angeles, 1976).

13. Martin A. Baumhoff, "Ecological Determinants of Aboriginal California Populations," UC-PAAE, 49 (2):223, 228.

14. Robert S. Connery, Governmental Problems in Wild Life Conservation, Columbia University Studies in History, Economics, and Public Law, 411 (New York, 1935), 122. On the history of the Alaska salmon fishery, see Richard A. Cooley, Politics and Conservation: The Decline of the Alaska Salmon (New York, 1963).

15. Baumhoff, supra, note 13, 185-189.

16. Id., 157; Sturtevant, supra, note 7, 142; Eugene S. Hunn, "Mobility as a Factor Limiting Resource Use in the Columbia Plateau of North America," in Nancy M. Williams and Eugene S. Hunn, eds., Resource Managers: North American and Australian Hunter-Gatherers, AAAS Selected Symposium 67 (Boulder, Colo, 1982), 23; see generally Don F. Dumond, "The Limitation of Human Population: A Natural History," Science, 187 (February 1975:713-721); Mildred Dickeman, "Demographic Consequences of Infanticide in Man," Annual Review of Ecology and Systematics, 6 (1975):107-137.

17. Jorgensen, supra, note 7, 143-144; Lowell J. Bean, "Social Organization in Native California," in Lowell J. Bean and Thomas F. King, eds., Antap: California Indian Political and Economic Organization, Ballena Press Anthropological Papers 2 (Ramona, California, 1974), 15-16; Kroeber, supra, note 7, 20-21.

18. AR-CIA (1885):492.

19. Driver, supra, note 6, 98.

20. On the world-renewal religion, see Jorgensen, supra, note 7, 262-263; A.L. Kroeber and Edward L. Gifford, "World-Renewal: A Cult System of Native Northwest California," UCAR, 13 (1949):1-156; Sturtevant, supra, note 7, 663-665.

21. Kroeber, supra, note 7, 294; Sturtevant, supra, note 7, 216-217; Kroeber and Gifford, supra, note 20, 56-61; Thomas T. Waterman and A.L. Kroeber, "The Kepel Fish Dam," UC-PAAE, 35 (1938):52; Robert Spott and A.L. Kroeber, "Yurok Narratives," UC-PAAE, 35 (1942):171-179.

22. A.L. Kroeber and Samuel A. Barrett, "Fishing Among the Indians of Northwestern California," UCAR, 21 (1960):12; Erikson, supra, note 5, 279, 300; Waterman and Kroeber, supra, note 21, 50-61, 78; Sturtevant, supra, note 7, 649; A.L. Kroeber, Yurok Myths (Berkeley and Los Angeles, 1976), 393-397.

23. George Gibbs, George Gibbs's Journal of Redick McKee's Expedition Through Northwest California in 1851, ed. Robert F. Heizer, University of California, Berkeley, Department of Anthropology (Berkeley, 1972), 146.

24. A.J. Bledsoe, Indian Wars of the Northwest: A California Sketch (1885; repr. Oakland, 1956), 73; William Dane Phelps, "Solid Men of Boston in the Northwest," in Robert F. Heizer, ed., The Four Ages of Tsurai: A Documentary History of the Indian Village on Trinidad Bay (Berkeley and Los Angeles, 1952), 82-83; Owen C. Coy, The Humboldt Bay Region, 1850-1875: A Study in the American Colonization of California (Los Angeles, 1929), 27-28, 36.

25. Stephen Powers, Tribes of California, US Geographical and Geological Survey of the Rocky Mountain Region, Contributions to North American Ethnology, 3 (1877; repr. Berkeley and Los Angeles, 1976), 404-405.

26. Arthur F. McEvoy, "Economy, Law, and Ecology in the California Fisheries to 1925" (Ph.D. diss., University of California, San Diego, 1979), 105-107. The differences are those between Cook's estimates of aboriginal population and Kroeber's compilation of US Census data for the 1880-1910 period. The latter figures are likely to be low and disproportionately more so for tribes outside the lowest reaches of the Klamath basin, who would have been dispersed and harder to count. The difference is significant, however, and corroborated by secondary evidence. Cf. Kroeber, supra, note 7, 102, 130; Cook, Population of the California Indians, supra, note 12, 71.

27. Erikson, supra, note 5, 257, 258.

28. California Department of Industrial Relations, Division of Fair Employment Practices, American Indians in California: Population, Employment, Income, Education (San Francisco, 1965), 8; California State Advisory Commission on Indian Affairs (Senate Bill No. 1007), Progress Report to the Governor and the Legislature on Indians in Rural and Reservation Areas (Sacramento, 1966), 24.

29. AR-CIA (1885):490.

30. Powers, supra, note 25, 73, 188-189; California Surveyor-General, Report (1859):27; id. (1 November 1865-1 November 1867):121; Gibbs, supra, note 23, 138, 172; William H. Brewer, Up and Down California in 1860-1864: The Journal of William H. Brewer, ed. Francis P. Farquhar (Berkeley and Los Angeles, 1966), 477-483.

31. AR-CIA (1871):374; Cook, "The Conflict Between the California Indian and White Civilization, III: The American Invasion," Ibero-Americana, 23 (1943):43 (Cook's "Conflict" series is reprinted in a single volume published by University of California Press, The Conflict Between the California Indian and White Civilization (Berkeley and Los Angeles, 1976); AR-CIA (1864):122.

32. US Congress, Senate, Joint Special Committee, "Condition of the Indian Tribes: Report of the Joint Special Committee appointed under Joint Resolution of March 3, 1865, "39th Congress, 2nd session, Senate Report 156, 1866-1867, 498; Bledsoe, supra, note 24, 91; Brewer, supra, note 30, 493-494; Coy, supra, note 24, 191-194, 197-198; California Surveyor-General, Report (1862):90, 113; id. (1863):121; AR-CIA (1864):122. The reservation on the lower part of the river was created pursuant to the act of 3 March 1855 (10 Statutes at Large 686, 699), by Executive Order dated 16 November 1855 (Executive Orders Relating to Indian Reservations, 1902, 21, 22). The reservation at Hoopa Valley was created pursuant to the act of 8 April 1864 (13 Statutes at Large 39, 40). See Jessie Short, et al., v. United States, 202 Ct. Cl. 870 (1973), 885-900.

33. AR-CIA (1871):157; Powers, supra, note 25, 48-49.

34. AR-DOI (1864):266; AR-CIA (1871):374; id. (1884):55; id. (1885):490-492.

35. Gibbs, supra, note 23, 149.

36. Powers, supra, note 25, 46.

37. AR-CIA (1872):454.

38. Erikson, supra, note 5, 258.

39. Cf. Jorgensen, supra, note 7, 136.

40. AR-CIA (1888):10; US Congress, Senate, Committee on Indian Affairs, Survey of Conditions of the Indians of the United States: Hearings before a Subcommittee of the Committee on Indian Affairs, 72nd Congress, 1st session, 1934, Pt. 29: California, 15653; Humboldt Times, 19 May 1887.

41. AR-CIA (1886); 261; Frances Turner McBeth, Lower Klamath Country (Berkeley, 1950), 46-47; re John McCarthy, 2 LD 460 (1883): AR-CIA (1885):490-492; id. (1887-1888):91; id. (1888):10; Humboldt Times, 9 June 1887; 10 Opinions, Attorneys General 35-37, 56-57 (1887); United States v. Forty-Eight Pounds of Rising Star Tea, 35 F. 403 (N.D. Cal. 1888), affirmed 38 F. 400 (C.C.N.D. Cal. 1889). Cf. Gordon B. Dodds, The Salmon King of Oregon: R.D. Hume and the Pacific Fisheries (Chapel Hill, 1959), 174-177. Harrison extended the Hoopa Valley Reservation down to the ocean in Executive Order of 16 October 1891, C. Kappler, Indian Affairs: Laws and Treaties, 1 (1904):815.

42. Crichton v. Shelton, 33 LD 205 (1906), 215; Donnelly v. United States, 228 US 243 (1913), 258-259; cf. Short v. United States, supra, note 32, 883, 902-903.

43. USFC, Report (1872-1873):193-194, emphasis in original; id. (1879):700.

44. John N. Cobb, "Pacific Salmon Fisheries," USBF Document 1072, USBF, Report (1930):572.

45. USFC, Report (1893):391.

46. Eileen M. Glaholt, "Office Report: History of the Klamath River Region,"
     (Sacramento: California Resources Agency, photocopied, 1975), 67, 74;
     Snyder, supra, note 11, 43. Organized sportfishers, with the help of the
     California Department of Fish and Game, secured passage of an initiative
     measure closing the lower river to hydroelectric development in 1924.
     1925 California Statutes xclii; Snyder, "Indian Methods of Fishing on
     Trinity River and Some Notes on the King Salmon of that Stream,"
     California Fish and Game, 10 (1924):162.

47. John H. Bushnell, "From American Indian to Indian American: The Changing
     Identity of the Hupa," American Anthropologist, 70 (1968):1111-1112.

48. USFWS, Arcata (California) Field Station, "Final Report: Hoopa Valley
     Indian Reservation: Inventory of Fish Rearing Waters, Fish Rearing
     Feasibility Study, and a Review of the History and Status of Anadromous
     Fishery Resources of the Klamath River Basin" (Arcata: USFWS,
     photocopied, 15 March 1979), 3-35.

49. On the Pacific Northwest fishing rights controversy, see Russel L. Barsh,
     The Washington Fishing Rights Controversy: An Economic Critique, rev.
     ed. (Seattle, 1979); Peter J. Aschenbrenner, "Comments: State Power and
     the Indian Treaty Right to Fish," California Law Review, 59
     (1971):485-524; Jack L. Landau, "Empty Victories: Indian Treaty Fishing
     Rights in the Pacific Northwest," Environmental Law, 10 (1980):413-456.

50. United States v. Washington, 384 F. Supp. 312 (W.D. Washington 1974),
     affirmed, 520 F. 2d 676 (9th Cir. 1975), certiorari denied, 423 US 1086,
     substantially affirmed sub nom. Washington v. Washington State Commercial
     Passenger Fishing Vessel Association, 443 US 658 (1979).

51. United States v. Washington (Phase II), 506 F. Supp. 187 (W.D. Washington
     1980), 203.

52. Peter C. Monson, "United States v. Washington (Phase II): The Indian
     Fishing Conflict Moves Upstream," Environmental Law, 12 (1982):502.

53. Winters v. United States, 207 US 564 (1908). See Robert S. Pelcyger,
     "The Winters Doctrine and the Greening of the Reservations," Journal of
     Contemporary Law, 4 (1977):19-37.

54. Arizona v. California, 373 US 546 (1963), 594-601.

55. Menominee Tribe v. United States, 391 US 404 (1968), 406. See Charles
     A. Hobbs, "Indian Hunting and Fishing Rights," George Washington Law
     Review, 32 (1963-1964):504-532; Hobbs, "Indian Hunting and Fishing
     Rights, II," id., 37 (1969):1251-1273; George C. Coggins and William
     Modcrin, "Native American Indians and Federal Wildlife Law," Stanford Law
     Review, 31 (1979):375-423.

56. United States v. Shoshone Tribe of Indians, 304 US 111 (1938); McClanahan
     v. Arizona Tax Commission, 411 US 164 (1973), 174.

57. Williams v. Lee, 358 US 219 (1959), 220; McClanahan v. Arizona Tax Commission, supra, note 56, 178. See Pelcyger, supra, note 53, 32-33.

58. Crichton v. Shelton, supra, note 42, 217.

59. Elser v. Gill Net No. One, 54 Cal. 568, 246 Cal. App. 2d 30 (1966); Arnett v. Five Gill Nets, 97 Cal. 894, 20 Cal. App. 3d 731 (1971), overruled, Mattz v. Arnett, Director, Department of Fish and Game, 412 US 481 (1973), on remand, Arnett v. Five Gill Nets, 121 Cal. 906, 48 Cal. App. 3d 454 (1975). Cf. Hobbs, "Hunting and Fishing Rights, II," supra, note 55, 1263-1264.

60. NMFS, Pacific Fishery Management Council, "Proposed Plan for Managing the 1982 Salmon Fisheries off the Coasts of California, Oregon, and Washington (amended)," (Portland: Pacific Fishery Management Council, photocopied, May 1982), 11-III, 14-III; Gary L. Rankel, "Depleted Chinook Salmon Runs in the Klamath River Basin: Causes, Consequences, and Constraints on Management," paper presented to the annual meeting of the Western Division, American Fisheries Society, Kalispell, Montana, 15 July 1980 (Arcata, California: USFWS, photocopied, July 1980); cf. Peter A. Larkin, "Maybe You Can't Get There From Here: A Foreshortened History of Research in Relation to Management of Pacific Salmon," Journal of the Fisheries Research Board of Canada, 36 (1979):99. For the demands of the outfitters and local civic authorities, see US Congress, House, Committee on Merchant Marine and Fisheries, "Klamath River Fishing Rights Oversight," Hearings before the Subcommittee on Fisheries and Wildlife Conservation and Environment, 96th Cong., 1st sess., 1979, House Serial 96-11, 16-23, 103, 119-120, 140-141, 177.

61. Hoopa Valley Tribe v. Malcolm Baldrige, Secretary of Commerce, et al., Civil No. C-82-3145 MHP (N.D. Cal., 1982).

62. Telephone interview, Douglas Ancona, NOAA Northwest Regional Counsel, Seattle, Washington, 19 August 1982.

63. Personal interview, Dr. Dan Huppert, NMFS Southwest Fisheries Center, La Jolla, California, 17 December 1982; Monson, supra, note 52, 503.

64. "Klamath River Fishing Rights Oversight," supra, note 60, 28. On the legal definition of commercial fishing as a "traditional livelihood," then-President Nixon stated that "federal and congressional concern now indicate that forcing Indians to surrender a traditional occupation, however exercised, is unacceptible." 116 Congressional Record, H. 6438, S. 10799 (daily edition, 8 July 1970), cited in Aschenbrenner, supra, note 49, 522.

65. "Klamath River Fishing Rights Oversight," supra, note 60, 16-23, 135.

66. Id., 6, 30-34, 78-79, 152. See Short v. United States, supra, note 32.

67. Elser v. Gill Net No. One, supra, note 59, 575.

68. Annette Hamilton, "The Unity of Hunting-Gathering Societies: Reflections on Economic Forms and Resource Management," in Hunn and Williams, eds., supra, note 16, 242.

69. Bushnell, supra, note 47, 1108, 1114-1115.

70. Russel Lawrence Barsh and James Youngblood Henderson, The Road: Indian Tribes and Political Liberty (Berkeley and Los Angeles, 1980), 286.

71. See, for example, Morgan S. Sherwood, Big Game in Alaska: A History of Wildlife and People (New Haven and London, 1981), 113-114; cf. Eugene S. Hunn and Nancy M. Williams, "Introduction," in Hunn and Williams, eds., supra, note 16, 1.

72. See generally Barsh and Henderson, supra, note 70, esp. 282; Robert Ericson and D. Rebecca Snow, "Comment: The Indian Battle for Self-Determination," California Law Review, 58 (1970):445-490; Charles F. Wilkinson and John M. Volkman, "Judicial Review of Indian Treaty Abrogation: 'As Long as Water Flows, or Grass Grows Upon the Earth'--How Long a Time is That?" California Law Review, 63 (1975):601-666; Daniel H. Israel, "The reemergence of Tribal Nationalism and Its Impact on Reservation Resource Development," U. Colorado L. Rev., 47 (1976):617.

73. Calvin Martin, Keepers of the Game: Indian-Animal Relationships and the Fur Trade (Berkeley and Los Angeles, 1978). Cf. Shepard Krech III, ed., Indians, Animals, and the Fur Trade: A Critique of Keepers of the Game (Athens, Ga., 1981).

74. Geertz, supra, note 3, 90, 123.

75. Dickeman, supra, note 16, 133.

76. Geertz, supra, note 3, 45-46. Daniel R. Gross and others analyzed the ecology of Indian-non-Indian interaction in a remarkable article, "Ecology and Acculturation Among Native Peoples of Central Brazil," Science, 206 (30 November 1979):1043-1050. See also Gary Coombs and Fred Plog, "The Conversion of the Chumash Indians: An Ecological Interpretation," Human Ecology, 5 (1977):309-328. See J. Kemper Will, "Indian Lands Environment: Who Should Protect It?" Natural Resources Journal, 18 (1978):503, where Will concludes that "the best environmental protection of Indian lands will normally be achieved through environmental action by those most interested in the land, in this case, by the Indians themselves."

77. Bushnell, supra, note 47, 1108.

PAWNEE USAGE OF BUNDLE BELIEFS AND PRACTICES

by

Morris W. Foster

ABSTRACT

The usual explanation of Plains Indian bundles had been that they served
(1) as a convenient material means of focusing ritual, belief and practice and
(2) as mnenomics for the telling of myths and historical tales and the
recounting of vision quests. The focus of this study is the Pawnee, for which
the best documentation of usages of bundle beliefs and practices exists.
Analysis of the Pawnee data suggest that the symbolism of bundles was used in
many different contexts to many different ends. Control of knowledge of
underlying rules of usage resulting in different, context-specific meanings or
interpretations allowed a small, carefully closed group of persons control
over much of Pawnee culture and society.

PAWNEE USAGE OF BUNDLE BELIEFS AND PRACTICES

Morris W. Foster

I originally began this study with the intention of treating the Native North American practice of forming, maintaining and using bundles composed of material objects considered to have symbolic value and, beyond that, power and ritual significance, in the broad form of a study of the relevant practices for all Plains groups wherein this phenomenon was primarily, though not exclusively, found. As such bundles, of one kind or another, figured in many creation and origin myths, annual and irregularly held rituals, personal and group religious practices, conceptions of medicine and curing, belief systems surrounding witchcraft and magic, conceptions of personal power and ability in hunting and war, and also in matters of group identity and solidarity, it seemed to me that the symbolism and the beliefs and practices surrounding these bundles were central to any approach to the study of Plains Indian religion and cosmology.

From the beginning, I was struck by the reluctance of previous studies of Plains religion and cosmology to treat bundles as anything but material manifestations. The usual explanation has been that bundles served 1) as a convenient material means of focusing ritual belief and practice and 2) that the existence and contents of bundles served primarily as mnemonics for the telling of myths and historical tales and the recounting of vision quests. Consequently, nearly all references to bundles in the ethnographic literature are mainly descriptions of particular beliefs about particular bundles and of some of the uses to which these bundles were put. It became increasingly clear that what is most interesting about Plains bundles is not their material existence or dispersion and not their particular integration into specific belief or ritual systems but, rather, the more general matter of the nature of the symbolism and meanings involved in the beliefs about bundles and in the uses to which bundles were put.

Consequently, I have shifted the focus of this study from a survey of the various Plains groups to only one group, the Pawnee, for which the best documentation of usages of bundle beliefs and practices exists. This shift has happened to coincide with a framework that I have attempted to work out specifying the nature of meanings perceived by participants and analysts in relation to objects of analysis. In what follows, I have attempted to use this framework to examine the nature of the symbolism and meanings involved in usage of bundle beliefs and practices and to use the detailed Pawnee data as illustrative examples of the framework. The act of analysis is not a neutral, disembodied thing. It, too, involves the differential perception of meaning and so we must extend any general semantic model in which different kinds of meanings are related to one another to cover the act of analysis as well as the object of analysis. The conditions prevailing in the phenomena which we study are not suspended or any less valid in the study itself.

215

1. Source of Data and Background

The source for data on Pawnee bundle practices and beliefs is a recently published manuscript by James R. Murie (Ceremonies of the Pawnee, edited by Douglas R. Parks and probably co-authored by Clark Wissler, Smithsonian Contributions to Anthropology, Vol. 27, parts 1 and 2, 1981). Himself a Pawnee, Murie worked for the Bureau of American Ethnology in the first two decades of this century. The account itself was researched and written from 1914-1921. It was based upon observations of bundle rituals and interviews with elderly bundle specialists, both priests and doctors. The study is divided into two volumes, one on the Skiri band and the other on the South Band Pawnee (the latter division including, actually, three bands). Both divisions of Pawnee were semi-sedentary horticulturalists who grew corn in season and exploited the bison herds throughout the year. Ceremonialism tended to center around agricultural ritual rather than hunting ritual and thus tended to emphasize village identity and solidarity (agricultural enterprises being carried out within villages and hunting often being carried out by the band as a whole). Each village possessed its own sacred bundle which was considered the sanction or charter for its collective power and identity and was protected from falling into the hands of outsiders by endogamous marriage practices. Within each band, the village sacred bundles in combination with the four band sacred bundles formed the basis, in ceremonial use and as authority for political organization, for group-identity and cooperation between villages within each band.

There is a hierarchy of power here, the band sacred bundles being considered more powerful than the village sacred bundles and these, in turn, being considered more powerful than personal bundles of doctors, warriors and others. It was also the case that a differential of ascribed power was perceived between different bundles at each of these three levels. Personal bundles derived their power from their owners' own vision quests and from the power that each person was considered to possess, power which was considered to reside in the personal bundles. Stories about the village and band sacred bundles often were about the vision quests of mythical figures. Ritual taboos surrounded the maintenance and possession of any bundle, more stringent for sacred bundles than for personal ones. Personal bundles, except sometimes those of particularly renowned doctors and warriors, were buried with their owners. Sacred bundles were passed down patrilineally through the office of a chief responsible for a particular bundle. The political hierarchy of chiefs corresponded to the religious hierarchy of priests and sacred bundles, the chiefs nominally considered the keepers of the sacred bundles and the priests the keepers and practicianers of bundle rituals.

As to personal bundles, three features are particularly interesting. The first is the existence of doctors' associations which were, in effect, guilds which carefully regulated their membership and so which had some control over the presumed efficacy of doctors' bundles. Doctors were shamans or ritual specialists who derived their livings in part through performance of curing ceremonials. They were largely outside of the political-religious complex of sacred bundles and offices, their positions based more on personal reputation than institutionalized status, and were those most often accused of witchcraft and involved in witchcraft prevention and curing. Warriors' bundles were specifically intended to give power and success in warfare. War and raiding parties were organized by individuals on the basis of their reputations for success and were preceded by bundle ceremonials. There also existed what Murie calls 'bundle societies' whose charters were based on the sanction of particular sacred bundles and whose authority often extended to duties of social control.

2. Argument

It is clear from this brief background, and from the more detailed discussions by Parks and Murie, that the usage of bundle beliefs and practices was a central focus in the cosmological, religious and political spheres of Pawnee culture. More than this, the perception of meaning(s) in the symbolism accorded to these bundles was an integral part of everyday Pawnee practice and belief. To put the point more precisely, the most striking aspect is the use of belief in particular contexts.

I specify use in context because, as the balance of this paper is intended to demonstrate, different meanings are communicated in (expressive) occurrences of use than exist solely in the perception of belief systems as systems (or as texts). In such instances of actual occurrence, of a ritual or explanatory statement or some other manifestation, a body of knowledge is drawn upon and placed in the context of occurrence to create a novel usage.

I am concerned, then, to show how this body of knowledge differs from its use in context in terms of the kinds of meanings that are or may be perceived. Because of the nature of the Pawnee data and the nature generally of anthropological analysis, I am also interested in the possibilities of differential perception of kinds of meanings between persons in the role of participant and persons in the role of analyst.

Finally, it is my contention that there existed, in the strategic contextual use of bundles, an awareness of underlying order or code in usage, a folk semiotic if you will. As Parks puts it:

> "Because he [the priest] alone knew all of the ritual and
> complex lore surrounding the sacred bundles and consequently
> mastered a prodigious amount of knowledge, he commanded a
> great deal of respect from the people. This knowledge was
> accumulated only after a long, arduous, and expensive
> process. The priests, like the doctors, guarded their
> knowledge: Knowledge was power and a life-sustaining essence,
> and to divulge everything one knew shortened one's life."
> (p. 10, 'Introduction')

Because bundles were involved in ritual at every level, in political organization, in beliefs concerning personal efficacy and power, in beliefs about agriculture, hunting, witchcraft, curing, warfare, nearly every aspect of social life, knowledge of rules concerning usage of bundle beliefs and rituals constituted control.

It is not surprising, then, that this knowledge was jealously guarded in ideologies of secrecy and in guild-like associations or that great care was taken in the proper performance of ritual. Many rituals were performed only when 'pledged' or 'called' by an individual though the participation was often village-wide and sometimes included other villages as well. An individual who pledged a particular ceremonial, however, had always to consult a ritual specialist, either a priest or doctor depending upon the nature of the ceremonial, for the rules of proper or competent usage of belief and practice in the particular context in which the ceremonial was called. By controlling knowledge of rules of usage, ritual specialists had control over significant portions of the meanings that might be invoked in social and cultural institutions, belief systems and action systems. In this manner, usage of bundle beliefs and practices was central not only to Pawnee religion and cosmology but also to Pawnee culture and society.

3. Definitions

3.1 Communicative meaning. That which an utterance functions to express through its occurrence in a particular time and place. This may include the meaning that the text of an utterance in relation to its particular usage functions to express or the meaning that the fact of the occurrence of an utterance in relation to its particular usage functions to express. The former differs from significative meaning in the relation of text to usage rather than divorcing text from the occasion of utterance. The latter differs from indexical meaning in that it is a reading of actual or imputed intention of expression rather than drawing upon existential relations to achieve a degree of understood conventionality.

This is a useful distinction in that it allows us to separate out context-specific actual or imputed intentional meaning and to, in some way, isolate those meanings in usage which are conditioned or dependent upon the circumstances of usage.

3.2 Significative meaning. That which the text of an utterance functions to express when taken apart from the occasion of utterance. This definition necessarily involves both indexical and referential meanings, though only as the former functions independently of particular usage, and so differs from referential meaning on account of this inclusion.

This is a useful distinction in that it allows us to separate out context-independent meaning which is not conditioned or dependent upon the circumstances of usage.

3.3 Indexical meaning. That which existential relations within the text of an utterance or between the text of an utterance or the fact of an utterance and its particular usage function to express. Existential relations which result in indexical meaning are conventionally recognized and comprise a mutually understood subtext or context.

This is a useful distinction in that it allows us to separate out that meaning which is (existentially) conventionally understood in usage as context or subtext but not a matter of expressive intention or imputation of intention.

3.4 Referential meaning. That which arbitrary relations of signifier to signified function to express through usage of particular signifiers in particular utterances.

This is a useful distinction in that it allows us to separate out that meaning which is fully independent of usage and of existential relation to subtext or context.

4. Objects of Analysis

4.1 Occurrences of use. Observable occurrences of use. These are unique events. In his research, Murie had two primary sources of information: his own observations of ritual events and event contexts in which bundles played a part and statements of informants about bundle beliefs and practices. These are the two primary sources of information upon which most ethnographers rely. These are also the primary sources of information available to participants in a social situation in learning those aspects of cultural knowledge and language involved in bundle beliefs and practices, in perceiving meanings in contexts in which bundles are used or beliefs about bundles are in some way expressed (and so used), and in competently using bundles or expressing bundle beliefs themselves.

Each event or instance of such activity is necessarily unique in the combination of circumstances, place, time, actors, motivations and intentions, perceptions, etc. Consequently, each occurrence of use is in some degree novel and creative.

4.2 Pragmatic salience. Participants' awareness of order in usage or pragmatic salience. This may be either idiosyncratic to individuals (the understanding or awareness, not the order itself) or general to a group of individuals and may be said to affect observable occurrences of use. Statements reflecting pragmatic salience are elicitable from participants.

This is a special category of statement about bundle usage which expresses knowledge of underlying rule or code in competent usage of bundle beliefs and practices in differing contexts of usage with differing intentions of usage. These statements are distinctive from other statements about or of bundle beliefs and practices in that 1) they are primarily concerned with the matter of usage and 2) the meaning that is conveyed concerning usage is not limited to the circumstances or context of expression but is context-independent in that it may be lifted from the specific context of communication and understood and applied in other contexts.

4.3 Systems of use. Systems of use may be presumed to underly observable occurrences of use but are not necessarily limited to participant's awareness of order in usage or to the manners in which participants phrase this awareness. These systems are represented by analytic models covering observed data and it is actually these models which are the objects of study rather than the directly unexaminable systems themselves. The term 'system' is used here to imply the linguistic notion of an integrated, interrelated logic by which actual occurrences of use are ordered or patterned.

It is clear from Murie's descriptions that there were ways in which usage of bundle beliefs and practices made sense and ways in which usage did not. This would indicate the existence of some underlying system of use. Both because participants' statements are unavailable concerning all dimensions or parameters of competent usage and because it is unlikely that explicit, conscious statements of pragmatic salience existed for all dimensions or aspects of the underlying system of use in any event, we are speaking here of analytic models constructed primarily to account for the data at hand.

4.4 Meaning per se. Models of different kinds of meaning and different general semantic models in which different kinds of meaning are related to one another. Meanings perceived in usage of bundle beliefs and practices are, first, merely connected parts of a larger body of commonly or conventionally perceived and understood meanings and, second, may be classed according to the different kinds of ways in which they are perceived and understood. The latter observation implies an explicit statement of intuitive perception and understanding, i.e., a general semantic model, which is necessary for the systematic and rigorous analysis of the former. Indeed, it may be that the best way in which to approach extensive domains of meaning or closely related and extensively connected domains is not descriptively but deductively through a general semantic model and models of different kinds of meanings.

5. Relation of Analysts to Objects of Analysis

5.1 Occurrences of use. The analyst may perceive both indexical and referential meanings and communicative and significative meanings or infer the fact of their existence in observed occurrences of use. Indeed, this is the point at which the data for these different kinds of meaning are initially perceived, identified and recorded.

In regard to the distinctions made in kinds of meanings, while all operative at this level, we are not here concerned to make the analytic separations implied by each definition. Context is left inviolate. It is when context is violated, when descriptions are written and when interpretations are made on the basis of these descriptions, in short when analysis is carried out, that the matter of meaning in relation to the acts of analysis becomes central.

We are necessarily in the position of having to deal with occurrences of use as set forth in Murie's descriptions and interpretations. In large part, his manuscript may be taken as a primary text about usage of bundle beliefs and practices in that he is careful to present us with accounts of usage and of conceptions of usage. We are, however, dependent upon his selection of

cases of usage to present as examples and often we are presented with
generalized rather than specific cases. To this extent, some
decontextualization has occurred and insofar as it has we are no longer
dealing with occurrences of use as objects of analysis but either with
pragmatic salience or models of systems of use.

5.2 Pragmatic salience. While the elicitation of participants' awareness of
order in usage by an analyst must, in every instance, be embedded in some
context in which communicative and indexical meanings are possible and while
the same must also be true for those contexts in which an analyst observes or
carries out analysis upon these data of awareness of order, these contextual
meanings are merely incidental and are irrelevant to the meaning of
participants' awareness of order in use as a model or body of knowledge, which
such awareness is, as pragmatic salience is, presumably, an explicit
restatement of an understanding of systems of communicative and indexical
meanings. As such, this is stated in referential and significative frames.
The study of the meaning of the existential context of elicitation or the act
of analysis, while perhaps interesting in and of itself, does not speak to the
meaning of the particular pragmatic salience in question but to the meaning of
another coincidental object of study with which we are not directly
concerned. Consequently, the meaning of pragmatic salience as an object of
study to an analyst can only objectively be referential and significative
(indexical meanings are relevant only insofar as they fall within the frame of
significative meaning, see 3.2 -- this caveat will apply whenever reference
is made to significative meaning).

A statement made to Murie by an informant about the competent usage of
bundle beliefs and practices may have had the expressive intention (or
communicative meaning) of including Murie in that privileged group of persons
privy to secret knowledge about bundles but this meaning is irrelevant to the
meaning of the statement as a folk analysis or model of order in usage. The
latter meaning is not context-specific or -dependent. Insofar as pragmatic
salience is defined as an explicit knowledge, and therefore an explicit
statement, then we are concerned only with the significative meaning of such
statements as objects of analysis.

5.3 Systems of use. Again, while each act of analysis and each study of a
completed analysis must be embedded in some context in which communicative and
indexical meanings are possible, the meaning which the analyst perceives in
relation to models of underlying order as objects of analysis can only
objectively be referential and significative.

The study of a completed analysis is, presumably, not that of imputed
intention or existential circumstance. While these latter meanings may be
objects of study in their own right, such as might fall under the headings of
methodology or sociology of knowledge, we are here interested in studying
Murie's analytic conclusions only insofar as they relate to occurrences of use
as objects of study and not to their own occurrences in context.

5.4 Meaning per se. Again, while the construction and study of models of different kinds of meaning and of meaning in general must be embedded in some context, the contextual meaning possible is irrelevant to the meaning of those models as objects of analysis and only referential and significative meanings are valid.

6. Relation of Participants/users to Objects of Analysis

6.1 Occurrences of use. In any speech event or situation it is possible and indeed likely that a participant perceive all possible kinds of meaning. This seems a self-evident matter except insofar as knowledge of competent usage was restricted to ritual specialists. To some extent, it appears to have been the case that knowledge, primarily knowledge of context-specific usage, was strategically controlled while a general understanding of the belief systems surrounding bundle usage remained as a basis for the social efficacy of ritual. This, of course, has a bearing not only upon occurrences of use as objects of participant analysis but also upon pragmatic salience.

6.2 Pragmatic salience. Though the circumstances and experiences through which a participant acquires and uses his or her awareness of order in usage may be indexically and communicatively meaningful, the point to learning this knowledge is to take it out of the unique context in which it is learned, treat it not as observed data of a past experience but as principles or rules of contextual usage, and to consciously apply it elsewhere. Consequently, a participant's awareness of order in usage constitutes a model which is in no way different in kind from any model that might be formulated by an analyst though perhaps lacking in some of the sophistication of linguistic or ethnographic technique and theory, and so a participant's awareness or model of order in usage (i.e., of code or underlying system) holds primarily referential and significative meanings for that participant. The same is true for a participant's perspective on the awareness of order in usage of another participant.

6.3 Systems of use. In approaching presumed systems which underly observed data and which are considered to be covert in their manner of operation and must be considered so as they are approachable only through models inferred from observable data and not as observable data themselves, the participant is in the same position as the analyst and, indeed, is in the position of acting as an analyst. While these models may be devised or perceived in existential circumstances having indexical and communicative meanings, these again are irrelevant to any concern with a model as a model and so these models of systems of use are perceived as having only referential and significative meanings for purposes of analysis.

It is already clear, at this point, that for the participant any distinction between pragmatic salience and models of systems of use will be redundant as pragmatic salience does constitute knowledge of some (folk) model of a system of use.

6.4 Meaning per se. A participant's perception of kinds of meaning and of models of general meaning is, again, the same as that of any analyst for the reasons set out in 6.3 and in 5.4, and so involves primarily referential and significative meanings.

7. Discussion

It becomes immediately obvious from the above characterizations that the position or role of analyst is no different in kind from the role of participant (and vice-versa) in relation to the various objects of analysis. It is also clear that pragmatic salience, while perhaps an interesting phenomenon in the same manner in which folk systems of classification and models are interesting, is an illusory conception when it is used to suggest that participants' awareness of order in usage has a kind of meaning which is in any way different in kind from the meaning that an analytic model holds for the analyst. Except in terms of greater immediate knowledge of situation and native fluency, the role of participant is in no way privileged as against the role of analyst.

Further, it is clear that communicative and indexical meanings are delimited solely to the level or domain of actual occurrences of use as objects of analysis and that analysis conducted at other levels can be said objectively to involve only significative and referential meanings although the systems of use or models of kinds of meaning which are addressed may have functions and affects at the level of occurrences of use which are indexical or communicative. Pragmatic salience per se, for instance, denotes a conscious system of use which is perceived significatively and referentially as a model or body of knowledge though the function and effects of which in usage are communicative and indexical.

In extending a general semantic model to cover the act of analysis, it is possible to say that communicative and indexical systems or, more accurately, models of these systems have significative and referential meanings for those who make use of them or analytically observe them and that significative and referential systems may have incidental communicative and indexical meanings (though these last are irrelevant for purposes of objective analysis by either analyst or participant).

In speaking of communicative and indexical meanings or systems of use per se it is important to note that we are not focusing upon actual occurrences of use as objects of analysis but upon models of systems of use and models of kinds of meaning and, as we cannot get at the observable data of the actual systems or the actual kinds, we are restricted to the necessary, objective relations of meaning of analytic models to analysts. In determining or explaining order in usage or rules of use we have passed beyond the level of evidence of indexical and communicative meanings in occurrences of use and find ourselves formulating and analyzing referential and significative models which are eminently admissible and subject to the methods and conventions of referential and significative analyses.

Finally, to return to the Pawnee data, it may be said that the symbolism of bundles was used in many different contexts to many different ends. Control of knowledge of underlying rules of usage resulting in different, context-specific meanings or interpretations allowed a small, carefully closed group of persons control over much of Pawnee culture and society. Of primary interest are the questions of who in the community controls knowledge of these folk models and of whether those aspects or meanings which folk models cover are, in any way, arguments for pragmatic salience as a special case of or kind of meaning. For instance, why do models of context-specific usage appear to be controlled by ritual specialists while knowledge of or models of belief systems do not?

From the systematic examination of kinds of meanings perceived, in sections (5) and (6), it is clear that pragmatic salience is not perceived any differently than are models of systems of use. Pragmatic salience, then, is not a special kind of meaning. It is, however, also clear that control over knowledge of rules of usage of beliefs and practices can be a very powerful instrument for the control and manipulation of populations and of social and cultural phenomena. In this sense usage, and particularly the context-dependent aspects of usage (and communicative and indexical meanings are, certainly, primarily concerned here), may be seen as the fulcrum by which turns the realization of any general semantic system.

NOTE: I would like to acknowledge the influence of J. Joseph Errington in the evolution of this study to a more semantic approach to the problem and data in question. I would also like to note that the notion of 'pragmatic salience' is of his authorship and that whatever I may have done to it here is of mine. Finally, I would like to thank William E. Bittle for first interesting me in Plains sacred and personal bundles and in the relation of language and culture generally.

NATIVE NORTH AMERICAN TRICKSTER-AND-VULTURE TALES

by

Pierre Ventur

225

ABSTRACT

     Etiological tales--explanatory/cautionary stories--are worldwide in their
distribution. This paper examines a large corpus (some several dozen) of such
tales (here termed "Trickster-and-Vulture tales") collected from speakers of a
number of eastern North American language groups: Algonquian, Siouan,
Iroquoian, Caddoan and Muskogean. Using a typological scheme in which the
stories are classified according to the presence or absence of the central
narrative elements (antecedant, intervening incident and consequence), the
tales are compared to one another and to similar folk-tales from the Caribbean
(hence of ultimately African origin) and Central America. With respect to the
etiological or explanatory element, the conclusion is reached (contra T. T.
Waterman and Stith Thompson) that the moral is an integral part of the stories
and not merely "a piece added on to give an interesting ending." The
affinities to African-Caribbean tales suggest a two-way flow of influence.
Certain Jamaican/Louisiana-French stories (the John Crow/carencro tales) seem
to have contributed elements to some Southeastern (notably Biloxi) folktales.
Conversely, the main corpus of indigenous Trickster-and-Vulture tales have
probably been the source of some American Negro stories.

226

NATIVE NORTH AMERICAN TRICKSTER-AND-VULTURE TALES

Pierre Ventur

The universal occurrence of the explanatory element throughout Native American folk-literature—etiological tales or tale motifs that account for or "explain" phenomena—has long been a focus of interest to folklorists. Nearly 60 years ago in a pioneering study of the explanatory element in North American Indian folktales, T. T. Waterman (1914) addressed many of the key questions concerning how such elements should be defined, studied, and, most importantly, interpreted. By comparing some 36 well-known tales and tale episodes drawn from the oral traditions of about 60 tribes from seven cultural subareas of aboriginal America north of Mexico, Waterman sought to ascertain what part the explanatory tendency played in the formation of folktales; that is, to what extent "the tendency to explain a certain thing had something to do with the origin and shaping of explanatory tales" (Waterman 1914:20). In seeking to answer this question, Waterman considered, among other things, what in fact constitutes an explanation, and what exactly is being explained; whether explanations seem to be conscious elaborations; how explanatory elements are integrated in relation to other aspects of folktales, such as story-plot and dramatis personae; and how to approach such problems as the regularity, variability, comparability, and temporal stability of explanatory elements.

Waterman's conclusion, succinctly stated, was that at least as far as Native North American oral traditions are concerned "the story is the original thing, and explanation an after-thought," and that "in the absence of evidence to the contrary...in North America, generally speaking, tales do not originate as explanations." Explanations "seem to be purely secondary:" while explanatory tales do exist, and while some tales may be based on the desire to explain, "many explanatory tales are not so by nature, but through accident and re-interpretation" (Waterman 1914:41; cf. Thompson 1929:xvii).

Stith Thompson (1946:9) similarly dismissed the significance of explanatory elements, suggesting that "explanation...seems to be the entire reason for the existence of the story, but more often than is usually recognized these explanations are merely added to a story to give an interesting ending. Such explanations may indeed be attached to almost any narrative form."

This study analyzes one set of etiological tales—what I shall call the Native North American/Trickster-and-Vulture tales—in which the explanatory element is anything but secondary or peripheral. A careful, detailed comparison of some two dozen versions of this folktale, the majority obtained from speakers of Algonquian and Siouan languages spoken in the Great Lakes region and on the eastern prairies, reveals that these tales share a basic morphological structure, as well as numerous parallels in the clustering of narrative elements. The primary goal of this study is to establish that while there is considerable variation within this corpus in the minutiae of narrative detail, individual tales typically being tailored to fit the requirements of a particular cultural milieu, Native North American Trickster-and-Vulture tales are, taken as a whole, internally consistent in terms of overall narrative structure and of such criteria as the identity and nature of dramatis personae, as well as other important narrative elements. From this perspective, the corpus of Native North American Trickster-and-Vulture tales can be readily contrasted with other North American and Caribbean etiological tales which also explain why "buzzards" (the red-headed turkey vulture, Cathartes aura, and the black-headed common vulture, Coragyps atrata) lack head plumage. Thus, I argue, the former constitute a set of related aboriginal folktales, while the latter form an unrelated body of folktales that derive from diverse oral traditions (Native American, French, Caribbean, and possibly African).

The original impetus that gave rise to this study was my collection of a Mesoamerican folktale, aj ch'om k'aʔlal tu yit aʔ tzimine ("The Vulture Caught in the Mule's Rectum"), one of 33 modern Itza Maya folktales collected in the Peten region of northern Guatemala in 1976.[1] Containing the last of the three basic components of the fully developed Native North American Trickster-and-Vulture tale, and being exactly parallel in terms of the most salient narrative elements, this Itza folktale would according to the typology developed here be classified as a Mesoamerican version of Type IIIc. Significantly, this Itza folktale can be shown on the basis of linguistic, iconographic, and hieroglyphic evidence to have relatively great local time depth (in excess of 1,500 years). Establishing, then, that the corpus of Native North American Trickster-and-Vulture tales is indeed aboriginal, and that my Itza Maya folktale is a Mesoamerican exemplar of Type IIIc, serves first of all to reinforce the conclusion based upon other types of evidence that the Itza tale is ancient, not recently introduced into the Maya area. More importantly, through tying the Itza tale directly to the corpus of Native North American Trickster-and-Vulture tales—and possibly to certain South American myths—Brinton's early formulation (Brinton 1868) of a common aboriginal substrate underlying New World mythology and religion finds new support.

This study is intentionally limited to the corpus of Native North American Trickster-and-Vulture tales. Through analyzing this corpus, a typology based upon internal morphological criteria, that is, narrative structure, has gradually emerged. This typology (Fig. 1) encompasses the entire spectrum of Native North American Trickster-and-Vulture tales and serves as a system for classifying the various tales into comparable tale types. The scheme also provides a convenient framework by which other New

World etiological tales, Native American and otherwise, can be evaluated.
Such an approach has broad implications for the analysis and classification of
other kinds of Native American folktales and myths--first, as a basis for
determining the likelihood that given texts are related; second, in the event
that this seems to be the case, as a means of showing systematically how a
given set of narratives are similar and, equally importantly, in what respects
they differ; and finally, as regards the diffusion of folktales and myths or
of the narrative elements which comprise them, as a framework for interpreting
individual elements or clusters of elements that have become detached from
their original folkloric content, that is, collected in isolation or
incorporated within other folk narratives. Once the overall structure and
basic features of an "original" folktale or myth have been established, such
isolated or incorporated elements can be readily related back to the original
core myths or tales from which they diverged, diffused, or descended. A good
case in point here is the incorporation of the third component of the
Trickster-and-Vulture tale into traditional American Negro narratives.

    In Table 1 are presented the sources of the various Native North American
etiological tales discussed in this paper. There are undoubtedly other
relevant texts, both published and otherwise, which I have not located, but
this corpus of tales is sufficiently comprehensive for the purposes of this
study.

    The texts are discussed below according to the analytical categories into
which they have been grouped (Fig. 1). First, Type I, fully developed
Trickster-and-Vulture tales, all of which contain three components occurring
in the same, invariable order: (a) an antecedent--malicious injury inflicted
upon the Trickster-figure by a vulture or, in some instances, another avian
protagonist, usually an eagle or a hawk; (b) an intervening incident--
typically, the Trickster's fall into a hollow log or tree stump and his
subsequent encounter with some women from a hunting party who free him; and
(c) a consequence--the revenge meted out by the Trickster, who succeeds in
bringing about the vulture's loss of head feathers by disguising himself as a
sham-dead animal and trapping the vulture by the neck in his rectum. (For
analytical purposes explained below [see under "Type I, Composite"], three
separate incidents in Radin's Winnebago Trickster cycle are grouped together
as a composite Type I tale, while two Plains Ojibwa tales collected and
numbered consecutively by Skinner are classified as a Type I variant because,
although the intervening incident is structurally parallel to that in all the
other Type I tales, a different cluster of narrative elements substitutes for
the hollow-tree incident [see under "Type I, Variant"]). Second, Type II
tales, in which only two of the above components occur. This category is
subdivided into Type IIa tales, containing components (a) and (b), but not
(c); Type IIb tales, which contain (a) and (c), but lack (b); and Type IIc
tales having only (b) and (c). Third, Type III tales, in which only one of
the three components occurs, the subcategories here being IIIa, IIIb, and IIIc
containing, respectively components (a), (b), or (c).

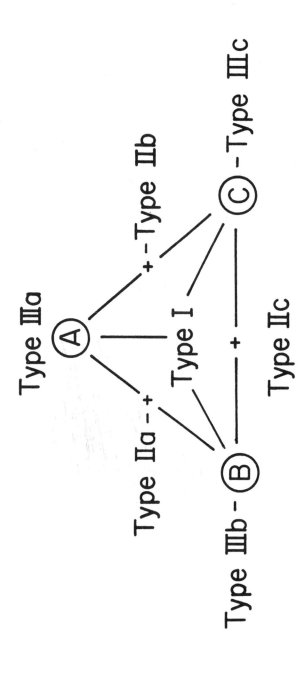

Type IIa

Type IIa – +

Type IIIb – B

Type I

Type IIc

+ – Type IIb

C – Type IIIc

A = Antecedent
B = Intervening Incident
C = Consequence

FIGURE 1. Narrative Structure of Native North American Trickster-and-Vulture Tales

LINGUISTIC AFFILIATION	SOURCE	TALE TYPE
ALGONQUIAN		
Kickapoo	Jones and Michelson 1913:9-13; No. 2	I
Ojibwa	Jones 1917:132-139; No. 16	I
Winnebago	Radin 1948:68-69, 79-80; 1956:20-21, 35; Nos. 17-18, 35	I, Composite
Plains Ojibwa (Timiskaming)	Skinner 1919:281-283; Nos. 4, 4a	I, Composite, with Variant in (b)
Eastern Ojibwa	Bloomfield 1956:224-227; Nos. 37-38	IIa
Mattagami Ojibwa	Speck 1915:38-39; No. 2	IIa
Menomini	Hoffman 1896:165	IIa
Menomini	Hoffman 1896:200-203; cf. Thompson 1929: 57-59	IIb
Plains Ojibwa	Skinner 1919:283; No. 4b	IIb
Ojibwa	Young 1903:222-229	IIb
Menomini	Bloomfield 1928:232-233; No. 83	IIb
Menomini	Skinner and Satterlee 1915:292-293	IIb
Sauk/Fox	Jones 1901:235-237	IIb, Variant
Menomini	Skinner 1913:78	IIIc
Ojibwa	Radin 1914:16-17; No. 6d	IIIc
CADDOAN		
Pawnee	Dorsey 1906:443-444; No. 124	IIa

TABLE 1. Native North American Trickster-and-Vulture Tale Types

LINGUISTIC AFFILIATION	SOURCE	TALE TYPE
IROQUOIAN		
Cherokee	Mooney 1900:293; No. 46	IIIc
MUSKOGEAN		
Koasati	Swanton 1929:211; No. 46	IIb
SIOUAN		
Iowa	Skinner 1925:486-487; No. 27; cf. Coffin 1961:142-143 No. 37	I
Omaha/Ponka	Dorsey 1890:74-78; cf. Dorsey 1892:302, Radin 1956:128	I
Teton-Dakota	Deloria 1932:36-43; No. 7	IIa
Assiniboine	Lowie 1910:107, No. 8; cf. Radin 1956:98	IIb
Assiniboine	Lowie 1910:108, No. 9; cf. Radin 1956:98	IIb, Variant
Assiniboine	Lowie 1910:107, No. 7; cf. Schoolcroft 1856:63-64	IIIa

TABLE 1. Native North American Trickster-and-Vulture Tale Types

All told, some two dozen texts can be classified according to this typology (Table 1). Others are clearly related to this corpus of Trickster-and-Vulture tales but for various reasons are not amenable to classification within this system; these, along with representative examples of texts which superficially resemble Trickster-and-Vulture tales but are not, in my view, related to them are discussed following the section on Type IIIc tales.

Type 1:   The Fully Developed Tale

The fully developed Type I Trickster-and-Vulture tale has the antecedent, intervening hollow-tree incident, and consequence all occurring within a single, coherent, bounded tale rather than as tale fragments or separate incidents within a larger myth. Two Type I tales are recorded in Algonquian language texts (Kickapoo [Jones and Michelson 1915:9-13; No. 2] and Ojibwa [Jones 1917:132-139; No. 16]), and two others were obtained from speakers of Siouan languages (Omaha/Ponka [Dorsey 1890:74-78; cf. Dorsey 1892-302, Radin 1956:128] and Sauk [Skinner 1925:486-487; No. 27; cf. Coffin 1961:142-143; No. 37]).

(a)   The Antecedent (Injury of the Trickster-Figure)

In the Kickapoo tale, Wīza'kä'ạ,[2] the Trickster-figure, sees an arrow-head up in the sky that he would like to have as he is lying down on his back gazing upward. W. pleads with Buzzard, whom he addresses as Uncle, to carry him up to get the arrow-head, and Buzzard complies, leaving him hanging onto the edge of the sky while he supposedly flies off to fetch the best one. Eventually tiring and realizing that Buzzard has no intention of returning, W. lets go and flutters downward as a leaf, landing in a hollow tree. In the Ojibwa version, the Trickster-figure (Nänabushu) is travelling along and sees Buzzard, his little brother, seated on a cloud; Nänabushu is envious of his ability to see the earth below and coaxes the reluctant vulture down from his cloud. Buzzard carries Nänabushu up to a large cloud, endeavouring to play a trick on him because Nänabushu is always tricking others. The cloud breaks apart in the wind, growing smaller and smaller, and Buzzard flies off to a large cloud, leaving Nänabushu stranded. When the cloud breaks apart, Nänabushu falls into a hollow tree. In the Omaha/Ponka tale, Ictinike the Trickster comes to the edge of a great body of water which he wishes to cross. Seeing Buzzard, his grandfather, flying around, Ictinike prays to him to be taken across, and Buzzard allows him to mount on his back; but instead of carrying Ictinike across the water, Buzzard searches for a hollow tree and, finding one, tips his wings, causing Ictinike to fall off and into the tree. The Sauk version begins exactly like the Ojibwa tale, with the Trickster-figure, Îshjînki, engaging Buzzard, his grandfather, in conversation so as to be taken up into the air. At first declining because Îshjînki's natural element is the earth, not the sky, Buzzard finally agrees. Îshjînki begs and teases Buzzard to fly higher and higher, and after the fourth time Buzzard swoops down near the tree tops and tips Îshjînki headfirst into a hollow stump.

(b) The Hollow-Tree Incident

In each of the tales, the Trickster-figure devises a clever ruse by which to escape from the hollow tree/tree stump into which he has fallen. In the Kickapoo tale, an old woman out cutting firewood makes a hole in the tree in which Wīza'kä'ạ is stuck and plucks a hair from the body of what she thinks is a bear. Returning home with the bear-hair as proof of her fortuitous find, the woman returns with her husband and, spurred on by Wīza'kä'ạ (who addresses her as Aunt), proceeds to enlarge the hole in the tree while her husband prepares to shoot the animal. Wīza'kä'ạ then emerges from the hole and makes a real bear appear, which he then kills and gives to the elderly couple. In the Ojibwa version, Nänabushu's two sisters (see Jones 1917:135, note 1) come by laughing, in search of the Gray Porcupine. Hearing their animated conversation, Nänabushu speaks up, saying that he is the Gray Porcupine that dwells inside the hollow tree. The women begin cutting down the tree, agreeing that whichever one finds the Gray Porcupine may claim him as her husband; Nänabushu hopes that the younger of the two will succeed. The younger sister goes about splitting up the tree, vainly searching for the Gray Porcupine and breaking her axe in the process; her elder sister continues the endeavour but is also unable to find the animal, and Nänabushu leaps up and runs away laughing at having deceived the women. In the Omaha/Ponka tale, Ictinike happens to land in a hollow tree near where a large hunting party is encamped, and two sisters-in-law arrive and pound on the tree in which Ictinike is sitting. Conveniently, Ictinike also happens to be wearing some raccoon skins and sticks the tails out through some cracks in the tree. Seeing the tails hanging out, the women begin to make a hole in the tree to get at the raccoons inside; Ictinike encourages them, saying in a deep voice that he is a large raccoon and that they must therefore make a bigger hole so that he can get out. Ictinike then emerges from the tree and converses with the women, who recognize him for what he really is--the Trickster--and immediately flee. In the Sauk version, the hollow-tree incident begins in the same way, with Īshjīṅki landing near a hunting party, but here he puts his coonskin up to a crack in the tree so that the two women out gathering firewood can see it. The women make the hole bigger and bigger in order to see the coonskin more plainly; when the hole is large enough, Īshjīṅki identifies himself as their grandfather and tells the women to let him out. They do so and get their axes and dance, while Īshjīṅki sings.

(c) The Consequence (The Trickster's Revenge)

The details of how the Trickster-figure gets revenge on Buzzard for having maliciously dropped him into the hollow tree are somewhat varied in these four tales: here there is internal consistency in the two Algonquian versions in that certain important details are omitted (e.g., specifying into what kind of sham-dead animal the Trickster transforms himself; that the vulture's head-feathers are lost as a result of this encounter). By contrast, these details are given in the two Siouan versions.

In the Kickapoo version, after giving the dead bear to the elderly couple who had freed him from the tree, Wīza'kä'ạ walks away, wondering where Buzzard has gone to. Acting as if he were dead, he becomes very fat and begins to be eaten by carrion-eating birds. Buzzard arrives shortly and goes headfirst up to his shoulders in Wīza'kä'ạ's anus, at which point Wīza'kä'ạ jumps up, clamping his anus tightly around Buzzard's head. Wīza'kä'ạ then sings derisively while Buzzard flaps his wings pathetically. Wīza'kä'ạ then walks on "verily even ten years"—that is, for a very long time—before freeing Buzzard, and the tale ends with Wīza'kä'ạ giving the vulture a new name, "Buzzard," by which it will henceforth be known. In the Ojibwa tale, Nänabushu continues on his way after the hollow-tree incident, wondering how to repay Buzzard for having tricked him. Coming to a frozen lake, he goes far out on the ice to lie down; there he lies down, feigning death, and wills that he be eaten by birds. Crows and various other birds begin devouring him, but Nänabushu enjoins them from eating his buttocks. Buzzard is attracted by the great racket created by the birds as they feast on Nänabushu, but he is fearful of the carcass. First alighting from far away, Buzzard lingers about tentatively, finally picking at the calf muscle, then hopping away. Becoming gradually bolder, he finally decides to eat from the small of the back "where he is fat," and thrusts his head and neck far into the anus. Nänabushu immediately springs up, closing his rectum tightly over Buzzard's head. He then runs along the lake, dragging Buzzard behind him, releasing him near the far end of the lake where Buzzard plops out onto the ice. The tale ends with Nänabushu cursing the vulture: "'Buzzard shall you be called till the end of the world.... For your filth will you be loathed by all the people.'"

Again, in neither of the two Algonquian Type I tales above is it explicitly stated that the vulture's head-feathers were lost as a result of the encounter with the sham-dead animal; in the two Siouan Type I tales this is made quite clear, however. In the Omaha/Ponka tale, Ictinike sits down after the two women who had freed him from the hollow tree run away to formulate a plan of getting even with Buzzard. He decides to accomplish this by pretending to be dead. Assuming the form of a dead elk, Ictinike implores Crow and Magpie to eat him, and they enlist the aid of Eagle, who with his "sharp knife" tears open a hole through the skin on the rump of the carcass, uncovering the rich fat underneath. Eventually Buzzard arrives, but believing the dead elk to be Ictinike, he refuses to join in. When Magpie enters far inside the hindquarters to eat the fat, Buzzard samples the head, then bites the nostrils and next the eye-lids. Emboldened by Ictinike's not having stirred at any of this, Buzzard moves on to the opposite end of the carcass, where he bites off a piece of fat from near the anus. Convinced at last that it is indeed just a dead elk, Buzzard enters the rectum to bite off a piece of fat; he is successful the first time, but when he enters again Ictinike tightens his sphincter muscles and stands up, holding Buzzard's head securely. He then upbraids Buzzard ("'As you have injured me, so will I do to you.'"), and the tale ends with an etiological coda: "And when he let go suddenly, the Buzzard had no feathers at all on his head on account of their having been stripped off. Therefore, the Buzzard has no feathers on his head; it is very red. The End." (In the abridged version of this tale [Dorsey 1892:302], the resultant condition of the vulture's head is described as resembling "a piece of raw beef." The reference here is clearly to the red-headed turkey vulture.) In the Sauk version, after singing along with his two dancing grand-daughters, Îshjîⁿki transforms himself into a sham-dead horse in a plan to punish Buzzard. He lies still three times while crows peck at his buttocks, but Buzzard is not fooled by this deception. He then becomes a dead elk; birds come and eat most of his buttocks and crows go in and out of his body. Eventually Buzzard arrives; first he pecks around the edge of the anal opening, and then he stretches his head and reaches far inside. Exclaiming gleefully, Îshjîńki closes up the opening and walks off with Buzzard dangling from his buttocks. After punishing him thus for a long time, Îshjîńki lets Buzzard go, and again we are told in an etiological coda: "That is why Buzzard's head is bald and smells bad."

Type I, Composite ([(a) + (b)] + (c))

Taken together, three separate incidents in the Winnebago Trickster cycle can be analyzed as constituting a composite Type I Trickster-and-Vulture tale. Incidents 17 and 18 (Radin 1948:68-69; 1956:20-21) contain the now-familiar antecedent and hollow-tree incidents discussed for the previous tales, and No. 34 (Radin 1948:79-80; 1956:35) contains the Trickster's revenge. While for the purposes of his study Radin kept these as discrete incidents, he recognized that all three actually belong together: in his first, more amplified study of the Winnebago hero cycles, Radin (1948:21) grouped the first two incidents together as the Seventh Episode of the cycle, noting that "the pendant of 17 and 18 is to be found in 34" (his Fourteenth Episode).[3] These incidents parallel those in the preceding Type I tales but differ from them in also having certain narrative elements in common with many of the Type II and Type III tales analyzed below; additionally, there is an internal inconsistency between the first and third incidents in that, unlike other Type I tales, a different avian protagonist figures in each (a turkey vulture in No. 17, as opposed to a hawk in No. 34).

In the antecedent (incident No. 17), Trickster is, as usual, walking along aimlessly. Hearing a turkey vulture (Radin's term is turkey-buzzard) strieking overhead, he becomes envious of him and engages the bird in conversation, addressing him as Younger Brother. Trickster mounts on the vulture's back, and after considerable exertion because of Trickster's great weight the bird becomes airborne. While Trickster contents himself in the euphoria of flying, the vulture looks around for a hollow tree, intending to play a trick on him. He finds one and drops Trickster into it. Radin's notes to the text are instructive at this point: "There is no intimation that Trickster intended to play a trick on the turkey-buzzard, but tricks are always to be expected of him." (Radin 1956:56, note 46); thus it made perfect sense from the vulture's point of view to rid himself of his passenger before falling prey himself to Trickster's predictable wiles. Trickster's ensuing escape from the hollow tree in incident No. 18 parallels three of the preceding four Type I tales (Ojibwa, Omaha/Ponka, and Sauk versions) in that he mimicks a raccoon. From inside the hollow Trickster hears the echoes of trees being cut down; the wood-cutters come closer and Trickster hears some women conversing. He calls out to them, saying that he is a bod-tailed raccoon. When the women begin to cut him out of the tree, Trickster puts the raccoon-skin blanket that he happens to have with him next to the hole for them to see, and the women believe they've found a large, fine raccoon. Trickster "the so-called raccoon" next tells them to plug up the hole with women's clothing, then to leave and come right back for him, assuring them that he won't run off. The women disrobe and go home, and Trickster comes out of the tree and wanders off; when the women return for the raccoon there is nothing to be found.

The consequence (incident No. 34) opens with Trickster meeting a hawk "in search of something dead or decaying." (Hawks, like crows, ravens, and vultures, are carrion-eaters.) Remembering that the hawk had once played a trick on him (cf. incident No. 17), Trickster lies down at the edge of a large body of water and assumes the form of a large buck-deer, dead but not yet decomposed. Crows are there anxious to begin feeding but cannot penetrate the deer's tough hide. They call repeatedly to the hawk, for "He alone generally has a sharp knife." Hawk finally arrives and with great energy goes all around the carcass looking for a place to attack it; finally coming to the soft hindquarter, he works his head into the rectum, and when his head is far inside Trickster closes his anus tightly. Gloating at having gotten even with Hawk, Trickster continues on his journey, with the trapped bird unable to extricate itself from its predicament: "At first he kept his wings flapping all the time but, after a while, he only flapped them intermittently." As the avian protagonist here in this incident from the Winnebago Trickster cycle is a hawk rather than a vulture, it is not surprising that no mention is made of any loss of head feathers. It is worth emphasizing, too, that as noted earlier, this detail was also lacking in the consequences of the two other Algonquian Type I tales (Kickapoo and Ojibwa versions).

Type I, Composite, with Variant in (b)

A single example, in Plains Ojibwa, has been found of a tale in which there is a different cluster of narrative elements in (b), the intervening incident; otherwise this tale is structurally parallel to the other Type I tales. Normally, as seen in the preceding tales, the Trickster-figure falls into a hollow tree after being dropped by the vulture, and escapes from it by means of a ruse. Here, however, Trickster lands unharmed and encounters a group of birds as he stands at the edge of a deep gorge. This substitution of narrative elements in (b) is of more than passing interest, as the occurrence of these elements in this Type I tale serves to tie in numerous other Native North American tales with the corpus of Trickster-and-Vulture tales--a linkage which might not otherwise be suspected.[4]

Once again, as with the three incidents in Radin's Winnebago Trickster cycle, I have combined what are recorded by the tale-collector (Skinner) as two distinct tales, or more precisely, as I interpret Skinner's numbering system and notes, as one basic tale and a variation of it (numbers 4 and 4(a), both entitled "Nänibozhu and the Buzzard," under "Tales of the Culture-Hero," in Skinner 1919:281-282).

The antecedent and intervening incident are contained in Skinner's first tale (No. 4). The antecedent begins as usual: Nänibozhu, walking along, sees a vulture and, addressing it as Brother, asks to be taken aloft; Buzzard agrees and off they go. Buzzard eventually tires, but Nänibozhu insists on continuing higher and higher, and the bird, undoubtedly annoyed at this, banks, causing Nänibozhu to fall off. Announcing that he had created the world, Nänibozhu desires to land in "a soft place" and does so, landing unharmed. The intervening incident bridging Nänibozhu's fall with the revenge that he will later take on Buzzard also begins with his walking along, to arrive at the edge of a deep gorge with a river at the bottom. Stepping back from the precipice, he vows to jump across if someone will promise to give him a young girl (the significance of his saying this is not immediately apparent, but this element may be related to the appearance of the women gathering firewood in the hollow-tree incident in the other Type I tales). Some partridges come along and see what Nänibozhu is about to do and sneak up on him when he approaches the edge of the gorge for the second time. Nänibozhu delays leaping, and when he is about to jump the gorge for the fourth time, the partridges rise up with a tremendous rush and startle him; Nänibozhu falls over the edge, once more landing unharmed, this time in soft sand.

The consequence is found in 4a, Skinner's first variation of tale No. 4. Looking up from where he has fallen, Nänibozhu arises and climbs up a hill, where he turns himself into a dead moose. All the birds come to feed on the carcass, but they fly away when Buzzard arrives. Though not explicitly stated in the text, they apparently had already devoured most of the carcass, for the only flesh left is at Moose's anus. Fearing that the carcass might be Nänibozhu, Buzzard pecks cautiously at first, then really gets busy; Nänibozhu immediately comes to life, catches hold of Buzzard, and walks off with the bird hanging out his rectum, flapping its wings. Nänibozhu does not intend to kill Buzzard, however; he merely wants to get even with him. Looking at Buzzard and finding that all of the feathers are now worn off his head, Nänibozhu is elated; he mocks him scornfully, saying that whereas he was formerly "'the finest bird I ever saw'"—in the very first line of Skinner's basic tale (No. 4), the vulture is described as "a fine bird"—he will henceforth be disgusting and evil-smelling, bare-headed and obliged to subsist on carrion. And the vulture is also given the name, "Buzzard," by which he will now be known.

Type IIa: (a) Antecedent + (b) Intervening Incident

Type IIa tales contain the antecedent and the hollow-tree incident but lack component (c), the consequence. Five such tales have been collected in Native North American languages, three from speakers of Algonquian languages (Eastern Ojibwa [Bloomfield 1956:224-227; Nos. 37-38, dictated and recorded versions, respectively]; Mattagami Ojibwa [Speck 1915:38-39; No. 2]; and Menomini [Hoffman 1896:165]); one in Teton-Dakota, a Siouan language (Deloria 1932:36-43; No. 7); and one Caddoan tale, in Pawnee (Dorsey 1906:443-444; No. 124).

(a) The Antecedent

In "Nenabush and the Ducks," the first of the three Algonquian Type IIa tales, the protagonists are Nenabush the Trickster and some ducks instead of a vulture or a hawk. Having been hungry for some time, Nenabush devises a plan to capture some ducks swimming in a river: taking some cord, he dives into the river and swims out to the ducks underwater, ties their legs together, and then surfaces among them. Frightened, the startled ducks take flight, with Nenabush hanging suspended from the cord, but the cord breaks and he falls into a hollow tree from which he cannot crawl out. The Trickster's plan has gone awry—instead of capturing the ducks, he in effect captures himself. In Speck's Mattagami Ojibwa version, the protagonists are a goose and the Trickster, Nenebuc. The goose gives Nenebuc a pair of wings, instructing him how to fly with them, and warning him not to look down. Predictably, Nenabush disobeys this injunction and tumbles down into a big hollow pine stump, where he remains stuck. In the Menomini version, the protagonists are the Menomini Trickster, Mänäbŭsh, and Buzzard, who is addressed as Trickster's brother. Travelling along as usual, Mänäbŭsh sees Buzzard flying high in the air and, musing what it would be like to fly and look out over the earth like Buzzard, flaps his arms as if flying while meditating. These movements attract Buzzard, who flies down to talk with Mänäbŭsh. Amused by the Trickster's wish to fly, Buzzard soars to the top of a high mountain peak with the Trickster on his back, and when Mänäbŭsh climbs off to look about, Buzzard flies away, leaving Trickster in a very precarious situation. Unable to climb down from the precipitous peak, Mänäbŭsh is forced to leap off and lands in a hollow tree from which he cannot extricate himself.

In the Teton-Dakota tale, Ikto the Trickster, dressed in a raccoon-skin robe, is following a narrow creek that unexpectedly converges with a wide, deep river. Unable to cross it, Ikto sits down and begins to cry, at which point a hawk flies by. Flattered by Ikto's self-deprecation, the hawk, who is addressed as Ikto's younger brother, agrees to carry him across the river. Once seated on the hawk's back, however, Trickster's flattery soon turns to insults, one of which—Ikto's snapping his fingers in the manner of a rude, unsocialized child—the hawk sees in their shadow cast on the ground. Angered by this reprehensible behaviour, the hawk realizes that it is Ikto, up to his old tricks, and he decides to get rid of him by dropping him into a hollow tree. Ikto, being telepathic, senses what is in the bird's mind and asks to be put down, continuing nevertheless to snap his fingers at the bird. The hawk again sees this in their shadow, and when he finds a hollow tree banks toward it, suddenly dipping his body sideways; this causes Ikto to fall off, and he falls howling into the hollow, where once again he sits and wails forlornly.

In the single Caddoan Type IIa tale, the protagonists are Coyote-Man, the Pawnee Trickster-figure, and four vultures. Coyote-Man leaves his lodge after having killed and eaten a sick boy; he wanders through the timber and after awhile begins to climb a hill, at the top of which four vultures are seated. Coyote-Man engages them in conversation, asking them to carry him up into the sky so that he can look down as they do and see what the earth is like. Two of the vultures leave, and the two which remain tell Coyote-Man to put his arms around their necks and they all fly off together. Addressing the birds as his grandchildren, Coyote-Man expresses great trepidation at being dropped and asks them to stop. They make several flights, Coyote-Man being terrified each time, and the vultures finally tell him to close his eyes when the first pair of vultures that had flown off earlier circle around and return. The other vultures had scouted out a hollow log into which they wanted to drop Coyote-Man, for they wanted to kill him. The pair of vultures carrying Coyote-Man separate when they fly over the log, and Coyote-Man drops into it, remaining trapped there for several days.

(b) <u>The Hollow-Tree Incident</u>

In Bloomfield's Eastern Ojibwa texts, Nenabush cries out from inside the hollow tree to a pair of approaching women, saying that he is a white porcupine. Fetching an axe, one of the women chops a hole in the tree, but worried that the animal might crawl out and escape, she removes her skirt to plug up the hole. When the hole gets larger, the other woman does the same thing. Finally, when the hole has been made still larger, Nenabush comes running out on all fours, grabs the women's skirts, and runs away with them. In Speck's Mattagami Ojibwa version, the hollow-tree incident ends in a humorous twist, with the Trickster not actually being freed: Two sisters come along with an axe, in search of firewood, and begin to cut into the hollow pine stump into which Nenebuc has fallen; Nenebuc remains silent as they chop, hoping that he will be set free. When the girls look inside the hole they've made, they see Nenebuc's belly and pull out a hair from it, running back to camp to show their father the porcupine quill that they had found in a tree. Looking at the so-called porcupine quill and laughing, he says, "'That's not a porcupine quill, that's a hair from Nenebuc's groin!'"

The third Algonquian version, Hoffman's "Mänäbŭsh and the Buzzard," again finds the Trickster mimicking a porcupine. On the fourth day of Mänäbŭsh's imprisonment in the hollow tree, some women come along in search of dry timber to cut up for firewood. Finding that the tree in which Mänäbŭsh is trapped is indeed dry, the women begin to cut it down, and Mänäbŭsh, not wishing to alarm them, mimics the sounds of a porcupine. Afraid that he may be wounded if they continue to chop down the tree, Mänäbŭsh then tells the woman who has the axe to cut a small opening in the trunk so that he can show her his beautiful quills. The woman does as she is told, and Mänäbŭsh next tells her to take off her skirt and cover the opening until he puts the quills out to where she can get them; when she complies, Mänäbŭsh crawls out and runs away laughing.

Deloria's Teton-Dakota text is by far the richest of all the Type IIa tales in ethnographic detail, and a new minor protagonist is introduced here. As Ikto sits inside the hollow tree bewailing his fate at the hands of the vultures, a red-headed woodpecker comes along and sits on the tree; seeing the bird, Ikto politely addresses him as his younger brother, asking him to please make a little hole for him to see out of. The woodpecker obliges, and Ikto immediately sees two women going by on their way to gather firewood.[5] Deciding "to deceive them to his advantage," he pretends to be a fat raccoon and banters back and forth with them about the efficacy of raccoon fat for tanning hides. The women then chop down the tree, and Ikto sticks the tail from his raccoon-skin robe out through the hole that the woodpecker had made for him; he pokes the tail out tantalizingly, then draws it back inside several times. The women cannot figure out how to get the raccoon out of the tree, so Ikto advises them to smoke him out. At first they decide that only one of them should go back to fetch fire, while the other stays to watch the raccoon, but Ikto intervenes and suggests that it would be better if they both went because "'it is just possible that one's fire may go out; but if so, at least the other's will still be burning.'" Convinced by Ikto's logic, the women set off together for home, and Ikto steps out of the tree the minute they are out of sight; he runs off into the woods, where he sits laughing, waiting for them to return.[6]

Finally, in the Pawnee Coyote-Man text, the Trickster also mimicks a raccoon. Here there are small holes in the sides of the hollow log into which Coyote-Man has been dropped by the pair of vultures. Coyote-Man enlarges the holes to enable him to look out, and one day when he hears "a great noise, as if there were many people travelling" he makes one big hole (exactly how he manages to enlarge the hole is never explained). A large number of people have set up camp nearby, and some women go out to gather dry limbs for firewood after having set up their tipis. As Coyote-Man watches the women approach the log, he cuts off the raccoon tails from his quiver and sticks them out through the hole in the log; the women, seeing the tails hanging out, believe that they have found a hollow log with some raccoons holed up inside. They grab hold of the tails and pull on them, and Coyote-Man pulls back from inside the log. Now definitely convinced that there are indeed raccoons hidden there, the women cut the tree down, and as it falls over Coyote-Man stands up and scolds the women angrily for having cut down his house--thankful, of course, that he has been set free.

Type IIb: (a) Antecedent + (c) Consequence

Type IIb tales consist of the antecedent, (a), and the consequence, (c), but lack an intervening incident bridging together the Trickster's fall and his subsequent revenge-taking. Synopses of seven examples of Type IIb tales are presented below in Table 2, ordered as follows according to the language in which they were collected:

LANGUAGE	TALE NUMBER IN TABLE 2	SOURCE OF TEXT
ALGONQUIAN		
Menomini	1	Hoffman 1896:200-203; cf. Thompson 1929:57-59
Menomini	2	Skinner and Satterlee 1915:292-293
Menomini	3	Bloomfield 1928:232-235; No. 83
Ojibwa	4	Young 1903:222-229
Plains Ojibwa	5	Skinner 1919:282; No. 4(b)
MUSKOGEAN		
Koasati	6	Swanton 1929:211; No. 46
SIOUAN		
Assiniboine	7	Lowie 1910:107; Trickster Cycle, No. 8, cf. Radin 1956:98

(a) Antecedent

No. 1. Animals meet in council to decide what each will eat; Buzzard (turkey vulture) chooses to subsist "on fish and animals that have died and become soft." Mä´näbúsh, seeing B. flying above him, asks to be taken up into air; B. obliges. B., reassuring M. that he'll be careful, while determined to play a trick on him if possible, banks sharply, causing M. to lose grip. M. falls to earth, is knocked unconscious. B. continues flying around, watching M. M. revives, finds own buttocks staring him in face, his body having become doubled up upon impact with ground. M. vows to get revenge; B. laughs scornfully, vows to prevent this by being on guard. M. continues on journey; B. flies off.

No. 2. Buzzard, flying around in heavens, seen by Mä´näbus, who engages him in conversation; B. initially ignores M.'s entreaties to descend, finally does so. M. asks to be taken flying to see world; B. agrees, but protests M.'s great weight. M. shrinks self to size of red squirrel; B. takes him up. M. and B. fly around; B. tires and wants to stop, but M. insists they continue, enjoying himself immensely. B. becomes fatigued, makes sommersault, shaking back and wings, causing M. to fall. M. knocked unconscious upon impact with ground, revives to finds pair of buttocks near face; tells them to go away, slaps them, realizes they are his own. M. cures self with handful of earth. M. vows revenge, admitting misfortune was partly own fault, laughing one minute and crying the next.

(c) Consequence

M. decides to transform self into dead deer, knowing B. has chosen to subsist on dead animals and fish. M. lies down on high hill, assuming form of a deer carcass. Various birds, beasts, and crawling things that subsist on carrion congregate; B. eventually joins them after cautiously circling around several times to see if deer might be M. B. approaches carcass, pecks hole into fleshy part of thigh, sticks head deep inside until head and neck are completely buried; goes in and out plucking fat from intestines. M. jumps up, pinches flesh together around B.'s head, holding it securely. M. mocks B., tells him to pull head out; B. does so with great difficulty, leaving scalp and neck "covered with nothing but red skin." M. curses B. Etiological coda reinforces M.'s curse.

M. continues travels, decides to change into big elk; M. very fat, as it is autumn. M. decides not to kill B., because B. had not killed him. M. goes up big hill, lies down feigning death; animals and all manner of birds gather to feast on carcass, evour upper part of body but leave hindquarter untouched. B. eventually arrives, suspicious at first, fearing power of M., but finally decides to eat, beginning by pecking around rectum. As rectum is wide open, B. sticks beak in, pulls at fat, pushing in farther. M. closes rectum, securing B.'s neck; B. immediately realizes he is in power of M., begs for mercy. M. mocks B., walks away with him dangling. B. again pleads for mercy; M. takes him out to look at head, decides punishment is insufficient, thrusts him back inside. M. resumes journey, looks at B.'s head again, sees that feathers have rooted off, lets him go. M.'s pronouncement as etiological coda.

TABLE 2. Synopses of Type IIb Trickster-and-Vulture Tales

(a) Antecedent

No. 3. Me'napus, tramping along, sees Buzzard flying aloft. M. engages B. in conversation, asks to be taken for ride; B. declines at first, protesting M.'s great weight, finally agrees. M. and B. fly around; B. decides to dispose of M., jerks body, causing M. to fall. Thoughts rush through M.'s head, suddenly blacks out. M. revives to find body broken in two, with buttocks in front of face; fixes self up, starts walking again. M. curses B., vows to get revenge.

No. 4. Romanticized introduction sets stage for telling of tale, with narrator saying it is turkey vulture's own fault that he lacks head plumage. Nanabhoozhoo, walking along, sees Buzzard making great circles in sky like an eagle. N. approaches B. when bird alights on rock, engages him in conversation. N. asks to be taken up to see what earth looks like, but is fearful lest he fall off; B. reassures him, while planning to play trick on him because of an old grudge which N. has forgotten. N. and B. fly off; B. sees wigwam of his grandmother, raises arms in excitement; B. takes advantage of situation, tilts body causing N. to lose grip and fall to earth. N. knocked unconscious; revives, annoyed and disgusted at allowing B. to trick him. B. laughs at his treachery; N. vows to get revenge by putting mark on him, he responds by vowing to be on guard. N. resumes journey; B., watching N., not observing anything unusual, flies off.

(c) Consequence

M. encounters herd of elk, engages them in conversation; insistently begs to be made an elk, and becoming one wants to be biggest, with largest antlers. Elk herd, with M. among them, chased by wolves; M.'s antlers get caught in trees. Wolves overtake and kill M. Creatures devour M., including crows who dig out his eyes; only M.'s bones remain, with small lump of fat meat sticking inside anus. B. arrives, sticks head inside to get at fat; M. draws anus closed, rises up, carries B. around with him for long time. M. amused at B.'s flapping wings, finally releases him. B. sits reeling, with head now entirely bald. M. pronounces etiological curse before leaving.

N. decides to turn self into dead deer, knowing B. subsists on dead animals. N. goes to top of high hill, transforms self; carrion-eaters arrive to devour carcass. B., seeing scavengers gathering, arrives; suspicious at first, B. is convinced by other animals that it is carcass of a deer. B. tears hole in side of body to get at rich fat around kidneys, wishing best for himself; when B.'s head is buried deep inside body, N. jumps up, closing flesh around head, holding B. securely. N. orders B. to withdraw head, which he does with great difficulty. In process, all head feathers are stripped off; only red, rough-looking skin remains. N. curses B., saying B.'s condition will be permanent sign to remind all of his treachery; also, that he will be detected and shunned for having disagreeable odor from eating rank food. Etiological coda by narrator reinforces N.'s curse.

TABLE 2. Synopses of Type IIb Trickster-and-Vulture Tales

(a) Antecedent

(c) Consequence

No. 5. Wenibozo, having seen all of earth and water, now wishing to explore air, begs Buzzard to take him aloft; B. agrees, upon condition that W. make himself small. They go so high that W. becomes dizzy and faints. B. places slumbering W. on edge of a precipice so that he'll fall off upon awakening. W. saves self, is furious at discovering the trick played on him by B.

To get revenge, W. turns himself into dead bull, lies where B. will see him. B. arrives, pecks out W.'s eyes; W. remains still until B.'s head is thrust up his rectum. W. contracts muscles, B. pulls feathers from head in struggle to get loose; B.'s head bald ever since.

No. 6. Rabbit, lying down resting, approached by Buzzard. B. accedes to R.'s request to be taken for ride. R. taken upward, left hanging to a door (presumably to B.'s house). B. flies off with other B.'s. R. tires, falls to ground, and bursts.

R. nursed back to health by his grandmother, who instructs him to seek revenge on B. B. lies down in marsh, feigning death, seizes B. when he alights on top of him. Assisted by grandmother, R. procedes to pull out B.'s feathers. R. ties B. in marsh, calls for cold weather. Grandmother gives B. a switching when it becomes very cold.

No. 7. Sitconski, feeling lonesome, asks to travel with Eagle; E. agrees. E. takes S. upward, abandons him on icy mountain in clouds. S. begs to be taken down; E. ignores him. Ice melts, S. wills that he strike earth in soft spot; falls headfirst into swamp, stuck up to hips.

S. begins to plot against E; tells all animals he will turn into dead moose, instructs them not to eat from his hips. E. flies down, wanting to eat "some of the forbidden food," but draws back when S.'s eyes move. E. finally takes bit, then eats more. S. tells E. that he wishes revenge on him for having been abandoned on mountain; S. arises. E. perishes. Etiological coda explains that color of E.'s head is due to his rubbing it against S.'s anus.

TABLE 2. Synopses of Type IIb Trickster-and-Vulture Tales

Taken as a group, the five Algonquian tales contrast with the two Koasati and Assiniboine ones in two ways: First, the principal protagonists in 1-5 are the Trickster-figure and a vulture; and second, in the consequence, in order to take revenge on the vulture for having dropped him, Trickster transforms himself into a large quadruped--a deer in 1 and 4; an elk in 2 and 3; and a bull in 5. A similar transformation occurs in 7, with Sitconski, the Assiniboine Trickster-figure, becoming a sham-dead moose. In this tale, however, the avian protagonist is an eagle (probably a bald eagle), not a vulture. Swanton's Koasati tale, "Rabbit and Buzzard" (No. 6), is like the Algonquian tales in having a vulture-protagonist, but the consequence differs from that in all of the other tabulated tales in that Rabbit does not actually undergo a transformation (he only lies down, pretending to be dead). Also, here the vulture does not lose his feathers through having them stripped off in the struggle to extricate himself from the Trickster's rectum: instead, Rabbit jumps up and grabs Buzzard, and then, assisted by his grandmother who had devised the plan, pulls his feathers out.

Within the set of five Algonquian tales, the three Menomini versions all share one motif absent in the remaining Type IIb tales--the Trickster's body is either broken in two or doubled up by the force of impact with the ground, Trickster ending up ass-backwards with his own buttocks staring him in the face. This same motif figures in other Menomini Trickster-and-Vulture tales, but this element does not occur in any non-Menomini tales, not even in those collected from speakers of other Algonquian or nearby Siouan languages.

A number of other noteworthy elements occur in this set of Type IIb tales, and while it is not possible within the limited scope of this study to elaborate upon them in any detail, they nevertheless do merit special attention because they have clear parallels in other Trickster-and-Vulture tales. Also, in certain cases these elements suggest a basis for tying in other Native North American folktales with our corpus of Trickster-and-Vulture tales, in the same manner as the substitution of narrative elements in (b), the intervening incident in the Type I Trickster-and-Vulture tales (see discussion of Skinner's Plains Ojibwa tale, "Nänibozhu and the Buzzard," under "Type I, Variant").

The first such element occurs in Hoffman's second version of the Menomini Trickster-and-Vulture tale (Table 2, No. 1). In a beautiful illustration of how logically consistent and generally devoid of superfluous detail these tales are, we (along with the Trickster, Mänäbush), learn at the very beginning of the tale that when all the animals met in council to decide what each would live on, Buzzard chose to subsist "on fish and animals that have died and become soft." The significance of this fact is that in (c), the consequence, Mänäbush utilizes this knowledge in devising a plan to get even with Buzzard: knowing that the bird is now a carrion-eater and would therefore be attracted to carcasses, Mänäbush transforms himself into a sham-dead deer. Also within the antecedent are certain physical and behavioural attributes of the Trickster which contribute to his being dropped by the vulture. The physical attribute is Trickster's enormous size--something that makes the vulture reluctant to take him aloft to begin with and which, once airborne, causes the bird to become fatigued. The behavioural attribute is Trickster's constant nagging throughout these Type IIb tales to continue flying despite his knowing that the vulture is obviously

exhausted and no longer wishes to fly. In Skinner's Menomini version
(Table 2, No. 2), Mänäbŭs shrinks himself "to the size of a red squirrel" when
Buzzard balks at his great weight, yet Buzzard still tires. Mänäbŭsh's small
size underscores how aggravating his nagging must have been: because Mänäbŭsh
is only squirrel-size, he cannot weigh very much, and so the vulture could
easily carry him without tiring. For the bird to have become exhausted
carrying the squirrel-size Trickster, therefore, he must have done a great
deal of flying. It is quite understandable, then, when Buzzard has finally
had enough and dumps Mänäbŭsh off. In the Bloomfield version (No. 3), Buzzard
again protests Me'napus's great weight but agrees to take him up anyway, and
in No. 5, the last Algonquian tale, Buzzard offers to allow Wenibozo to mount
on his back only upon condition that he make himself small.

Another salient behavioural attribute of the Trickster that figures in
many Trickster-and-Vulture tales, as in Trickster tales generally, is his
predilection for perpetrating tricks and deceptions. This is hinted at in
only one of the seven Type IIb tales: in No. 4, Young's romanticized Ojibwa
version, "The buzzard told Nanabhoozhoo that he would be very careful,
although at the same time he was resolved, if it were possible, to play a
trick on him; for he had a grudge of some long standing against him which
Nanabhoozhoo seemed to have forgotten" (Young 1903:224-225).

Two other noteworthy elements occur in the antecedent section of the
fifth Algonquian Type IIb tale (Table 2, No. 5), and in Lowie's eighth
incident in the Assiniboine Trickster cycle (Table 2, No. 7). These elements
involve the physical characteristics of where the Trickster falls and serve to
contrast these two tales from the other five Type IIb tales. In the three
Menomini versions, as noted above, the Trickster's body is either contorted or
broken in two when he impacts with the ground; in 4 he is knocked unconscious
but eventually revives; and in 6, Rabbit, who substitutes for the
Trickster-figure in this Koasati tale, actually bursts when he hits the
ground. Here, however, in 5 and 7, Trickster is not injured at all: In 5
Buzzard places the slumbering Wenibozo on the edge of a precipice, hoping that
he will fall off when he wakes up, but Trickster somehow saves himself (we are
not told how). In 7, Sitcoñski, the Assiniboine Trickster, is abandoned by
Eagle on an icy mountain in the clouds; when the ice melts, he wills that he
strike the earth in a soft place and falls headfirst into a swamp, stuck up to
his hips but otherwise uninjured. There are analogues to both of these
elements--the mountain/precipice and the swamp--in several other
Trickster-and-Vulture tales, and also in other Native North American tales, at
least some of which are probably related to the present corpus (see below,
following "Type IIIc Tales").

One final element deserving special comment is the characterization of
the moose carcass as "the forbidden food" in Lowie's Assiniboine tale.
Numerous explanations could be offered as to why this might occur here; e.g.,
a culturological explanation that this might be related to culture-specific
food taboos; a structuralist-type interpretation that this is somehow a
symbolic inversion (the normal pattern in the Trickster-and-Vulture tales, as
discussed above with respect to the first Menomini Type IIb example, is that
vultures are carrion-eaters, but here vultures are enjoined from eating
carrion). An equally likely and perhaps more plausible explanation is that

this may well be an intrusive non-aboriginal element, in which case this is one of the very few instances of such borrowing in the entire corpus of Trickster-and-Vulture tales.[7]

Type IIb, Variants

Two other Type IIb tales parallel the preceding ones in that they both contain an analagous antecedent and consequence. However, like Skinner's Plains Ojibwa tale, "Nänibozhu and the Buzzard" (see above, under "Type I, Variant"), these show significant variation in one of the components; in this case, in (c), the consequence. The first is excerpted from Jones' (1901) rendition of the Fox/Sauk version of the Algonquian culture-hero myth (the pertinent section begins with the third paragraph on p. 235 and ends at the bottom of the third paragraph on p. 237). The second, collected from speakers of a Siouan language, is the ninth of 52 incidents in the Assiniboine Trickster cycle, as reported by Lowie (1910:108).

The Algonquian myth is one of the most complex Type II tales in terms of the cast of characters involved and its overall richness of narrative detail:

The fateful encounter between Wī'sa'kä, the culture-hero, and the vultures occurs after the dissipation of the Flood, with Wī'sa'kä seated in front of his lodge making arrows for the people whom he will soon create. Sun, his grandfather, calls down to him, and on the fourth call he looks upward. Sun tells Wī'sa'kä to come up to his lodge, where he has a great supply of blue colour for his arrows; Buzzard is to bring him up on his back. Wī'sa'kä relates their conversation to Buzzard the very next time he comes by to visit, but the bird is extremely unhappy with the news: at this time he is the most beautiful of creatures, with brilliant, multi-coloured plumage. Buzzard is proud at being able to live off alone with his fellow-vultures, and extremely lazy, accustomed as he is to spend all of his time admiring himself. But knowing better than to refuse Sun and Wī'sa'kä, he accedes to their wishes and takes Wī'sa'kä upward on his back, the culture-hero clasping him about the neck. Seeing his grandson approaching after a flight of many days' duration, Sun reaches out for his grandson's hand, but as Wī'sa'kä unclasps one hand from around Buzzard's neck and reaches for that of his grandfather with the other, the vulture quickly flies out from beneath him. Wī'sa'kä, tumbling head over heels, seems destined to perish, but his other grandfather, the tree, catches him in his arms before he crashes to the ground.

The consequence opens with Wī'sa'kä, now in a furious rage, being visited by his friend, Elk. After relating the story of his original conversation with Sun, and of Buzzard's treacherous behaviour, Wī'sa'kä tells Elk to bring Buzzard to him any way he can, as quickly as possible. Happy to be on an errand for Wī'sa'kä, Elk sets out to a place frequented by all the animals and lies down there, feigning death. Two animals arrive to feed on Elk—first Wolf, then Crow; they pull off flesh and peck through his skin, but Elk remains still as if truly dead. The third creature to arrive is Buzzard, who alights "on a mound close by in the rear." Buzzard hops up to the carcass and begins to pull on the flesh, but Elk endures it all until Buzzard has "his beak in past the head," at which point he jumps up and runs off to Wī'sa'kä's lodge, holding Buzzard securely by the head. Wī'sa'kä receives them courteously and instructs Buzzard to summon his companions to hear an important message. Greatly relieved at not having been punished, Buzzard sets off and soon arrives back at Wī'sa'kä's lodge, bringing all of his fellow-vultures with him; they assemble outside, waiting to hear Wī'sa'kä's message, but his long monologue is hardly what they expect. First Wī'sa'kä up-braids Buzzard personally for his treachery, then says how displeased he is with his behaviour, and that indeed he does intend to punish him for it. The role of the vultures in shaping the earth, as well as the reason for their present condition, are made clear as Wī'sa'kä's harangue continues (Jones 1901:237):

> You see the land is level everywhere. Now I wish you to dig courses for rivers, to build hills and mountains, and to give shape to all the earth. I shall create a people when you will have done this work, and I shall put them to dwell on the earth. They will look upon you, and you will be to them the most loathsome of all living-kind. The beautiful colors of your feathers shall change to the color of the soil of the earth. And your neck and head, once so fair of form, shall remain disfigured as Elk made them in dragging you to me. So now set to the work that I have commanded you.

The myth then concludes by describing how the vultures went about carrying out Wī'sa'kä's commands:

> Thereupon the Buzzards set to work, and sad they were at their task. Some formed in line, one behind the other, and pushing their breasts against the soil, formed the river courses. Others dug up the ground with their talons and piled up huge mounds of earth. Afterwards they came and soared slowly along the slopes of the mounds and gave them shape with the under side of their wings. It was these that made the hills and the mountains and formed the slopes of the valleys in between.

This particular Algonquian myth differs from the other Type IIb tales analyzed above in that there is no explicit reference to vultures having lost their head feathers. This can be inferred, however, from how Buzzard was captured and brought to Wī'sa'kä by Elk: the bird alighted on a mound "in the rear"—i.e., near the tail-end of the carcass—and Elk had jumped up only once Buzzard had "his beak in past the head." Elk had then run off to Wī'sa'kä's lodge holding Buzzard by the head, that is, with the head and neck secured inside Elk's rectum. Wī'sa'kä's monologue contains a clear allusion to the present, barren condition of the vulture's head: "And your neck and head, once so fair of form, shall remain disfigured as Elk made them in dragging you to me."

A second point of departure here is the nature of what normally is the Trickster-figure, and how this might be interpreted to reflect on what happens to Buzzard. At least in this myth, Wī'sa'kä is portrayed not as a Trickster-figure at all, but as the culture-hero, loved by all the animals (with the exception of Buzzard, who probably should also but doesn't), the creator of men and implements (arrows), and, indirectly through his command, of the natural features of the earth. It is perfectly logical, therefore, that Wī'sa'kä, not being a Trickster-figure here, should not transform himself into a sham-dead animal in order to catch and punish Buzzard: he delegates this role to Elk. (This convention of using third parties to serve as intermediaries is consistent, by the way, with the pattern initially established at the beginning of the myth, where Sun tells Wī'sa'kä to tell Buzzard that he is to bring him up to his lodge. Yet another instance of this occurs much later in the myth after Buzzard is brought to Wī'sa'kä's lodge and the culture-hero sends him off to bring back his fellow-vultures to hear the important message that he will deliver.)

The second Type IIb variant and the last Type II Trickster-and-Vulture tale is the ninth incident in the Assiniboine Trickster cycle as compiled by Lowie (1910:108). Like the seventh incident, which is discussed immediately below under Type IIIa, the protagonists in the antecedent are the Trickster-figure and some geese. In the consequence, however, the animals who become intimately involved with the Trickster's anus are of a type completely different from those in the consequence of all the other published Trickster-and-Vulture tales that I have been able to locate: some mice. The antecedent opens with the Trickster, Sitconski, travelling by a large lake. Hearing some noisy geese nearby, he buries his face in his hands and begins to cry; this ploy evokes the sympathy of the geese, and when asked why he is crying, Sitconski explains that he would like to go home with the birds because they are singing and laughing so much. The geese are reluctant to take Sitconski along because life is very difficult for them, what with the Indians shooting at them all the time. But Sitconski insists and they finally consent. When the geese, carrying Sitconski, fly near the Indians, the people recognize Sitconski and begin shooting at the birds, who immediately scatter, dropping the Trickster. Sitconski then wills that he fall in a soft place and tumbles headfirst into a mud-hole, landing in such a manner that only his anus is visible.

Up to this point, aside from the fact that the avian protagonists are not birds of prey or carrion-eaters (vultures, hawks, eagles), this tale is not drastically dissimilar from the preceding ones: the Trickster-figure, by guile, satisfies his need to be taken aloft, and it is ultimately his own responsibility that he gets dropped--had he been dissuaded at the onset and not insisted on flying with the geese, then the Indians obviously would never have seen him among them, there would have been no need for the geese to scatter in self-defense, and Sitconski would never have fallen into the mud-hole.

I have chosen to classify this Assiniboine Trickster-cycle incident as a Type IIb variant for two reasons. First, it is structurally parallel to the other Type IIb tales in that it clearly has the same basic antecedent, followed by a consequence which though similar in many respects, is admittedly quite different in others. Second, it lacks anything resembling an intervening incident of the sort occurring in the Type IIa tales. There can be no doubt that this tale is at least related to the corpus of Trickster-and-Vulture tales, inasmuch as (a) avian protagonists and the local Trickster-figure are the dramatis personae in the antecedent; (b) the Trickster is dropped by the birds, wills that he fall in a soft place, and lands headfirst, stuck up to his waist in a mud-hole; and (c) notwithstanding the fact that vultures are not present in the tale (nor, logically, an etiological element accounting for their bareheadedness), it is the Trickster's anus into which some mice attempt to enter that is the focal point of action in the consequence.

Type IIc: (b) Intervening Incident + (c) Consequence

I have been unable to locate examples of Type IIc tales, which would contain the hollow-tree incident (or a substituting cluster of narrative elements, cf. "Type I, Composite, with Variant in (b)"). Because such versions may eventually be uncovered, however, I include this type here as a logical possibility.

Type IIIa: (a) Antecedent Only

I have located only one clear example of a Type IIIa tale: the seventh incident in the Assiniboine Trickster cycle, again as compiled by Lowie (1910:107).[8] Here the Trickster-figure, Inktúmni, sees some geese flying and wishes to go along with them, but they seek to dissuade him, saying that flying is difficult. Inktúmni stubbornly insists, however, so eight of the geese take him up and fly off. While Inktúmni is enjoying himself, the geese, knowing what a trickster he is, catch sight of a mud-hole and drop him into it, then fly away. Inktúmni remains stuck there up to his waist for several days. Here again, as noted above with respect to the Type IIb tales, it is Inktúmni's behaviour which gets him into difficulty--first his insistence on flying with the geese when he should have been dissuaded from doing so, and then his renowned reputation as a trickster, which is what made the birds want to drop him into the mud-hole.

As in the ninth incident in the Assiniboine Trickster-cycle (see above, under "Type IIb, Variants"), the avian protagonists are geese. This is neatly related to the temporal context of the tale, as it transpires in the fall when the geese are flying. In only one other Trickster-and-Vulture tale is there such a contextualization: in the second Menomini Type IIb tale (see Table 2, No. 2), where Mänäbús, transformed into a sham-dead elk in the consequence, is appropriately very fat because it is autumn.

Type IIIb: (b) Intervening Incident Only

I have been unable to locate examples of Type IIIb Trickster-and-Vulture tales, i.e., tales which contain only (b), the hollow-tree incident or alternatively as in "Type I, Composite, with Variant in (b)," the substituted partridges. Again, I include this type here because it is a logical possibility that should be kept in mind. There are, however, numerous Native North American folktales and myths--undoubtedly several dozen--in which one of the three components, including (b), or individual narrative elements or clusters of elements from within one of the components--becomes incorporated within a different tale. Representative examples of this sort are discussed below in the section immediately following Type IIIc.

Type IIIc: (c) Consequence Only

Type IIIc tales contain only the consequence--the vulture (or other avian protagonist substituting for the vulture) losing its head feathers by becoming caught in the rectum of a sham-dead animal. Three examples of Type IIIc tales have been collected from speakers of Native North American languages, two in Algonquian languages (Ojibwa [Radin 1914:16-17; No. 6d] and Menomini [Skinner 1913:78]), and one in Cherokee, an Iroquoian language (Mooney 1900:293; No. 46). Radin's Ojibwa tale is the most elaborate of the three:

Nenebojo, walking along as usual, meets Crow and tells her to tell Eagle that she has found a dead kingfisher along the lake, and that he should come and eat it. Crow obediantly relays this message, but Eagle refuses to go, fearing that the dead bird may be Nenebojo, the Trickster. Crow interprets Eagle's refusal to mean that he "must have done something to Nenebojo to make him angry." She then returns to Nenebojo, who sends her back to Eagle to say that she has found a dead sturgeon, but Eagle again declines to respond, still believing that the dead fish is Nenebojo. Crow returns to Nenebojo, and he sends her back to Eagle a third time with the message that she has found a dead man along the beach. This time Eagle sets out immediately, "never imagining that Nenebojo was the man." Upon reaching the beach, Eagle begins to eat the cadaver's back and is soon drawing out the intestines, but as soon as Eagle's head is way inside his rectum, Nenebojo closes his anus tightly, securing Eagle's head. Eagle moves his head around inside for some time, and when Nenebojo finally releases it it is all white and completely devoid of feathers. The tale then ends with a brief etiological coda: "Today the eagle looks just as he did when Nenebojo released him."

The avian protagonist here is an eagle (probably the American bald eagle, Haliaetus leucocephalus),[9] rather than a vulture, and there is an interesting innovation in the capture of the bird: as in the Sauk/Fox culture-hero myth (see above, under "Type IIb, Variants"), a mediary is employed. Unlike all of our other Trickster-and-Vulture tales, however, the Trickster-figure undergoes a series of transformations here, first as a bird, then as a fish, and finally as a man. The classification of this tale is somewhat problematic. There is no question but that it contains the same basic consequence as the Type I, IIb and other IIIc Trickster-and-Vulture tales, and that there was an antecedent which brought about the consequence is clear from the fact that when Eagle first refused to eat the dead kingfisher, telling Crow that it must be Nenebojo, Crow inferred that Eagle must have done something to Nenebojo to make him angry. Because this earlier event is not made explicit in the tale, whereas the consequence is fully developed, I have chosen to classify this as a Type IIIc tale.

The Cherokee mythical tale, "Why Buzzard's Head is Bare," is, in the form given by Mooney, also an example of Type IIIc, although based on Mooney's notes it could also be classified as Type I. In ethnographic notes preceding the tale (p. 284), Mooney discusses the role of the vulture in shaping the earth, as narrated in the Cherokee genesis myth; the medicinal efficacy of vulture flesh and feathers; and certain beliefs about the contagious effects of vulture feathers in bringing about baldness. "Its own baldness," Mooney states, "is accounted for by a vulgar story." The "vulgarity" was apparently edited out, as is sometimes the case in other Trickster-and-Vulture tales (e.g., in Jones' Ojibwa Type IIb tale; see above), because Mooney's notes to the tale (p. 456) establish not only that it is well known but also that "it has an exact parallel in the story of 'Ictinike and the Buzzard'" (cf. Dorsey 1890--see above, under "Type I"; emphasis in Mooney quote added). In Mooney's account, the myth lacks both the antecedent, (a), and the intervening incident, (b): here it is the vulture's supreme arrogance, not its having inflicted injury upon the Trickster-figure that brings about its bare-headed condition. And while a large quadruped is involved in the de-feathering of the vulture (in this case, a buffalo), the bird's becoming caught by the head inside the animal's rectum can only be inferred on the basis of Mooney's notes because this is not explicitly stated in the text.

Mooney's version of this Cherokee myth is sufficiently brief to be quoted in full (Mooney 1900:293):

> The buzzard used to have a fine topknot, of which he was so
> proud that he refused to eat carrion, and while the other
> birds were pecking at the body of a deer or other animal which
> they had found he would stand around and say: "You may have
> it all, it is not good enough for me." They resolved to
> punish him, and with the help of the buffalo carried out a
> plot by which the buzzard lost not his topknot alone, but
> nearly all the other feathers on his head. He lost his pride
> at the same time, so that he is willing enough now to eat
> carrion for a living.

The third and final example of a Type IIIc tale is embedded in Skinner's discussion of Menomini mythology (Skinner 1913:78). As Skinner distinguishes this in a footnote from "the more common [Menomini] version of this myth in which Mänäbus turns himself into a dead elk in order to entrap the buzzard who has injured him," it is classified here as a Type IIIc tale. This version differs from most other Trickster-and-Vulture tales in that the Trickster-figure (or his surrogate) does not undergo a transformation. Also, the animal-protagonist into whose rectum the vulture sticks his head is a horse--a large quadruped, to be sure, but a species that does not occur in any of the other tales. The tale is not lengthy and is given below in full:

> So too, is the vulture (Opäskwûsiu) though his head was made
> bare and foul-smelling by Mä´näbus as punishment. The great
> hero was hunting one day when he caught the vulture in the
> very act of thrusting his head in the bowels of a dead horse.
> "Disgusting creature," he cried, "may your head remain in the
> place you have chosen to put it until the carcass rots away."
> As Mä´näbus had commanded, so it fell about. The vulture's
> head was caught in the bowels of the horse, and he was unable
> to withdraw it until the flesh had decayed. The feathers were
> rotted from the vulture's head by the same process and it has
> remained bald and ill-smelling to this day.

Related, Unclassified Tales

An additional, potentially large class of folktales and myths are those which incorporate narrative elements from Trickster-and-Vulture tales but are not amenable to classification according to type, as in Table 1. Representative examples include the Eastern Ojibwa and Timiskaming Algonquin texts discussed earlier in connection with Type I Composite Trickster-and-Vulture tales (see note 4); these contain the partridges motif from (b), the intervening incident. Additional elements from the intervening incident figure in such texts as "Îshjîñki and the Undesirable Son-in-Law" (Skinner 1925:82-84; No. 23), where the motif of raccoon tails hanging out of tree hollows becomes embedded within a Jack-in-the-Beanstalk type folktale.

Narrative elements from (c), the consequence, appear in the Assiniboine version of "The Two Brothers" (Lowie 1910:145-147; No. 5). This text can be related to the Trickster-and-Vulture tale corpus on the basis of internal narrative evidence, as well as through comparison with other versions of the Two Brothers myth.[10] The pertinent section involves two brothers who become separated; one is spirited away as a future son-in-law by an old fisherman. Eventually, the captive brother returns to the lake-shore where he had last seen his younger sibling, only to find a set of tracks that are half-human, half-wolf. Realizing that his brother has become a wolf, the young man transforms himself into a dead moose and orders all the animals to come eat him. When the wolves arrive and begin feeding on the carcass, the brother resumes his human form and seizes his wolf-brother. The obvious incorporated Trickster-and-Vulture tale elements here are the transformation of the main protagonist into a sham-dead moose, and his capturing his wolf-brother as soon as he begins to devour the moose's buttocks. While there is no mention of vultures, a bald eagle figures prominently in the subsequent portion of the text.

OTHER NORTH AMERICAN ETIOLOGICAL TALES ACCOUNTING FOR THE VULTURE'S LACK OF HEAD FEATHERS

Other North American etiological tales also account for the vulture's lack of head feathers, but in ways different from the preceding folktales and myths. Some of these are aboriginal, others are of European or possibly of African origin, and still others are hybrid tales meshing indigenous Native American and introduced elements.

Because avian Trickster-figures are so highly prominent in the oral traditions of the Northwest Coast,[11] this area might be expected to yield additional Trickster-and-Vulture tales. A cursory review of the literature suggests, however, that while some texts do exhibit superficial similarities with the Trickster-and-Vulture tale corpus, a clear connection between the two bodies of data cannot be established. One initially promising lead proved to be both erroneous and unproductive: Stith Thompson's reference to a Tahltan text in his entry under motif A2317.5 "Why raven is bald" (Thompson 1955-58, I:285). The original source (Teit 1920:220-221; No. 28) concerns the scorching off of Raven's feet feathers, not those on his head.

A more intriguing candidate for comparison is Frachtenberg's Alsea myth, "Vulture" (Frachtenberg 1920:117-121; No. 49), in which a vulture is shut up inside a whale for a lengthy period of time and loses his head feathers, no doubt as a result of the whale's digestive juices.[12] The points of similarity between this text and the Trickster-and-Vulture tales are that the primary Alsea protagonist is a vulture; that treachery is involved, Vulture's brothers-in-law having lured him into becoming trapped inside the whale; and that Vulture ends up devoid of head plumage. The remainder of the myth bears no significant resemblance to any of the Trickster-and-Vulture tales.[13] Also, here it is the vulture-protagonist, not those who maliciously deceive him, who suffers the indignity of becoming bald. Were the evidence of relationship with the Trickster-and-Vulture tale corpus stronger--most importantly, had Vulture transformed himself into a whale and then feigned death for the purpose of seeking revenge upon his brothers-in-law, and had additional Northwest Coast versions of such a myth been collected--then it would be tempting to regard the Alsea whale as a logical extension of the pattern established in the Trickster-and-Vulture tales, where the Trickster-figure typically assumes the form of a large local quadruped. But this is not how the Alsea text goes, nor to my knowledge are there other Northwest Coast texts that fit such a pattern.

The loss-of-hair motif also figures in the Blackfoot myth, "Old Man Gets Fast in an Elk-Skull, and Loses His Hair" (Wissler and Duvall 1909:32-33; No. 16). Here, however, it is the Trickster-protagonist, not a vulture who loses his hair. Although this myth has four elements in common with Trickster-and-Vulture tales--the presence of the local Trickster-figure, Old Man; some mice, which figured in one Type IIb tale;[14] the loss of the protagonist's hair, which is chewed off by the mice; and the occurrence of an elk in the form of a skull--it should be classified instead as one of numerous Native American narratives centering around motif J2131.5.1 "Trickster puts on buffalo skull" (Thompson 1955-58, IV:182; cf. Thompson 1929:297, No. 86; Wissler and Duvall 1909:33, No. 1).[15]

An Arapaho version of "Blood-Clot Boy" (Dorsey and Kroeber 1903:302-303; No. 130) also contains narrative elements that are superficially similar to those in some Trickster-and-Vulture tales, but the resemblance appears to be coincidental. In this text, Blood-Clot Boy, accompanied by his father, meets an old man who leads him to the brink of a precipice, intending to push him over the edge. Anticipating this, Blood-Clot Boy steps aside as the man lunges at him, and the man falls headfirst into the body of a dead animal below. All of the skin from the man's head, and presumably his hair as well, are torn off in the process. Blood-Clot Boy, finding the man still alive, then upbraids him before cutting off his arms and feet, saying that his fate is to be bareheaded and no longer dangerous. The now-hairless man, the text informs us, "was the buzzard."

According to an Iroquois myth (Canfield 1902:77-79; Ingersoll 1923:225; cf. Smith 1883:79-80), the present condition of the vulture's plumage was arrived at through default: Originally, all birds lacked feathers, "having been created naked" (Smith 1883:79; cf. Canfield 1902:77). A vulture referred to as a turkey buzzard--i.e., the red-headed turkey vulture, Cathartes aura--in both the Smith and Canfield versions of the myth is dispatched to obtain feathers for its avian companions; directed by the gods, the vulture undergoes an arduous journey, during which he "was compelled to ear carrion" (Canfield 1902:78) "and filth of all kinds; hence his present nature" (Smith 1883:79). Eventually locating "the feathered garments," the vulture rejects a series of four sets of feathers, each being inappropriate for a specific reason, and the bird is finally forced through default to accept "the plain, homely, coarse suit he has since worn" (Canfield 1902:78).

While there is indirect evidence for possible Siouan analogues to this Iroquois myth (see notes to the Seneca version in Canfield 1902:203-204), it does not appear to be related to any of the Trickster-and-Vulture tales. Significantly, though, it does have one important feature in common with the Cherokee version (see previously under "Type IIIc"). In the Cherokee myth it was the vulture's finicky attitude towards eating carrion that angered the other birds and ultimately brought about its bare-headed condition. Here also in the Seneca myth the vulture is responsible for its own fate for having been unable to make up its mind about which set of feathers to choose (Canfield 1902:78):

> As a reward for making the journey, the buzzard had been
> given first choice of the garments. He at once selected the
> most beautiful of the lot, but upon trying it discovered that
> he could not fly well with so many long feathers to manage,
> and so he laid the dress aside and tried others. One he
> feared would soil too easily; another was not warm enough to
> satisfy his taste; a third was too light-colored and would
> render him too conspicuous; a fourth was composed of too many
> pieces and would require too much of his time to care for it.
> So he went from one to another, finding some fault with each,
> until there was but one suit left--the plainest of all.

Another North American etiological tale explaining how the black vulture lost its head feathers is particularly interesting from a folkloristic standpoint: "Why the Buzzard Is Bald" (Dorsey and Swanton 1912:33-38; No. 10), a tale collected in Biloxi, a Siouan language spoken in north-eastern Alabama which is related most closely to the nearby Ofo language (also known as Offagoula or Ofagoula), to the extinct Tutelo of Virginia, and among the western Siouan languages, to the northern representatives of the family (Dakota, Hidatsa, Mandan, Crow, Winnebago; see Dorsey and Swanton 1912:10, 12). While there are no European linguistic borrowings in the original Biloxi text (pp. 33-34), the tale itself is a local version of "The Seven-Headed Dragon," a European tale widely dispersed throughout the indigenous oral traditions of both North and Central America. Stith Thompson (1919:327) classified this tale as one of several Native North American versions of Type II.[16] The Biloxi tale is unique among all 20 of Thompson's Native American versions of "The Seven-Headed Dragon" in having a vulture as the hero-imposter. Dorsey and Swanton gloss his name as "The Ancient of Black-headed Buzzards,"--i.e., as the black vulture, Coragyps atrata--and the vulture's punishment for falsely claiming to have killed the horrible monster that had been devouring the people was to have his head thrust into a fire by the real hero (Dorsey and Swanton 1912:36): "He threw him about at randon, making him fall to the ground. And then the Ancient of Black-headed Buzzards was making a sort of blowing noise, just as buzzards now make. And because he was thus, his head is bald."

Within the overall context of the tale, the burning off of the vulture's head feathers plays a decidedly secondary role; this element is certainly less crucial, at least in this particular telling of the tale, than in the Trickster-and-Vulture tales discussed earlier. How, then, should this element be interpreted? There are three possibilities. One is that this element is of purely local invention--from which it follows that any similarity between this and analagous elements in other Native American folktales, including those recorded in languages historically related to Biloxi, must be regarded as coincidental. The second possibility is that, given the linguistic affinity of Biloxi with northern Siouan languages in which numerous versions of the Trickster-and-Vulture tale are known to occur, the black vulture's baldness through burning here in the Biloxi tale is somehow related, albeit very distantly, to the vulture's baldness brought about through an encounter with a sham-dead animal, as recounted in the Trickster-and-Vulture tales. The end-product is the same, after all, and in each case the vulture brings about the consequence through deceit--in the Biloxi tale, for having impersonated the real hero; in the Trickster-and-Vulture tales, for having maliciously inflicted injury on the Trickster. Adopting this view, the Biloxi tale would be viewed as containing a residual motif--a vulture bringing about the loss of its own head feathers--of an ancient indigenous folktale, with the specific means by which this is achieved--the vulture's feathers being burned off as the bird's head is thrust into the fire by the real dragon-slayer--being a strictly localized departure from the original tale. In this case the tale would then be classified within Thompson's scheme as a mixed tale composed of amalgamated indigenous and European elements, the tale itself being European and this particular element being a vestige of an ancient Native North American tale.

The third possibility is that Thompson was correct in classifying the entire Biloxi tale as being of European origin, in which case any parallels from among the Trickster-and-Vulture tales to the burning incident in the Biloxi tale would again have to be regarded as purely coincidental rather than as evidence of genetic relationship.

As between the second and third possibilities, the evidence suggests that Thompson was indeed correct in classifying the tale itself as non-indigenous. Thus the burning-off-of-the-head-feathers incident is neither a local innovation nor a residual element from an aboriginal tale common to the Biloxi and their Siouan relatives to the north. The crucial lead here is Thompson's conclusion (Thompson 1919:234) that the North American versions of "The Seven-Headed Dragon" are probably the result of French influence: "We can see in all the tribes who have variants of this tale the great possibility that it has been borrowed from the French. The Mississippi Biloxi are near to the Louisiana French, and all the other tribes have been, at one time or another, in close contact with the French Canadians."

Such a connection, which may well account for the head-feather-burning motif in the Biloxi tale, is suggested in "Compair Lapin et Madame Carencro," a Louisiana-French folktale presented in both local French dialect and English translation by Fortier (1895:23-24). In this tale, a mother vulture shuts up a rabbit in its hole at the foot of the tree where she is nesting, intending to make a meal of the rabbit when it starves to death. The rabbit, referred to as Godfather, manages to escape unscathed and seeks asylum at the home of a friend. In revenge for the mother vulture's having tried to catch and eat him, the rabbit throws a large tin pan full of burning embers and hot ashes on her and her children as they pass by. Vultures have thick feathers except on top of their heads, the story explains, and so while they were able to shake off the embers and ashes, they did not do so quickly enough "to prevent the feathers on their heads to burn down to the skin." And that is why they are bald "and never eat bones of rabbits."

The avian protagonist in this Louisiana-French tale is called a carencro in the original French text and is consistently identified as a "buzzard" throughout the English text. (The word carencro is not actually French but is derived from the English 'carrion-crow', which in colloquial usage denotes both the common European black crow and the black vulture.) That the carencro in this Louisiana-French folktale is a vulture, not a crow, is critical in tying it to certain Caribbean folktales that offer strikingly similar accounts for the origin of the black vulture's featherless head. Two such tales are a pair of Jamaican Anansi stories collected by Beckwith (1924): "Carencro's House with a Key" (No. 17d, pp. 21-22) and "Why John-Crow has a Bald Head" (No. 47, pp. 56-57). In a footnote to the first story, Beckwith incorrectly identifies the carencro in her story title and its equivalent "in French stories" as a crow (footnote 2, p. 21), however the referent of the Jamaican word used throughout Beckwith's original text, kyan-crow, is actually a vulture. Similarly, the Jamaican word John-crow in Beckwith's second story also designates a vulture, not a crow.[17] Like the Louisiana-French carencro in Fortier's folktale, both of these Jamaicanisms are derived from the English 'carrion-crow', the specific referent of each being the black vulture.

In Beckwith's Jamaican Anansi stories, the means by which the vulture's head is made bare is not liquid, not burning ashes and hot embers, but the analogy between them--as well as that between the Jamaican and Louisiana-French tales, taken as a group, and the Biloxi tale with the burning off of the vulture's head feathers in a fire--suggests a more than coincidental linkage. In the opening episode of "Carencro's House with a Key," Anansi is caught running out of Kyan-Crow's house, where he had surreptitiously entered to eat up some food. In the follow-up, Anansi sets up a dance for Kyan-Crow, explaining that his banjo will not play without hot water. When Kyan-Crow's back is turned, Anansi scoops up a gourdful of hot water and throws it on Kyan-Crow. "So from dat day," the story concludes, "every kyan-crow got peel-head." The second story, as presented by Beckwith, consists of two parts, "The Baptism" and "The Dance." At the beginning of the first part we are told that Anansi (a spider) has a grudge against John-Crow because every time he makes his nest (i.e., web) the vulture comes along and destroys it. Anansi plots against John-Crow by inviting him to dinner, after which there is to be a baptism. Anansi explains that he baptises only with hot water and bids John-Crow to immerse his head in a copper pot full of boiling water--"an' dat why John-Crow have bald-head today." The second variation lacks the initial explanation of John-Crow's having previously destroyed Anansi's web. Here Anansi and John-Crow have dinner together; afterward there is a big dance, and Anansi becomes jealous and angry because John-Crow is a much better dancer. Anansi convinces him to dance up to a pot of porridge that is still hot from dinner. When he does so, Anansi "got a ladle an' dash on John Crow wid de hot pop right up on de head, an' all John Crow head 'trip off. All de John Crow in dis worl' never have no feder upon i' head heah; Anansi bu'n 'em off wid hot pop."

Now, one question which immediately occurs at this point to anyone familiar with the long-standing controversy over the influence of African and Afro-American narrative traditions upon Native North American oral literatures, and vice versa (cf. Dorson 1967, 1977; Dundes 1973, 1977), is whether the Jamaican Anansi stories collected by Beckwith and others, Fortier's Louisiana-French "Compair et Madame Carencro" and—if I am correct in relating these to the burning incident—Swanton and Dorsey's Biloxi version of "The Seven-Headed Dragon"—bolster Dundes's or Dorson's side of the argument. This is more than a peripheral issue because one problem that must be squarely faced here is that there are numerous American Negro folktales which parallel the Native American Trickster-and-Vulture tales analyzed in the preceding section of this paper. If it can be demonstrated that these American Negro folktales, or at least the pertinent narrative elements relating to the vulture's loss of head feathers, originated in Africa, and furthermore, that given this it is very likely that the Native American Trickster-and-Vulture tales may in fact not be aboriginal at all, then the initial proposal that my Itza Maya folktale collected in Guatemala is related to the corpus of Native North American Trickster-and-Vulture tales that account for the vulture's barren head can easily be shown to lack merit.

The American Negro folktales in question all contain narrative elements explaining why vultures ("buzzards") are bare-headed. Two representative folktales of this type are found in Dorson's Negro Folktales in Michigan (1956): "The Reason the Buzzard Is Got a Bald Head" (pp. 41–42) and "Crow, Buzzard and Mule" (pp. 43–44). A third, "The Bear and the Buzzard," is in Dorson's American Negro Folktales (1967:111–112; No. 25), in which volume are reprinted the two folktales referred to above (numbers 24 and 28, respectively, pp. 109–110, 112–113).[18]

Of these three American Negro folktales, the one which most closely parallels the Native American Trickster-and-Vulture tales is the last. In "The Reason the Buzzard Is Got a Bald Head," the main protagonists are a "buzzard" and a fox who is maliciously shut up inside a hollow tree by the vulture. (A crow also figures, but only peripherally at the beginning of the story.) Unlike the Trickster-and-Vulture Tales, no larger animal is involved; instead, the vulture's head feathers are pulled off by the fox when the vulture sticks its head into the hollow. In "The Bear and the Buzzard," the protagonists are a pair of hunters, a large bear, and a vulture. The hunters catch and tie up the bear, leaving it to die, and the vulture flies around waiting for the bear to weaken and expire. When the vulture flies down to feed on what he must think is a carcass, the bear hits him with his paw, knocking "that patch of hair outa his head," and the remaining feathers become dislodged when the vulture is thrown backwards against a tree—"And he been blad-headed ever since." In the third folktale, the protagonists are all animals: a crow and a vulture in search of food, and a mule. Goaded on by the crow, the vulture first pecks at the mule's eyes to see if the animal is dead, then proceeds to "try him" by sticking his head up the animal's rectum. The mule is still very much alive, however, and the vulture's head is pinned "between his tail and his ass." Driven into a frenzy by the malevolent crow, the mule runs itself to death with the unfortunate vulture unable to free itself.

This particular version of "Crow, Buzzard and Mule" has the crow eating up both mule and vulture in the end, and no mention is made of the vulture's bareheadedness. In other versions, "when the buzzard 'tries' the mule in the rear, the mule clamps his buttocks around the buzzard's head, and the buzzard pulls all the feathers off his head trying to get away" (Dorson 1956:207, note 12; cf. Dorson 1967:114, prefatory note to folktale No. 28).

Returning now to Beckwith's Jamaican Anansi stories, I agree with Dorson (see his note to folktale No. 24) that these Jamaican folktales molded around motif A2317.11 ("Why john-crow has bald head") "do not correspond to United States Negro tales of the buzzard becoming bald"--but not, as Dorson argues, because of the "chanted conversation between the buzzard and his captive" in American Negro tales of the sort typified by his folktale No. 24. I would regard this as a matter of narrative style. Instead, I submit that what we are dealing with are completely different, unrelated sets of etiological tales which happen to explain the same phenomenon. I also do not believe that the "motif of the baldheaded buzzard" is merely "intrusive" in Dorson's folktale No. 28, as Dorson contends, although it does appear that this narrative element was "neatly added," to use Dorson's words, in tale No. 25.

I would interpret Dorson's folktale No. 28 as being of Native American origin, derived from the Trickster-tale tradition. Dorson's folktale No. 24 is somewhat more problematic. The fox's being shut up in a hollow tree is reminiscent of the hollow-tree/stump incidents in some versions of the Trickster-and-Vulture tale (see discussion of (b), Intervening Incident, under "Type I" and "Type IIa"), and so it seems likely that this element, too, is derived from aboriginal American oral tradition. As for folktale No. 25, there is a parallel between it and the Trickster-and-Vulture tales generally in that the protagonists directly involved in the loss-of-feathers incident are almost always a vulture and a large quadruped (in Dorson's folktale, a bear; in the Trickster-and-Vulture tales, a buffalo, elk, deer, moose, etc.), but the specific means by which the vulture loses its head feathers in the American Negro folktale--through being kicked and hurled backwards by a bear--coupled with the fact that the opening part of this folktale is so dissimilar from all of the Trickster-and-Vulture tales, suggests that it probably does not have a common origin with folktale No. 28.

There are, then, at least two distinct, unrelated sets of etiological tales which explain the black vulture's lack of head feathers, both of which have contributed narrative elements to American Negro and Native American oral traditions of the southeastern U.S. One set is the Jamaican/Louisiana-French John-Crow/carencro folktales, from which the burning incident in Swanton and Dorsey's Biloxi tale is probably derived. The second is the corpus of aboriginal American Trickster-and-Vulture tales, elements of which were incorporated into American Negro folktales. Other Trickster-and-Vulture tales survived more or less intact among southeastern Native American peoples such as the Biloxi. That some narrative elements in these same folktales may ultimately be of African origin is an intriguing possibility that folklorists more familiar with African and Caribbean narrative literatures might pursue. In any case, short of finding complete, irrefutable African parallels to the Native North American Trickster-and-Vulture tales, substantiating an African connection for certain narrative elements in these American Negro and southeastern Native American folktales would not, in my view, call into question the conclusion that Dorson's folktale No. 28, and perhaps elements of numbers 24 and 25 as well, resulted from contact between Native Americans and American Negroes--the direction of cultural borrowing in this case being from the former to the latter.

CONCLUSION

This study has examined in considerable detail the corpus of Native North American Trickster-and-Vulture tales. Our primary goal in analyzing these texts was to establish on the basis of internal narrative-structural criteria that they do indeed constitute a unified corpus of aboriginal folktales and myths. This was not intended as an end in itself, however, for we are also concerned with broader historical and culturological issues in New World prehistory. What gives the present study special meaning from this perspective is that now deep historical relationships between other cultural areas of the New World and Native North America can be inferred from this analysis.

Such a link can definitely be drawn to Mesoamerica. In 1976 I was able to collect from one of the few remaining speakers of Itza Maya, a Yucatecan language now restricted to only a handful of villages in the central Peten region of Guatemala and adjacent Belize, an etiological tale which is quite clearly a Mesoamerican Type IIIc Trickster-and-Vulture tale. Because this folktale can be shown on the basis of other kinds of evidence--linguistic, hieroglyphic, and iconographic--to have relatively great local time depth within the Maya area, it represents one of the few instances of which I am aware of a folktale that can be dated with any degree of precision (see Ventur 1983). It was not introduced into Mesoamerica recently, though exactly when and how it arrived in the Peten is open to conjecture. But since there is no doubt that this Itza folktale is a Trickster-and-Vulture tale, a rather ancient historical linkage between Mesoamerica and aboriginal North America can be inferred. Perhaps this comes as no great conceptual surprise to archaeologists and historical linguists, or to Americanists familiar with the early writings of Daniel Brinton, who well over a century ago (Brinton 1868:38-39) advanced the notion of a common Native American mythical and religious substrate.[19] Yet most folklorists have failed to recognize or follow up on what to Brinton and many others seemed so obvious.

In closing, a tantalizing hint of how far our analysis of Trickster-and-Vulture tales can be taken to ferret out evidence in support of Brinton's proposition. Various Tupi myths (cf. Lévi-Strauss 1969:139-143) involve as principal protagonists: culture-heroes feigning death as large Amazonian quadrupeds; and the ubiquitous urubus, the king vultures.

FOOTNOTES

1. Itza folktale No. 1.6 in Ventur 1976, narrated by Felix Fernando Tesucún,
    then ago 48, a native of the village of San José, El Petén, the pueblo
    cabecera of the municipio of the same name, located along the northern
    shore of Lake Petén Itzá opposite the Peninsula of Tayasal. Maya
    transcription, vol. 1, pp. 51-52; colloquial petenero Spanish
    translation, vol. 2, pp. 38-39; English synopsis, vol. 3, pp. 15-16.
    Photocopies of the entire text corpus, including additional annotated
    texts in Mopan Maya, may be consulted in the National Anthropological
    Archives, Smithsonian Institution, and in the library of the Proyecto
    Lingüístico Francisco Marroquín (PLFM), Huehuetenango, Guatemala.

2. The orthographic conventions adopted here for transcribing Native North
    American names follow those used in the sources cited.

3. Were it not for Radin's having linked these three incidents together--the
    result being a Type I Trickster-and-Vulture tale according to the
    classificatory scheme developed here--each could be classified as a
    separate type: No. 17 as an example of Type IIIa; No. 18, of Type IIIb;
    and No. 34, of Type IIIc. Alternatively, if Radin's grouping according
    to episodes were followed, then 17 and 18 taken together as his Seventh
    Episode would belong with our Type IIa tales, while No. 34 would still be
    a Type IIIc version.

4. For example, Bloomfield's Eastern Ojibwa texts, "Nenabush and the
    Partridges" (Bloomfield 1956:220-224; nos. 35-36). See also, from the
    Timiskaming Algonquin Trickster cycle, "Wiske·djak Anum Suum Urit ... "
    (Speck 1915:10-15; No. 4).

5. My interpretation of what happens here is that Ikto fell inside the
    hollow of an upright tree, and that he saw the woodpecker alight around
    the rim of the opening, silhouetted against the bright sky; the hole that
    the woodpecker makes for Ikto to look out of is farther down the trunk
    (cf. text line 18), where the two women try to determine exactly where in
    the tree he is hiding.

6. For our purposes the relevant part of the hollow-tree incident ends here;
    the story goes on to recount what happens when the women return.

7. The allusion here to "the forbidden fruit" may be biblical. Other
    European elements which have found their way into the Trickster-and-
    Vulture tale corpus are non-native animals which substitute for
    indigenous quadruped-protagonists (e.g., bulls, horses). The origin of
    the rabbit-protagonist here in Swanton's Koasati Type IIb folktale is a
    matter of debate among folklorists, some believing the rabbit-figure to
    be African rather than aboriginal American (see Dundes 1976). An
    overlooked fact on this point is the etymology of Mänäbush, the Menomini
    Trickster: mashä 'great' + wabus 'rabbit' (Hoffman 1896:87,
    No. 2)--literally, "Great Rabbit."

8. For a similar, unattributed version, see Schoolcroft 1856:63-64. Lowie (1910:107, note 1) also cites a similar tale collected by Skinner among the Albany Cree.

9. This tale characterizes the eagle's head as being devoid of feathers, but this description is technically incorrect; "bald" eagle is also a misnomer. The bald eagle's head may appear to be barren from a distance, but it is actually covered with white feathers--unlike the heads and necks of all three common species of North American vultures which are either completely bare (the black vulture, Coragyps atrata, and the turkey vulture, Cathartes aura) or else sparsely covered with black bristles (the king vulture, Sarcoramphus papa). For detailed information on the physical characteristics and habits of American vultures, see Austin 1961:73-74; Brown and Amadon 1968:17-19, 175-192; and Grossman and Hamlet 1964:197-204).

10. Note the similarity to the traditional history of Menomini genesis (Hoffman 1896:87) in which Mänäbŭsh transforms Wolf (Moqwaio´) into his human brother.

11. On ravens as the Northwest Coast Trickster, see Radin 1956:156.

12. My interpretation as to why Vulture lost his head feathers inside the whale finds confirmation in another Native American folktale concerning a young boy swallowed by a giant pike (Speck 1915:65-66; No. 13): "'I'm scalded with the intestines,'" the boy cries out as he is freed from the belly of the fish. "'I'm scalded. I've been here three days.' He was already beginning to be digested."

13. This Alsea myth combines elements of several different narratives; Northwest Coast parallels to the Alsea vulture inside the whale include, from the Tlingit Trickster cycle, Raven's flying inside a whale and feasting on its insides and what it swallows (see Radin 1956:104-105; cf. Frachtenberg 1920:118, No. 1). Three prominent motifs figure in the text: F921 "Swallowed person becomes bald" (Thompson 1955-58, III:235; cf. Thompson 1929:322, No. 159b); H310 "Suitor tests" (Thompson 1955-58, III:398; cf. Thompson 1929:324, 328, notes 170, 186); and K952 "Animal (monster) killed from within" (Thompson 1955-58, IV:355; cf. Thompson 1929:321, No. 159).

14. In the ninth incident in the Assiniboine Trickster cycle--see discussion under "Type IIb, Variants."

15. In Tales of the North American Indians (pp. 297, 365) Thompson lists the pertinent motif as J2152; the motif listed in his Motif Index is J2131.5.1.

16. Subsequently codified as Tale Type 300 "The Dragon-Slayer" in Aarne and Thompson 1973:88-90.

17. Cassidy and LePage (1967:250) analyze 'John-Crow' as a Jamaican "folk-etymological formation from its former name (still extant) CARRION CROW, which was reduced in popular pronunciation to CYANCRO /kyankro/ whence by affrication of /ky-/ to /ty-/ and voicing to /j/--both common phenomena in the folk speech--the form /jangkro/." They identify the specific referent of the word as "the red-headed turkey buzzard"; cf. source citations under their first entry describing the characteristics of the bird's color and plumage, and Edwards' identification as a turkey vulture (cited in Cassidy 1961:307). 'John-Crow' also occurs as a constituent in the name 'John-Crow Headman', which Cassidy and LePage describe (p. 251) as "an albino JOHN-CROW), to which the black john-crows defer." This is undoubtedly the king vulture, Sarcoramphus papa, also known colloquially as the Headman John-Crow, King Crow, White Crow, and John-Crow Parson (cf. Cassidy 1961:306-308). In jocular or derisive contexts, especially in proverbs, vultures are also referred to as "Jamaica Turkeys" (Cassidy and LePage 1967:242). By contrast, the common Jamaican black crow, Coryus jamaicensis, is terminologically distinguished from vultures in Jamaican speech, usually being referred to as the Jabbering Crow or some derivation thereof (e.g., Jabbling Crow, Gabbling Crow, Javeline Crow); see Cassidy and LePage 1967:193, 238.

18. The vulture's bare-headedness is explained in a different manner in another American Negro folktale unrelated to those under discussion here (Ingersoll 1923:240-241, citing M. Young). According to this folktale, Buzzard originally had "a fine plume sweepin' from de top of his head" but lost it in a quarrel with a dog. "'Sense dat day Buzzard don't never miss fust pickin' out de eye of ev'ithing that he gwine eat,' so that it cannot see to resist if it is not quite dead."

19. Brinton's original statement, which I have elaborated upon elsewhere in regard to Native American mortuary games (Ventur 1980:94), is that the "Red Race," as he termed it, "be studied as a unit, its religion as the development of ideas common to all its members, and its myths as the garb thrown around these ideas by imagination more or less fertile, but seeking everywhere to embody the same notion."

REFERENCES

Aarne, Antti and Stith Thompson
1973   The types of the folktales: a classification and bibliography.
        2nd revision. FF Communications 184. Helsinki: Academia
        Scientiarum Fennica.

Austin, Olivia L., Jr.
1961   Birds of the world. New York: Golden Press.

Beckwith, Martha Warren
1924   Jamaica Anansi stories. Memoirs, American Folklore Society 17.

Brinton, Daniel G.
1868   Myths of the New World: a treatise on the symbolism and mythology
        of the Red Race. New York: Leypoldt and Holt.

Bloomfield, Leonard
1928   Menomini texts. Publications, American Ethnological Society 12.

1956   Eastern Ojibwa grammatical sketch, texts, and word list. Ann
        Arbor and Leyden: University of Michigan Press and E.J. Brill.

Brown, Leslie and Dean Amadon
1968   Eagles, hawks and falcons of the world, vol. 1. New York:
        McGraw-Hill.

Canfield, William W.
1902   The legends of the Iroquois: told by "The Cornplanter." New
        York: A. Wessels Co.

Cassidy, Frederic G.
1961   Jamaica talk: three hundred years of the English languages in
        Jamaica. London and New York: MacMillan and Co. and St. Martin's
        Press.

Cassidy, Frederic G. and R.B. LePage
1967   Dictionary of Jamaican English. London: Cambridge University
        Press.

Coffin, Tristram P.
  1961   Indian tales of North America: an anthology for the adult
            reader. Bibliographical and Special Series 13, American Folklore
            Society. Philadelphia.

Deloria, Ella
  1932   Dakota texts. Publications, American Ethnological Society 14.

Dorsey, George A.
  1906   The Pawnee: mythology (part 1). Publications, Carnegie
            Institution of Washington 59.

Dorsey, George A. and Alfred L. Kroeber
  1903   Traditions of the Arapaho. Publication 81 (Anthropological
            Series, 5). Chicago: Field Columbian Museum.

Dorsey, James Owen
  1890   The Ȼegiha language. Contributions to North American Ethnology
            6. Department of the Interior, U.S. Geographic and Geological
            Survey of the Rocky Mountain Region. Washington: Government
            Printing Office.

  1892   Nanibozhu in Siouan mythology. Journal of American Folklore
            5:293-304.

Dorsey, James Owen and John R. Swanton
  1912   A dictionary of the Biloxi and Ofo languages, accompanied with
            thirty-one Biloxi texts and numerous Biloxi phrases. Bulletins
            13, Bureau of American Ethnology. Washington: Government
            Printing Office.

Dorson, Richard M.
  1956   Negro folktales in Michigan. Cambridge: Harvard University
            Press.

  1967   American Negro folktales. Revised ed. Greenwich, Conn.: Fawcett
            Publications.

  1977   The African connection: comments on African folklore in the New
            World. In Daniel J. Crowley, ed., African Folklore in the New
            World, pp. 87-91. Austin and London: University of Texas Press.

Dundes, Alan
    1973   African tales among the North American Indians. In Alan Dundes,
                ed., Mother wit from the laughing barrel: readings in the
                interpretation of Afro-American folklore, pp. 114-125. Eaglewood
                Cliffs, N.J.: Prentice-Hall.

    1977   African and Afro-American tales. In Daniel J. Crowley, ed.,
                African Folklore in the New World, pp. 35-53. Austin and London:
                University of Texas Press.

Fortier, Alcée
    1895   Louisiana folk-tales, in French dialect and English translation.
                Memoirs, American Folklore Society 2.

Frachtenberg, Leo J.
    1920   Alsea texts and myths. Bulletin 67, Bureau of American
                Ethnology. Washington: Government Printing Office.

Grossman, Mary Louise and John Hamlet
    1964   Birds of prey of the world. New York: Clarkston N. Potter.

Hoffman, Walter James
    1896   The Menomini Indians. Annual Reports 14, Bureau of American
                Ethnology. Washington: Government Printing Office.

Ingersoll, Ernest
    1923   Birds in legend, fable and folklore. New York: Longmans, Green
                and Co.

Jones, William
    1901   Episodes in the culture-hero myth of the Saulks and Foxes.
                Journal of American Folklore, 14 (No. 55):225-238.

    1917   Ojibwa texts. Publications, American Ethnological Society 7(1).
                Leyden and New York: E.J. Brill.

Jones, William and Truman Michelson
    1915   Kickapoo tales. Publications, American Ethnological Society 2.

Lévi-Strauss, Claude
    1968   The raw and the cooked: introduction to a science of mythology,
                1. New York: Harper and Row.

Lowie, Robert
 1910 The Assiniboine. Anthropological Papers, American Museum of
     Natural History 4(1).

Mooney, James
 1900 Myths of the Cherokee. Annual Reports 19, Bureau of American
     Ethnology. Washington: Government Printing Office.

Radin, Paul
 1914 Some myths and tales of the Ojibwa of southeastern Ontario.
     Memoirs 48 (Anthropological Series 2), Canadian Department of
     Mines, Geological Survey. Ottawa: Government Printing Bureau.

 1948 Winnebago hero cycles: a study in aboriginal literature. Memoirs
     1 (Supplement, International Journal of American Linguistics
     14(1)), Indiana University Publications in Anthropology and
     Linguistics.

 1956 The Trickster: a study in American Indian mythology. London:
     Routledge and Kegan Paul.

Schoolcroft, Henry R.
 1856 The myth of Hiawatha and other oral legends, mythologica and
     allegoric, of the North American Indians. Philadelphia and
     London: Lippincott and Co. and Trübner and Co.

Skinner, Alonson
 1913 Social life and ceremonial bundles of the Menomini Indians.
     Anthropological Papers 13(1), American Museum of Natural History.

 1919 Plains Ojibwa tales. Journal of American Folklore 32
     (No. 126):280-305.

 1925 Traditions of the Iowa Indians. Journal of American Folklore 38
     (No. 150):425-506.

Skinner, Alonson and John V. Satterlee
 1915 Folklore of the Menomini Indians. Anthropological Papers 13(3),
     American Museum of Natural History.

Smith, Erminie A.
 1883 Myths of the Iroquois. Annual Reports 2, Bureau of American
     Ethnology. Washington: Government Printing Office.

Speck, Frank G.
    1915   Myths and folk-lore of the Timiskaming Algonquin and Timagami
                    Ojibwa. Memoirs 71 (Anthropological Series 9), Canadian
                    Department of Mines, Geological Survey. Ottawa: Government
                    Printing Office.

Swanton, John R.
    1929   Myths and tales of the southeastern Indians. Bulletins 88, Bureau
                    of American Ethnology. Washington: Government Printing Office.

Teit, James A.
    1920   Tahltan tales. Journal of American Folklore 32:198-250.

Thompson, Stith
    1919   European tales among the North American Indians. Colorado College
                    Publications 2:318-471.

    1929   Tales of the North American Indians. Cambridge: Harvard
                    University Press.

    1946   The folktale. New York: Holt, Rinehart and Winston.

Ventur, Pierre
    1976   Itza Maya folklore texts. Unpublished MS. 3 vols.

    1980   A comparative perspective on Native American mortuary games of the
                    Eastern Woodlands. Man in the Northeast 20:77-100.

    1983   aj ch'om k'a'lal tu yit a' tzimine - "The Vulture Caught in the
                    Mule's Anus": a note on vultures in Maya folk-literature. In
                    press.

Waterman, T.T.
    1914   The explanatory element in the folk-tales of the North-American
                    Indians. Journal of American Folklore 27 (No. 102):1-54.

Wissler, Clark and D.C. Duvall
    1909   Mythology of the Blackfoot Indians. Anthropological Papers,
                    American Museum of Natural History 2(1).

Young, Egerton R.
    1905   Algonquin Indian tales. New York: F.H. Revell Co.

THE INDIAN RIGHTS ASSOCIATION AND THE GHOST DANCE UPRISING

by

William T. Hagan

ABSTRACT

In the winter of 1890-91 the Plains Sioux reservations were swept by the
last wave of warfare between Indians and the United States Army. The Sioux
"uprising" - the term contemporaries use - had grown out of government efforts
to suppress the Ghost Dance religion. This paper looks at the aftermath of
the uprising, considering in particular the role of the Indian Rights
Association as advocate of Sioux interests. They sought to publicize the
details of U.S. - Sioux conflicts, mobilize public opinion on behalf of the
Indians, and contribute to the medical care of wounded Indians. Finally, they
sought to ensure that justice was done in the treatment of Indian participants
in the courts. The Sioux affair and its aftermath demonstrated that the
I.R.A. was the most active and influential of American Indian welfare
associations.

THE INDIAN RIGHTS ASSOCIATION AND THE GHOST DANCE UPRISING

William T. Hagan

In the winter of 1890-91, the Plains Sioux reservations were swept by the last wave of warfare between Indians and the United States Army. Within hours of its occurrence telegraph wires had carried lurid accounts of what would become known as the Wounded Knee Massacre in which over 150 Indians were killed, at least half of them women and children.[1]

The Sioux "uprising," the term contemporaries used, had grown out of government efforts to suppress the new ghost dance religion. Originating with a Paiute messiah named Wovoka, the new religion promised the faithful a return to plains swarming with buffalo and free of white invaders.

Virtually all western tribes were to some degree exposed to Wovoka's doctrines. But only among the Plains Sioux did they assume a warlike tone. Only among the Sioux did you find the ghost dance shirts purportedly capable of turning bullets.

The Sioux had suffered a series of shocks and disappointments which made them prime material for a messiah movement, one holding out the hope of supernatural help. Confined to reservations for nearly fifteen years, subsisting at what were at times near starvation levels, the Indians were being badgered to begin farming and give up cherished religious and social customs--in short, give up a way of life they had developed and which they cherished, and in place of it adopt alien ways.

Moreover, in 1889 they had been coerced into agreeing to sell to the United States half of their land and accept the division of the remainder into family-sized farms on which they would be settled. To secure the signatures of Indians on the agreement promises had been made which were not kept. As one Indian put it later: "They made us many promises, more than I can remember, but they never kept but one; they promised to take our land, and they took it."[2]

Defrauded of their land, frequently going hungry, and provided with clothing and tools that were a disgrace--hoes and spades of soft metal that would not last a day in the field, pants with seats that split the first time you attempted to sit down in them, shoes that could not be worn because the nails attaching the soles had not been turned down inside the shoe--the Sioux understandably were frustrated and despairing.

Many were not prepared to accept the loss of half of their land and the abandonment of their band-oriented life which allotment in severalty entailed, and were inspired to resist by chiefs who spoke of action in the spring.

271

Sitting Bull, Red Cloud, Big Foot, and Crow Dog were not very definite as to what might take place. Indeed, the chiefs themselves were not in agreement on a course of action. However, by December of 1890 a growing number of Sioux had come to believe that in the spring an effort should be made to seize a large area west of the Sioux agencies, and make it a place where the Indians could pursue their old ways without being badgered by government agents, teachers, and missionaries.

That was the situation among the Plains Sioux. Now let us look at the other group under discussion, the Indian Rights Association.

In the fall of 1890 the I.R.A. was recognized as being the most active and the most influential of the several organizations interested in Indian welfare. Founded in 1882 in Philadelphia, its 900 members in 1891 were mostly from Philadelphia and its suburbs. Perhaps another 300 or 400 people belonged to branches of the association, usually located in eastern communities like Providence, Rhode Island, and Cambridge, Massachusetts.[3]

The membership of the I.R.A. was drawn largely from the upper middle classes--business, professional, and academic types whose social theories conditioned by their strong religious views led them into a variety of reform movements.

Although there was a full slate of officers, together with an executive committee that was supposed to meet monthly, the real leadership of the I.R.A. was provided by a man with the innocuous title of corresponding secretary, Herbert Welsh.

Welsh had had the leading role in the foundation of the association, and he was the only officer able to devote full time to the I.R.A. The son of a prominent Philadelphia merchant and financier who had served also as minister to England, Herbert Welsh had inherited an estate that permitted him to devote his life to good causes while still being able to maintain his family in a style appropriate to "proper Philadelphians."

Coupled with this time to devote to good causes, Welsh brought to the task an abundance of energy, a highly developed social conscience, a very real sense of his own rectitude, and a positive talent for polemics. He was a man of many causes, but the one that commanded most of his talents in the period 1883-1891, was the welfare of the American Indian.[4]

By the fall of 1890 the I.R.A. was recognized as the most important voice in the Indian reform movement. It maintained a full-time agent in Washington, and virtually every year the agent and Welsh could be counted upon to visit some of the sixty-odd agencies scattered across two-thirds of the U.S. With a network of contacts on the reservations, plus their own field work, the I.R.A. leaders were better informed on Indian conditions than were any people outside the Indian Bureau itself.

Presidents, secretaries of the interior, commissioners of Indian affairs, and members of congress had learned the wisdom of giving a hearing to I.R.A. views. The penalty for ignoring the association was to subject oneself to critical editorials inspired by the I.R.A. and appearing in prominent eastern newspapers and Protestant religious journals, and being inundated by letters and petitions from prominent citizens. Herbert Welsh believed that public opinion was shaped by a few thousand people, and he was indefatigable in seeking to bring them to support what the I.R.A. considered to be a proper Indian policy.

The I.R.A.'s idea of a proper Indian policy was one that had as its objective the complete assimilation of the Native American. Herbert Welsh, like other eastern reformers of the day, believed that while Indian cultures might not be as advanced as that of American whites, Native Americans had the same potential. By education and proper management the tribesmen could rapidly close the gap and take their place as citizens on the same footing with other Americans. In the process, of course, they would shed their pagan religions. Welsh was a staunch Episcopalian and his church's missionary work among the Indians had first attracted the young Philadelphian to the cause.

The troubles stemming from the ghost dance among the Sioux caught Welsh and most everyone else by surprise. Only one of the five Sioux agents had mentioned the possibility of trouble in his annual report prepared in the summer of 1890.[5] In the months preceding the outbreak, the I.R.A.'s principal interest in the Sioux reservations was an effort to retain capable agents. The Harrison administration was in the process of replacing Democratic appointees by loyal Republicans. In the process, two Sioux agencies where the ghost dancers were particularly numerous, Cheyenne River and Pine Ridge, had received new agents. Both of them were rather inexperienced, and Dr. Daniel F. Royer, the new agent at Pine Ridge, was hardly in office before he was pleading for troops to be sent to support him.

Not until mid-November did Welsh receive his first communication from the Dakotas indicating that a crisis was brewing. It was a letter from an I.R.A. member, one Thomas Stewart, the harness maker at Pine Ridge. Stewart warned Welsh that at Pine Ridge there would be trouble by spring between Agent James McLaughlin and the ghost dancers headed by Sitting Bull, for whom Stewart had considerable sympathy.[6]

Alerted by Stewart to the possibility of trouble, Welsh dispatched letters to the man most responsible for his entrance into Indian work, W.H. Hare, the Episcopal bishop in charge of his church's missionary work among the Sioux. Welsh also contacted Charles Cook, a Sioux at Pine Ridge who was an Episcopal missionary, Agent James McLaughlin of Standing Rock, and General Nelson A. Miles whose command included the area of the Sioux reservations.[7]

Reverend Cook, Agent McLaughlin, and General Miles all agreed that the situation was serious. Bishop Hare, however, believed the danger had been exaggerated. Only Reverend Cook urged Welsh to come out for a personal inspection.

Welsh decided the situation did provide a vivid illustration of the problems resulting from the political spoils system, and in the next few weeks wrote a number of editors and others urging the need of an extension of civil service over more positions at the Indian agencies. The I.R.A. also published and circulated over 2,000 copies of a St. Paul newspaper's condemnation of the spoils system, and a similar number of copies of an assessment of the situation by Bishop Hare.

Welsh seized on the growing criticism of the Pine Ridge agent, Dr. Royer, to urge his replacement by Dr. Valentine T. McGillycuddy, a former Pine Ridge agent who had been a political casualty. Dr. McGillycuddy did not regain the position, but did go to Pine Ridge as a special representative of the Governor of South Dakota and from there provided Welsh a steady stream of reports on conditions.[8]

Despite the flow of information from Dr. McGillycuddy, Bishop Hare and others, Welsh decided the I.R.A. needed its own investigator on the scene. The man he selected for the task was the Reverend William J. Cleveland, an Episcopal missionary at Pine Ridge with seventeen years experience among the Sioux and command of the Dakota language.

The terms on which Reverend Cleveland would serve the I.R.A. were agreed upon shortly before Christmas. As of that time the only bloodshed had resulted when Agent McLaughlin at Standing Rock was pushed into an effort to take Sitting Bull into custody. The result was a fire fight between the Indian police attempting the arrest and Sitting Bull's supporters, and fourteen Sioux, including Sitting Bull and five policemen, were killed.[9]

Welsh directed Reverend Cleveland to go to Standing Rock to investigate that calamity, but before Cleveland could do so, an even greater tragedy occurred on Wounded Knee Creek. There on December 29th an effort to disarm a party of ghost dancers from Cheyenne River agency enroute to join those at Pine Ridge had led to the Wounded Knee Massacre.

Herbert Welsh described what occurred on Wounded Knee Creek as "a horrible sequel of the whole wretched affair."[10] Incidentally, the man to whom he addressed this remark was Civil Service Commissioner Theodore Roosevelt, to whom Welsh frequently turned in his campaign to remove politics from the Indian Service. In the next three months Welsh would hammer on this theme of civil service reform in mailings to I.R.A. members, editors, ministers, and prominent citizens who might have influence with the administration and members of Congress.

In a typical letter, Welsh said that he asked "no pity for those ignorant and frantic creatures whose fierce act of resistance to disarmament was the last link of a series of causes which produced this horror."[11] However, he continued, he did ask whether the country could afford the continuation of a spoils system which could contribute to such disasters.

Civil service reform might be a long range goal, but the I.R.A. would be called upon to do something immediately about the Indian casualties at Wounded Knee. Bishop Hare reported his shock at the "chamber of horrors" which the Episcopal church at Pine Ridge had become by being converted into a temporary hospital for Wounded Knee casualties.[12] Elaine Goodale, an I.R.A. member and Indian Service employee at Pine Ridge, asked the association for financial help in caring for the wounded. The I.R.A. quickly raised over $1,000, which helped provide a trained nurse and other necessities.

In assigning blame for Wounded Knee, Welsh strove to be fair to all parties. The I.R.A. reproduced and circulated a letter by a Sioux Indian, Dr. Charles Eastman, who was acting as agency physician at Pine Ridge and had searched the battlefield for survivors. Dr. Eastman's communication had referred to the large numbers of women and children victims of the firing.[13]

In his correspondence Welsh referred to the "horrible butchery of women and children" and asked Reverend Cleveland to explore thoroughly the question of responsibility for their deaths at Wounded Knee.[14] It was Welsh's opinion that "in a fierce sanguinary hand-to-hand fight common soldiers would become unrestrainable."[15] In a letter to the Washington Post, Welsh spelled it out in more detail:

> I, personally, should be very slow to criticize those who
> are risking life and limb in suppressing an Indian outbreak
> which was not of their making, and should be altogether
> unwilling to make any reflections upon the Army as a whole,
> knowing well as I do many of the officers are not only
> honorable and brave men, but are serious, steadfast and
> judicious friends of the Indian; men who are advocates of
> humane treatment of the Indian race, and of all wise efforts
> for its education and development.[16]

In the aftermath of Wounded Knee, Welsh also urged discrimination in dealing with the Sioux. Those progressive Indians who had suffered property losses at the hands of the ghost dancers should be compensated. The I.R.A.'s corresponding secretary was particularly upset that some of the leading ghost dancers had been released to travel in Europe with Buffalo Bill's Wild West show.[17]

Welsh's sense of justice also was outraged by the prospect that Plenty Horses, a young Sioux who had killed Lieutenant Edward C. Casey, would be dealt with severely while white cowboys who had killed Few Tails, a Sioux, would go unpunished. Lieutenant Casey was a cavalry officer shot without warning by Plenty Horses while Casey was conferring with other Indians.

A few days later, in a totally unrelated incident, two Indian families returning from a hunt were attacked by cowboys and Few Tails was killed and his wife and another woman wounded. The men primarily responsible for the attack were the Culbertsons, three brothers.

Initially the I.R.A.'s involvement stemmed from Welsh's concern that the Culbertsons would escape justice, frontier juries being notorious for overlooking crimes by whites against Indians. Welsh wrote the secretary of the interior insisting that the "white desperadoes" be punished, and the I.R.A. distributed a circular contrasting the treatment of the cowboys, who had yet to go to jail, with that of Plenty Horses who was being held for trial.[18] "Evidently," the circular concluded, "there is one law for the white man and another for the Indian."[19] Welsh also elicited from the Interior Department the admission that it had no record of a white man being hanged for the death of an Indian.

One man with whom Welsh corresponded about the murder of Few Tails was Civil Service Commissioner Theodore Roosevelt. Roosevelt assured Welsh that he favoured martial law if that was the only way to bring the Culbertsons to justice. "The hanging of a few white scoundrels implicated in such deeds as that of the murder of Few Tails' party would do incredible good," stormed T.R.[20]

In addition to seeking prosecution of the Culbertsons, the I.R.A. was drawn into the defense of Plenty Horses. Both an attorney interested in representing the Sioux and the army officer commanding the post where he was being held prisoner wrote Welsh to ask that the I.R.A. contribute financially to his defense. Ultimately the I.R.A. did provide a few hundred dollars for the defense of the young Sioux, but reluctantly as the association was afraid of establishing a precedent for this type of financial obligation.[21]

Welsh first had sought to convince the Indian Bureau that it should provide counsel. His argument was similar to the one he has used to try to get federal government assistance in prosecuting the Culbertsons—the Indians were wards of the government and entitled to its protection.[22]

After two trials Plenty Horses was free, a federal judge having held that his killing of Lieutenant Casey was an act of war. Welsh was not happy with the outcome of the trial. He did not believe that Plenty Horses, who had shot the officer in the back of the head as he rode away from him, should go free, although Welsh certainly had not favoured a death sentence. It was also feared that Plenty Horses's release would have an unfortunate impact on the trial of the Culbertsons and their two accomplices who had been indicted.

In an effort to create public opinion in favour of punishment for the murderers of Few Tails, the I.R.A. purchased 500 copies of a letter on the case Welsh had published in a Philadelphia newspaper. These copies Welsh mailed to newspapers with readers in the Dakotas, as well as to ministers in the area. But all this was to no avail, the South Dakota jury failed to convict the cowboys. Welsh made one last futile attempt to extract some reform from this miserable affair. He approached a young writer with the suggestion that she use the Few Tails tragedy as the subject of a novel which might "prevent in the future such a tragic miscarriage of justice."[23]

The I.R.A. could feel some satisfaction in at least seeing the Culbertsons brought to trial and in securing a degree of justice for Plenty Horses. It also claimed some of the credit for President Harrison's decision, in the wake of the Sioux troubles, to extend civil service over several additional job classifications in the Indian Service. Welsh had launched one of his media blitzes to ensure this, sending out petition forms and letters to editors and members and friends of the association urging them to contact President Harrison and members of Congress. The association also mailed out several thousand copies of pamphlets it prepared dealing with various aspects of the troubles in the Dakotas, all calling for an end to the political spoils system.

The I.R.A. annual report for 1891 described President Harrison's order extending civil service as the "silver lining to the otherwise dark cloud of the Dakota outbreak."[24] The annual report also carried a summary by Reverend Cleveland whose letters from the Dakotas had been so influential in shaping Herbert Welsh's views of events. Cleveland had begun his investigation in mid-January and in the next two months it took him to all the Plains Sioux agencies.

Welsh was so pleased with Reverend Cleveland's performance that he brought him east to speak to audiences in nine cities. Cleveland's message to his listeners was that there had not been an Indian outbreak, rather the Indians had been "broken in upon." Cleveland did not defend Sitting Bull, Crow Dog, and the other leaders who had been planning some action in the spring. However, he made clear that government mismanagement, heightened by the political spoils system, had driven the Indians to the point that they would be receptive to a Sitting Bull or a Crow Dog.

The whole sordid affair had demonstrated the range and the nature of I.R.A. concerns, and the way it could mobilize public opinion. Caught by surprise by the trouble on the Sioux reservations, Herbert Welsh had reacted quickly. The hundreds of letters and 13,000 copies of seven circulars relating to the difficulty which the association had sent out had helped educate the public to the I.R.A. version of the issues.

The association also had made a contribution to the medical care of the Wounded Knee casualties, helped ensure that some justice was done in the Lieutenant Casey and Few Tails cases, and played a role in the campaign which resulted in the further extension of civil service over positions in the Indian Bureau. Last, but certainly not least for scholars, the association's voluminous correspondence, carefully preserved, provides us one of the best sources for what happened in Dakota Territory in the fall and winter of 1890.

FOOTNOTES

1. The best general account is Robert M. Utley, The Last Days of the Sioux Nation (New Haven: Yale University Press, 1963).

2. The I.R.A. Annual Report, 1891, p. 28, to be found in Reel 103:D9 in the microfilm edition of the I.R.A. papers published by the Microfilming Corporation of America (1973) in 135 reels. Hereafter, these will be cited as IRAP, Reel____. This essay is largely based on this collection.

3. This type of organization had not worked well as the branches found themselves with little role to play except to raise money and to generate petitions and letters for campaigns developed by the Philadelphia headquarters.

4. Welsh was the archetypal reformer. In addition to his Indian work in 1890 he was a vice-president of the Forestry Congress, an official in the Philadelphia city parks association, a supporter of the local board of education, a member of the Universal Peace Union, and an organizer of an independent Republican group with the mission of defeating Matthew "Boss" Quay. As he did not have the usual business or professional commitments, Welsh was always called upon to do more than his fair share in these reform groups.

5. This was H.D. Gallagher of Pine Ridge.

6. Stewart to Welsh, November 11, 1890, in IRAP, Reel 6.

7. These letters were sent November 19, 1890; see IRAP, Reel 70.

8. McGillycuddy's letters appear in IRAP, Reel 6. All incoming correspondence is arranged by date of letter.

9. Again, Utley's Last Days of the Sioux Nation provides the best summary.

10. Welsh to Roosevelt, December 31, 1890, in IRAP, Reel 70.

11. Welsh to the editor of the Civil Service Record, December 31, 1890, in IRAP, Reel 70.

12. Hare to Welsh, January 6, 1891, in IRAP, Reel 6.

13. The letter to Frank Wood of Boston, dated January 3, 1891, was published in the Boston Transcript. This version, with accompanying editorial comment by Welsh, was circulated by the I.R.A. under the date January 9, 1891. See IRAP, Reel 102:A131.

14. The quotation is from Welsh to Captain John G. Bourke, January 19, 1891, in IRAP, Reel 70.

15. Welsh to Edward M. Bacon, January 23, 1891, in IRAP, Reel 70.

16. Welsh to the editor of the Washington Post, January 10, 1891, in IRAP, Reel 70.

17. Welsh to the editor of the Philadelphia Press, March 16, 1891, in IRAP, Reel 70.

18. Welsh to the secretary of the interior, February 14, 1891, in IRAP, Reel 70.

19. To the Public Press, in IRAP, Reel 102:A138.

20. Roosevelt to Welsh, February 13, 1891, in IRAP, Reel 7.

21. I.R.A. law committee report, April 6, 1891, in IRAP, Reel 7.

22. Welsh to the attorney-general, April 3, 1891, in IRAP, Reel 71.

23. Welsh to Winifred Jennings, July 13, 1891, in IRAP, Reel 71.

24. I.R.A., Annual Report, 1891, p. 7, in IRAP, Reel 103:D9.

THE GITSKAN INCIDENT OF 1888

by

I. V. B. Johnson

ABSTRACT

In 1888 a Gitksan Indian named Kitwancool Jim killed a shaman in
retribution for the death of his son. Three special constables from Hazelton
were sent to Kitwancool to arrest the Indian. Despite the fact that Jim
intended to give himself up one of the constables shot and killed him. The
outcome of the incident was a series of Gitksan uprisings, in the course of
which several deaths occurred. Ultimately the government dispatched a force
to the Skeena Forks to quell the "Indian troubles." Why would the government
react so strongly to what on the surface would appear to be a typical local
situation? The Kitwancool Jim incident demonstrates the white pattern of
intervention in Indian social institutions. A viable and culturally inherent
judicial process that had effectively dealt with a dispute to the satisfaction
of all native parties concerned had been disrupted by Eurocentric whites,
resulting in animosity and general confusion on the part of the Gitksan. The
Eurocentric assimilation policy of the Canadian government continues to the
present day in its attempt to undermine the strength of Indian peoples.

282

THE GITKSAN INCIDENT OF 1888

I.V.B. Johnson

A fascinating story is told among the Gitksan of northern British Columbia's Skeena River Valley.[3] It's a true story about an Indian called Kitwancool Jim who was murdered by the whiteman. The story focuses on government attempts to disrupt the traditional judicial system of the Gitksan. The legend begins with an internal Raven tribe rivalry between a young boy from Kitwancool and his maternal uncle, the shaman from the neighbouring village of Kitseguecla. That winter, 1887, during the potlatch ceremonies to choose a Chief, the most destructive measle epidemic in memory swept through the Northwest Coast and the Skeena River Valley. The boy succumbed to the disease and the shaman was accused of murder through witchcraft by the boy's mother. In accordance with Gitksan law, the grieved father, known as Kitwancool Jim, of the wolf tribe, sought retribution and killed the shaman at Wendzelneleetu on the trail between Kitsequecla and Kitwancool. This incident set in motion a series of events.

The people of Kitseguecla were influenced by their missionary not to seek revenge for the death of their shaman. Nevertheless the Raven tribe of Kitseguecla demanded some form of compensation for their loss. The wolf tribe of Kitwancool was able to appease the anger of the Raven tribe with blankets, guns and supplies in compensation. Thus the traditional court of law settled the affair and the Indians returned to their homes in peace.

Legend tells us however that some of the whites in the area were incredulous over how the situation had been resolved.

A local prospector and trader, B.W. Washington, engaged a plan whereby he would renew the conflict and capitalize by selling his services to the government to help institute the Queen's law in the region. This enterprising but unscrupulous individual, with the support of the local manager of the Hudson's Bay Company store, went to the Hon. A.E.B. Davie, Attorney General in Victoria, with a proposal that he be commissioned to lead a force to Kitwancool to arrest Jim. Although the government hesitated and procrastinated for some time, they finally issued an Order in Council that sent the Skeena River Patrol north in the spring of 1888.

When Jim learned of this news he is said to have gone to the legendary Temlaham, birthplace of the Gitksan people, for refuge and asylum. After considering his position Jim finally returned to Kitwancool.

The three special constables from Hazelton were informed of Jim's return and quickly moved in to capture him. Jim reportedly had in his possession at the time, a letter from the local Indian Agent in which he had been advised to surrender.[4] Legend recounts how Jim decided to capitulate, but that he would do so in the traditional Gitksan manner befitting a person of his rank by feigning a token show of force. This theatrical demonstration was misinterpreted by constable Billy Green as an attempted escape. Green shot Jim in the back. The legend also tells how Green discharged Jim's gun to counterfeit an act of self-defence. The constables then returned to their base at Hazelton.

The murder of Kitwancool Jim set in motion a series of reprisals that shocked the country from Victoria to Ottawa. The Gitksan of the Skeena Forks rose threateningly against the whites in the area to seek retribution for the death of Kitwancool Jim. Several more killings occurred in rapid succession. All of the whites in Gitksan territory barricaded themselves into the Hudson's Bay Company post at Hazelton with the special constables and sent an urgent request for assistance to the government at Victoria. In the meantime constable Green was charged with murder and acquitted by a jury of six of his cohorts in an attempt to satisfy the Gitksan call for justice.

Finally the government dispatched a military force to the Skeena Forks to quell the 'Indian troubles'.

It is interesting to digress for a moment to ask the question: why would the governments react so strongly to what, on the surface, would appear to be a relatively typical, local situation? Part of the answer lies in the history of the northwest coast.

Troubles of this nature were not unusual on the Skeena. The Gitksan had been involved in continuous conflicts with the whites. The resulting tension had a substantial history in the area by 1888. The longer the situation wore on, the more deeply embedded the resentment became. This mutual animosity was deeply ingrained in the characters that played out the Kitwancool Jim incident and accounts partially for the extreme reaction of the government to this local conflict.

Hazelton, the Hudson's Bay Company post closest to Kitwancool, was the site of one incident in 1843. By constructing the post at the Forks of the Skeena River, near the location of Itagwilget, a major Gitksan fishing village, the Hudson's Bay Company had disrupted a strategic trade network between the Gitksan and the Carrier. Consequently:

> The natives here...were not particularly loyal to the
> Hudson's Bay Company, since they traded largely with the
> coast, and their attitudes to the various men who in turn
> took charge of the fort was treacherous and often
> belligerent.[5]

This animosity was the background to a trade dispute at the post in 1843. At this time, the fort at Hazelton was controlled by William Morwick who held the rank of postmaster. A Hagwilget Indian, Lewke, became incensed during barter negotiations for caribou furs that he had brought in. After a day of reflection, Lewke returned to the fort to renegotiate a deal and an argument erupted again during which Lewke was shot by Morwick's interpreter, Charles Toin. Lewke in turn stabbed the Indian interpreter. Neither man was killed, inspite of the serious wounds. Nevertheless, rumour spread quickly through the territory that Lewke had been killed and his son-in-law, known as

"Green then raised his Winchester rifle and
fired, striking Jim in the back, the bullet
going clear through his body."
                    -Victoria Daily Colonist

"...the ball entering near the right shoulder blade,
passing quarterly through the lung, and coming out on the
right breast, between the third and fourth ribs."
                    -Victoria Daily Colonist

Leaning totem poles, Kitwancool, B.C., ca. 1941. (National Film Board Collection
PA-112855, National Archives of Canada.)

Note: The Gitksan judicial system focussed on compensatory action. Any individual or group loss was redressed through compensation. Compensation was necessitated by a whole spectrum of things from personal insult to murder. The form of compensation could be in kind or through payments of material wealth. In the absence of proper compensation retaliation was a viable alternative.

Part of Hazelton, B.C., with Rocher Déboule Range in background. Photo by R.C.W. Lett. (Geological Survey of Canada Collection, Public Archives of Canada PA-51448) posterity as 'Grand Visage', shot Morwick in the head from long range thereby fulfilling his obligations to native law. 'Grand Visage' approached the fort stealthily, fed the barrel of his rifle through a whole in the pallisade wall, and escaped immediately after completing his task. In response to this, Chief Factor Archibald McDonald sent a message to Chief Factor Peter Skene Ogden at Fort St. James. Ogden reacted by dispatching a party of twelve police lead by one of his clerks, William B. McBean, to quell the disturbance. Grand Visage was coazed from hiding with promises of leniency under the King's law, but was shot on sight.[6]

A second noteworthy incident occurred. In 1874, the Church Missionary Society missionary, the Reverend Robert Tomlinson, was on a tour of the Skeena tribes and reported a state of affairs that again illustrates the tensions between the whites and the Indians. Tomlinson wrote that, at the time of his visit, many whites had already left the area because the Peace River Mines had been deserted. This left many former Indian employees, who had become accustomed to a higher standard of living, bitter and disillusioned with the whites. Tomlinson reported that Indians had 'levied Black Mail upon, and otherwise maltreated some packers and men'.... Such a state of things cannot exist long without resulting in outrage and murder which will necessitate the government inflicting severe punishment on offenders.[7]

Finally, an illustration of the tension in the area that is very telling. The murder of A.C. Youmans at the Forks in 1884 illustrates the nature of Gitksan relations with the whites prior to the Kitwancool Jim incident and the similarity between the two is striking. Youmans ran a trading company which employed natives to ship goods along the Skeena by canoe. In 1884 while on a trip with Youmans, a young native, Billy Owen, drowned. Billy's father sought retribution from Youmans for the death of his son as was the Gitksan custom upon the death of a relative. Youmans refused. The situation was made more accute because Billy's older brother had drowned on the Skeena in 1881 while in Youmans employ and Youmans had refused to compensate the father on that occasion as well.[9] The father murdered Youmans and was arrested and taken to Fort Simpson for trial.

The Gitksan were angered by the treatment Owen had received and when a report circulated intimating that he had been sentenced to hang the Indians began to gather in threatening statue.[10] All of the whites deserted the Forks when the Indians threatened to stop navigation of the Skeena and Indians went to Lorne Creek and the Omneca minefields where they threatened the miners with reprisals.[11]

This was the mood in which the Kitwancool Jim incident occurred. These incidents suffice to demonstrate the precarious relationship between the whites and the Gitksan of the Skeena Forks. With the immediate history of Indian-white relations in the area in mind, and the Gitksan oral tradition as a barometer, it is interesting to examine the documentary account of the incident.

The written records of the period provided a more detailed version of the Kitwancool Jim story. In 1887, the Methodist missionaries Thomas Crosby and W.H. Pierce surveyed Gitksan territory for a potential mission site. They passed through Kitwancool and Kispiox before deciding on Kitseguecla as a

possibility. Pierce, a Tsimshian convert, spent the winter in the village
while Crosby returned to his station at Fort Simpson. Pierce reported that a
severe measle epidemic accompanied by scarlet fever broke out on the Skeena
that winter. Over two hundred died in the villages around the Forks.
Kitwancool suffered worse than most: 'some of the houses are empty – father,
mother and four children all dead'.[12]

The following spring the Wolf tribe of Kitwancool held a potlatch to
which the Ravel tribe of Kitseguecla was invited. One of the Chiefs of the
wolf tribe at Kitwancool, Kitwancool Jim, sought compensation from the
Kitsequecla shaman accused of murdering his son through witchcraft. Jim met
the shaman outside the village and killed him. The missionary recounted that
the warriors of Kitseguecla promptly prepared for an attach on Kitwancool to
seek revenge but he (the missionary) convinced them to seek British justice
instead. The missionary was then appointed to report the incident to the
authorities.

A warrant was issued for the arrest of Kitwancool Jim by Judge S.Y.
Wooton of Metlakatla.[13] A merchant from Victoria on business in Hazelton at
the time, returned to Victoria with news of the manhunt for Kitwancool Jim on
the Skeena. He told the newspaper that three constables had gone to arrest
Jim and that constable Green had shot Jim in the back.[14]

The three constables were then forced to retire to Hazelton because of
the threatening attitude of the Gitksan in the wake of Jim's murder. The
special constable in charge of the manhunt, arrived on the scene later that
day to identify the body but left quickly for Hazelton in fear for his life.
Upon arrival at Hazelton his packers told the local Indians of Jim's murder
and the constable had great difficulty calming the resultant tumult.
Nevertheless he was cautious to summon all whites in the area into the
barricaded H.B.C. store. The constable reported that Kitwancool Jim's
relatives were demanding one thousand dollars, a whiteman and a gun used to
kill Jim as compensation.[15] He then requested assistance from Victoria to
deal with the expanding conflict. The agent for the H.B.C. post at Fort
Simpson, echoed the constables plea for reinforcements to deal with the
volatile situation.

The government at Victoria reacted by dispatching a military force on
board a Royal Navy gunboat to the Skeena River. Ten North West Mounted Police
(NWMP) were also sent north. Twenty thousand pounds of supplies and eighteen
thousand rounds of ammunition were requisitioned for the troops. In total
eighty-five soldiers and eleven constables were dispatched north with full
military accounterments.

The gunboat proceeded from Esquimault on Vancouver Island to Port
Essington on the Skeena where it moored off Robert Cunningham's Cannery. Camp
was struck one mile below Cunningham's at the junction of the Hochstaa and
Skeena Rivers. This landing came to be known as Soldier's Point. It was
decided that the N.W.M.P. would make the one hundred and sixty miles trek to
investigate the situation before taking the rest of the force to the Forks.
With great difficulty Cunningham was able to hire six Tsimshian to man canoes
for the remainder of the trip.

Indian Chief, Skeena River, B.C., ca. 1900. In <u>Annual Report of the Department</u> <u>of Indian Affairs</u>, Dominion of Canada, 1900, page 16.

One of the supply officers informed the Victoria Daily Colonist that the hundreds of Indians around Port Essington who had come to see the gunboat lying at anchor were impressed with her armaments, particularly the Gardiner and Nordenfeld guns, which he hoped would influence the Indians to abandon their demands. By the time the N.W.M.P. arrived at the Forks a quiet had settled over the scene.[16] The whites were still anxious about an attack but most of the Indians had left the area for their fishing territories. Kitwancool Jim's widow had lowered her demands for compensation to one hundred dollars and the right to determine the fate of constable Green. No further developments occurred in the area although the tension lasted for many years to come.

The Toronto Mail ran an interesting article speculating that the land question was the root cause of the Indian troubles rather than simply the immediate events as they unfolded. The Government of British Columbia had notoriously rejected the land claim issue and consequently many sources including the Victoria papers jumped on this explanation and it was silenced.

However another voice was raised that reinforced the Mail's search for a broader explanation. Gabriel Dumont, one of the driving forces behind the second Riel uprising in Saskatchewan, echoed the claim to a deeper problem.

> "It is the old story: for you know among us Indians'
> byword is, "you touch one, you touch all." All that I can
> say is that the government had better be careful with these
> Indians as they are dangerous. It is better to try and od
> what is right with to treat them kindly, because if a
> genuine Indian uprising takes place the government will not
> have to face a few men like the last campaign, but from
> 30,000 to 40,000 of them."[18]

The fact that the troubles on the Skeena subsided quietly should not be construed to mean that they were not serious. Both the writer for the Toronto Mail and Gabriel Dumont pointed to a very real issue. The treatment by the Canadian governments of the Indians across the country had been cavalier at best. Certainly the land issue was a major issue of contention but the general culture shock of white expansion throughout the country cannot be underestimated.

It should be noted that the shock waves of resentment created during the 1885 Riel Rebellion were still very real in Canada. The Canadian Government was apprehensive about controlling the 'west' and nervous about Indian and Métis dissension in particular. The re-emergence of Gabriel Dumont into the limelight, extolling the virtues of native resistance, no doubt created anxiety in government circles. This connection may also help to explain the government reaction to the Skeena incident.

Government legislation regarding Indians is one example of this expansion. The late nineteenth century say many changes among the Gitksan. The Indian Improvement Act and the Potlatch law followed close on the heels of the Indian Act. Indian Agents became active in the area adding a new dimension to Indian-white relations and the federal government and the B.C.

provincial government fought continously over the jurisdictional question. But the expansion of government into northern B.C. was not the only confusing change.

The murder of Kitwancool Jim set

in motion a series of reprisals

that shocked the country from

Victoria to Ottawa.

Another illustration of white expansion into Indian territory came through the churches. The churches began to extend their administrative and ecclesiastical influence into the north as well. This resulted in many quarrels between the churches and the missionaries active in the area since 1854. An increasing influx of whites into the area to trade in the valley's rich natural resources was a third element that put a great deal of pressure on the Gitksan. The traditional economy began to falter under the changing circumstances.

Consequently the Gitksan world came under increasing attack and with it their value system was questioned. The Kitwancool Kim incident is an example of this pressure as the traditional judicial system, which was still intact and operating successfully, was undermined by whites seeking control of the area. However, the resistance of the Gitksan did not end in 1888. A great emphasis was placed on the integration and adaption of British ideas into Gitksan society but only as those ideas could strengthen resistance to cultural genocide. Troubles and violence continued to spring up from time to time in the area, and many contentious issues remained unresolved to the present day.

In the final analysis the Kitwancool Jim incident points to the disrupting effect of white intervention into Indian social institutions. Repeatedly Indian societies have been infiltrated and integral parts of those societies attacked and disturbed. No culturally viable alternative can replace traditional mechanisms and British institutions that are forced onto Indians only serve to confuse them resulting in a litany of harmful effects.

The problems on the Skeena in the nineteenth century as illustrated by the events surrounding the murder of Kitwancool Jim fit this pattern. A viable and culturally inherent judicial process that had effectively dealt with a dispute to the satisfaction of all parties concerned was disrupted by eurocentric whites resulting in animosity and general confusion for the Gitksan. The eurocentric assimilation policy of the Canadian government continues to the present day in its attempt to undermine the strength of Indian people.

FOOTNOTES

1.   Borland, <u>Victoria Daily Colonist</u>, July 12, 1888, p. 1, c. 4, 5.

2.   Washburn to Davie, Ibid., p. 1, c. 5.

3.   Marius Barbeau, <u>The Downfall of Temlaham</u>, (Hurtig: Edmonton, 1973).

4.   Hon. J.H. Turner, <u>Victoria Daily Colonist</u>, July 30, 1888, p. 1, c. 4, 5.

5.   R. Geddes Large, <u>The Skeena River of Destiny</u>, (Mitchell: Vancouver, 1964) p. 13.

6.   Ibid., p. 14.

7.   Tomlinson to C.M.S., April 30, 1875, <u>CMS Correspondence</u>, (A-106).

8.   British Columbia Sessional Papers, B.C. Legislative Assembly, Request for Correspondence concerning the North-West Coast Indian Troubles, p. 279.

9.   W.H. Collison, <u>In the Wake of the War Canoe</u>, (London: Seeley, 1915), p. 303.

10. Jennings to Provincial Secretary, September 16, 1884, p. 280, B.C. Sessional Papers.

11. Ibid., Green to Government of B.C., September 20, 1884.

12. Annual Report, Greenville, 1887-1888, Methodist Missionary Society Notes.

13. S.Y. Wooton to A.E.B. Davie, Mettakahtla, July 5, 1888, <u>Victoria Daily Colonist</u>, July 30, 1888, p. 1, c. 4, 5.

14. Victoria Daily Colonist, July 12, 1888, p. 1, c. 4.

15. Washburn to Davie, <u>Victoria Daily Colonist</u>, July 12, 1888, p. 1, c. 5.

16. <u>Victoria Daily Colonist</u>, July 30, 1888, p. 2, c. 1.

17. Ibid., July 31, 1888, p. 2, c. 3.

18. Ibid., July 27, 1888, p. 4, c. 4.